Synchronous Online Counseling and Supervision in the 21st Century

Synchronous Online Counseling and Supervision in the 21st Century

SHERRY M. TODD, TRICIA M. MIKOLON, AND DEBRA M. PEREZ, EDITORS

cognella®
SAN DIEGO

Bassim Hamadeh, CEO and Publisher

Amy Smith, Senior Project Editor

Casey Hands, Production Editor

Jess Estrella, Senior Graphic Designer

Stephanie Kohl, Licensing Associate

Natalie Piccotti, Director of Marketing

Kassie Graves, Vice President of Editorial

Jamie Giganti, Director of Academic Publishing

Cover image: Copyright © 2014 Depositphotos/studio-fi.

Design Icons: Copyright © by Microsoft.

Printed in the United States of America.

3970 Sorrento Valley Blvd., Ste. 500, San Diego, CA 92121

This book is dedicated in loving memory of Eugene Chambers whose enthusiasm about this project was the driving force behind it.

BRIEF CONTENTS

DETAILED CONTENTS

UNIT II   SYNCHRONOUS COUNSELING AT A DISTANCE   61

CHAPTER 7   Clinical Skills for Synchronous Counseling   109

Sarah Littlebear, Debra M. Perez, and Tricia M. Mikolon

CHAPTER 8   Crisis Response From a Distance   128

Sherry Todd, Tina Pharr, and Andrea D. Josephs

CHAPTER 12   Group Work   223

Sherry Todd, Kristal James, and Debra M. Perez

PREFACE

The global pandemic of 2020 brought new challenges to the field of counseling. With state mandates to stay at home, counselors had to quickly adapt their practices to the online platform without guidance or direction. Many were left to apply in-person regulations, theories, and best practices to their online therapy. Guidance specific to counselors for working with clients in an online capacity is necessary and timely.

Our clinical experience as counselors in both the traditional and online settings brought about the idea of writing *Synchronous Online Counseling and Supervision in the 21st Century* to provide education to current and future counselors in effective use of technology to provide ethical counseling to various populations online. The importance and the need for this training was dramatically emphasized with the mandated leap to online counseling and supervision caused by COVID-19, which moved counselors from their offices into the online realm with little to no prior education, experience, or guidance on how to successfully accomplish this. Counselors had to navigate this leap while maintaining competency and compliance with both the American Counseling Association (ACA) Code of Ethics standards and best practices. There are other books written about online therapy, but none written for counselors. *Synchronous Online Counseling and Supervision in the 21st Century* focuses solely on counselors and their needs in working in telebehavioral health and online supervision.

With counselors, educators, and supervisors striving to maintain compliance with both ACA and Council for Accreditation of Counseling and Related Educational Programs (CACREP) standards, our text provides sound, evidence-based practices on which to base interactions with clients and supervisees online. *Synchronous Online Counseling and Supervision in the 21st Century*, unlike others, assists counselors in developing therapeutic relationships while tailoring counseling skills and techniques to provide treatment at a distance. Fundamental understanding of online counseling and supervision is provided, including the unique needs of clients seeking synchronous treatment. Clinical skills, licensing, practice issues, technology, regulations, ethics, multicultural, and social justice issues are explored. Working with special populations in an online format is addressed, and couples and marriage formats are discussed. Online group sessions and child counseling, from kindergarten to college, are explored. Finally, included in the book is a comprehensive exploration of online crisis counseling, providing specific crisis intervention strategies and techniques.

Current and future counselors are provided a variety of worksheets, games, tools, and techniques to help develop effective online counseling skills tailored to the unique needs of each client. Educators are provided with a resource incorporating the CACREP standards guiding counseling students' education, specifically Standard B.2.g., which states that supervision training must include clinical supervision and the use of technology, as well as F.1.j. addressing technology's influence on the counseling profession (CACREP, 2016). Supervisors are provided distance supervision skills, the identification and management of online gatekeeping issues, as well as resolutions of legal and ethical concerns. Additionally, any licensed counselors seeking information or education on working with clients or supervisees in an online capacity will be guided through the appropriate steps to take with various populations, as well as considerations for setting up an online practice.

With the growing accessibility and the expansion of technology, counseling is interfacing with technology to meet the demands of a new generation of clients seeking online mental health services. *Synchronous Online Counseling and Supervision in the 21st Century* will ensure the next generation of counselors and supervisors will have necessary information to provide counseling and supervision services online and also for counselor educators to educate future counselors and supervisors about competent and ethical online work.

Since *Synchronous Online Counseling and Supervision in the 21st Century* focuses on both synchronous counseling and supervision, the use of technology and visuals are important aspects to assist students in providing synchronous online counseling in an ethical manner. This reinforces ACA standards as they apply to various scenarios. With this in mind, our text has been designed to include numerous visual features to enhance learning, including basic counseling skills and adaptation summaries, worksheets to use with clients on chapter topics, basic counseling forms modified for the synchronous format, modifications of various counseling techniques in special areas, and a list of online resources for each chapter.

Basic counseling skills and adaption summaries: These summaries will be provided at the end of each chapter reviewing basic counseling skills and noting modifications necessary to successfully adapt them to the needs of the online counselor, supervisor, and client.

Worksheets: Each chapter will provide a worksheet for the counselor, supervisor, or client intended to enhance the online counseling or supervision sessions. These will be designed to assist the counselor or supervisor in addressing a specific area of concern such as confidentiality, ethical considerations, or practice development. Additionally, some worksheets will address specific needs of special populations including LGBTQIA+, multicultural issues, and diagnostic and symptoms management.

Basic counseling forms: These will be provided with a review of the necessary format to comply with ACA ethical standards but will include modification suggestions for the synchronous format with a checklist to assist counselors in ensuring the formats for their practice comply with ACA standards.

Modification of techniques: Specific techniques for counselors and supervisors will be explored with the focus on modifying these for the synchronous counseling and supervision platforms. Some of these will include basic counseling skills, group work, and crisis assessment and intervention.

List of online resources: Each chapter will provide a list of online resources to supplement the learning and worksheets provided.

Case exploration: Each chapter will provide a case exploration on the hypothetical Levai family for consideration and discussion. These are provided from the point of view of the counselor, supervisor, or client as they fit each topic, allowing the reader to apply the knowledge from the chapter into the case.

To supplement the learning of the students and effectiveness of the instructors, we have created a database of ancillary instructional materials for use in an online counseling and supervision course aligned to the CACREP standards. An instructor's manual will supplement the text and include a sample syllabus based on an 8-week term and 16-week traditional semesters including CACREP standards, case exploration for discussion in each chapter, discussion prompts for both in class and discussion board formats, and an objective test bank including multiple choice, matching, and fill-in-the-blank questions for each chapter. Additionally, useful forms and worksheets will be included in the textbook, providing the necessary tools for a successful and inclusive classroom experience.

References

Council for Accreditation of Counseling and Related Educational Programs (CACREP). *2016 CACREP Standards*. Author.

ACKNOWLEDGMENTS

The editors would like to thank each contributing author. Your hard work and dedication to this project is greatly appreciated and indicative of your strong counselor identity and professionalism. We gratefully acknowledge the feedback and guidance from the following reviewers: Dr. Tiffany Darby, Dr. Sarah Littlebear, Dr. Lee Underwood, and Dr. Cyrus Williams. Finally, the editors appreciate the support and hard work of Kassie Graves, Amy Smith, and the entire Cognella team.

Sherry M. Todd acknowledgement:

Many thanks to my students who provided the foundation for this work. The support and encouragement of my parents, Edward and Sonia Todd, is undeserved and I am forever grateful. A special note of appreciation to my many mentors for their exceptional guidance.

Tricia M. Mikolon acknowledgement:

I would like to thank my parents, Emil and Patricia, and my nephew E. J. Mikolon, for their undying support and encouragement throughout this process, as well as Sherri Howe and Amy Talipski for always being there for me. And I would be remiss to not thank my husband, Frank A. Levai, Jr., for all his encouragement, feedback, support, and love.

Debra M. Perez acknowledgement:

I would like to thank my sons, Tarin and Tristin, and my husband, Andy, for their unconditional love, encouragement, and support throughout this project. I would not have made it through this without those late-night talks, Tarin, thank you so much! Tristin, you were my constant cheerleader, thank you! To my husband, you are truly my rock! I so appreciate every meal, snack, bowl of popcorn, and hug you gave throughout this project. Without your support and sacrifice, this book would never have happened.

Fundamentals of Synchronous Counseling

1

Introduction to Synchronous Counseling and Supervision

Tricia M. Mikolon, Debra M. Perez, and Sherry M. Todd

The shoe that fits one person pinches another;
there is no one recipe for living that suits all cases.

—Carl Jung

Telebehavioral health became the recommended venue for providing treatment, crisis intervention, and various other counseling services during the COVID-19 pandemic. The national *stay-at-home recommendation* created a crisis of provision for many counselors. Providing counseling while separated by distance offers an opportunity for connection that would otherwise be lacking. When a client cannot come to the counselor's office because of location or another limitation, the counselor's office literally meets the client "where they are." The utilization of technology empowers counselors and supervisors to reach further, helping and supporting more clients and supervisees. With the growing accessibility and the expansion of technology, counseling strives to keep pace to meet the new and changing demands of the client. The COVID-19 pandemic forced many counselors who may have been reluctant to become telebehavioral health providers to shift to this modality with little preparation or planning. This book hopes to aid counselors in all aspects of online counseling. Throughout the book, distance or online counseling will be referred to as telebehavioral health to align with the descriptions and definitions from the American Counseling Association (ACA).

History of Distance Counseling

Counseling from a distance is not a new concept; therapists as far back as Freud have utilized letters to communicate with patients (U.S. Library of

Congress, n.d.). Today's access to technology and ease of use has increased the acceptance and utilization of distance counseling exponentially. Von Hafften (n.d.) provided an extensive timeline of the American Psychiatric Association's (APA) usage of telemedicine, beginning with the Nebraska Psychiatric Institute's use of videoconferencing for services ranging from group and individual treatment to professional consultation and education. The author elaborates on the progression with the use of psychiatric consultation by the Massachusetts General Hospital in 1969 and the expansion to its use globally in the 1990s. Telepsychiatry has been found to be "equivalent to in-person care in diagnostic accuracy, treatment effectiveness, and patient satisfaction" (Von Hafften, n.d.); citing it allows for the conservation of resources, including time and money. Further, the author identifies findings that "patient privacy and confidentiality issues parallel in-person care" as well as expedite health care reform.

Since Freud's treatment of "Little Hans" through correspondence in letters, advances in technology have provided new opportunities for counseling across a distance. Skinner and Zack (2004) explain that the invention of the telephone provided a novel treatment modality for counselors that is now supported in the research as an effective treatment option for a variety of clients. With the increased utilization of personal computers and the invention of the internet, distance counseling was again influenced by changing technology (Skinner & Zack, 2004). Although the initial use was for support groups and answers to mental health questions online, the internet now provides counselors with the technology to meet with their clients face-to-face through confidential videoconferencing platforms (Skinner & Zach, 2004).

A study in 2018 by Wong et al. found synchronous counseling and supervision to be a means of providing counseling to individuals in a highly accessible and cost-effective manner. Individuals who may have previously avoided counseling due to stigma or availability now have access to services through synchronous counseling (Mallen et al., 2005; Novotney, 2017). As Childress (2000) notes, this shift brings with it a unique set of etiquette and ethical concerns. The Council for Accreditation of Counseling and Related Educational Programs (CACREP, 2020) notes that online counselor education programs are certified against the same set of standards as traditionally provided programs. However, not all counseling education programs prepare their students to effectively provide counseling and supervision on the synchronous platform. This became very apparent during the COVID-19 pandemic as many programs scrambled to fulfill internship requirements while face-to-face counseling ceased for most providers.

As counselors with a wide range of clinical experience, including online counseling work, we believe that education regarding online counseling is imperative for the next generation of counselors. Technology and the accessibility to that technology has created an access to mental health services not seen in previous times. Counselors currently require training tailored to their discipline on best practices to work with various populations online in an ethical manner. In their Code of Ethics, the American Counseling Association (ACA, 2014) has addressed the need for counselors to widen the lens and to not view in-person counseling as the single means for providing services, to understand the influence of technology on the profession, to be competent in the use of technology, and to practice online counseling in an ethical manner, similarly to the expectation with face-to-face (Standard H).

The expansion of counseling onto the online landscape requires an evidence-based guide to direct counselors in the best practices of online work. *Synchronous Online Counseling and Supervision in the 21st Century* was developed as a text primarily used in a Counselor Education and Supervision course focusing on the synchronous/online format of counseling and supervision. Counseling and Supervision represent two of the eight core curricular areas required of all entry-level counselor education graduates set forth in the 2016 CACREP program accreditation standards, and gatekeeping is a mandate of the ACA standards. This book will provide insight into meeting each of those standards through an evidence-based discussion on the etiquette, skills, and issues surrounding synchronous counseling and supervision. With CACREP accrediting nearly 900 counseling programs and over 101 additional programs engaged in the process of seeking first-time accreditation, this text will provide counselor educators with an evidence-based guide to utilize in graduate-level classes focusing on online counseling and supervision. By building on the knowledge developed through their education and experience in the field, this text provides students with the guide to working with clients and supervisees at a distance while focusing on the specifics necessary for successful and ethical online practice. Additionally, the text can be utilized by seasoned professionals looking to expand their counseling practice to include the online environment. The text is unique in that it focuses solely on counselors, is based in the research of best practices for online counseling and supervision, includes recommendations for specific populations, and provides resources with each chapter. A case exploration is also included and offers a real-world view of each chapter topic.

The effectiveness of online synchronous mental health treatment has been established throughout the literature (Chakrabarti, 2015; Richardson et al., 2009; Simpson, 2009). In 2008, Barak et al. found the average impact of online treatment to be equivalent to that of face-to-face interventions and the effectiveness between the two modalities was relatively equal, providing "strong support for the adoption of online psychological interventions as a legitimate therapeutic activity" and suggesting "several insights in regard to its application" (p. 109). This text provides professionals and students with valuable and useful adaptions of evidence-based interventions tailored to the online synchronous format, thus providing a springboard to transition into this realm of counseling rooted firmly in science and research.

History of Online Supervision

Just as Freud was the first to provide distance counseling, he was also the first to provide distance supervision, offering suggestions to other therapists studying his psychoanalytic approach, though he did not refer to it as supervision (Bradley et al., 2010). Though initial supervision was provided predominantly in person, as the budding therapist studied with the experienced therapist, those who were not able to relocate consulted via correspondence (Watkins, 2013). Watkins suggested that the first formal supervision occurred when Freud worked with "Little Hans" and provided in-person supervision to Hans's father on how best to work with the young boy. Online supervision has been shown to be equally effective as in-person supervision, and Coker and Schooley (2012) reported that the quality of the supervisory relationship, not the medium that supervision was delivered, was more important for successful client and supervisee outcomes.

Synchronous Online Counseling and Supervision in the 21st Century offers supervisors the tools and techniques to successfully supervise emerging counselors in an online format. Utilizing evidence-based approaches, supervision theories and skills will be explored with modifications for the online environment. Additionally, gatekeeping from a distance will be explored and online challenges addressed.

Multicultural/Ethical/Social Justice Applications

Counselors and supervisors need to consider the multicultural, social justice, and ethical implications of the theoretic approach they choose as well as the issues brought forth by the client or supervisee. Counselors need to consider the multiple identities of the client online, bearing in mind not only their culture, socioeconomic status, traditions, and values, but their age, comfort with technology, and view of counseling. This will be explored more thoroughly in subsequent chapters. Social justice refers to the consideration of the client and their environment, social situation, and the counselor's ability to facilitate the client's access to services and to empower the client to self-advocate. Multicultural competence and social justice will be discussed in each chapter as applicable to the specific topic. Counseling ethics, according to the ACA standards, as well as state regulations and certification board requirements, apply regardless of setting and will be explored further in Chapter 3. The online counseling realm brings both opportunities and challenges that forward-thinking counselors can learn in order to provide effective assessment, treatment, and crisis intervention to clients at a distance.

Discussion of Applicable Skills

Each chapter will have bonus sections to further learning and provide examples of chapter content. Specific skills will be listed with the necessary adaptations for the online environment. Sample forms will be included to aid the online transition.

Modification of Techniques

Specific techniques for counselors and supervisors are explored in each chapter with the focus on modifying these for the synchronous counseling and supervision platforms. Each chapter will explore modifications specific to its topic, providing the counselor with various adaptions necessary to meet online clients' needs. These modifications will provide the counselor with an understanding of the modified skills anchored in the fundamental evidence-based practices of the field.

Basic Counseling Skills and Adaption Summaries

The summaries provided at the end of each chapter review basic counseling skills and note modifications necessary to successfully adapt them for the online counselor, supervisor, and client. These modifications are provided as a guide for counselors to tailor to their client needs. Each summary will focus on the highlights of the chapter and provide a quick reference for counselors in training as well as those actively working in the field.

Case Exploration

The case exploration provides the reader with the opportunity to consider various scenarios to apply their skills but also provides an instructor with a foundation on which to build class discussions to enhance student learning. The case exploration was designed to include multicultural, ethical, and social justice considerations regardless of topic, as these are fundamental issues necessary to consider in each counseling session. Each chapter will utilize the following case exploration for consideration and discussion as applicable to the topic being covered:

> The Levai family consists of Juan, the biological father of Amy and Raymond, and their biological mother, Tristin. Tristin and Juan divorced several years ago. Amy is a 9-year-old female and Raymond is a 16-year-old male. Tristin is currently in a long-term relationship with Pat and sharing custody of Amy and Raymond with Juan. The family system as a whole has numerous challenges and is seeking online counseling because they live in a remote area several hours from any counseling services. Katrina is a provisionally licensed mental health counselor in her state and is currently under the supervision of Eugene, a licensed professional counselor certified in telebehavioral health who resides 2 hours away from Katrina in the same state.
>
> Facts that may surface throughout Katrina's work with the family: Pat is a transgender female; Pat and Tristin are life partners but are not married; and Katrina is pursuing her LPC and is not currently independently licensed.

Chapter Summary Worksheets

Each chapter will provide a worksheet for the counselor, supervisor, or client intended to enhance the online counseling or supervision experience. These will be designed to assist the counselor or supervisor in addressing a specific area of concern such as confidentiality, ethical considerations, or practice development. Additionally, some worksheets will address specific needs of special populations including LGBQIT+, couple and families, and school-aged clients. Diagnostic and symptoms management worksheets are included as well. Topic-specific worksheets are intended to assist the reader in considering the spectrum of issues a client brings to session as well as provide instructors with focused discussion material.

Basic Counseling Forms

Some chapters will include sample forms. These will be provided with a review of the necessary format to comply with ACA ethical standards. The forms will include modification suggestions for the synchronous format with a checklist to assist counselors to ensure the formats for their practice comply with ACA standards.

List of Online Resources

Each chapter will provide a list of online resources to supplement the learning and worksheets provided. These resources will provide additional information, materials, and tools related to chapter topics. Technology and the practice of distance counseling are changing at a rapid pace. The resources included will be a means of remaining informed and up to date with the evolving practice of telebehavioral health.

SUMMARY

The authors understand that basic skills used by counselors are rooted in their education (Erlina Yaumas et al., 2018). These fundamental required skills go beyond just the counseling session and need to include theoretic applications to client needs, assessment, and ethical interventions (Lenz et al., 2010). Clients utilizing the online format bring with them special considerations for the counselor, including receiving counseling in a private space, the adjustment to the online format and interaction pace, and receiving feedback in various formats (Haberstroh et al., 2007). For this reason, this text will focus on assisting counselors to develop a connection and understanding of the synchronous client while tailoring counseling techniques to provide support throughout the counseling process. Additionally, clinical and crisis management skills, diagnostic and symptom management techniques, and licensing and practice issues will be addressed.

Counseling, regardless of format, carries the responsibility for the counselor to provide ethical and evidence-based practices to facilitate a positive change in the client (Lau et al., 2013). Therefore, legal and ethical issues will be a focus with each modification tailored to fit the format, while providing an inclusive view of special populations such as LGBQIT+, those with varying abilities or challenges, remote settings, and couples. Finally, group and child counseling, from kindergarten through college, will be explored and crisis intervention online explained. Readers will be provided a variety of worksheets, games, tools, and techniques to help develop effective synchronous counseling tailored to the unique needs of each client.

Supervision is a vital component of counselor development and a pillar of counselor education and supervision. Therefore, cybersupervision will be addressed with specific attention to models of supervision, distance supervision skills to include cultural competence, the identification and management of online gatekeeping issues, as well as legal and ethical problems. This section of the text will offer guidance to counselors interested in providing supervision at a distance.

With the growing accessibility and the expansion of technology, counseling is again utilizing the latest technology to meet the demands of a changing group of clients seeking mental health services in a different format. Subsequently, supervision of counselors has needed to expand to the online format as well. *Synchronous Online Counseling and Supervision in the 21st Century* aims to ensure counselors, supervisors, and counselor educators will have necessary information to not only provide counseling and supervision services online but also to educate future counselors and supervisors about ethical online work.

References

American Counseling Association. (2014). *ACA code of ethics*. https://www.counseling.org/docs/default-source/ethics/2014-code-of-ethics.pdf?sfvrsn=2d58522c_4

Barak, A., Hen, L., Boniel-Nissim, M., & Shapira, N. (2008). A comprehensive review and a meta-analysis of the effectiveness of internet-based psychotherapeutic interventions. *Journal of Technology in Human Services, 26*(2–4), 109–160. http://dx.doi.org/10.1080/15228830802094429

Bradley, L. J., Ladany, N., Hendricks, B., Whiting, P. P., & Rhode, K. M. (2010). Overview of counseling supervision. In N. Ladany & L. J. Bradley (Eds.), *Counselor supervision* (4th ed.) (pp. 3–13). Routledge.

Childress, C. A. (2000). Ethical issues in providing online psychotherapeutic interventions. *Journal of Medical Internet Research, 2*(1). https://doi.org/10.2196/jmir.2.1.e5

Chakrabarti, S. (2015). Usefulness of telepsychiatry: A critical evaluation of videoconferencing-based approaches. *World Journal of Psychiatry, 5*(3), 286–304. http://dx.doi.org/10.5498/wjp.v5.i3.286

Coker, J. K., & Schooley, A. (2012). Investigating the effectiveness of clinical supervision is a CACREP accredited online counseling program. In G. R. Walz, D. C. Bleuer, & R. K. Yep (Eds.), *Ideas and research you can use: VISTAS 2012, Vol. 1* (pp. 1–10). American Counseling Association. https://www.counseling.org/docs/default-source/vistas/vistas_2012_article_42.pdf?sfvrsn=dbff9031_11

Council for Accreditation of Counseling and Related Educational Programs. (2015). *2016 standards for accreditation.* http://www.cacrep.org/wp-content/uploads/2018/05/2016-Standards-with-Glossary-5.3.2018.pdf

ErlinaYaumus, N., Syafril, S., Mohd Noor, N, Mahmud, Z, Umar, J., Wekke, I., & Rahayu, T. (2018). The importance of counseling basic skills for the counselors. *International Journal of Pure and Applied Mathematics, 119*(18), 1195–1207. https://acadpubl.eu/hub/2018-119-18/1/87.pdf

Haberstroh, S., Duffey, T., Evans, M., Gee, R., & Trepal, H. (2007). The experience of online counseling. *Journal of Mental Health Counseling, 29*(3), 269–282. https://doi.org/10.17744/mehc.29.3.j344651261w357v2

Lau, P., Jaladin, R., & Abdullah, H. (2013). Understanding the two sides of online counseling and their ethical and legal ramifications. *Procedia-Social and Behavioral Sciences, 103*, 1243–1251. https://doi.org/10.1016/j.sbspro.2013.10.453

Lenz, J. G., Peterson, G. W., Reardon, R. C., & Saunders, D. E. (2010). *Connecting career and mental health counseling: Integrating theory and practice.* http://counselingoutfitters.com/vistas/vistas10/Article_01.pdf

Mallen, M. J., Vogel, D. L., Rochlen, A. B., & Day, S. X. (2005). Online counseling: Reviewing the literature from a counseling psychology framework. *The Counseling Psychologist, 33*(6), 819–871. https://doi.org/10.1177/0011000005278624

Novotney, A. (2017). A growing wave of online therapy. *Monitor on Psychology, 48*(2), 48. https://www.apa.org/monitor/2017/02/online-therapy

Richardson, L. K., Frueh, B. C., Grubaugh, A. L., Egede, L., & Elhai, J. D. (2009). Current directions in videoconferencing tele-mental health research. *Clinical Psychology: A Publication of the Division of Clinical Psychology of the American Psychological Association, 16*(3), 323–338. https://doi.org/10.1111/j.1468-2850.2009.01170.x

Simpson, S. (2009). Psychotherapy via videoconferencing: a review. *British Journal of Guidance & Counselling, 37*(3), 271–286. http://dx.doi.org/10.1080/03069880902957007

Skinner, A., & Zack, J.S. (2004). Counseling and the internet. *American Behavioral Scientist, 48*(4), 434–446. http://dx.doi.org/10.1177/0002764204270280

U.S. Library of Congress. (n.d.). *Collection: Sigmund Freud papers.* https://www.loc.gov/collections/sigmund-freud-papers/about-this-collection/

Von Hafften, A. (n.d.). *The history of telepsychiatry.* American Psychological Association. https://www.psychiatry.org/psychiatrists/practice/telepsychiatry/toolkit/history-of-telepsychiatry

Watkins, C. E., Jr. (2013). The beginnings of psychoanalytic supervision: The crucial role of Max Eitingon. *The American Journal of Psychoanalysis, 73*, 254–270. https://doi.org/10.1057/ajp.2013.15

Wong, K. P., Bonn, G., Tam, C. L., & Wong, C. P. (2018). Preferences in online and/or face-to-face counseling among university students in Malaysia. *Frontiers in Psychology, 31*. https://doi.org/10.3389/fpsyg.2018.00064

Fostering Connections and Supportive Relationships at a Distance

Tera Rumbaugh Crawford and Diedre L. Wade

The therapeutic relationship is essential in all counseling settings due to its effect on counseling outcomes. Distance counseling is a growing mental health specialty resulting in counselors turning to technology to provide client support and treatment. Clients are drawn to distance counseling because of cost, convenience, safety of not seeing someone they know in the office, and flexibility, despite being geographically away from the counselor. Distance counseling and the integration of technology can positively affect the therapeutic alliance (Leibert et al., 2006). Research shows that through distance counseling a strong therapeutic alliance can be established that generates positive client outcomes (Pruitt et al., 2014; Richard & Simpson, 2015; Ross, 2016). Future research is necessary to create measures to assess the therapeutic alliance in distance counseling (Hadjistavropoulos et al., 2017). More data collection and analysis of the distance therapeutic alliance is necessary as we are transitioning to telebehavioral health services at a rapid pace, catapulted by the COVID-19 pandemic.

Fostering Connections and Supportive Relationships

Distance counseling can provide multiple advantages for the client and counselor. Advantages, including convenience and autonomy, are drawing clients to distance counseling (Leibert et al., 2006). It is the counselor's responsibility to ensure the establishment of the therapeutic alliance through the online format. Fluckiger et al. (2018) define alliance as "holistic collaborative aspects of the therapist-client relationship" (p. 317). A functional therapeutic alliance consists of the counselor and client having shared goals, tasks completed by both the therapist and the client, and a strong attachment between client and the therapist (Norwood et al.,

2018). All of these tasks are easily accomplished at a distance by a well-prepared telebehavioral health counselor.

Psychodynamic therapies popularized the concept of alliance (Fluckiger et al., 2018). Tsai et al. (2019) discuss the concept of alliance as the client and counselor being in a vulnerable therapeutic relationship that encourages the client's process of transformation. Having a strong counseling alliance early on reduces early dropout rates and a stronger likelihood of ongoing treatment (Tsai et al., 2019). The authors go on to say that the majority of clients require an average of 10 sessions to get the most benefit from counseling (Tsai et al., 2019). If given a choice, it is highly unlikely that a client will attend more than two sessions with a counselor if they do not feel a therapeutic connection (Tsai et al., 2019). Therefore, it is imperative that a counselor ensures an alliance is developed quickly and intentionally, as a relationship may be more difficult to establish at a distance.

Bedi (2006) discussed an interview of 40 participants in a study to find out what qualities form a strong alliance in the counseling relationship. Seventy-four factors were identified and categorized into 11 areas, including the following: "setting, presentation and body language, nonverbal gestures, emotional support and care, honesty, validation, guidance and challenging education, referrals and recommended materials, client's personal responsibility, and session administration" (Bedi, 2006, p. 26). As already mentioned, the counselor must ensure that distance counseling is just as effective as in-person counseling in the formation of a strong therapeutic relationship. Ross (2016) discusses a study of 81 participants who engaged in internet-based counseling. Half reported a strong therapeutic alliance, and all reported less inhibition and more self-disclosure than if they participated in face-to-face counseling (Ross, 2016). Another study of 16 therapists and 17 clients all rated their experience with online counseling as positive in the areas of the therapeutic alliance and how well the treatment went (Ross, 2016). Both studies suggest a therapeutic alliance is possible and often positive regardless of the platform in which it is delivered.

It has been suggested that there are two phases in the alliance between counselor and client (Fluckiger et al., 2018), both involving expectation. The first phase, Type I alliance, is the client having a belief that the counselor can help them, and they have a supportive relationship (Fluckiger et al., 2018). Type I alliance is easily replicated in the online format. Type II alliance is the second phase and refers to the client having faith in the process of therapy and being a willing participant in the process (Fluckiger et al., 2018). The alliance consists of shared therapeutic goals. The client must first trust the counselor before they can trust the process of counseling. Type II alliances may require intentional effort on the part of the counselor. The client will not only have to trust the therapeutic process, but they will also have to develop a trust for the mode of delivery. Exploring concerns about the technology and service delivery will improve trust in the online therapeutic process, facilitating a Type II alliance.

The development of a **therapeutic relationship** is essential "because clinical evidence suggests that the relationship is one of the largest and most consistent factors predicting [a] successful outcome of counseling" (Leibert et al., 2006, p. 70). Freud was one of the first to identify that the relationship between the counselor and the client was more important than the actual therapy process (Fluckiger et al., 2018). Carl Rogers had a positive influence on the concept of alliance with the ideas of empathy, unconditional positive regard, and being genuine with the client (Fluckiger et al., 2018). The therapeutic alliance consists of the counselor and the client forming a bond that helps accomplish the treatment goals. Clients and counselors tend to view the therapeutic alliance differently, so the counselor must evaluate the status of the differing perceptions throughout the counseling process (Bedi, 2006). Tsai et al. (2019) state that "attachment security" is the therapist exhibiting supportive behaviors to the client (p. 56). These supporting behaviors show the client that the counselor is committed to the counseling process and has their best interests in mind.

Distance Counseling Enhancing the Therapeutic Relationship

Technology is being integrated with traditional counseling methods to enhance the therapeutic relationship. Research (Kafka, 2020; Kay-Lambkin et al., 2017; Pruitt et al., 2014; Richard & Simpson, 2015) has shown an effective and strong alliance can be developed from a distance. The counselor can still exhibit the positive aspects of in-person counseling, such as showing empathy, active listening skills, and the use of reflection with the client. Studies have found that clients rate the level of therapeutic alliance in distance counseling to be equal to or greater than traditional counseling (Pruitt et al., 2014). Distance counseling and the integration of technology into counseling can have positive effects on the therapeutic alliance.

Counselors are integrating technology to improve traditional counseling experiences by using text messages to add to treatment. Counselors are now looking to technology to enhance more than the logistical side of services. Technology is used as a tool to enhance between-session experiences of face-to-face counseling. Pruitt et al. (2014) found that clients are more likely to reach out to the counselor in between sessions when distance counseling is utilized. If the client is going through a crisis, it is often easier for the client to quickly see the counselor via an online platform rather than wait for a scheduled session in the office. Kafka (2020) discussed distance counseling as a "stepping stone," with a quick intervention being more helpful sometimes than a weekly 50-minute in-person session (p. 2). Distance counseling may be used for a one-time consultation or as a regular counseling option.

Richard and Simpson (2015) investigated an advanced technological system's effects on clients' between-session experiences. The study utilized goACT, a mobile and web-based interactive software application, which can be used between counseling sessions. Richard and Simpson (2015) found that by using goACT the clients showed enhanced patient experience, therapeutic alliance, and patient engagement. These findings suggest that traditional counseling can be improved with the use of technology.

Kay-Lambkin et al. (2017) conducted an exploratory analysis of eHealth interventions' impact on the therapeutic alliance and outcomes for clients suffering from depression and alcohol/substance abuse problems. The clients received computer-delivered cognitive behavioral therapy with motivational interviewing (SHADE CBT/MI) that utilized brief therapist assistance. Kay-Lambkin et al. found that SHADE CBT/MI "produced superior outcomes in depression and alcohol/cannabis use compared to supportive counseling" (p. 729). The findings identified a higher therapeutic bond early in treatment for SHADE CBT/MI clients, which was associated with reduced cannabis use over time (Kay-Lambkin et al., 2017). This study supports the use of technology-based interventions for positive therapeutic relationships and treatment outcomes.

Researchers at an eastern Kentucky university found that nearby combat veterans diagnosed with posttraumatic stress disorder (PTSD) found distance counseling to be just as effective as in-person counseling (McClellan et al., 2020). While some of the counselors they studied had less than favorable views of distance counseling, clients with depression in rural areas found distance counseling to be helpful (McClellan et al., 2020). When counselors embraced distance counseling as a viable therapeutic option, they sought out more training and experience to feel more comfortable utilizing this format (McClellan et al., 2020). Security issues and lack of training were the main factors identified by Norwood et al. (2018) as reasons counselors were hesitant to provide distance counseling.

Norwood et al. (2018) conducted a study to see if videoconferencing psychotherapy (VCP) had an inferior therapeutic alliance compared to in-person counseling. Their hypothesis was that VCP would be inferior to in-person counseling (Norwood et al., 2018). Primarily using the Working Alliance Inventory (WAI) by counselors, clients, and observers, the researchers showed that VCP was just as effective for a strong working alliance compared to in-person counseling (Norwood et al., 2018). Sample questions and more information about the WAI can be found in the worksheet section at the end of this chapter. While counselors clung more to the idea of it not being as effective for the alliance between counselor and client, clients did not see this as an issue (Norwood et al., 2018). It should be noted that the WAI is measuring the therapeutic relationship between counselor and client, while the term *working alliance* is often associated with the relationship between counselor and supervisor.

The traditional therapeutic relationship can be enhanced by utilizing technology. When individuals tried distance counseling initially as their first experience with counseling, researchers wanted to know if they would be interested in ongoing counseling in person and found that 65% said they would continue counseling (Alleman, 2002). Counseling services do not have to be solely traditional or distanced but can be blended. Counselors should embrace technology and use it to improve their clients' therapeutic experience. The integration of technology is associated with positive client outcomes. Distance counseling is desirable due to the speed of receiving services and the access (Kafka, 2020). Technology offers an additional tool for counselors to provide, or at the very least enhance, counseling services.

Therapeutic Alliance Through Distance Counseling

A **working alliance** is the quality of the relationship between counselor and client "that develops around the goals, cooperation, mutual trust, confidence in, and liking of one another" as defined by Klemperer et al. (2017, p. 130). In this study working and therapeutic alliance are used synonymously. A strong therapeutic (working) alliance will assist clients in making meaningful changes in their lives. Originally, counselors doubted the ability to form meaningful working relationships from a distance. However, research has changed those opinions by proving that strong therapeutic alliances can be created utilizing distance counseling.

Klemperer et al. (2017) conducted a randomized controlled trial with smokers to compare the effects of usual care versus brief motivational and reduction counseling. All counseling services were delivered via telephone. The researchers analyzed the effects of the alliance and empathy on the smokers' quit attempt (QA). Klemperer et al. (2017) found that the increase of working alliance had a positive effect on QA while increased empathy had a negative effect on QA. When the follow-up occurred at 6 months, "39% of participants in the usual care, 44% in the motivational, and 38% in the reduction condition made a QA that lasted 24 hours" (Klemperer et al., 2017, p. 133).

The percentages of clients that made a QA shows that an effective therapeutic alliance is possible to create via distance counseling.

The inability to utilize nonverbal cues is a common complaint about text-based distance counseling. Cook and Doyle (2002) quantitatively and qualitatively evaluated the effect of online counseling without video chat on the therapeutic alliance. For quantitative analysis, Cook and Doyle (2002) used the WAI. The results from the WAI revealed that the working alliance was significantly higher for online counseling dyads versus face-to-face counseling dyads. From qualitative data, the results indicated clients experienced strong alliances with their online counselors and disinhibition effects. Therefore, despite the loss of nonverbal cues, the working alliance was effectively established.

Written communication via technology can be effective for the counselor and the client. Alleman (2002) discussed a study that showed people can express how they are feeling via written text even when the reader is communicating with someone they cannot see or hear. The use of emojis, punctuation, and capitalization can help emphasize a message the writer is wanting to convey. Clients can use text-based messages as a way to quickly communicate how they are feeling with their counselor. The counselor can respond back to bridge the time the client waits for their next session. Of course, rules and boundaries are established during the initiation of services to avoid potential problems.

Berger (2017) organized a narrative review of studies that assessed the therapeutic alliance established through distance counseling. When analyzing studies that utilize real-time videoconferencing therapies, Berger (2017) found statistically significant differences in client participation. The clients participated less in face-to-face counseling than in the videoconference therapies. Client participation measures included "the clients' activity level, initiative, trust, spontaneity, and disinhibition" (Berger, 2017, p. 519). Ross (2016) discusses the "disinhibition effect," which involves the internet leading people to behave differently than when they are away from the screen, more often in a positive sense, with more self-disclosure and honesty (p. 38). Distance counseling can lead to clients taking more responsibility in the counseling relationship. The increased sense of responsibility may create more client participation in the counseling process.

Centore and Milacci (2008) described a study of Arab Israeli clients that showed that distance counseling may be an appropriate method of treatment for those who are hesitant to seek mental health services. Accessibility of services from the client's home can allow distance counseling to help conquer the stigma that may come from seeking mental health services (Centore & Milacci, 2008). McClellan et al.'s (2020) study of rural combat veterans showed that a decrease in stigma occurred when distance counseling was utilized. The veterans experienced more comfort from seeking services from their homes. Clients are more likely to participate in treatment that has fewer negative associations.

Along with allowing the time to carefully choose their words to properly convey their message, clients may express themselves with less restriction when they can write their feelings and thoughts through text-based distance counseling compared to sitting in the counselor's office (Centore & Milacci, 2008). The counselor can also take time to fully process what the client is saying and can be comprehensive in their responses to the client. Ross (2016) found that for subjects suffering from bulimia, writing out thoughts and feelings can be helpful as emotional catharsis, which is likely applicable to other concerns as well. Long after counseling has terminated, the client may continue to have access to their writings with their counselor to continue to review and solidify their progress and the ongoing pursuit of their treatment goals.

Understanding the Client's Perspective Regarding Synchronous Counseling

The client's views on the therapeutic relationship are important to consider. Clients who have a more favorable view of distance counseling are more likely to have a more favorable view of their counselor (Centore & Milacci, 2008). Berger's (2017) narrative review discovered that "client-rated alliance scores were high, roughly equivalent to alliance ratings found in studies on face-to-face therapy" (p. 511).

Some clients are more drawn to distance counseling than others based on their perceptions and knowledge of technology. Distance counseling can also be perceived by clients as more covert than traditional counseling. Leibert et al. (2006) conducted a study to compare the self-reported therapeutic alliance of online counseling and face-to-face counseling. The study found that clients of distance counseling are often regular internet users and enjoy the convenience of the sessions. The clients specifically appreciated the advantage of receiving counseling from home when sharing personal information that might produce feelings of shame or embarrassment. Some distance counseling clients report feeling less self-conscious and more able to express themselves compared to in-person counseling (Alleman, 2002). Additional research has hypothesized distance counseling may appeal to people who are more introverted (Hamburger & Ben-Artzi, 2000; Ross, 2016). Clients with problems surrounding body image, eating disorders, and anxiety disorders also find counseling from the privacy of their home appealing (Rochlen, Zack et al., 2004.; Ross, 2016). Distance counseling also appeals to those with fears of being judged, including survivors of sexual or intimate partner abuse and LGBQIT+ clients (Ross, 2016). Clients may perceive the distance counseling relationship as more private than traditional counseling. For some clients, this is the ideal situation.

Rochlen, Land et al. (2004) found that while men and women express similar views of distance counseling, women tend to have higher favorable views of their experiences with in-person counseling compared to men. Online counseling may potentially appeal to "populations who underutilize or stigmatize counseling services" (Rochlen, Land et al., 2004, p. 191). Distance counseling can create a less threatening environment, which can be appealing to men and allow them to open up more in counseling (Rochlen, Land et al., 2004). Men who are less expressive may appreciate distance counseling more than men who display more emotionality (Rochlen, Land et al., 2004).

The benefits of distance counseling can impact the therapeutic relationship. Using technology in counseling can benefit clients by "improved access to services, increased flexibility with timing and location of services, increased patient self-disclosure, and reduced costs" (Richards & Simpson, 2015, p. 57). The client will be more satisfied with their services due to those benefits. The previously mentioned study by Leibert et al. (2006) found that their clients "rated themselves as satisfied with online mental health counseling and had established a working (therapeutic) alliance with their mental health counselors" (p. 78). In a qualitative analysis, Leibert et al. (2006) had clients report that self-disclosing was possible with greater ease during online counseling than during face-to-face counseling.

Clients do occasionally have negative perceptions of distance counseling. A study of five individuals counseled by doctoral interns via synchronous internet-based counseling showed that the therapeutic relationship between client and counselor was primarily affected negatively by technical concerns (Ross, 2016). The clients in the study by Leibert et al. (2006) reported that the main disadvantage of online counseling was the loss of nonverbal information. The lack of nonverbal cues was believed to interfere with the development of the therapeutic relationship (Leibert et al., 2006). Ross (2016) found that some would argue that nonverbal cues were necessary to form an effective counseling relationship. Nonverbal communication can either help or hinder the counseling process (Alleman, 2002). This finding should not discourage distance counselors. There are sites and applications that distance counselors can use that offer video chat and video messaging. The use of punctuation, emojis, and capital letters can mimic what is experienced in-office counseling (Ross, 2016). Alleman (2002) found that counselors felt more focused when they were able to thoroughly think through a written response back to the client. Similarly, the client appreciates the time given to think through what they would like to share with the counselor (Alleman, 2002). Leibert et al. (2006) found evidence that some clients will need video chat to build a strong therapeutic alliance. If the counselor does not have a favorable view of distance counseling, the client's view of the therapeutic relationship will not be as strong (Centore & Millaci, 2008). Ultimately, the client's perspective of either in-person or distance counseling comes from the alliance with the therapist (Bedi, 2006). Although a therapeutic alliance can be developed through nonvisual means, using a video platform is proving to be a more advantageous means of facilitating distance counseling services.

Future Research

Technology is constantly advancing. Therefore, the research in technology-based counseling must continue to advance. Berger (2017) believes that further research should be conducted to "identify unique characteristics of the therapeutic alliance in the different treatment formats" (p. 511). This research would help determine what factors are contributing to the therapeutic alliance in distance counseling. Counselors could understand what formats and characteristics have the greatest effect on the therapeutic alliance. Studies that analyze various techniques and modalities in distance counseling to understand the client's perspective and to see what else might contribute positively to the therapeutic alliance are crucial (Centore & Millaci, 2008: Rochlen, Zach et al., 2004). Studies that focus on specific populations are also necessary to identify cultural nuances that contribute to or interfere with a healthy therapeutic alliance. Norwood et al. (2018) stress the importance of studying the therapeutic alliance between counselors and youth clients using distance counseling. The authors of this text suggest studying the therapeutic alliance and distance counseling across all cultural groups.

Hadjistavropoulos et al. (2017) believe that research should be conducted in order to develop a new measure of therapeutic alliance specific to distance counseling formats. These researchers were most intrigued by assessments for internet-delivered cognitive behavior therapy (ICBT). This is just one of many technology-based formats. Research needs to be conducted to create a distance counseling therapeutic alliance measure (Hadjistavropoulos et al., 2017). The assessment should be able to measure the therapeutic alliance throughout the treatment process.

Multicultural, Ethical, and Social Justice Applications

In 1997 the International Society for Mental Health Online (ISMHO) was created to "promote the understanding, use and development of online community, information and technology for the mental health community" (Ross, 2016, p. 40). A final update was added to the American Counseling Association's (ACA) guidelines in 2005 to include ethical considerations for distance counseling (Ross, 2016). Clients must be appropriate candidates for distance counseling. The counselor must be well informed of the rules and statutes regarding distance counseling, including verifying the client's identity and obtaining proper informed consent information. The counselor must also properly handle privacy and confidentiality concerns. Local resources and how to mitigate technology concerns must be well known to the counselor as well (Ross, 2016). These areas are covered in greater detail in Chapters 3 and 4.

Just as with in-person counseling, the counselor must be properly trained and aware of potential cultural factors that could affect the counseling relationship (Luxton et al., 2016). Jones et al. (2014) discuss the likelihood of "limited multilingual and culturally competent services in rural areas" (p. 399). Minority clients may prefer to see a counselor who is of similar race or ethnicity, but these options may be minimal or nonexistent. The therapeutic alliance is stronger when the client is able to work with someone whom they feel comfortable with, whether that is speaking the same language or sharing the same race or ethnicity. Distance counseling may allow the client to have a counselor who speaks their native language. Pollard et al. (2017) discuss the value of "delivering treatment in a family's native language [to] improve the clinician's ability to describe a complex treatment" (p. 301). The counselor can easily access translated treatment plans and resources for the client and either share their screen during the session or utilize email communication to send to the client (Pollard et al., 2017). As long as privacy standards are followed, the counselor can receive aid from an interpreter to provide the client with the best treatment options (Pollard et al., 2017). The counselor must get as much information on the client's culture as possible, including their cultural values, to properly identify what multicultural issues will need to be emphasized in counseling (Ross, 2016). Today, people are affected by numerous cultural affiliations, and generalizations should be avoided (Luxton et al., 2016). Luxton et al. suggest telebehavioral health assessment should evaluate the "impact of culture on the client/patient's (a) overall comfort/socialization with the behavioral health system; (b) comfort and familiarity with the technology; (c) communication, rapport, and trust; and (d) perceptions of confidentiality" (p. 111).

Out of a nationwide study of 184 individuals who identify as LGBQ, psychological well-being was associated with how the therapist displayed affirmative practices (Alessi et al., 2019). Clients who identify as LGBQ can benefit from distance counseling due to the stigma they may perceive when seeking services from a local provider (Alessi et al., 2019). The therapeutic relationship is more about empathy and sensitivity to the needs of LGBQ clients rather than sharing the same sexual orientation or the counselor's theoretical orientation (Alessi et al., 2019). Distance counseling should provide a safe space for clients of all cultural backgrounds and sexual orientations.

Those recovering from an injury or a long-term physical disability, such as amputation, burn, stroke, multiple sclerosis (MS), or paralysis often experience psychological issues, chronic pain, immobility issues, and transportation problems bolster the need for distance counseling (Dorstyn et al., 2011). The authors go on to say that for amputees, distance counseling can improve self-care routines, decrease symptoms of depression, improve self-efficacy, and improve pain management. Distance counseling allows this population to receive specialized care even though they are at home. This research also reports that studies show distance counseling has been as favorable as in-person counseling. Specifically, patients with MS report improvements in their self-esteem and a decrease in their fatigue through the use of distance counseling. Overall, distance counseling has been shown to enhance "coping and community integration skills and the management of depression for adults with either a newly acquired or long-term physical disability" (Dortstyn et al., 2011, p. 11).

Dual relationships in mental health treatment are unethical (ACA, 2014) yet in small communities difficult to avoid. For clients in rural or small communities, telebehavioral health may offer an opportunity to obtain services from a counselor with no common connections, ensuring dual relationships are avoided (Luxon et al., 2016), facilitating a greater sense of safety and confidentiality, and leading to an improved therapeutic alliance. This may also be applicable to persons with notoriety or in community leadership, further reiterating the point that it is vital to thoroughly assess all the aspects that contribute to a person's unique cultural mosaic.

Discussion of Applicable Skills

Distance counseling requires an additional set of skills to build a strong therapeutic alliance. The counselor is expected to integrate prior strategies from theoretical orientations into their newly developed virtual approach to the therapeutic alliance. Basic and advanced counseling skills are necessary to form a healthy and effective therapeutic relationship. Additionally, advanced skills in technology are necessary so that services can be provided in a safe and reliable manner (Pollard et al., 2017). There are few things more disruptive to a distance relationship than a bad internet connection or operator error.

Trust is the foundation of any healthy relationship, and the therapeutic relationship is no different. Trust is based on similar beliefs and values and words matching actions or "predictable behavior" (Flannery, 1999, p. 57). There is a "conviction that genuine human contact is imperative for successful psychotherapy" (Weinberg & Rolnik, 2020, p. 14). However, if trust can be established through recognition and acceptance of a client's values and beliefs and the counselor demonstrates predictable behavior, the establishment of a therapeutic alliance seems possible even at a distance. In traditional counseling, a client learns a great deal about the counselor's values from their physical space. Consider the physical environment in which counseling is provided; what is seen in the background can be used to connect or disconnect with clients. Consider other basic counseling skills used to build rapport and the application of those skills in the online format. Counseling skills for telebehavioral health are covered in Chapter 7.

Fluckiger et al. (2018) analyzed 295 studies consisting of 30,000 clients from 1978–2017 that either participated in distance counseling or in-person counseling. From these studies, the researchers recommend the counselor build, maintain, and evaluate the therapeutic alliance throughout the entire process of therapy. The counselor and client must agree on treatment goals early on in therapy (Fluckiger et al., 2018). Fluckiger et al. also suggest that the counselor should evaluate the client's readiness for change early on in the therapeutic process. The client and counselor must understand and maintain confidentiality. The client must understand the expectations of counseling, including not sharing content that had been written or recorded in the therapy context (Alleman, 2002). Alliance in counseling is "often the result of negotiation … [and] attention should be equally accorded to the alliance in internet-mediated psychotherapy" (Fluckiger et al., 2018, p. 333). The therapeutic alliance in distance counseling must be formed in a similar fashion to in-person counseling. The client and the counselor must work together to negotiate and build the foundation of the therapeutic relationship. A client is more likely to contact the counselor between sessions when distance counseling is utilized (Pruitt et al., 2014). For this reason, boundaries and rules concerning between-session contact must be established during the initial contact. It could be extremely beneficial for the client in crisis to speak to a counselor right away instead of waiting for their next scheduled session. Crisis and emergency plans must be established, clearly conveyed to the client, and maintained. The counselor may help de-escalate the situation in the moment, rather than the client experiencing further distress. Crisis intervention can be more helpful than a weekly in-person session (Kafka, 2020) and is discussed in more detail in Chapter 11.

Just because the counselor has years of experience in practice does not mean they will effectively counsel from a distance. A pilot one-semester study of psychology students showed that a training program increases skills, but additional training would be needed to effectively provide online services to clients (Ross, 2016). The counselor must undergo special training to ensure they are equipped to handle issues that may arise and properly develop a therapeutic alliance with the client. Training can be found online and in person through various counseling associations and organizations.

Modification of Techniques

Pollard et al. (2017) recommend having a "clinical infrastructure" designed to ensure that policies and procedures are carried out effectively to maintain client safety and confidentiality (p. 298). This includes the proper selection of candidates for effective distance counseling, distance counseling education for the counselor, safety planning, proper technology, and adequate internet capacity for both the client and the counselor (Pollard et al., 2017). The counselor begins safety planning at the onset of counseling by gathering a list of local resources for the client, along with crisis hotline numbers (Ross, 2016). This clinical infrastructure supports the development of the therapeutic alliance.

Skills in technology can help the counselor create questionnaires and surveys to better understand their clients, further developing the therapeutic alliance. Tsai et al. (2019) recommend that distance counselors use a brief life summary. The brief life summary allows the client to share all the "highlights" of their life, including the "challenges, celebrations, relationships, enduring circumstances, turning points, accomplishments, losses, adventure, and the peaks and valleys that have shaped [the client] as a person" (Tsai et al., 2019, p. 56). This summary allows the client to reflect on their life and saves time during the session. This format also allows the counselor to have this information on hand to "give reinforcing feedback and express safety, acceptance, empathy, validation, and deep understanding" (Tsai et al., 2019, p. 56), all vital factors in relationship development. It also allows the client to disclose as much or as little to the counselor as they wish. As already discussed in this chapter, the counselor must have as much information as possible on the client's cultural background to be able to properly counsel from a multicultural perspective.

According to Thera Platform (2018), some of the techniques that promote the therapeutic relationship translate to distance counseling and some techniques do not. Theoretical orientation may influence this to some degree. Weinberg and Rolnick (2020) discuss "two camps," described as the "techniques camp" and the "relationship camp," each representing a different view of the "curative factor" resulting in change (p. 14). Each camp has a specific view of providing mental health services at a distance. The relationship camp is associated with a psychodynamic or a Freudian approach and may struggle with forming relationships at a distance (Weinberg & Rolnick, 2020). The techniques camp is associated with cognitive behavioral therapy and Albert Ellis. The techniques camp embraced the internet and worked to make face-to-face intervention convert to the internet platform. Ellis is reported to have rebuked the idea that you have to see clients face-to-face (Weinberg & Rolnick, 2020). Both camps initially began with services that did not include real-time interaction or videoconferencing. It should be stated that it is highly beneficial to use videoconferencing to aid in the therapeutic relationship development. Many of the suggestions included in this book are based on the use of video.

Counselors should build a rapport with clients by appearing professional, relaxed, and friendly (Thera Platform, 2018). Counselors should simulate eye contact by alternately looking into the camera and at the screen (Thera Platform, 2018). It may appear that the counselor is not making eye contact sometimes when looking at the screen. This should be explained to the client to avoid interference in the development of a therapeutic relationship. Therapeutic alliance is also established through the use of nonverbals (Thera Platform, 2018). Distance counseling with video features allows for body language use in the session. More descriptive language can be used when video features are unavailable. Counselors can also directly address the therapeutic relationship by discussing the benefits of establishing a therapeutic alliance, checking in on the client's feelings, and inviting feedback (Thera Platform, 2018), all similar to face-to-face interactions performed in the office.

Basic Counseling Skills and Adaptation Summaries

Counselors must modify their techniques and the delivery of services in order to maintain a therapeutic alliance in distance counseling. This may require more effort and intentionality on the part of the counselor. It is important for counselors to correctly identify clients that would benefit from distance counseling (Pollard et al., 2017) and those not suitable for telebehavioral health services. A virtual approach has to be taken to administer traditional strategies, such as crisis interventions and obtaining basic client information. In order to do this effectively, counselors must obtain advanced skills in technology. Resources for online training can be found in the sources identified at the end of this chapter. Online training can show counselors how to build and maintain an effective therapeutic alliance throughout the entire process of therapy.

SUMMARY

Clients report that the advantages of distance counseling draw them to this format. The cost, convenience, anonymous nature, and flexibility are some of the clients' perceived benefits. Distance counseling and the integration of technology can have a positive effect on the therapeutic alliance. Distance counseling clients report a strong therapeutic alliance, less inhibition during sessions, and increased self-disclosure (Ross, 2016). Counselors appear to experience more difficulty moving to an online format than clients, with many counselors expressing concerns about rapport building and the therapeutic alliance (Bedi, 2006).

Technology is being used to enhance traditional face-to-face counseling and the therapeutic alliance (Leibert, 2006; Pruitt et al., 2014; Richard & Simpson, 2015; Ross, 2016). The therapeutic alliance created through distance counseling can place more responsibility on the client and counselor. This increased level of responsibility can provide better outcomes for some individuals. Counselors were once skeptical about distance counseling's ability to create an effective therapeutic alliance (Bedi, 2006). Research has proven that distance counseling can establish a strong therapeutic alliance that positively impacts client outcomes (Leibert, 2006; Pruitt et al., 2014; Richard & Simpson, 2015; Ross, 2016).

CASE EXPLORATION

Consider the fact that Pat is a transgender female and the life partner to Tristin, but they are not married. Raymond has some difficulty accepting Pat in a parental role for no other reason than Pat is not Juan, and he harbors some resentment towards Juan and Tristin for breaking up and having to travel between two households. However, Raymond states he does not feel "ready" to discuss this with Pat or Juan yet and is afraid to discuss it with Tristin because he "doesn't want to make her cry." Katrina, the counselor, will introduce some solution-focused and person-centered techniques to foster connections and establish a supportive relationship.

> **Katrina:** So, Raymond, last week we talked about you wanting to talk to your mom and dad about your feelings about them breaking up, and you shared you were having difficulty getting close to Pat because she's not your dad. How are you doing with all that today?

> **Raymond:** I'm feeling frustrated with all these feelings. I can't talk to my dad because he just gets angry and I can't talk to my mom because she just cries and tells me she's sorry, but she had to leave if she was ever going to happy. My mom keeps asking me what the problem is with Pat and I can't tell her that basically it's that she's not my dad and never will be. I just don't know.

> **Katrina:** That all sounds very stressful for you to deal with. It is understandable that you would feel frustrated. Your dad and mom are lucky to have a son who cares about their feelings and that you do not want to make them upset.

> **Raymond:** I definitely don't want to make my mom upset. She cries enough as it is.

> **Katrina:** It's interesting to hear you say you "can't" talk to your dad and you "can't" talk to your mom. Is that really true?

> **Raymond:** Well, I know I "can" talk to them, but I get stressed out about how they might respond to me.

> **Katrina:** So, if you could snap your fingers and make things go the way you think they should in the conversation, what would happen?

> **Raymond:** I could talk to my dad without him getting angry and talk to my mom without making her cry.

Katrina: How about we switch around the wording? Instead of saying you could talk to your dad without him getting angry, how about we say, "I could talk to my dad and feel good about the conversation"? While we can't control how others respond to what we say, we can work on ways of communicating with them to make you feel better about your part in the conversation. Same with your mom: Instead of not making her cry, how about we focus on talking to her where she will understand where you are coming from?

Raymond: Yeah, makes sense.

Katrina: I know you said you weren't "ready" to talk about these things with them yet. What needs to happen to make you more ready?

Raymond: I guess having practice saying what I'd like to say to them.

Katrina: Great! This is a wonderful opportunity to talk about these things without being fearful of how they might react, because it's just me hearing. Does that sound okay with you?

Raymond: Sure does.

Worksheets

WORKING ALLIANCE INVENTORY SAMPLE
Form C: Questions 3, 4, and 6
Instructions

On the following pages there are sentences that describe some of the different ways a person might think or feel about their therapist. As you read the sentences mentally insert the name of your therapist (counselor) in place of _____ in the text.

Below each statement inside there is a 7-point scale:

1	2	3	4	5	6	7
Never	Rarely	Occasionally	Sometimes	Often	Very often	Always

If the statement describes the way you *always* feel (or think) circle the number 7; if it *never* applies to you circle the number.

Use the numbers in between to describe the variations between these extremes.

Work fast; your first impressions are the ones we would like to see.

(PLEASE DON'T FORGET TO RESPOND TO *EVERY ITEM*.)

Thank you for your cooperation.

© A. O. Horvath, 1981, 1984.

3. I am worried about the outcome of these sessions.

1	2	3	4	5	6	7
Never	Rarely	Occasionally	Sometimes	Often	Very often	Always

4. What I am doing in therapy gives me new ways of looking at my problem.

1	2	3	4	5	6	7
Never	Rarely	Occasionally	Sometimes	Often	Very often	Always

7. I find what I am doing in therapy confusing.

1	2	3	4	5	6	7
Never	Rarely	Occasionally	Sometimes	Often	Very often	Always

SCORING KEY FOR THE WAI

(Revised Version T and C forms)

Note: Items with negative (–) polarity should be reverse scored.

TASK scale: 2, 4, 7, 11, 13, 15, 16, 18, 24, 31, 33, 35

Polarity + + – – + – + + + – – +

BOND scale: 1, 5, 8, 17, 19, 20, 21, 23, 26, 28, 29, 36

Polarity – + + + + – + + + + – +

GOAL scale: 3, 6, 9, 10, 12, 14, 22, 25, 27, 30, 32, 34

Polarity – + – – – + + + – + + –

Basic Counseling Forms

NEW CLIENT *COMFORTABILITY* ASSESSMENT

Please fill out the information to share with your counselor about how comfortable you are with working with a counselor and the format of distance counseling.

1. If you have had counseling in the past, what was *most* helpful?

_____

_____

_____

2. If you have had counseling in the past, what was *not* helpful?

_____

_____

_____

3. What qualities would you like your counselor to exhibit?

_____

_____

_____

4. How will you know when you are being understood by your counselor?

_____

_____

_____

5. What fears/anxieties (if any) do you have about starting counseling or working with a counselor?

_____

_____

_____

6. What fears/anxieties (if any) do you have about counseling via technology/distance counseling?

_____

_____

_____

Online Resources

- **Mind ReMake Project**: This site has an extensive list of sites containing free assessments for clinicians to use with clients, covering topics such as anxiety, depression, substance use and relationships, among many other issues. https://mindremakeproject.org/2018/07/21/free-online-assessment-and-screening-tools-for-mental-health/

- **THERA Platform**: The site contains a Health Insurance Portability and Accountability Act (HIPPA) compliant distance counseling platform, blogs on establishing a therapeutic alliance, and articles and resources on tips, techniques, and laws for distance counseling. https://www.theraplatform.com/

References

Alessi, E., Dillon, F., & Van Der Horn, R. (2019). The therapeutic relationship mediates the association between affirmative practice and psychological well-being among lesbian, gay, bisexual, and queer clients. *Psychotherapy, 56*(2), 229–240. https://doi.org/10.1037/pst0000210

Alleman, J. (2002). Online counseling: The internet and mental health treatment. *Psychotherapy: Theory/Research/Practice/Training, 39*(2), 199–209. https://doi.org/10.1037//0033.3204.39.2.199 https://doi.org/10.1037/0033-3204.39.2.199

Bedi, R. (2006). Concept mapping the client's perspective on counseling alliance formation. *Journal of Counseling Psychology, 53*(1), 26–35. https://psycnet.apa.org/doi/10.1037/0022-0167.53.1.26

Berger, T. (2017). The therapeutic alliance in internet interventions: A narrative review and suggestions for future research. *Psychotherapy Research, 27*(5), 511–524. https://doi.org/10.1080/10503307.2015.1119908

Bouchard, S., Payeur, R., Rivard, V., Allard, M., Paquin, B., Renaud, P., & Goyer, L. (2000). Cognitive behavior therapy for panic disorder with agoraphobia in videoconference: Preliminary results. *CyberPsychology & Behavior, 3*(6), 999–1007. https://doi.org/10.1089/109493100452264

Centore, A., & Milacci, F. (2008). A study of mental health counselors' use of and perspectives on distance counseling. *Journal of Mental Health Counseling, 30*(3), 267–282. https://doi.org/10.17744/mehc.30.3.q871r684n863u75r

Cook, J. E., & Doyle, C. (2002). Working alliance in online therapy as compared to face-to-face therapy: Preliminary results. *CyberPsychology & Behavior, 5*(2), 95–105. https://doi.org/10.1089/109493102753770480

Dorstyn, D., Mathias, J., & Denson, L. (2011). Psychosocial outcomes of telephone-based counseling for adults with an acquired physical disability: A meta-analysis. *Rehabilitation Psychology, 56*(1), 1–14. https://doi.org/10.1037/a0022249

Flannery, R. B. (1999). *Preventing youth violence: A guide for parents, teachers and counselors.* Continuum.

Fluckiger, C., Wampold, B., Del Re, A., & Horvath, A. (2018). The alliance in adult psychotherapy: A meta-analytic synthesis. *Psychotherapy, 55*(4), 316–340. https://doi.org/10.1037/pst0000172

Hadjistavropoulos, H. D., Pugh, N. E., Hesser, H., & Andersson, G. (2017). Therapeutic alliance in internet-delivered cognitive behaviour therapy for depression or generalized anxiety. *Clinical Psychology & Psychotherapy, 24*(2), 451–461. https://doi.org/10.1002/cpp.2014

Hamburger, Y. A., & Ben-Artzi, E. (2000). The relationship between extraversion and neuroticism and the different uses of the internet. *Computers in Human Behavior, 16*(4), 441–449. https://doi.org/10.1016/S0747-5632(00)00017-0

Horvath, A.O. (1992). Working Alliance Inventory. Retrieved from https://wai.profhorvath.com/

Jones, A., Shealy, K., Reid-Quinones, K., Moreland, A., Davidson, T., Lopez, C., Barr, S., & de Arellano, M. (2014). Guidelines for establishing a telemental health program to provide evidence-based therapy for trauma-exposed children and families. *Psychological Services, 11*(4), 398–409. https://www.apa.org/pubs/journals/releases/ser-a0034963.pdf

Jordan, S., & Shearer, E. (2019). An exploration of supervision delivered via clinical video telehealth (CVT). *Training and Education in Professional Psychology, 13*(4), 323–330. https://doi.org/10.1037/tep0000245

Kafka, A. (2020). Therapy for the Snapchat Generation: As counseling centers try to meet overwhelming demand, telecounseling makes inroads. *The Chronicle of Higher Education, 66*(22), A14–. https://www-chronicle-com.eu1.proxy.openathens.net/article/therapy-for-the-snapchat-generation/

Kay-Lambkin, F., Baker, A., Palazzi, K., Lewin, T., & Kelly, B. (2017). Therapeutic alliance, client need for approval, and perfectionism as differential moderators of response to eHealth and traditionally delivered treatments for comorbid depression and substance use problems. *International Journal of Behavioral Medicine, 24*(5), 728–739. https://doi.org/10.1007/s12529-017-9676-x

Klemperer, E., Hughes, J., Callas, P., & Solomon, L. (2017). Supplemental material for working alliance and empathy as mediators of brief telephone counseling for cigarette smokers who are not ready to quit. *Psychology of Addictive Behaviors, 31*(1), 130–135. https://doi.org/10.1037/adb0000243

Leibert, T., Archer, J., Munson, J., & York, G. (2006). An exploratory study of client perceptions of internet counseling and the therapeutic alliance. *Journal of Mental Health Counseling, 28*(1), 69–83. https://pdfs.semanticscholar.org/d58b/1900f052a1a205d2ec1f3a342d919e2626d1.pdf?_ga=2.203866966.792469355.1608054527-1464124737.1608054527

Luxton, D. D., Nelson, E., & Maheu, M. (2016). *A practicioner's guide to telemental health: How to conduct legal, ethical, and evidence-based telepractice.* American Psychological Association.

McClellan, M., Florell, D., Palmer, J., & Kidder, C. (2020). Clinician telehealth attitudes in a rural community mental health center setting. *Journal of Rural Mental Health, 44*(1), 62–73. https://doi.org/10.1037/rmh0000127

Mind ReMake Project. (2020). *Free online assessment and screening tools.* https://mindremakeproject.org/2018/07/21/free-online-assessment-and-screening-tools-for-mental-health/

Norwood, C., Moghaddam, N., Malins, S., & Sabin-Farrell, R. (2018). Working alliance and outcome effectiveness in videoconferencing psychotherapy: A systematic review and noninferiority meta-analysis. *Clinical Psychology & Psychotherapy, 25*(6), 797–808. https://doi.org/10.1002/cpp.2315

Pollard, J., Karimi, K., & Ficcagliia, M. (2017). Ethical considerations in the design and implementation of a telehealth service delivery model. *Behavior Analysis: Research and Practice, 17*(4), 298–311. https://doi.org/10.1037/bar0000053

Pruitt, L., Luxton, D., & Shore, P. (2014). Additional clinical benefits of home-based telemental health treatments. *Professional Psychology: Research and Practice, 45*(5), 340–346. https://doi.org/10.1037/a0035461

Richards, P., & Simpson, S. (2015). Beyond the therapeutic hour: an exploratory pilot study of using technology to enhance alliance and engagement within face-to-face psychotherapy. *British Journal of Guidance & Counselling, 43*(1), 57–93. https://doi.org/10.1080/03069885.2014.936824

Rochlen, A. B., Land, L., & Wong, Y. (2004). Male restrictive emotionality and evaluations of online versus face-to-face counseling. *Psychology of Men & Masculinity, 5*(2), 190–200. https://doi.org/10.1037/1524-9220.5.2.190

Rochlen, A. B., Zack, J. S., & Speyer, C. (2004). Online therapy: Review of relevant definitions, debates, and current empirical support. *Journal of Clinical Psychology, 60*(3), 269–283. https://doi.org/10.1002/jclp.10263

Ross, W. (2016). Web-based counseling: Evaluating efficacy in light of ethical challenges and therapeutic advantages. *The Online Journal of Counseling and Education, 5*(2), 35–49

TheraPlatform. (2018, April 2). *How to build the therapeutic relationship in the teletherapy modality.* https://www.theraplatform.com/blog/266/how-to-build-the-therapeutic-relationship-in-the-teletherapy-modality

Tsai, M., Hardebeck, E., Kohlenberg, R., Yoo, D., & Loudon, M. (2019). Creating safe, evocative, attuned and mutually vulnerable therapeutic beginnings: Strategies from functional analytic psychotherapy. *Psychotherapy, 56*(1), 55–61. https://doi.org/10.1037/pst0000203

Weinberg, H., & Rolnick, A. (2020). *Theories and practice of online therapy: Internet-delivered interventions for individuals, groups, families, and organizations.* Routledge.

Legal and Ethical Issues in Synchronous Counseling and Supervision

Colette Brooks, Marcus Folkes, and David Walther

As counselors, we enter the field with the goal and desire to help people improve their lives. In our roles we can see clients develop and grow in a variety of ways. They can find the strength to move forward in difficult times while learning to trust and beginning to challenge long-held beliefs that do not serve them. The privilege of being in this role also comes with the professional responsibility and the commitment of ethics.

Online counseling ensures lower costs, access to services rapidly, as well as the convenience of being in your own home (Pelling, 2009). Online counseling may provide better access to a wide range of clients assisting them with improving coping skills and issue management. According to Novotney (2017), telebehavioral health can increase access to therapeutic services, sometimes to individuals who have never sought out counseling. Online counseling, however, creates ethical concerns, the most noticeable concern is protecting client's privacy (Novotney, 2017). We must also consider the increased use of technology in the operational aspects of managing an agency or practice as well as our communication with clients. The use of technology includes not only videoconferencing, but also electronic health records, text messages, and email (Kramer & Luxton, 2015). Generally, the counseling profession looks to the code of ethics of the various associations for guidance on ethical concerns. Membership in professional associations is voluntary and not mandated in order to be licensed. However, professional associations establish ethical codes to set the standards and principles for its members and the profession. The code of ethics of the American Counseling Association (ACA, 2014) dedicates section H of the code to distance counseling, technology, and social media. The code of American Association of Marriage and Family Therapy (AAMFT, 2015) also calls out technology-assisted services in section VI of its code. The call out of ethics as it relates to distance counseling clearly indicates the importance ethics in the online environment. It also supports the notion that there is a difference between face-to-face and online counseling and supervision. It is important for counselors to be mindful not only of the code of ethics but also their practicing state guidelines. We explore the special considerations when providing telebehavioral health services resulting from the difference in location and the impact of technology. Discussion of the foundational skills of online counseling will be explored. This chapter explores the ethical topics of consideration when providing counseling services and supervision at a distance.

Confidentiality, Privacy, and Data Security

Counselors are guided by both legal and ethical doctrine to maintain confidentiality of client-protected health information. This extends to the provision of telebehavioral health and supportive services, such as communication outside of the therapy session (Kramer & Luxton, 2015). The introduction of technology into the process will impact the approach to privacy and confidentiality (Lustgarten & Colbow, 2017). Therefore, as clinicians, we must consider security and protect the confidentiality of client data when processing, transmitting, storing, archiving, or even discussing during online supervision. The U.S. Department of Health & Human Services (HHS, 2013) defines confidentiality as the protection of patient information and data from unauthorized disclosures. Within the United States the Health Insurance Portability and Accountability Act of 1996 (HIPAA) mandates the privacy and security of protected health information (U.S. Department of HHS, 2013). To meet the standards of the confidentiality requirements of the act necessitates the implementation of processes, secure communication mechanisms, remediation plans, and staff education (U.S. Department of HHS, 2013). Additionally, the act mandates professionals to enter business associate agreements (BAA) with their technology partners (Pollard et al., 2017; U.S. Department of HHS, 2013). The agreements, however, do not remove the liability from the practitioner in the case of a data breach or other failure of the technology, so diligence is key.

The provisions for security should also be considered in how clients receive communication outside of the therapy session. Clinicians must consider how they use text messages, cellphone devices, and email. These communication methods require attention to ensure security of client information. The best practice for clinicians is to utilize end-to-end encryption software along with two-factor authentication on all software being used in the deployment of telebehavioral health services (Lustgarten & Elhai, 2017). The breach of client information can also occur on the client's devices. The authors stress that clients must be informed of the potential risk and given guidance to keep their devices secure. Additionally, clinicians need to discuss the importance of the client's location during the session, the use of headphones to reduce the risk of a confidentiality breach, and other common measures to improve privacy.

The privacy of client data is also important for security measures, including the way data is collected, stored, and shared. Clinicians need to be aware of privacy risks and to develop mitigation policies and practices (U.S. Department of HHS, 2013). According to Lustgarten and Elhai (2017) clinicians must ensure end-to-end encryption along with proper technological security for both software and hardware. Since a potential breach may occur by individual users, organizations are responsible for ensuring staff members are appropriately trained on regulations as well as policies and procedures that have been adopted to meet these requirements.

Clinical supervision also poses unique ethical concerns in the online environment. Since any computer connected to the internet is vulnerable to being hacked, supervisors must also use HIPAA-compliant software for the storage of supervisee and client records (Rousmaniere et al., 2014). Additionally, the authors suggest adding an encryption software as an additional layer of protection against breaches. Supervisors and supervisees must ensure the privacy of client information during asynchronous consultation or while viewing a video of a session. This can be accomplished by utilizing a space that is closed and private, ensuring their screen is not visible, and the use of headphones. Supervision concerns will be further addressed in Chapter 14.

Online counseling also has limitations specifically related to privacy, practicing at a distance, duty to warn and protect, and the use of social media and applications. As indicated by the HHS Office for Civil Rights, the division in charge of implementing HIPAA, professionals may speak with clients electronically as long as sensible protections are utilized. Some instances of safeguards or protection may incorporate securing a private location to conduct counseling, utilization of the proper HIPAA-complaint database or equipment, and implementing items to mitigate any breaches of privacy.

Privacy

Counselors using email for communication need to be completely consistent with the **security rule** (U.S. Department of HHS, 2019). The Security Rule establishes the national standard for protecting health information held and transferred electronically. It is the standard that operationalizes the **privacy rule**, which mandates that providers release information to sources they are authorized to do so by the client (U.S. Department of HHS, 2013). The security rule provides guidelines and standards that must be met; however, the method of meeting the compliance standard can be adapted to the needs of the practice. When evaluating office rules and procedures, the standard is focused on reasonableness. Neither the privacy rule nor the security rule restricts the utilization of email in communicating with patients or fundamentally requires encryption to be utilized. However, the counselor has an obligation to ensure the confidentiality of protected health information. Counselors must utilize other sensible shields to secure protection, for example double-checking email addresses for accuracy or limiting the amount or types of information contained in unencrypted communications.

In the majority of cases, telebehavioral health relies on live video- or teleconferencing. It is uncommon for practicing counselors to use asynchronous approaches such as email or text messages due to concerns related to not having real-time responses or knowing who is on the other line. While many practices and organizations offer private secure networks to receive, store, and transmit client data, practitioners working in solo or small practices must use commercially available technology and applications (Milby, 2010). Videoconferencing is viewed as a transmission of electronic **protected health information (PHI)**, so the security rule is very relevant. The privacy rule is also relevant and must be adhered to while providing telehealth services (U.S. Department of HSS, 2019; the Office for Civil Rights, 2010). Clinicians and supervisors must ensure the applications, tools, and processes deployed within their practice meet the requirements of the compliance regulation. Some basic guidelines to follow according to the American Counseling Association (ACA, 2014) are (a) give a valiant effort to comprehend the technology you are utilizing, including any important safety efforts; (b) take care with your utilization of web-based media and know that even your search history is a potential risk of security; (c) realize that electronic correspondence has a higher danger of being made public; and (d) utilize strong passwords, information encryption, and other comparable safety efforts. For additional information, please refer to the online sources for HIPAA guidelines.

Social Media

The use of technology can make any counselor's life easy, but if not used consistently as outlined in both ethical codes and law, it could create an abundance of problems. In a rapidly changing technological world, it is important to understand the uses and limitations of social media. Social media can help you keep in touch with other professionals, pursue continuing education opportunities, or reach out to people who may be searching for your services. It is important to implement social media policy in your informed consent (Lannin & Scott, 2013). Counselors need to keep their social media use strictly limited to business purposes only, keeping it separate from personal accounts, not adding clients to the accounts, and not using it to research clients. According to the ACA (2014, H.6.c., H.6.d.) it is an ethical violation for counselors to contact clients through social media and violate their **privacy**. It is vital to protect client privacy and not to disclose confidential client information via social media (H.6.c.) and any exceptions would require a detailed consent outlining the information to be released (ACA, 2014, H.6.d.).

Duty to Warn and Protect

Duty to warn aligns with the counselor's obligation to warn identifiable victims, while duty to protect is the obligation of a counselor to reveal confidential information in the event that counselors have reasons to believe that someone may be harmed. Counselors have a duty to warn authorities if they believe a client presents a threat. They must also report suspected harm to children or elders (Reynolds et al., 2013). A significant concern occurs if the counselor has never met the client or does not know the client's physical location as it may be difficult for the counselor to meet their ethical obligations. For this reason, counselors need to comply with the HIPPA standards regarding identification of clients in verifying their identity and location and developing an applicable emergency plan.

The knowledge of a counselor's obligation to warn begins with affirmation of the distinction between the ethical responsibility of confidentiality and the legal term of **privileged communication**, which is fundamental to the counseling relationship and enhances the confidentiality of shared information with exceptions as noted in the informed consent (Glosoff et al., 2000). Privileged communication is a legal doctrine (also known as therapist-patient privilege) that declares client–counselor helpful communications are to be kept private by the counselor. The client, instead of the counselor, owns this legal benefit, and for the most part just the client has the option to release data from the relationship. Privileged communication rules may vary from state to state; therefore, it is important that clinicians understand the specific requirements for the state where they practice.

However, one consistent feature of privileged communication is that it is not absolute; a special case exists, for instance, when a client threatens to hurt oneself or others. HIPPA (1996) discusses situations where releasing information is appropriate and allowable. Specifically, when there is a serious threat to health or safety then the entity may release this information. While HIPAA does not require a release of information when there is a threat of harm, they do allow disclosure. The ACA's (2014) Code of Ethics perceive exceptions and note that counselors are not required to maintain confidentiality when clients pose a danger or risk to recognizable others.

When counselors stumble on an ethical dilemma, they may choose to implement an ethical decision-making model to help with this process; this can help ensure that their obligation as a counselor is upheld. Barnett and Johnson (2010) suggested that the initial step should include defining and understanding the problem and gathering as many relevant facts and details as possible. The authors suggest this allows counselors to not only identify the main areas of interest, but also begin to consider the ethical issues at hand and any obligations they may have. If a counselor is unsure how to uphold their obligation, supervision and consultation can be beneficial. As counselors it is also our duty to know and inform our clients of the exceptions of confidentiality and privileged communication. One example is suicidal or homicidal ideation with an intent and plan.

The legal precedent for establishing a duty to warn and a duty to protect was set in the wrongful death case of *Tarasoff v. Regents of the University of California*. Tatiana Tarasoff was murdered by Prasenjit Poddar, a student from India enrolled at the University of California. Upon the rejection of Ms. Tarasoff's affection, Mr. Poddar became distraught and sought counseling at the university student counseling center. During therapy, the psychologist working with Mr. Poddar became concerned that Mr. Poddar intended to harm Ms. Tarasoff. The psychologist, along with a psychiatrist, unsuccessfully attempted to have Mr. Poddar committed. The psychologist also advised the campus police of his concerns. The campus police questioned Mr. Poddar, but he assured them he would not harm Ms. Tarasoff and was subsequently released. Mr. Poddar terminated therapy and eventually went to Ms. Tarasoff's home, shot her with a pellet gun as she ran from the house, and ultimately killed her with a kitchen knife (*Tarasoff v. Regents of the University of California, 1974-1976*). In the *Tarasoff* case (1974–1976), Ms. Tarasoff's parents were able to file a wrongful death lawsuit against the university that she attended as well as the psychiatrist and the psychologist with their carelessness to caution Ms. Tarasoff of the fast-approaching peril presented by Mr. Poddar. The defendants won in this lower court case where an appeal was then submitted. The original ruling was overturned. In 1974, the California Supreme Court issued a ruling that established a duty for therapists to warn potential third-party victims. Additionally, the California Supreme Court extended counselors' responsibility to take reasonable steps necessary to protect intended victims, thereby establishing duty to protect in the 1976 rehearing of the *Tarasoff* case. The court held that danger to the public supersedes the protective privilege of a therapeutic relationship (*Tarasoff v. Regents*, 1976).

The duty to warn and protect has been maintained in different states and has become the standard of training for counseling professionals. Duty to warn is an ethical responsibility of professional counselors and an exception to privileged communication, as outlined in the informed consent. In choosing whether duty to protect is applicable under the law, judges for the most part think about whether (a) there was an uncommon relationship and the client conveyed a planned risk legitimately to the counselor, (b) unsafe or harmful activity (for example, extreme injury, psychological abuse or death) was predictable and unavoidable, and (c) the victim was recognizable. When and how to apply the duty to warn to a case may be confusing, and counselors are encouraged to seek both supervision and consultation in making decision in cases where this applies. Court cases coupled with ethical guidelines may guide counselors in application of the duty to warn as it applies to both directly identified and predictable victims. In a telebehavioral health format, the duty to warn and protect may arise in contexts other than threat of injury or homicide of identifiable victims. Counselors should be conscious of responsibilities to warn and protect against clients' threats of danger to identifiable or foreseeable victims of (a) HIV/AIDS (DiMarco & Zoline, 2004), (b) child abuse or neglect, (c) incest, and (d) battery. There are also reporting considerations regarding nonsuicidal self-injurious behavior (NSSIB), late-term abortion, sex-trafficking, and addictive behavior amongst certain professions. Other controversial reporting topics include obligation to warn third-party risk of transmission of HIV or teenage substance use.

Guidelines

There is no simple way to decide when the duty to warn and the duty to protect will emerge, as each case is unique, and resolutions fluctuate among states. Counselors need to approach a potentially dangerous client (a) by being mindful and being sensitive in nature, (b) developing and implementing a remediation plan, and (c) applying a technique for analyzing dangerous behaviors and documentation of these behaviors in the client record. Likewise, if available, past records should be reviewed to assess a client's history and assess the client's potential for violence and intent to act on this possibility.

Malpractice and Liability Insurance

Malpractice occurs when a counselor is negligent in performing responsibilities. As in the face-to-face counseling relationship, clinicians have a duty to be responsive to client needs and ethical in their practice (ACA, 2014). Malpractice insurance is required to practice in most states. Practitioners need to confirm that their coverage extends to online. Additionally, the counselor must be licensed in any states their clients and supervisees are physically located at the time of service. It is important for counselors to understand that they should obtain professional liability insurance.

Licensure and Scope: Domestic and International

The counseling profession in the United States is regulated by the state in which the counselor resides and practices. Regulatory boards in each state are responsible for enforcing laws applicable to the profession of counseling. Counselors, therefore, need to be aware of their state's online counseling rules and laws (Luxton et al., 2016). In addition to licensing, scope of practice must be carefully considered with the anticipation of providing counseling online. The counselor must consider what basic competencies must be in place before working in an online capacity. Competencies are generally based on training, supervision, and experience (Luxton et al., 2016). Training options include online counseling content-specific continuing education, graduate-level courses, and certification. Supervision will be covered in detail later in the last section of this text.

Many states have rules and laws that address online counseling. Should counselors wish to provide counseling services to clients who are located outside of the state in which the counselor is licensed, it is necessary to adhere to the counselor's state's rules and laws. In addition, it is necessary to investigate and adhere to the state's rules and laws in which the client is located. According to the most recent information available from the ACA, 19 states "regulate electronic communications for counselors, but only within their particular states. The general rule is that to practice distance counseling in these states, the counselor must be licensed and follow the regulations of that state" (ACA, n.d.a, para. 2). Nineteen states do not have any rule or law regulating online counseling. The remaining states have either specific stipulations for providing online counseling or explicitly do not support online counseling. The COVID-19 pandemic has caused states to review and establish new guidelines concerning the provision of telebehavioral health.

Licensure portability is a serious issue affecting counselors and clients. The absence of portability severely limits online counseling across state lines. The ACA is addressing portability through "The Interstate Compact for Portability" (ACA, n.d.b). The portability movement has been significantly and thus far positively impacted by the COVID-19 pandemic. Changes to online counseling are shifting rapidly; up-to-date information is best accessed by directly contacting the state in which the counselor and client are located. Additional information on "telehealth," which includes professional counseling, is available through a number of sources. The COVID-19 pandemic and resulting health crisis of 2020 has thrust telebehavioral health to the forefront of professional counseling essential services. In response to this health crisis, states have sensed the urgency to provide and/or update telebehavioral health rules and laws Counseling for State Governments ((CSG) n.d.; APA, 2020 June).

The most up-to-date, comprehensive online counseling laws, regulations, and regulatory policies listed state by state are available through the Epstein, Becker, Green's (n.d.) "Telemental Health Laws available through a free app. Epstein, Becker, Green have been providing these updates since 2016 and in 2020 included telebehavioral health law changes from both state and federal responses to the COVID-19 pandemic (Lerman & Ozinal, n.d.).

Because laws vary from state to state, general guidelines are provided here. Regardless of which state the counselor resides in, it is suggested that the following steps be followed. First, review the ACA Code of Ethics (2014). Section H, Distance Counseling, Technology, and Social Media, are pertinent to telebehavioral health. ACA emphasizes the importance of knowledge and competency in the use of technology and considerations related to ethical and legal use of technology in online counseling (Standard H.1.). Counselors are subject to the state's laws and statutes (Standard H.1.b.) in which they practice as well as the state's laws where the client resides. Knowledge and adherence to these laws and statutes are necessary when providing telebehavioral health. Clients must be made aware of their legal rights and limitations of online counseling when the counselor and client both reside in the same state or are located in different states or countries (Standard H.1.b.).

Informed Consent

When providing online counseling, written documentation of informed consent is required by many states. Some states have specific items that are required for informed consent in general when working with clients face-to-face. Some states have additional required items for informed consent when providing online counseling. For example, the Arizona Board of Behavioral Health Examiners lists specific stipulations continued in R4-6-1106 in its rules related to informed consent when providing online counseling (Arizona Secretary of State, 2018). In summary, Section R4-6-1106, C. 1. stipulates that providers who offer telebehavioral health, in addition to adhering to the requirements of R4-6-1101 (consent for treatment related to behavioral health counselors described in the Arizona Administrative Code, chapter 6. Board of Behavioral Health Examiners), must document in their informed consent inherent limitations and risks pertaining to online counseling. The limitations and risks to providing online counseling must include added risks associated with electronic communication and the possibility of the technology not functioning properly or not functioning at all. Other limitations and risks to be documented in the informed consent include specifics of procedures to be followed in the event of an emergency when the counselor is not available. Also, to be documented is the means of client identification when video is not used.

Section R4-6-1106, C. 1 stipulates that behavioral health providers who offer telebehavioral health, in addition to adhering to the requirements of R4-6-1103 (client record related to behavioral health counselors described in the Arizona Administrative Code, chapter 6. Board of Behavioral Health Examiners) also document in the progress note whether the session was conducted through audio, video, or electronic communication. Each progress note must also document the specific physical location of the client at the time of the counseling session.

The ACA (2014) Code of Ethics also specifies items for inclusion in online counseling-specific informed consent, which include documenting the credentials related to telebehavioral health held by the counselor, contact information, and the counseling practice's physical location. Differences in time zones may be a matter to be addressed as are potential cultural and language differences. Other areas to be documented should include the potential risks and benefits of online counseling, technology in general, as well as social media. Additionally, informed consent should address the potential of failure of the online technology and alternate means of counseling services in the event of technology difficulties, the time frame in which a client may expect a response from the counselor, and the specific protocol should an emergency occur in the counselor's absence (Standard H.2.a.).

Additional suggestions for inclusion in online-specific counseling informed consent include a statement that online sessions are not to be recorded by any party except with explicit documented permission. Also, to be included is an agreement of the specific online counseling platform to be used and instructions on how to use the specified platform. A statement related to the client participating in counseling from a private, distraction-free space is advised, as is a statement related to using a secure internet connection. Other suggestions for inclusion in the informed consent include an established backup plan on how to reconnect in the event that the online counseling connection is lost as well as obtaining emergency contact information for the client if needed (APA, 2020 March). As always, when establishing an informed consent specific to online counseling, the counselor should consult with an attorney familiar with the counselor's state statutes and rules related to the practice of online counseling. The means the client should access emergency services in their specific physical location, time zone and language differences between client and counselor, potential insurance payment barriers, and policies related to social media and include them in the informed consent.

Counselors may also face additional challenges of maintaining client confidentiality of electronic records, the transmission of records, and associated information inherent in online counseling. Counselors must inform clients of these inherent risks of records being accessed by unauthorized entities, as well as inform clients of access of records by authorized persons such as counselor supervisors (Standard H.2.b.), as well as be informed of the limitations of confidentiality associated with online counseling (Standard H.2.c.). Although current standards of encryption for telebehavioral health platforms are not foolproof means of ensuring security, they must be utilized by counselors as a means to ensure confidentiality (Standard H.2.d.). Some means of verification of client identification need be employed throughout delivery of telebehavioral health services. Current industry standards toward this end include the use of specialized identifiers such as code words, or when videoconferencing, photo identification is the preferred means (Standard H.3.).

Distance counseling relationships (Standard H.4.) require special attention. The benefits and limitations of technology in online counseling need to be addressed (Standard H.4.a.). Professional boundaries with clients must be established (Standard H.4.b.) and a concerted effort to determine if clients are capable and qualified to use the telebehavioral health application or platform is necessary (Standard H.4.c.). If synchronous online counseling is determined to be unsuitable or ineffective with the client, face-to-face services or appropriate referrals may be offered (Standard H.4.d.). In addition, information related to how clients may access the requisite technology for online synchronous counseling is provided by counselors and is done so to assist clients in their comfort with the technology as well as to further build the therapeutic alliance (Standard H.4.e.). Chapter 2 explored the nuances unique to the online counseling relationship in detail.

ACA standards regarding technology, records, and maintenance of websites are also important considerations when providing synchronous online counseling (Standard H.5.). In compliance with applicable laws and statutes, specifics of encryption and storage of electronic records is relayed to clients (Standard H.5.a.). Counselors also self-disclose to clients with whom they are engaged in online synchronous counseling, electronic links to licensure, and certification boards. This permits clients to address potential ethical concerns and exercise their client rights (Standard H.5.b.). Counselors need to ensure that the electronic links on practice websites are regularly assessed to be functional and updated (Standard H.5.c.). Giving consideration to cultural and differing ability factors, counseling websites must be accessible to all people. When applicable, means of translation to persons whose primary language differs from the counselor's primary language is available. Counselors, acknowledging the limitations of these accessibilities and translations, need to be aware of these issues and address them with all clients (Standard H.5.d.).

Carefully reviewing one's state's board rules and statutes is imperative. In order to comply, the counselor should carefully follow the rules and statutes established by the state in which they are licensed and are practicing. When clarification is needed counselors should contact the board directly. Consultation with colleagues and legal experts acquainted with the given state's law is advised. Experienced colleagues may provide another set of eyes, which gives perspective to the counselor in insuring laws and statutes are being followed. Review by an attorney with specialization in this area of online professional counseling is advised. Attorneys may review counselor's informed consent and other pertinent documents associated with providing online counseling in order to reasonably ensure counselor compliance with applicable laws and statutes. Membership in professional associations at the state and local level are recommended for further guidance surrounding state regulations.

Additionally, knowledge and competency (ACA, 2014, Standard H.1.a.) in providing telebehavioral health may be addressed through applicable continuing education or graduate-level courses. Another means toward knowledge and competency in providing online counseling is certification. One such certification for professional counselors is the Board Certified Telemental Health Provider (BC-TMH) offered through the Center for Credentialing & Education (n.d.), which is an affiliate of the National Board for Certified Counselors (NBCC).

When practicing counseling in the United States and desiring to offer online counseling to individuals located outside of the United States, due diligence is necessary in determining the specific country's licensing requirements. First, the counselor must consult their licensing board for directives on providing counseling services outside of the state in which they are located. For example, the Arizona Board of Behavioral Health Examiners outlines their rules in reference to telepractice ((R4-6-1106) Arizona Secretary of State, 2018) as follows:

A. Except as otherwise provided by statute, an individual who provides counseling, social work, marriage and family therapy, or substance abuse counseling via telepractice to a client located in Arizona shall be licensed by the Board.

B. Except as otherwise provided by statute, a licensee who provides counseling, social work, marriage and family therapy, or substance abuse counseling via telepractice to a client located outside Arizona shall comply with not only A.R.S. Title 32, Chapter 33, and this Chapter but also the laws and rules of the jurisdiction in which the client is located.

The counselor needs to identify whether counseling and/or related fields are recognized and regulated in the country that the client is located. This is often not an easy task, as in many countries there does not exist an equivalent board of behavioral health that regulates the profession of counseling. In fact, the profession of counseling may not be known or recognized, although other behavioral health professions such as psychiatry and psychology may exist and be regulated. Additionally, in some countries, the lack of recognition or regulation are motivators to seek a counselor located in the United States.

How does the counselor determine if the profession of counseling is recognized and regulated by a country outside of the United States? There are several imperfect ways. One way is to simply do a web browser search by entering counseling or behavioral health in (said country) as an initial means of investigation. An additional way is to contact the United States embassy in the country to determine if the counseling profession is recognized and regulated (M. Maheu, personal communication, March 17-19, 2017). A third way is identifying a U.S. citizen or expatriate who may be practicing in the country to determine how the profession of counseling is understood and regulated (Huggins & Dalton, 2018). Regardless of the manner of investigation, a counselor who chooses to see international clients will need to understand how their mandated duties translate in the client's country. In some countries, mental health is not viewed favorably and any acknowledgement of a diagnosis would detrimentally affect the client for life, so those needing mental health support look to receive services outside of their country. Not all countries have a requirement to report someone who is suicidal or homicidal, and therefore would have no entity to report concerns to in order to fulfill mandated requirements. The counselor will have to consider how to collect emergency contact information and ways to follow up when an international client is suicidal or homicidal.

SUMMARY

Counseling, regardless of platform, is guided by legal and ethical standards. It is important to consider the means to protect client privacy and confidentiality on the online platform by evaluating the security of the various platforms utilized. The manners in which communication occurs must also be secure, so extra steps are required to ensure no violations occur in the online format. Supervision online is an additional risk for violations and must be considered and security attended to. Additionally, the use of social media has specific considerations for the protection of client confidentiality and privacy. Counselors must understand their duty to warn or report and consider the potential difficulties practicing online of these mandates. It is imperative to seek consultation and supervision for cases in which legal or ethical concerns arise. Understanding the need for liability and malpractice insurance is key, as are additional considerations when practicing online. The importance of both HIPAA and ACA standards as they apply to online counseling expand beyond the informed consent to include the transmission of information, the counselor's use of technology and social media, and data security. Counselors need to apply the ethical standards they practice under and the legal statues for both their location of practice and the physical location of the client. Consistent application of legal and ethical statues is expected of counselors, especially those practicing in the online synchronous realm.

CASE EXPLORATION

Family travels out of town (country) and needs a session. Counselor (Katrina) seeks supervision (Eugene).

Katrina: During supervision today, I would like to bring up a question regarding the Levai family. Juan indicated to me that he is planning a trip to another state in a few weeks, but he still wants to keep his telecounseling appointment with the other family members. Since we are doing it online anyway is that okay? Does it matter which state they are in for just that one appointment?

Eugene: Thanks Katrina, I am glad you brought this matter to supervision today. Let us spend a few minutes talking about it. Yes, it does matter. It may seem like a small detail, but we must make sure as ethical and law-abiding counselors we do the right thing.

Katrina: Okay! I am glad I mentioned it; I was not even going to bring it up.

Eugene: Let me break it down like this: Katrina, your provisional license allows you to practice in our state. However, you are not licensed to practice in the state that Juan is traveling to. First, we need to look at our board of behavioral health code in our state to see what it says regarding telecounseling over state lines. We will need to follow these statutes and laws. Next, we will need to look at the board of behavioral codes in the state that Juan is traveling to and comply with those state's statutes and laws.

Katrina: That sounds like a lot of work.

Eugene: Yes, well we do want to do our due diligence and make sure that we are complying with our state's statutes and the rules and statutes of where Juan will be located. Generally, states require that we be licensed not only in the state in which we reside but also in the state where the client is located, even if the client is located there only temporarily. However, some states allow us to conduct counseling (or permit us to practice) for a very limited amount of time in their state even if we are not licensed there. Said another way, those states will permit us to practice there for a short period of time. This is sometimes called the temporary provisions to practice. Some states allow this; other states do not.

Katrina: Okay, how do I find this information out to see if the state that Juan is traveling to allows for this temporary arrangement? How do I do this?

Eugene: First you will want to look at our state board's rules and statutes for counselors. See what they say about practicing over state lines and phone them or email them for clarification. Then look at the state that Juan will be located in. Look at that state's board rules for counselors. See if there is a provision for temporary practice. Give them a call or email them for clarification. Since you are doing telecounseling, be sure to see if they have explicit telecounseling rules. Some states do, and some states do not. You will want to be sure you observe any telecounseling rules the state has in place.

Katrina: Anything else?

Eugene: Yes, you will want to be sure that you record Juan's physical location when he is in the other state for that appointment and review with him emergency procedures and services near him in the event that they are needed.

Katrina: How do you know so much about this?

Eugene: I like to stay abreast of what is happening with telecounseling law, ethics, and best practices. A couple of really good resources for staying current Katrina, are the Epstein, Becker, Green Telemental Health Laws app and the Person-Centered Tech website.

Worksheets

ETHICAL DECISION-MAKING WORKSHEET

What is the ethical question, dilemma, or problem?

Known facts?	Additional facts needed?

What is the impact of technology in this dilemma?

Can the client be involved in the decision-making process? If so, how will they be engaged?

How does your professional code apply?

What applicable laws and regulations apply?

Who can provide consultation on this dilemma?

What are the possible options and courses of action?

What are the consequences of each potential option?

Choose and implement a course of action.

Monitor your choice and evaluate the outcomes to determine if additional action is needed.

Adapted from Forester-Miller & Davis, 2016; Remly & Herlihy, 2016

Online Resources

- **American Counseling Association**: *COVID-19 state resources: State actions on telebehavioral health.* https://www.counseling.org/docs/default-source/government-affairs/telebehavioral-health-per-state.pdf?Status=Temp&sfvrsn=5db75e2c_2

- **American Counseling Association**: Distance counseling, technology, and social media information. https://www.counseling.org/knowledge-center/licensure-requirements/distance-counseling-technology-and-social-media

- **American Counseling Association**: *Licensure & certification – state professional counselor licensure boards.* https://www.counseling.org/knowledge-center/licensure-requirements/state-professional-counselor-licensure-boards

- **American Counseling Association**: *Portability.* https://www.counseling.org/government-affairs/state-issues/portability

- **American Psychological Association**: *Informed consent checklist for telepsychological services.* https://www.apa.org/practice/programs/dmhi/research-information/informed-consent-checklist

- **American Psychological Association**: Telehealth guidance by state during COVID-19: State emergency orders relevant to licensed psychologists during the COVID-19 public health crisis. https://www.apaservices.org/practice/clinic/covid-19-telehealth-state-summary

- **Arizona Secretary of State**: *Arizona administrative code; title 4. Professions and occupations; chapter 6. Board of behavioral health examiners.* https://apps.azsos.gov/public_services/Title_04/4-06.pdf

- Berger, S. E., & Berger, M. A. (2011). Tarasoff "duty to warn" clarified. *The National Psychologist, 71*(2), 133–150. https://nationalpsychologist.com/2009/03/tarasoff-%E2%80%9Cduty-to-warn%E2%80%9D-clarified/101056.html#:~:text=He%20points%20out%20that%20historically,California%20Supreme%20Court%20in%201976

- **CCE-Global**: BC-TMH: Board certified telemental health provider. https://www.cce-global.org/credentialing/bctmh

- **Center for Ethical Practice**: Ethical and legal resources: Practice resources. https://centerforethicalpractice.org/ethical-legal-resources/practice-resources/

- **Elaws.us**: *Arizona revised statutes (Last updated: March 31, 2016), title 32 professions and occupations, chapter 33 behavioral health professionals.* http://az.elaws.us/ars/title32_chapter33

- **Epstein, Becker, Green**: Telemental health laws app. https://www.ebglaw.com/telemental-health-laws-app/

- **Epstein, Becker, Green**: Telemental health laws: Overview. https://www.ebglaw.com/telemental-health-laws-overview/

- **Person Centered Tech**: Legally practicing across borders: A detailed survey of interstate and international mental health practice. https://personcenteredtech.com/courses/bordercross/?utm_source=Person+Centered+Tech+Newsletter&utm_campaign=534706aeeatherapy_from_may_

forward&utm_medium=email&utm_term=0_e9b2dcace3-534706aeea-125876633&goal=0_
e9b2dcace3-534706aeea-125876633&mc_cid=534706aeea&mc_eid=91dfe1fe05

- **U.S. Department of Health and Human Services**: Security rule checklist and guidance material. https://www.hhs.gov/hipaa/for-professionals/security/guidance/index.html

References

American Association for Marriage and Family Therapy. (2015). *AAMFT Code of Ethics*. https://www.aamft.org/Legal_Ethics/Code_of_Ethics.aspx.

American Counseling Association. (n.d.a). *Distance counseling, technology, and social media information*. https://www.counseling.org/knowledge-center/licensure-requirements/distance-counseling-technology-and-social-media

American Counseling Association. (n.d.b). *Portability*. https://www.counseling.org/government-affairs/state-issues/portability

American Counseling Association. (2014). *ACA code of ethics*. https://www.counseling.org/resources/aca-code-of-ethics.pdf

American Counseling Association. (2020, February 18). *The interstate compact*. https://www.counseling.org/docs/default-source/licensure/interstatecompactprogress.pdf?Status=Temp&sfvrsn=1d855d2c_4

American Psychological Association. (2020, March). *Informed consent checklist for telepsychological services*. https://www.apa.org/practice/programs/dmhi/research-information/informed-consent-checklist

American Psychological Association. (2020, June 11). *Telehealth guidance by state during COVID-19: State emergency orders relevant to licensed psychologists during the COVID-19 public health crisis*. https://www.apaservices.org/practice/clinic/covid-19-telehealth-state-summary

Arizona Secretary of State. (2018, December 31). *Arizona administrative code; title 4. Professions and occupations; chapter 6. Board of behavioral health examiners*. https://apps.azsos.gov/public_services/Title_04/4-06.pdf

Barnett, J. E., & Johnson, W. B. (2010). *Ethics desk reference for Counselors*. American Counseling Association.

Center for Credentialing & Education. (n.d.). *BC-TMH board certified-telemental health provider*. https://www.cce-global.org/credentialing/bctmh

DiMarco, M., & Zoline, S.S. (2004). Duty to warn in the context of HIV/AIDS-related psychotherapy: Decision making among psychologists. *Counseling and Counseling Psychology Journal, 1*(2), 68–85. http://eds.a.ebscohost.com/eds/pdfviewer/pdfviewer?vid=1&sid=687f319a-5a27-444b-b496-22fedde2a031%40sessionmgr4007

Epstein Becker Green. (2020). *Telemental health laws App*. https://www.ebglaw.com/telemental-health-laws-app/

Forester-Miller, H., & Davis, T. E. (2016). *Practitioner's guide to ethical decision making* (Rev. ed.). Retrieved from http://www.counseling.org/docs/default-source/ethics/practioner's-guide-toethical-decision-making.pdf

Glosoff, H. L., Herlihy, B., & Spence, E. B. (2000). Privileged communication in the counselor-client relationship. *Journal of Counseling & Development, 78*(4), 454–462. https://doi.org/10.1002/j.1556-6676.2000.tb01929.xzs

Huggins, R., & Dalton, L. (2018, November 29). *Legally practicing across borders: A detailed survey of inter-state and international mental health practice.* https://personcenteredtech.com/courses/bordercross/

Huprich, S., Fuller, K., & Schneider, R. B. (2003). Divergent ethical perspective on duty-to-warn principles with HIV patients. *Ethics and Behavior, 13*(3), 263-278. doi: 10.1207/S15327019EB1303_05

Kramer, G., & Luxton, D. (2015). Telemental health for children and adolescents: An overview of legal, regulatory, and risk management issues. *Journal of Child and Adolescent Psychopharmacology, Advance online publication, 26*(3), 198-203. doi: 10.1089/cap.2015.0018.

Lannin, D. G., & Scott, N. A. (2013). Social networking ethics: Developing best practices for the new small world. *Professional Psychology Research and Practice, 44*(3), 135–141. https://www.researchgate.net/publication/255721188_Social_Networking_Ethics_Developing_Best_Practices_for_the_New_Small_World

Lerman, A. F., & Ozinal, F. R. (n.d.). *Telemental health laws: Overview.* https://www.ebglaw.com/telemental-health-laws-overview/

Lustgarten S., & Colbow, A. (2017). Ethical concerns for telemental health therapy amidst governmental surveillance. *American Psychologist, 72*(2), 159–170. doi: 10.1037/a0040321

Lustgarten, S. D., & Elhai, J. D. (2018). Technology use in mental health practice and research: Legal and ethical risks. *Clinical Psychology: Science & Practice, 25*(2), e12234. https://doi.org/10.1111/cpsp.12234

Luxton, D. D., Nelson, E-L, & Maheu, M. M. (2016). *A practitioner's guide to telemental health: How to conduct legal, ethical, and evidenced-based telepractice.* American Psychological Association.

Milby, S. (2010). The new meaning of a house call: Wanna Skype, Dr. Gupta? *NewBizViews.* http://www.newbizviews.com/2010/04/12/the-new-meaning-of-a-house-call-wanna-skype-dr-gupta/

Novotney, A. (2017). A growing wave of online therapy. *Monitor on Psychology, 48*(2), 48. https://www.apa.org/monitor/2017/02/online-therapy

Office of the National Coordinator for Health Information Technology (ONC), 2018. Protecting your privacy and security: Protecting the privacy and security of your health information. Author. https://www.healthit.gov/topic/protecting-your-privacy-security

(1), (1), The Use of Technology in Mental Health Special Issue, 1-25.

Remley, T. P., & Herlihy, B. (2016). *Ethical, legal, and professional issues in counselling* (5th edition). Pearson.

Reynolds, D. J., Stiles, W. B., Bailer, A. J., & Hughes, M. R. (2013). Impact of exchanges and client–therapist alliance in online-text psychotherapy. *Cyberpsychology, Behavior, and Social Networking, 16*(5), 370–377. https://doi.org/10.1089/cyber.2012.0195

Rousmaniere, T., Abbass, A., & Frederickson, J. (2014). New developments in technology-assisted supervision and training: A practical overview. *Journal of Clinical Psychology, 70*(11), 1082–1093. https://doi.org/10.1002/jclp.22129

Tarasoff v. Regents of the University of California, 118 Cal. Rptr. 129, 529 P.2d 533 (1974).

Tarasoff v. Regents of the University of California, 17 Cal. 3d 425, 551 P.2d 334 (1976).

U.S. Department of Health and Human Services (2019). *HIPPA for professionals.* Authors. https://www.hhs.gov/hipaa/for-professionals/index.html

U.S. Department of Health and Human Services (2019). *Security Rule Guidance Material.* Authors. https://www.hhs.gov/hipaa/for-professionals/security/guidance/index.html

4

Establishing an Online Practice in Today's World

Debra M. Perez and Tricia M. Mikolon

In today's ever-changing world of daily challenges, global stressors, and the "new reality," counseling services, and specifically distance counseling services, are more needed and sought after than ever before. The need for online counseling was accelerated by the coronavirus pandemic. Technology has aided in providing access to those who may have otherwise avoided counseling in the past (Leibert et al., 2006; Mallen et al., 2005; Novotney, 2017). Online counseling has been found to be an effective means of treatment (Cook & Doyle, 2004; Evans & Hawkins, 2002; Heinlen et al., 2003; Maheu & Gordon, 2000; Rochland et al., 2004; Sampson et al., 1997) and the use of this treatment modality has recently increased exponentially. For these reasons and the COVID-19 stay-at-home requirements, it has become increasingly important for counselors to understand how to effectively and ethically establish an online practice. Counselors pursuing an online practice need to be flexible to the challenges of starting a business and understanding of the risks and benefits, as well as the technological, ethical, and skill adaptions necessary to be successful on this format (Alleman, 2002; Evans & Hawkins, 2002; Heinlen et al., 2003; Maheu & Gordon, 2000). Circumstances and the need to move toward telebehavioral health quickly has facilitated a mass transition to online counseling. Identifying and defining program or practice needs has proven to lead to more successful businesses (Luxton et al., 2016). The mass transition due to the pandemic may require counselors to make needs assessments after the initial start-up. This chapter will identify and suggest ways to eliminate barriers, provide a roadmap, and address multicultural, ethical, and social justice applications of establishing an online practice. **Barriers** are factors that limit or otherwise restrict access to counseling services. The American Counseling Association (ACA, 2014) stresses the need for counselors to "understand that the profession of counseling may no longer be limited to in-person, face-to-face interactions" (Section H), suggesting a shift to the provision of counseling at a distance was gaining popularity. This section of the ACA Code of Ethics stresses the need for counselors to be both knowledgeable and competent in the use of "distance counseling, technology, and/or social media" (H.1.a.) and in the laws and statues regulating distance counseling (H.1.b.). Also outlined are the necessary considerations and guidelines regarding the use of informed consent and security (H.2.), client verification (H.3.), the benefits and considerations of the distance counseling therapeutic relationship (H.4.), the maintenance of records and technology (H.5.), as well as the use of social media (H.6.). Each of these guidelines and necessary considerations will be explored in greater detail.

In addition to what is required to establish any business, the following also will need to be considered:

1. Understanding ACA Code of Ethics and your state's licensure laws for telebehavioral health
2. Informed consent and telebehavioral health treatment documentation
3. Liability insurance that specifically covers telebehavioral health
4. HIPAA-compliant software
5. Clinical outcomes in online counseling

Business Set-Up

Setting up an online practice requires similar steps to setting up an in-person practice. These include needs assessments, office set up considerations, insurance needs, and necessary knowledge and competencies. Other special considerations for online practice will also be discussed.

Needs Assessment

Luxton et al. (2016) suggest that costly decisions can be avoided by conducting a needs assessment to "identify and define" (p. 47) clinical needs, resources available to meet identified needs, and support for the practice. "To rush into to doing online therapy without considering all the many factors involved" can create personal, professional, and financial problems (Derrig-Palumbo & Zeine, 2005 p. 129). Needs assessments should include data from a variety of stakeholders to "answer who, where, when, what, why, how" questions that will ultimately inform the business plan (Luxton et al., p. 49). The needs assessment and subsequent business plan should guide the development of the practice process and procedures. The "telebehavioral health policies and procedures should approximate the in-office setting" (Luxton et al., p. 54). Additionally, "the business structure is another critical initial decision that has important financial and tax implications" (O'Brien & Hauser, 2016, p. 135). While the business considerations of starting a private practice are beyond the scope of this book, the general considerations specific to online work will be explored.

Office Considerations

Although office location is less important since the client is not physically entering the space, the environment that the client sees is something to consider. If working from home, there should be a dedicated office space that is respected by all household members. Furniture is less important since the client will not be sitting in the counselor's office and will only require a desk or table for the computer and a chair for the counselor. The client should view a plain and inviting space, like a wall with a plain picture on it, not one that is overwhelming or cluttered. A bookcase full of books may create an unnecessary distraction for the client as they speak with the counselor. Another important consideration is the security and HIPAA compliance of the dedicated office space. An online office needs to be behind a secure closed door where those walking by cannot hear the sessions and where the computer can be safely locked up when the counselor is not in session.

Since the counselor is not creating an office where clients will visit, another consideration is how to handle basic office duties. Phones can be answered solely by the counselor returning calls outside of sessions, or a virtual receptionist can add a more personal touch by answering the phones to handle basic questions and even schedule appointments. Fax lines can be virtual as well, coming straight to the counselor's computer. The counselor will need to determine how best to manage the various tasks associated to the operation of the business not directly related to providing counseling.

Issues that arise, such as the various options for taking payment for therapy services, have to be worked out prior to taking the first client for counseling. There are various options for receiving payment, including numerous online payment processing services, credit card processing services, and money transfers. Additionally, the process to get signed up with various insurance companies is a long and involved one, so if insurance is to be an option, that process will need to begin right away while other details of the practice are being resolved. There are billing companies that will not only bill insurance companies on the counselor's behalf, but will also do the work to get the counselor registered with each insurance company. That is an additional expense that will need to be weighed against the benefit of someone else filing and following up with insurance companies. If a billing company is utilized, then collections will also be handled by them, freeing up the counselor to focus on therapy and not the billing side of the business. The provider will have additional considerations for how taxes will be filed, business expenses tracked, and daily operations handled. These areas will determine whether or not a service will need to be hired to manage the practice, an accountant required, or if the provider will complete these tasks independently.

Professional Insurance

A counseling practice, whether in person or online, requires professional liability insurance. With the pandemic, malpractice and liability insurers have been covering telebehavioral health more frequently than in the past. However, not all insurers cover counselors who do not live in the same state as their clients. It is wise for a counselor considering providing services in a state they do not live to explore the coverage options with their malpractice and liability insurer.

Knowledge and Competency

Counselors who work in telebehavioral health are required to continually expand their knowledge, skills, and abilities regarding the technical, ethical, and legal considerations of online practice (ACA, 2014, Standard H.1.a.). It is important to have additional training in ethics concerning telebehavioral health practice. Education and certification above and beyond standard training received through graduate counselor education programs is required. Additionally, if telebehavioral health will be the main form of therapy provided, the counselor should pursue additional credentials, such as certification, to demonstrate their commitment to telebehavioral health counseling competencies.

Counselors who use telebehavioral health, technology, and social media within their counseling practice must know the laws and regulations of both the counselor's practicing location and the client's place of residence. Counselors must also confirm that their clients are aware of germane legal rights and limitations governing the practice of counseling across state lines or international boundaries (ACA, 2014, Standard H.1.b.). The details of legal and ethical standards are discussed in detail in Chapter 3; however, it is important to note that counselors must be licensed in the state where their client is located.

Developing a Client Population

When considering the type of online practice the counselor would like to build, client population is an important area to explore. There are some types of clinical problems and types of clients that are not suited for the online modality (Derrig-Palumbo & Zeine, 2010; Luxton et al., 2016). Knowing the types of client issues the counselor would like to focus services on will help guide future professional partnerships and relationships, as well as target marketing options for spreading word about the business. Once the treatment population is chosen, the counselor can begin to market the business by reaching out to potential referral sources, building relationships, and a creating a network of professionals such as general practitioners, psychiatrists, other medical doctors, other counselors, school counselors, social workers, and insurance providers, among others. Networking is a key component in building a successful practice.

In addition to the type of client, the number of clients the counselor will see as a weekly caseload needs to be thoughtfully considered. Being too busy is a good problem to have if there is a successful plan in place to manage the workload, but it can also be the downfall of the business if there is not a well–thought out plan. An overloaded counselor may leave potential clients and referral sources frustrated and will eventually lead to counselor burnout. It is important to address in the policies and procedures a process to manage potential clients when the counselor reaches caseload capacity. Details for managing a waiting list, if that is an option, should also be included. Developing a current and thorough referral list is recommended and is also a method of networking.

Consultation/Supervision

The emerging telebehavioral health counselor may benefit from developing a working relationship with other telebehavioral health providers who have established their own practice. Counselors with face-to-face practices can also mentor the budding businessperson in the nuances of starting a private practice, while also serving as a referral source for the new business. Additionally, having multiple counseling colleagues will provide options should peer supervision or consultation be required for any client concerns.

Technology

There are specific technology requirements for online counseling to ensure protection for the client, as well as a streamlined process. Issues such as client confidentiality, records, and communication fall under this topic. It is imperative that each section is addressed by the counselor prior to seeing clients online.

Hardware

In order to provide counseling online, a computer with a camera and microphone is required. A headset with a microphone is also an option if there is concern that the client could potentially be overheard by others in the counselor's office space. The computer will need to be hardwired into the modem utilizing an Ethernet cord to protect the signal, ensuring the utmost safety, as wireless signals can be hijacked. Additionally, the modem speed will need to be sufficient to ensure video and audio quality during appointments and to avoid freezing or reloading. Working closely with an internet provider to ensure speeds are sufficient will be necessary. Encryption tools will be required to remain HIPAA compliant, if the counselor will be utilizing email, as most email providers do not automatically offer encryption. The ACA (2014) Code of Ethics further addresses the need for counselors to be proficient in the use of this technology under the Distance Counseling, Technology, and Social Media standards in Section H.

Platforms

Various types of online platforms that allow the counselor to virtually see their clients are best practices. There are platforms that offer only videoconferencing or only billing, while others offer both. Other platforms offer multiple functions in one location, such as videoconferencing, note filing, insurance billing, and record keeping. Regardless of the platform chosen, any company storing client information will require a business associate agreement (BAA) signed by the business and the counselor in order to ensure the protection of client information by HIPAA. It is important that this agreement is thoroughly explored and understood by the counselor, as it is ultimately their responsibility to ensure their client's protected information is safe. A checklist is listed in the online resources at the end of the chapter to explore the HIPPA compliance of each available platform.

As an introduction to counseling in the online format, an initial consultation can be offered. This allows the client to experience a simulation of counseling online and decide (without obligation) if telebehavioral health is a viable option. This initial meeting can last 15 minutes and will focus mainly on the counselor's experience and the client's comfort with the online platform. As informed consent has not been signed, client information sharing should be kept very general, and the counselor should not ask specific questions that could lead to mandated reporting. As discussed previously, the ACA (2014) Code of Ethics Standard H.2. directly applies to the informed consent process for online services.

Client Records and Confidentiality

The ACA (2014) Code of Ethics (H.5.) reminds counselors that they must maintain the client's electronic records according to the laws of the client's state, the counselor's state, and the counseling profession. As part of the informed consent process, counselors explain to clients how their electronic records are maintained, stored, encrypted, and protected, as well as for how long records will be stored. Electronic records and transmissions must be HIPAA compliant, as addressed earlier. Counselors will need to explain to the client who specifically could access those electronic records and transmissions. Counselors will need to address the limits of confidentiality when using technology. This was explored in more detail in Chapter 3.

Client Communication

Since some platforms offer messaging capabilities, the counselor will need to consider how they will communicate with their clients and how quickly a client can expect a response. This aspect of online counseling is addressed by Standard H.4.f. of the ACA (2014) Code of Ethics. If the counselor will utilize the online messaging options, it needs to be clear to the client what times the counselor is available for messaging and what types of messages are appropriate. The established business plan and the policies and procedures will identify alternate ways to reach the counselor outside of the acceptable times or in case of emergency. If the counselor is not using the online messaging, then they must clearly explain the preferred method for reaching the counselor outside of appointment times, define the contact steps for emergencies, and clarify that the messaging options are not to be used. Additionally, the counselor will need to define an appointment cancellation policy, deciding how long before the appointment it must be canceled to avoid being charged, as well as the appropriate process for canceling appointments.

Informed Consent

Clients have the ability to decide whether or not to use distance counseling, social media, and any technology as part of the counseling process. Regardless of the type of counseling method chosen, informed consent is an important and ongoing component of the counseling relationship. In addition to the items that are included in a traditional face-to-face informed consent, the counselor will need to address specifics for distance counseling. ACA standard H.2.a. indicates it is to be made clear to the client during this process that all of their therapy sessions will occur online and what technology issues may arise. The counselor will need to specifically lay out the minimum technology requirements that the client will need in order to participate in telebehavioral health, as well as the procedure in the event of technology failure, both during sessions and outside of session time, and alternative methods of counseling during technology failure (H.2.a.). The counselor will need to explain the benefits of engaging in distance counseling, as well as the potential risks (H.4.a.). Additionally, this same standard indicates that the physical office location and contact information for the practice need to be included and the manner to reach the counselor and response times explained. The counselor should explain to the client their experience with distance counseling, as well as their advanced credentials that qualify the counselor to provide services online. Clarity on any time zone differences, including which time zone appointments are scheduled in, and any cultural or language variations that could affect service delivery, need to be clearly explained (H.2.a.). The emergency procedure to follow when the counselor is unavailable must be explored. Counselors need to also discuss any policy on social media use, if the counselor will be utilizing social media (H.6.). Finally, it is important to explain that telebehavioral health can be denied by the client's insurance and what the cost of services will be if the client's claim is denied (H.2.a.).

Policies

Informed consent policies are discussed in Chapter 3 but bear repeating due to their importance. Per the ACA (2014) Code of Ethics Standard H.2.a, "In addition to the usual and customary protocol of informed consent between counselor and client for face-to-face counseling, the following issues, unique to the use of distance counseling, technology, and/or social media are addressed in the informed consent process" (p. 17) and therefore need to be included in the counselor's policy development. The following procedures are not exhaustive but provide a starting place.

Emergency Procedures

Define what the client is to do in an emergency, who they call, and when to call. **Contact information** is obtained from the client including the client's phone number, address, and emergency contact; provided to local emergency services during instances of medical and mental health emergencies. This also needs to address what will happen if the client were to have a medical or psychological emergency during session. Clear and sequential steps may assist to reduce added stress and chaos during an emergency. Refer to the established practice protocol developed and described in the business plan.

Counselor Availability

The **counselor availability statement** explains when the counselor is available and where to call during that time, establishing business hours so to speak. Define who to call and what to do if the counselor is unavailable. Determine a plan in case of an emergency during business and nonbusiness hours. Client expectations of response time need to be clearly delineated and procedures in place.

Client Contact

The **client contact statement** provides clients the counselor's contact information, times available, and acceptable means of communication. Clearly explain if client can contact the counselor through electronic means and define how that process will work. The counselor should reiterate expected response times. It is important to establish boundaries around the client-counselor relationship.

Time Off

Define steps to take if the counselor has taken time off, such as who the client is to contact in the counselor's absence. It is a good practice to have a covering clinician able to respond to client crises. The counselor will provide clear parameters of the time off with an expected return date for availability. The client will be encouraged to use their support system and emergency procedures as applicable during this time frame.

Cancellation/No-Show

In the business plan, establish a policy for client cancellations. **The client cancellation/no-show policy** describes what will happen if the client does not cancel in a timely manner; include the no-show fee and the appropriate timeframe for canceling an appointment to avoid a fee. This discussion will also include any procedures related to rescheduling appointments. Establish the same expectations for participation in counseling as would be expected in the office. This information should be reiterated throughout the counseling process.

Client Verification

When engaging in telebehavioral health, it is important that the client's identity is verified prior to the beginning of treatment, especially if insurance is being utilized. Privacy and confidentiality can only be assured if the client's identity is verified. When using videoconferencing, the counselor can complete **client verification** by comparing a photo ID picture to the client on the screen and making sure the identification matches the name on the insurance card. This ensures that services are billed to the insurance for the correct person (H.3). Additionally, a code can be sent via a secure texting system to the phone number on file for the client or through encrypted email, if there is doubt.

Social Media

Some counseling professionals may choose to use social media as a form of communication or promotion for the online practice. Social media accounts for the business must be kept separate from personal accounts, ensuring personal social media accounts are kept private (H.6.a). It is important to understand the nature and function of the chosen social media platform and to ensure that private information is never shared in this online format. All information about the counselor and the practice should be accurate and up to date. It is important to understand, prior to posting on social media, that what the counselor may say online carries weight and could be shared with clients, employers, counselor education programs, ACA and other member organizations, and other counseling professionals. The social media posts and shares should be professional in nature and reflective of the profession as a whole.

Counselors should refrain from diagnosing in an online format, even if it is a public figure, as this violates professional ethical practice. Additionally, it is inappropriate to look at a client's social media profile without the explicit permission of that client (H.6.c). Finally, a social media policy should be developed and posted on any social media platform, on the practice website, and given to clients as part of the informed consent process (H.6.b).

Counselors will list the social media account and define the risks involved with interacting with the counselor on social media, especially to confidentiality, and the benefits in interacting on social media. Additionally, clear expectations about interactions between the client and the counselor on social media are clearly stated. This policy is posted on social media accounts and the website and shared during informed consent.

Website Considerations

Utilizing a website can offer potential clients and referral sources basic information about the counselor and the online practice. The website can list the counselor's credentials and experience, practice location, contact information, services provided, and general information on counseling. All information regarding the counselor's experience, education, licensure, credentials, accreditation, and memberships must be accurate and appropriate (H.5.b). In addition, there should be links to the professional board for the state if a client needs to address ethical concerns or understand their rights. It is important to ensure all links contained on the website are accurate and functioning correctly, as well as professionally appropriate (H.5.c). The website should be maintained in a manner that allows access for those with disabilities and translations for those whose first language is not English, if possible (H.5.d). While providing these options on the website, it is important to acknowledge the imperfect nature of the accommodations and translations. Finally, if any electronic communication is possible through the website, the counselor must ensure confidentiality by having encryption methods in place to protect the electronic transmission of information (H.5.a).

Multicultural, Ethical, and Social Justice Concerns

It is the counselor's responsibility to consider and address any multicultural, ethical, and social justice concerns that may result from the use of technology. These concerns are addressed by the ACA (2014) Code of Ethics explicitly in Standard H.5.d. This standard identifies the responsibility of the counselor to ensure technology used provides "accessibility to persons with disabilities" as well as "translation capabilities for clients who have a different primary language, when feasible." Further to this point, Standard H.5.d places the expectation that "counselors acknowledge the imperfect nature of such translations and accessibilities."

Examining the use of telebehavioral health services in relation to social justice concerns, various issues arise that counselors need to actively address to ensure their competent use of this platform. In 2015, the ACA governing body accepted the Multicultural and Social Justice Counseling Competencies (MSJCC) (Ratts et al., 2015) to guide counselors in multicultural and social justice counseling with diverse populations. These guidelines were highlighted by Ratts et al. (2016) as follows:

> The MSJCC acknowledge the following as important aspects of counseling practice for both counselors and clients: (a) understanding the complexities of diversity and multiculturalism on the counseling relationship, (b) recognizing the negative influence of oppression on mental health and well-being, (c) understanding individuals in the context of their social environment, and (d) integrating social justice advocacy into the various modalities of counseling (e.g., individual, family, partners, group). (p. 3)

Considering these points, counselors need to explore multicultural issues such as systemic racism, ableism, sexism and heterosexism, classism, nationalism, ageism, and religious, geographical, and linguistic differences (Grant & Zweir, 2011). Although each of these may not be blatantly obvious, it is the counselor's responsibility to be aware of each and continue to gain education as well as personal insight on how to manage these in an ethical and responsible manner with each client. Specifically, regarding the use of telebehavioral health services, counselors need to consider limitations online, including the client's access limits such as those without the means to afford technology and possible alternatives to circumvent these, including those in very rural areas without internet. Options could include utilizing a computer and private room from the local library and public Wi-Fi for internet access, though the risks of these options would need to be explained. Specific cultural group considerations would include evaluating who this platform is better for, who is not served well by it, as well as appropriate and applicable adaptions to assist in remediating these issues. Counselors need to consider their own world view, values, beliefs, and identity when addressing these variables, each of which will be explored in greater detail in Chapter 9, as well as a component of each chapter in this text.

Basic Counseling Skills and Adaption Summaries: Establishing an Online Practice in Today's World

Topic	Summary
Business Set-Up	
Office considerations	The HIPAA compliance, security, and visual space a client sees are most important. Office duties need to be explored.
Professional insurance	Liability insurance is always required. Not all providers cover online counseling.
Knowledge and competency	Get further knowledge and training, specifically a certification specific to providing counseling online. Counselors must be licensed in the state the client resides.
Developing a client population	Know the target population in order to guide marketing and referrals by outside sources. Consider logistic concerns of client workload.
Consultation/supervision	Utilize experienced colleagues as mentors and supervisors.
Technology	
Hardware	A computer with a microphone and camera is required, in addition to a wired connection to the modem. Speed fast enough to support a videoconference is also necessary.
Platforms	There are single-purpose platforms and multipurpose platforms. BAA are required for any platform that will have access to client information. Initial consultations can be offered to indoctrinate clients onto the platform.
Client records and confidentiality	The use of electronic medical records and HIPAA compliance will need to be explained. Limits to confidentiality need to be made clear
Client communication	Discuss how clients communicate with the counselor and the expected time for responses.
Informed consent	There are multiple considerations that will need to be addressed in the informed consent specific to online counseling.
Policies	
Emergency procedures	What to do in case of emergency
When counselor cannot be reached	Steps for the client to follow if they cannot reach the counselor
Client contact	Ways to contact the counselor outside of session
Time off	What to do for the client when the counselor takes time off
Cancellation/no-show	The counselor's policy when a client does not show or cancel in the amount of time required for a cancellation
Client verification	The importance of verifying the client's identity, especially if utilizing insurance
Social media	It is important to understand the responsibility with social media.
Website considerations	Websites require specific information included.
Multicultural, Ethical, and Social Concerns	Multicultural, ethical, and social justice concerns need to be considered prior to engaging in online counseling.

SUMMARY

The decision to venture into the telebehavioral health practice is one that brings with it the consideration of numerous personal and professional components, as well as the responsibility that comes with using technology in treatment and business management. The counselor needs to consider the fundamental aspects of the professional responsibilities related to independent practice including insurance, competency, clinical supervision and client outcomes. Additionally, the telebehavioral health platform brings with it a number of ethical provinces regarding informed consent and compliance with the ACA Code of Ethics and HIPPA regulations. Adaptions for compliance is necessary when technology is incorporated into the counseling session, as is an understanding, appreciation, and active incorporation of appropriate adaptations to actively address both multicultural and social justice issues that are present. By incorporating these factors in their decision to pursue the development of a telebehavioral health counseling practice, counselors can ensure the decision is a best fit for themselves and the clients they will serve.

CASE EXPLORATION

The Levai family consists of Juan, the biological father of Amy and Raymond, and their biological mother, Tristin. Tristin and Juan divorced several years ago. Amy is a 9-year-old female and Raymond is a 16-year-old male. Tristin is currently in a long-term relationship with Pat and sharing custody of Amy and Raymond with Juan. The family system as a whole has numerous challenges and is seeking online counseling because they live in a remote area several hours from any counseling services. Katrina is a provisionally licensed mental health counselor in her state and is currently under the supervision of Eugene, a licensed professional counselor certified in telebehavioral health who resides 2 hours away from Katrina in the same state.

Looking at the case study, let's look at Katrina setting up her online practice:

1. What considerations does Katrina need to consider before accepting any of the Levai family as online clients regarding ethical concerns?
2. What platform/technology considerations does Katrina need to check?
3. What specific issues need to be considered regarding client records for online treatment of the Levai family?
4. What liability considerations are important for Katrina to consider regarding her insurance as well as her supervision?

Worksheets

ONLINE COUNSELING PRACTICE WORKSHEET

The following checklist provides an overview of the areas to address when setting up an online counseling practice. This is not an exhaustive checklist, so please feel free to make your own to fit your needs.

ADAPTATIONS CHECKLIST

☐ **Office Considerations**
HIPPA compliance: Review the privacy, security (administrative, physical, and technical), and breach notification rules. Review security measures for privacy on your chosen platform to ensure HIPPA compliance. Prepare office space that is visually appealing to client: Is it appropriate, professional, and confidential? Also, consider the management of the office: Who will be doing filing, billing, and so on? Is there a BAA in place?

☐ **Professional Insurance**
Is your liability insurance up to date? Does it specifically cover online counseling?

☐ **Knowledge and Competency**
Is your license current? Does it cover the same state where the client is located? Have you gained certification to provide online counseling? Is that certification up to date, and have you completed the necessary CEUs?

☐ **Development of Client Population**
Have you developed a client population that falls within your competency areas? Is your marketing focused on this population, identifying any limitations and clarifying online counseling as the means of treatment? Have you considered the needs of your clients in developing your caseload, both in session time and documentation/billing/administrative duties?

☐ **Technology Hardware**
Check microphone and camera are functioning properly. Use a wired connection to a modem to ensure confidentiality and reduce disruptions. Ensure the speed of your connection will support videoconferencing.

Be prepared to assist clients with these same issues.

☐ **Platform**
Ensure current BAA is up to date. Review platform functions with clients to ensure their understanding; update on any changes as necessary.

☐ **Client Records and Confidentiality**
Ensure you are using an electronic medical records system that is HIPPA compliant with BAA in place. The limits of confidentiality are outlined clearly in your informed consent, and you review these regularly with clients throughout the counseling process.

☐ **Client Communication**
Clients are aware of how to contact the counselor and the expected time of responses. These are reviewed regularly throughout the counseling process.

☐ **Consultation/Supervision**
Who do you consult with regarding cases? Who can you turn to for supervision? Keep in mind, these are ongoing needs for professional counselors regardless of platform.

☐ **Emergency Policy**
The emergency policy is clearly explained to the client. If the counselor is unavailable, there is an alternative plan in place. This policy includes the physical location of the client, a list of available resources near the client (support system members, local authorities, other treatment providers). Clients understand that in an emergency they may go to their local emergency room first, notifying the counselor later once stable.

☐ **Counselor Contact Policy**
This clearly outlines how the client may contact the counselor and expected response times. Outlines alternatives if the counselor is unavailable, including use of emergency policy or counselor time off policy.

☐ **Counselor Time Off Policy**
This outlines what alternatives the client has for treatment needs when the counselor is not working. This would include review of the emergency policy, use of personal support, and local resources.

☐ **Cancellation/No-Show Policy**
This clearly outlines the procedures to cancel appointments, the necessary time frame to avoid payment for session, and payment consequences for no-shows.

☐ **Client Verification Policy**
Outlines the importance of client verification as well as the means of accomplishing this in session. How will the client obtain the session link and password? How close to the session will this occur? What password or code will be used to ensure the client is in a safe and confidential setting?

☐ **Informed Consent**
It clearly identifies online counseling as the means of treatment andidentifies the limits of confidentiality. It provides clarification of expectations regarding confidentiality for both counselor and client.

☐ **Social Media Policy**
Clearly outlines the counselor's social media use, and the responsibility to manage their personal and professional accounts separately. Clearly identifies protection of client confidentiality. Have you reviewed the ACA standards regarding this subject? Is your current policy in compliance?

☐ **Website Considerations**
Specific information provided on the website is outlined. Client testimonials and such are not included to protect confidentiality.

☐ **Multicultural/Social Justice Considerations**
Have you considered the cultural variables that make the client unique? How will you incorporate these in sessions? Have you explored social justice issues with the client? What necessary treatment goals or modification are necessary to support the client with these?

☐ **Ethical Consideration**
When was the last time you reviewed the code of ethics of all bodies that you fall under? Consider those of your state licensing board, your certifications, and the ACA. Are you in compliance with the strictest one that applies?

Basic Counseling Forms

INFORMED CONSENT

Additional Considerations for Telebehavioral Health Counseling Checklist
(Rooted in the ACA Standard H)

When developing an informed consent, be sure to include the following:

☐ Make it clear to the client during this process that all their therapy sessions will occur online and what the technology issues are that they may experience.

☐ Lay out the minimum technology requirements that the client will need in order to participate in telebehavioral health.

☐ Discuss the procedure for technology failure both during sessions and outside of session time, including alternative methods of counseling during technology failure.

☐ Explain the benefits of engaging in distance counseling, as well as the potential risks. The physical office location and contact information for the practice need to be included and the manner to reach the counselor and response times explained.

☐ Explain to the client their experience with distance counseling, as well as their advanced credentials that qualify the counselor to provide services online.

☐ Clarify on any time zone differences, including which time zone appointments are scheduled in.

☐ Clarify any cultural or language variations that could affect service delivery.

☐ Share an emergency procedure to follow when counselor is unavailable:
- Define what the client is to do in an emergency, who they call, and when to call.
- Address what will happen if the client were to have a medical emergency during session.
- Provide clear and sequential steps that may assist to reduce added stress and chaos during an emergency.

☐ Explain when the counselor is available and where to call during that time:
- Define who to call and what to do if the counselor is unavailable.
- Clearly delineate client expectations of response time.

☐ Provide clients the counselor's contact information, times available, and acceptable means of communication:
- Clearly explain if the client can contact through electronic means and define how that will work.
- Reiterate expected response times.

☐ Define steps to take if counselor has taken time off, such who the client is to contact in the counselor's absence:
- Provide clear parameters of the time off with expected return date for availability.
- The client will be encouraged to use their support system and emergency procedures as applicable during this time frame.

☐ Describe what will happen if the client does not cancel in time, including the charge of a no-show fee and what the cut-off time is for canceling an appointment without a fee being charged:

- Include any procedures related to rescheduling appointments.
- This information will be reiterated throughout the counseling process.

☐ Discuss any policy on social media use, if the counselor will be utilizing social media:

- List the social media account and define the risks involved with interacting with the counselor on social media, especially to confidentiality, and the benefits in interacting on social media.
- Clearly state expectations clients can have for interacting with the counselor on social media.
- Post this policy on social media accounts, the website, and share during informed consent.

☐ Explain that telebehavioral health can be denied by the client's insurance and what the cost of services will be if the client's claim is denied

Online Resources

- **iTherapy**: Guide to online counseling with ability to consult with contact an agent for assistance. https://itherapy.com/the-ultimate-resource-list-for-starting-an-online-therapy-practice/

- **Counseling Today**: The pros and cons of contracting with online counseling companies. https://ct.counseling.org/2019/01/the-pros-and-cons-of-contracting-with-online-counseling-companies/

- **Dasenbrook Consulting**: Private practice checklist handout. https://counseling-privatepractice.com/private-practice-checklist-handout/

- **Abundance Practice-Building**: Checklist covering topics from practice set up to references to key terms. https://abundancepracticebuilding.com/wp-content/uploads/2017/10/Check-list-Draft-2.pdf

- **Counseling Today**: Establishing a private practice. https://ct.counseling.org/2019/03/establishing-a-private-practice/

- **USA Today**: 10 steps to starting a private practice in counseling. http://sitelaunch2.com/usatodayclassifieds/10-steps-to-start-a-private-practice-in-counseling/

- **Level Up Your Practice**: Private practice startup checklist. https://static1.squarespace.com/static/5c3fcfaeb10598244d51edeb/t/5d0457b2d800ce00010288e1/1560565685108/PRIVATE+PRACTICE+START+UP+CHECKLIST.pdf

- **Fit Small Business**: Steps for starting a business. https://fitsmallbusiness.com/how-to-start-your-own-business/?gclid=Cj0KCQjw6PD3BRDPARIsAN8pHuEs2oNkED-92WIIc-6xr1L76IkNko_Tbr5BPKvQCwUCdy4Qo-n5BW2oaAvUwEALw_wcB

- **Online Therapy Directory**: HIPPA-compliant platforms. https://www.onlinecounselling.com/web-conferencing-platforms/

References

Alleman, J. R. (2002). Online counseling: The Internet and mental health treatment. *Psychotherapy: Theory, Research, Practice, Training, 39*(2), 199–209. https://doi.org/10.1037/0033-3204.39.2.199

American Counseling Association. (2014). *2014 ACA code of ethics.* https://www.counseling.org/docs/default-source/default-document-library/2014-code-of-ethics-finaladdress.pdf

Cook, J. E., & Doyle, C. (2004). Working alliance in online therapy as compared to face-to-face therapy: Preliminary results. *CyberPsychology & Behavior, 5*(2), 95–105. https://doi.org/10.1089/109493102753770480

Derrig-Palumbo, K. & Zeine, F. (2005). *Online therapy: A therapist's guide to expanding your practice.* W. W. Norton & Company

Evans, M., & Hawkins, M. (2002). The impact of the internet on the counselling profession: The counsellor, the client, and the practice. Promise or peril? *The Journal for the Professional Counselor, 17,* 39–51.

Grant, C. A., & Zweir, E. (2011). Intersectionality and student utcomes: Sharpening the struggle against racism, sexism, classism, ableism, heterosexism, nationalism, and linguistic, religious, and geographical discrimination in teaching and learning. *Multicultural Perspectives, 13*(4), 181–188. https://dx.doi.org/10.1080/15210960.2011.616813

Heinlen, K. T., Reynolds-Welfel, E., Richmond, E. N., & Rak, C. F. (2003). The scope of web-counseling: a survey of services and compliance with NBSS standards for the ethical practice of web counseling. *Journal of Counseling & Development, 81,* 61–69. https://doi.org/10.1002/j.1556-6678.2003.tb00226.x

Leibert, T., Archer, J., Munson, J., & York, G. (2006). An exploratory study of client perceptions of internet counseling and the therapeutic alliance. *Journal of Mental Health Counseling, 28*(1), 69–83. https://doi.org/10.17744/mehc.28.1.f0h37djrw89nv6vb

Maheu, M. M., & Gordon, B. L. (2000). Counseling and therapy on the Internet. *Professional Psychology: Research and Practice, 31,* 484–489. https://doi.org/10.1037/0735-7028.31.5.484

Mallen, M. J., Vogel, D. L., Rochlen, A. B., & Day, S.X. (2005). Online counseling: Reviewing the literature from a counseling psychology framework. *The Counseling Psychologist, 33*(6), 819–871. https://doi.org/10.1177/0011000005278624

Novotney, A. (2017). A growing wave of online therapy. *Monitor on Psychology, 48*(2), 48. https://www.apa.org/monitor/2017/02/online-therapy

O'Brien, E. R. & Hauser, M. A. (2016). *Supervision and agency management for counselors: A practical approach.* Springer Publishing Company.

Ratts, M. J., Singh, A. A., Nassar-McMillan, S., Butler, S. K., & McCullough, J. R. (2015). *Multicultural and Social Justice Counseling Competencies.* https://www.counseling.org/docs/default-source/competencies/multicultural-and-social-justice-counseling-competencies.pdf?sfvrsn=20

Ratts, M. J., Singh, A. A., Nassar-McMillan, S., Butler, S. K., & Rafferty McCullough, J. (2016). Multicultural and social justice counseling competencies: Guidelines for the counseling profession. *Journal of Multicultural Counseling and Development, 44,* 28–48. https://doi.org/10.1002/jmcd.12035

Rochland, A. B., Zach, J. S., & Speyer, C. (2004). Online therapy: Review of relevant definitions, debates, and current empirical support. *Journal of Clinical Psychology, 60,* 269–283. https://doi.org/10.1002/jclp.10263

Sampson, J. P., Kolodinsky, R. W., & Greeno, B. P. (1997). Counseling and the information highway: Future possibility and potential problems. *Journal of Counseling & Development, 75,* 203–212. https://doi.org/10.1002/j.1556-6676.1997.tb02334.x

Synchronous Counseling at a Distance

5

Theories and Treatment Considerations for Online Counseling

Tricia M. Mikolon and Michelle Harrison

Counseling theory is of primary importance to counselor education and practice, as it is the foundation for treatment. Theory is based on assumptions about human nature and what provokes change (Puleo et al., 2015). Counselors typically adapt theoretical practices that mirror their own beliefs about human nature and change (Corey et al., 2011), as well as personality development and diagnosis. Choosing a theory or a therapeutic approach based on a theory is an intentional act that guides ethical, competent, and responsible counseling practices (Puleo et al., 2015). Similarly, selecting an approach based in theory and techniques that are adaptable for online counseling must be intentional. Derrig-Palumbo and Zeine (2005) found theoretic approaches integrate well into the telebehaviroal health format, although some are better tailored to its unique requirements. The authors suggest that cognitive-based, solution-focused, and narrative treatments are most easily modified to fit telebehavioral health counseling.

A fundamental conviction underlying the use of theories is that the counselor matches the techniques and approaches of a specific theory to the client, considering their culture, abilities, and preferences, which requires an integrative approach. Such an approach allows the counselor to tailor their interventions to the client while using the most effective techniques from various therapies to assist the client in reaching their goals (Corey, 2004, 2009). When application of the counselor's theoretical orientation meets with the online counseling format, adaptions are necessary. Researchers completed a meta-analysis using various **evidence-based practices** and found the most effective adaptation necessary to fit the individual culture and needs of the clients was the combining of approaches (Lau et al., 2017). Wiltsey Stirman et al. (2017) went on to identify 11 modifications often used in treatment; these include tailoring, removing, adding, shortening (protocol and session), lengthening (protocol and session), integrating, repeating, reordering, and loosening. It is important to explore each of these modifications and how they apply to theories for synchronous online counseling.

Tailoring is defined by the authors as slightly changing aspects of a treatment without significantly altering core elements, meaning the therapist will modify the treatment protocol to meet the client's need but maintain the core focus and values of the therapeutic approach, while **removing** is defined as eliminating at least one distinct element of an evidence-based psychotherapy (EBPT) original protocol. **Adding** is defined as "including one or more distinct treatment components that are not part of the original EBPT protocol," indicating that the therapist will incorporate other interventions into the current theoretic approach to enhance its effectiveness with the individual client (Wilsey Sitrman et al., 2017, p. 401). **Shortening the protocol** is defined as reducing the number of sessions with the client while maintaining the evidence base, while **shortening the session** is summarized as reducing the time spent with the client in each session. In contrast, **lengthening the protocol** increases the number of sessions while maintaining the evidenced-based protocol, and **lengthening the session** maintains the protocol while extending the number of sessions with the client.

Finally, **integrating** is defined as "the infusion of a different, established therapeutic approach into an EBPT throughout the duration of the protocol," indicating the counselor will provide an integrated approach of one or more theoretic approaches throughout counseling (Wilsey Sitrman et al., 2017 p. 401). **Repeating** occurs when the counselor uses the interventions prescribed once by a protocol repeatedly during the duration of treatment, while **reordering** allows the counselor to modify and rearrange the order in which interventions are provided (Wilsey Sitrman et al., 2017). Finally, the authors identify **loosening** as occurring when the structure of the protocol for the approach is made less restrictive by the therapist to modify the treatment approach to the client and their individual needs.

Lau et al. (2017) found that adaptations did not change the effectiveness except when "adding components" (p. 664) to the evidence-based psychological treatments, which impacted the effectiveness in a positive way. These authors also found reducing or rearranging components of treatment to have an adverse impact on the client's perception of the effectiveness of treatment. Therefore, the focus will be on the additive modifications of theories to assist counselors in effectively modifying their theoretic approach in this manner.

Another term for the **additive approach** to theoretic work is the **integrative approach**. As Corey (2009) explains, the integrative approach is the combining of theoretic approaches to be able to provide the best treatment to an array of clients with various problems effectively. This approach draws from the strengths of individual theories and combines them in an additive manner to provide the counselor with a variety of skills and techniques personalized to the client, rooting this approach in empirically supported interventions (Corey, 2004). The integrative approach allows for the counselor to address social justice, multicultural, and ethical considerations utilizing the strengths of various theories without the impact of the weaknesses a theory may bring in one or more of those specific areas. Corey (2004) cites that a weakness to this approach is that the untrained counselor may justify their use of techniques without rooting them in sound understanding and application of the empirical evidence. Caution needs to be used in this approach, with regular consultation and supervision expected to ensure counselor efficacy.

The integrative approach provides counselors with strong theoretic guidance rooted firmly in empirical evidence to navigate the unique needs of the online synchronous format. Any adaption of the theories needs to consider the counselor's skills and proficiency with technology and the client's needs prior to being implemented (Popoola & Adebowale, 2012). Counselors need to be aware that adaptions do not end with theory, but include expressing and identifying emotions, forming a therapeutic relationship and clinical skills, and providing diagnostic assessments and crisis management, all of which will be discussed in-depth in future chapters.

Counselors need to consider their ability to transcend the physical setting of a face-to-face session and apply their approach to the distance relationship before them effectively (Anthony & Merz Nagel, 2010). Common themes of adaptions include empathy, respect for autonomy and individual experience, unconditional positive regard, congruence, and identification of thoughts and emotions (Anthony & Merz Nagel, 2010; Capuzzi & Stauffer, 2016 Corey, 2004, 2009, 2017). Anthony and Merz Nagel (2010) identified that online counselors need a "full commitment to knowing oneself thoroughly and being able to recognize dynamics that come into place as communication without a bodily presence takes place" (p. 12). Bridging this physical distance between counselor and client depends heavily on appropriate adaptions of theory and techniques to the synchronous online configuration.

An examination of the theories and their adaptions to the synchronous online counseling format will include an exploration of the theoretic schools of counseling, including structuralism/functionalism, Gestalt psychology, behaviorism, psychoanalysis, **humanism** and cognition, existentialism, and the modern theories including feminism, solution-focused brief therapy, and social construct theories, to name a few, focusing on the strengths of each in the online setting and necessary adaptions. Each school of thought will be reviewed with attention to its foundational beliefs, techniques, strengths, and adaption to synchronous online counseling. Readers are encouraged to consider how each combine within their personal integrative approach.

Although the first two schools of thought are more theoretical than practical, they do provide a historical foundation to the field of psychology and counseling. Both **structuralism** and **functionalism** provide insight into the structure on which current techniques are established and provide some basic interventions that become the foundation on which later theories are built. For these reasons they provide a point of departure for our discussion on theories and their application to online counseling.

Structuralism

Structuralism encompasses experimental psychology and its focus on human emotions, perceptions, motivations and the structure of experiences (Mangal, 2011). Structuralism strives to define the human experience, which is highly subjective. However, it does provide an excellent foundation for the understanding of the perceptions of the individual, making it worthy of discussion in this chapter.

Foundational Beliefs

Experimental psychology was founded by Wilhelm Wundt (1832–1920), who believed the human mind needed to be studied in a systematic manner, focusing on the interaction of cognitions, emotions, perceptions, and motivations (Mangal, 2011). Wundt created the first psychology laboratory designed to systematically study the nature of human thoughts, ideas, feelings, perceptions, and sensations, which culminated into his definition of experience. He and his students studied the nature of human experience through the use of introspection, which established psychology as a separate science by providing a definition of psychology, one that considered the interaction between physiology and human experiences. His former student Edward B. Titchener (1867–1927) focused on the structure of experiences, the combination of the elements of sensations and perceptions, and providing insight into conscious experiences (Fancher & Rutherford, 2017; Mangal, 2011). Titchener believed that the **consciousness** was the sum of physical sensations, memories and dreams, and emotions (Mangal, 2011). The summation of these three elements was viewed by structuralists as the definition of human experience; however the processing of these by the individual was not a consideration. This view, along with the highly subjective nature of the introspection technique, limits reliability and validity, thus providing limitations to this approach.

Overview of Common Techniques

Structuralism's main technique is that of introspection. **Introspection** is used to separate the mental processes, allowing the client to have a clearer understanding of their own root emotions, perceptions, thoughts, and sensations (Mangal, 2011). A concern with structuralism and introspections, as noted previously, is the lack of scientific validity of an individual's interpretation of these fundamental elements of their experiences. The compartmentalization of thoughts, feelings, and physical sensations without consideration of how an individual would process these limits the empirical evidence to support it. However, the value of appreciating an individual's thoughts, perceptions, and interpretation of events benefits both the client and clinician from a social justice approach, allowing for the better understanding of the individual's world view.

Strengths for Use Online

As Min Shim (2011) explained, a significant value of structuralism is the appreciation for the subjective experiences and views of the individual person. This approach allows for the understanding of the lived experiences of the individual, which enhances both the multicultural and social justice appreciation between the counselor and the client. When integrated with other clinical techniques, this subjective response can provide a more vivid and complete picture of the individual's experiences, perceptions, emotions, and thoughts as they impact their understanding of themselves and the world around them.

Adaptions to Consider

Introspection, combined with other skills such as self-awareness and mindfulness, increase an individual's understanding of themselves and their interactions with the world. Speyer and Zack (2003) and Suler (2000) highlight that a characteristic of online clients is their motivation for treatment and use of introspection. Online counseling allows for introspection and self-evaluation via the written word through text, much as journaling does in face-to-face counseling. Journaling can still be used, but counselors may want to increase the use of technology for this introspective exercise, allowing for creative means and comfort on behalf of the client. Clinicians need to be aware that clients will express themselves best when they are comfortable with the means of expression, be that paper/pen, text, blogs, or other self-observation techniques.

Functionalism

Functionalism arose from structuralism as a means to include individual differences within the understanding of human nature (Francher & Rutherford, 2017). Functionalism strives to understand an individual's motives and perceived benefits of chosen behaviors while considering the role of **free will** in decision making. Clients seeking online counseling value their independence and bring with them an internal motivation for change (Murphy et al., 2011), making this a valuable concept to discuss in this chapter.

Foundational Beliefs

William James (1842–1910) developed functionalism as a transformation from structuralism and as an approach emphasizing individual differences and the system in which an individual functions (Fancher & Rutherford, 2017). This change in thinking rooted in Darwinian thought emphasized the utility and purpose of a behavior for the individual (Mangal, 2011) and attempted to be more systematic and accurate in its assessment of human consciousness. James brought to light the concepts of **free wil**l, instinct, and voluntary behaviors (Seel, 2012), integral concepts related to autonomy. Additionally, John Dewey (1859–1952) influenced our educational system by asserting that instruction needs to be tailored to the student's ability and that interaction with peers and teachers and the student's own relation to the material had significant impact on a student's learning (Dewey, 1902). This is a principle counseling has included in the individualization of treatment planning and in matching the theory to the client's comfort and abilities.

Overview of Common Techniques

Functionalism is not technique focused but more theory driven. The fundamental concepts include exploring the purpose of behaviors and assessing their benefit to the individual. Concepts of free will and voluntary behaviors coupled with the fundamental concepts result in an appreciation for autonomy of the client. Counselors are encouraged to address autonomy and motivation in treatment regardless of theoretic approach (Ryan et al., 2010) and to modify techniques to ensure these considerations.

Strengths for Use Online

Those who seek online counseling tend to be motivated for change and value their independence (Murphy et al., 2011). These traits are supported by the online synchronous format, allowing clients the flexibility of their sessions from various locations and through different means, be it synchronous video, chat, or text messages. This freedom to individualize their treatment increases a client's sense of autonomy, a cornerstone of counselor ethics (American Counseling Association [ACA], 2014).

Adaptions to Consider

As with any theoretic approach, counselors need to consider how to incorporate the fundamental principles of the theory in a manner that matches the client's comfort and ability to utilize them.

For functionalism, this means supporting the autonomy of the client in an ethical manner and encouraging them to discuss their insights and choices in a nonjudgmental environment. Counselors will support the free will of the client while simultaneously holding them accountable for the logical consequences of their actions. Personalizing the treatment plan to the goal of the client and their current abilities and resources for change is also an adaption counselors need to consider, while encouraging a healthy therapeutic relationship between counselor and client.

Gestalt Psychology

Gestalt Psychology strives to unite the human experience (Corey, 2017) by providing a more wholistic approach to understanding human nature. With a variety of techniques easily adapted to online counseling, this approach provides a foundation for understanding the client's experience in the here and now. Self-regulation skills and the ability to personalize the techniques to fit the individual are strengths this approach brings with it.

Foundational Beliefs

Gestalt psychology is rooted in a response to structuralism and functionalism, which some viewed as fragmenting the human experience (Corey, 2017; Mangal, 2011). Leaders of this school of thought include Max Wertheimer (1880–1943), Kurt Koffka (1886–1941), Wolfgang Kohler (1887–1967), and Kurt Lewin (1890–1947), who viewed the human experience in a more holistic manner and were attempting to include the colorful aspects of each individual as compared to the sterile scientific approaches utilized by the theories that came before them (Mangal, 2011). Gestalt is built on the belief that individuals become more whole by integrating all aspects of themselves, including those previously denied or dismissed. This approach allows the individual to experience themselves and their lives as a whole with attention to the here and now, the what and how, and ownership of their experience (Corey, 2017). Later, Laura Pearls, Paul Goodman, and Fritz Pearls would become the faces of Gestalt psychology with their book, entitled *Gestalt Psychology: Excitement and Growth in Human Personality*, released in the 1950s. Their book brought to the mainstream the approach to wellness underpinning Gestalt psychology.

Various techniques are rooted in the value of viewing experiences as a whole without denying any aspect of the experience (**holism**) and in the acknowledgement and acceptance that the client is in an everchanging field of experiences containing numerous variables that influence the interpretation of the experience at any given moment. How these experiences are organized from moment to moment, known as the figure formation process, provides insight into the individual's perceptions and evaluation of the variables provided as either figure or ground. Finally, the concept of organismic **self-regulation** allows each individual to interpret the impact of changing experiences on their definition of themselves and the choices they perceive to have for their actions. These concepts combine to form a more complete understanding of the individual and how they experience their interaction with the world around them (Corey, 2017).

Gestalt psychology is firmly rooted in the concept of the now, focusing on current experiences and opportunities rather than being tethered to and thusly limited by the past. By remaining in the now, the strength of choice becomes evident and empowered, rather than rooting ourselves in the past and attempting to change moments that are written in our history. Expression of emotions regarding our past experiences is an important inclusion in Gestalt therapy, as it allows an individual to become clearer on their current options, to resolve lingering emotions, and to transition to a place of action versus stagnation or self-defeating behaviors (Corey, 2017).

The concepts of energy and its flow through the human experience is sometimes thought of as a new-age concept. However, Gestalt psychology investigates how energy is experienced by the individual. Is it being blocked and resulting in resistance or hesitation, or is it allowed to flow freely and being experienced as it occurs? Both of these extremes, and all the variances in between, provide insight into how the energy is being used in the formation of productive or self-defeating behaviors. Finally, Gestalt psychology provides insight into how an individual views themselves in relationship to others and how they maintain their individuality through boundaries. Exploring the use of boundaries allows an assessment of personal preferences, needs, and strengths, while allowing for the understanding of how we interact with others, the give and take of relationships (Corey, 2017).

Overview of Common Techniques

The experiment is the Gestalt technique in which an individual tries on a new behavior prior to accepting it into their daily life. This experimentation allows for a trial run of sorts, removing the pressure to commit to a change and allowing the client to modify the change as needed to increase success in various situations. The **internal dialogue exercises** allow the client to externally process an internal conflict. The empty chair exercise is one such internal dialogue exercise that allows an individual to express their emotions and perceptions in a safe manner without having to do so with the person who is at the root of those uncomfortable emotions. Often the presentation of this exercise may influence the comfort the client has with using it. If the counselor explains the empty chair technique as the conversations we all have in our cars or showers, where we carry on an entire conversation with our boss, professor, spouse, or other person we have conflicting emotions with in a place away from them, it allows the concept to feel more approachable. The simple act of expressing our emotions and processing our reactions within a safe environment where we can do so without judgment or consequence allows for the necessary emotional release that often is what is needed with or without the conversation actually happening in real life.

Rehearsal exercises are similar in that they are practiced within a support group or supported environment in which a client may attempt to use a new behavior without the fear of failure. These may include role playing in which a client practices setting a healthy boundary with their counselor or a peer, practicing for the possible responses, both positive and negative. Such practice allows for a reduction in anxiety while simultaneously increasing the individual's self-confidence so that they are prepared for various possible outcomes. **Reversal techniques** allow a client to explore repressed aspects of their personality by acting in the opposite manner they may be used to. For example, if a client is feeling uncomfortable with confrontation, they may be asked to act as confrontational as possible, with exploration of how they define confrontation and what healthy confrontation is. Often as humans we define ourselves in the extremes, viewing ourselves as one thing or another. This exercise allows a client to explore the continuum of human behaviors without having to be in one or other of the extremes.

Exaggeration exercises require the client to focus on underlying emotions by repeating and exaggerating a behavior or expression, such as a leg bounce or an eye roll, to gain insight into the emotions related to the action. These exercises allow a client to focus on the root emotion of the behavior, gaining clarity into the origins of the behavior and addressing the underlying emotion in a direct manner. Increased insight into the emotion allows the client to identify it at its inception, thus determining how to express it in a more controlled and determined manner. Finally, **staying with the feeling** encourages a client to go deeper into uncomfortable emotions rather than avoid them. This allows a client to gain insight into their range of emotions and realize that regardless of their initial emotional reaction intensity, they ultimately have control over how they choose to express their emotions. This allows the client to increase their sense of personal responsibility and accountability for their actions while simultaneously increasing their honesty with themselves and others.

Strengths for Use Online

With each of these techniques providing insight into how an individual experiences and interprets the world around them, the value for each in counseling is evident. Given the unique aspects of the online setting, these become even more valuable as they help to capture the view of the individual with appreciation of their values, insights, and interpretations. Gestalt psychology also allows for easy adaption of various client cultures and is inclusionary of the individual world view unique to each client, adapting itself to include what may be conflicting aspects of an individual's experience. Its adaptation to various treatment formats, be it individual, group, or family/couple's treatment, increases its use in the online format. By encouraging the exploration of our current needs and values coupled with an increase in self-actualization, Gestalt therapy allows for positive changes in both perception and behavior simultaneously. The dynamic exchanges and nature of Gestalt psychology assist clients in moving to action while personalizing their treatment plan to match their strengths, needs, and values, which enhances the online interactions between counselor and client.

Adaptions to Consider

Tempering the techniques to match the client is of utmost importance with Gestalt techniques. Gestalt can, at times, come off as intense or highly directive. The experiment can be adapted into a self-evaluative homework assignment where the client practices a new behavior between sessions, keeping a record of what situations it works well in and what, if any, modifications are necessary to enhance the utility of the change in their daily life. A running dialogue via journaling, blog, or text may assist the client in increasing their awareness of their use of the new skill while assessing the usefulness in various settings and situations.

Internal dialogue exercises can be used, such as the empty chair conversations, as described previously, as can phantom letters that clients write but share only with the therapist, never sending to the intended recipient. Another adaption would be the client having the conversation with the therapist acting as the client's intended target, allowing for the expression of the emotions without analysis, instead filling the empty chair. The necessary feature of the exercise is the processing of expressing the honest emotions without editing; the modifications are dependent on the client's preferences and comfort level.

Role playing is easily accomplished in the online format, allowing for real-time practice of new skills and boundaries. Using the "what if?" modification and running through various possible situations back to back allows the client to increase their confidence in handling the unpredictability of variables in various social situations. Role playing can be modified to include the exaggeration, rehearsal, and reversal techniques of Gestalt psychology. The exaggeration of emotion is valuable in the online format as the minute nuances of behaviors often evident in face-to-face counseling may be lost in the small focus on the screen. Asking a client to exaggerate their behaviors, not only to identify the emotion associated with them but to also bring awareness to the counselor, brings the regular practice of increased self-awareness and integration of mind-body connections into daily life. Coupling the practice of staying in the emotion with the exaggeration of behaviors is beneficial in the online format as it again adds one more layer to the rich lived experience of the client, which may be otherwise downplayed by distance. As Foulds (1971) noted, the use of Gestalt techniques in therapy allows for the development of more self-actualized individual who views themselves as "more whole, fully integrated persons who stand on their own two feet and take full responsibility for themselves and their lives" (p. 1).

Existentialism

Anxiety, grief, isolation and death are all common themes of the human experience (Corey, 2017). As counselors, being able to assist clients in processing the role each of these has in our daily lives is a strength of this approach. Existentialism stresses the personalization of experiences making it a great approach for diverse client populations.

Foundational Beliefs

Corey (2017) identifies **existentialism** as a philosophical approach to counseling for those considering the nature of humans and the experiences of anxiety, grief, isolation, and death that we all share. Existential theory is rooted in the beliefs that all humans are searching for meaning in their lives. Throughout that search, they explore the concepts of freedom and responsibility, development of their own identity and meaningful relationships, as well as self-awareness, a capacity believed to be a basic condition of human existence. In the pursuit of self-awareness, acceptance of anxiety as a condition of living and the awareness of death and nonbeing occurs (Corey, 2017).

Existential therapy aims to assist clients in becoming more authentic through gaining insight into their own self-deception, finding meaning in their experiences, and learning to accept the role of anxiety in their daily life (Corey, 2017). Existential counselors, according to Corey, also strive to assist clients in regaining a sense of control in their own lives, assisting them in learning to appreciate what they already know about themselves and their experiences. Schneider and Krug (2010) outlined four main goals for clients in existential therapy: being more present for themselves and others, identifying how they limit themselves from being present, accepting that they design their own lives through choices, and exploring and challenging their self-definition and existence in daily life.

Overview of Common Techniques

Techniques do not play a role in existential therapy. Instead, therapy focuses on the relationship between the counselor and the client in their most genuine forms. Other counseling techniques that assist clients in understanding themselves and how they relate to the world may be used, but Corey (2017) cautions that they should be used in an integrative manner to assist in forming a better understanding of the client, their understanding of their own value system and experiences and their interpretations of the world around them. The existential counseling client will ultimately show what they have learned about themselves through the actions they take in their life.

Strengths for Use Online

Existential theory, with its focus on building both interpersonal skills and a personal sense of responsibility, couples well with online counseling. The sharing of viewpoints between the therapist and the client allows for exploration of possible alternative interpretations of experiences and emotions while focusing on the universal experiences we share as humans. From a diversity perspective, the personalization of experiences and acceptance of individual worldviews strengthens the understanding and appreciation of how social and cultural experiences influence the individual's interpretation of world around them (Corey, 2017). The appreciation of individuals' perceptions characteristic of existential therapy in conjunction with its focus on personal responsibility and increased self-awareness matches well with many online counseling clients' goals. However, counselors need to be cautious when social injustices have occurred. Existential therapy's focus on personal responsibility to change your world may further victimize or frustrate those experiencing social justice issues, as it is not in their ability to change what is happening to them (Corey, 2017).

Adaptions to Consider

Corey (2017) cites that some clients may prefer a more concrete and structured approach to therapy. Since existential therapy is not technique driven, integration of other counseling techniques and adaptions to online counseling provided in this chapter should be considered. Counselors are encouraged to use an integrative approach when exploring topics such as death, anxiety, guilt, loneliness, and grief with clients, thus allowing them the benefits of existential therapy while providing them with the skills necessary to feel capable of change.

Behavioral Therapy

Behavioral Therapy focuses on the impact of positive and negative rewards and consequences on human behavior. This approach includes both operant and classical conditioning with attention to what triggers behaviors and how to modify the resulting behaviors. These skills are easily adapted to online counseling and provide the client with a structure upon which to modify their behaviors and develop healthy coping skills.

Foundational Beliefs

John B. Watson notably established that human emotions were pliable with conditioning (Levitt et al., 2015). Behavioral therapy focuses on identifying the connection between the client's feelings and environment and whether or not behavior produces a positive reward or a negative consequence (Levitt et al., 2015). The goal of therapy is to reinforce, quench, or reshape various behaviors, and the role of the counselor is to help clients learn, unlearn, and relearn behavior. Behavior is modified by determining what triggers behavior and then eliminating it (Corey, 2017). Behavior therapy incorporates therapeutic techniques from Ivan Pavlov's classical conditioning learning theory and the operant learning of E.L. Thorndike and B.F. Skinner, as well as ideas from Joseph Wolpe, Hans Eysenck, and Albert Bandura (Donnelly, 2015; Levitt et al., 2015). Skinner is noted as first using the term *behavior therapy* in a 1954 publication *Studies in Behavior Therapy* (Donnelly, 2015).

Overview of Common Techniques

Donnelly (2015) stated, in general, behavioral therapy techniques are founded in classical and operant conditioning and cognitive behavioral theory. Counselors using behavioral therapy embody the role of teacher, facilitator, and reinforcer. Various behavior modification techniques, like the token economy technique, which awards the client tokens upon reaching specified target behavior (Levitt et al., 2015), are commonly utilized. Techniques like this focus on reinforcing behavior. Other techniques, including modeling, behavior rehearsal, and role play, draw on the social learning theory. A social learning approach considers interactions between the client's behavioral, personal, and environmental factors. Corey (2017) refers to these techniques as social skills training, which help the client develop and gain skill, increasing the client's interpersonal competence. Modeling, behavioral rehearsal, and role play provide the client the opportunity to learn and "practice" a new skill in problematic situations and be better prepared and confident of utilizing the skill in their daily living.

Acceptance and commitment therapy, dialectical behavior therapy, exposure therapy, prolonged exposure therapy, and systematic desensitization are all under the umbrella of behavioral therapy. Each of these therapies highlight the individual's personal choices and help facilitate the client's ability to conceive and implement new learned behavior. These therapies utilize techniques like relaxation training, in vivo desensitization and flooding, and aversive techniques (Levitt et al., 2015). Each of these techniques modify behavior. For example, in vivo desensitization and flooding exposes the client to actual or imagined stimuli for an extended amount of time in order to achieve a new response (fear is replaced with relaxation, for instance).

Strengths for Use Online

For clients who might be hesitant to seek in-person counseling because of a phobia or stigmatization associated with a behavior, online counseling is an inconspicuous opportunity for the client to receive counseling with the additional benefit of the security provided by being in a familiar environment (Poh Li et al., 2013). Clients may feel more comfortable disclosing information about themselves, be more honest, and feel less embarrassed about sharing details of behavior and thoughts (Poh Li et al., 2013). Additionally, online counseling is conducive to record keeping, which may be helpful to track any rewards for behaviors or to review written goals and plans for behavioral change identified in a contingency contract or plan. Depending on the online therapy platform the client uses, records may be easily assessable to both the client and the counselor, enabling review of past sessions and gauging progress and change (Poh Li et al., 2013). Behavioral therapy leans on learning. Like cognitive behavioral therapy (CBT), which will be discussed later in the chapter, it is easy to utilize psychoeducational materials and incorporate homework into therapy online. Behavioral therapy focuses on modifying behavior rather than modifying feelings and emotions.

Adaptions to Consider

Even when conducting in-person counseling, missed facial expressions and physical cues may increase the opportunities for misunderstandings between the client and the counselor. Recognizing nonverbal cues and reading clients' body language when counseling online might not seem as easy as when in person, but online therapy may actually perpetuate a greater awareness of body and facial nuances. As the online space limits seeing the whole body, more awareness and focus is concentrated on what is seen. Instead of being aware of the whole body, the counselor can pay greater attention to smaller shifts in body posture and facial reflections.

If behavior is assessed as a high risk, it may be beyond the scope of the counselor to address online. But there are many behavioral therapeutic techniques easily adapted to use online. Establishing reward-based incentives to reduce or change behavior may be tracked as efficiently online as in person. The counselor may use modeling and behavioral rehearsal and engage in role playing with the client online. Using imaginative stimuli, or in vivo desensitization, may be practiced as a tool to reduce fear when triggered. Contingency contracts may be established and shared as easily online as in person as well.

Psychoanalysis

Psychoanalysis explores past events and how they influence the lived experience of the individual. Understanding the impact of childhood circumstances on the development of an individual's personality, coupled with an appreciation of the Id, Ego, and Superego provide counselors with an understanding of the subconscious world as it impacts client's behaviors and choices. Development of self-understanding and the use of Adler's individual psychology approach match well with online counseling.

Foundational Beliefs

Sigmund Freud's psychoanalytic theory, which originated in the early 19th century, is notably one of the most recognized and foundational psychodynamic paradigms. Developmental in nature, psychodynamic theories examine how the client's past experiences and unresolved issues from childhood affect current functioning (Levitt et al., 2015; Milton et al., 2011) and are lenses that are still informing theory development and counseling today. In **psychoanalysis**, the personality is distinguished by three parts: the id (pleasure principle), the ego (reality principle), and the superego (morality principle). In true psychoanalysis, the counselor facilitates bringing the unconscious drives into consciousness (often through dreams), identifies defense mechanisms, and pays attention to **transference** and **countertransference** (Levitt et al., 2015; Milton et al., 2011).

Working with Freud as a student and mentor, Alfred Adler expanded on Freud's theory, focusing on the whole person and the ability of the person to grow and connect socially with others. Noting the role of childhood in development, Adler is known for his analysis of birth order (Levitt et al., 2015). Carl Jung and Jungian theory (or ego psychology) as well as object-relations theory evolved out of the psychanalysis paradigm. Object-relations theorists, such as Donald Winnicott, examine the development of infants in relationship to their experience with their caregivers, mainly the mother (Mays, 2018).

Overview of Common Techniques

The psychoanalytic counselor employs techniques to draw the unconscious drives into the conscious in order to understand conflict within the psyche (Levitt et al., 2015). Techniques for psychoanalysis include utilizing free association, interpretation, dream analysis, examining resistance, and countertransference or transference to gain insight (Corey, 2017). Corey defines free association as the client freely describing and verbalizing thoughts and feelings without using any filters. Interpretation occurs when the counselor reflects, explains, or teaches the client the meaning of what was verbalized. Dream analysis is often associated with Freud and psychoanalysis. Corey quotes Freud's (1900) description of "using the royal road to the unconsciousness" (p. 74) in an effort to reveal the client's conscious material. Resistance represents anything preventing the progress and presentation of the conscious material. Transference is another technique associated with psychoanalysis. This occurs when the client responds to the therapist in a way that is like responding to another significant person. Countertransference occurs when the counselor reacts to the client and objectivity is blurred (Corey, 2017).

Techniques that examine conscious and unconscious, like **sand tray** (sandplay) and symbolic play, using a timeline to notice themes and utilizing creative activities to gain insight, are also employed. Other techniques, like acting "as-if," practicing the empty chair technique, role playing, teaching "I" statements, or other skills to help develop self-awareness are also utilized (Levitt et al., 2015). These techniques are used by Adlerian therapists who focus on seeing the client as a whole person, facilitating individual growth and connection to society and with others.

Strengths for Use Online

In psychoanalysis therapy, the client's past is explored to understand the present. The counselor is often seen as the expert and a teacher, facilitating and aiding the client to process psychological thoughts, both conscious and unconscious. The online format is conducive to employing techniques that foster and develop self-awareness through homework exercises and questioning. Adlerian therapy, also termed individual psychology, is considered a short term, goal-oriented, and positive psychodynamic theory (Corsini & Wedding, 2010) and can work well in an online context. Clients may feel "safer" disclosing personal information about their family background and developmental history, as the online setting provides the client the security of being in a known environment.

Adaptions to Consider

Some of the techniques that enable counselors to gain information and insight by observing physical cues and responses, like play therapy or artwork, may take more planning and preparation and require some creativity to use online. The counselor will need to see what materials are available to the client, send a list of materials or worksheets to be used in each session to the client in advance, and may suggest having all supplies nearby and stored in an easily assessable container in order to have what is needed during the session. A little preplanning can facilitate the adaptability of play therapy and artwork online; these techniques can be utilized to help identify the client's current emotional state (Levitt et al., 2015) online, as in person.

Most of the therapeutic techniques used to facilitate client understanding of what is happening in the present are adaptable to online. Using free association, interpretation, dream analysis, and examining resistance are not impeded by the online format. Similarly, Adlerian techniques like teaching "I" statements, acting "as-if," and role playing are adaptable online. Adaptions for the empty chair technique were discussed earlier in the chapter when examining Gestalt psychology.

Paying attention to **transference** and **countertransference** may be perceived differently in the synchronous format. For example, Anthony and Merz Nagel (2010) noted the importance of being aware of the additional software and hardware used in the online format. In some online formats, the client has more opportunity to contact the counselor at any time through email, text, or chat box. Though the client can communicate to the counselor at virtually any time of the day, the counselor may not be available to immediately respond to the correspondence. The client may have feelings toward the counselor based on the timing of the counselor's response, and the counselor may develop feelings toward the client if perceived as always available. Psychoanalytic counselors need to be able to pay attention to and address how transference and countertransference may occur in the counseling process online.

Brief psychoanalytic therapy is typically 10 to 25 sessions (Corey, 2017), and true psychoanalysis includes additional sessions. Counselors and clients need to evaluate whether the psychoanalytic techniques utilized are effective (ACA, 2014, Section H.4.d.) and meet the client goals in a time that is satisfactory and enjoyable in this format. Limitations and benefits of this therapeutic approach, as with the other therapeutic approaches discussed, should be reviewed with the client (ACA, 2014, Section H.4.a.).

Humanism

Humanism is rooted in the belief that humans are inherently good and trustworthy (Capuzzi & Stauffer, 2016). Keeping this concept in mind, counselors strive to uncover the coping skills needed for individuals to become self-actualized (Corey, 2017). This approach focuses on client's meeting their fundamental needs and becoming the best possible version of themselves, the very foundation upon which counseling is based.

Foundational Beliefs

Humanism developed out of the deterministic views of psychoanalysis and the utility of behavioral therapay (Hansen, 2005; Wilks & Ratheal, 2010). Humanistic theories hold to the fundamental belief that humans are inherently good and trustworthy (Capuzzi & Stauffer, 2016). Humanists believe people are capable of making changes in their lives to move toward being more self-actualized, and that by fostering a growth-encouraging environment the counselor can assist the individual in moving toward their fulfilled creative self, one who is capable of moving forward and creating healthy coping skills for problems that may arise (Corey, 2017). Humanism combined the focus on human freedom from existentialism with the subjective nature of phenomenology to produce an approach rooted in the appreciation of personal experiences of an individual balanced by the freedom of choice and personal responsibility (Hansen, 2000; Wilks & Ratheal, 2010).

In 1943, Abraham Maslow (1908–1970) published his work entitled *A Theory of Human Motivation* in which he discussed his hierarchy of needs represented by a pyramid with the most basic needs at the base and higher needs at the top, culminating in his fifth stage of self-actualization. Carl Rogers (1902–1987) built on this concept with his person-centered approach to therapy in which the counselor helps to create a growth-promoting climate in which a client's potential is fostered and encouraged through the genuine interaction with the counselor who unconditionally accepts the client for where they are yet challenges them to become better versions of themselves (Corey, 2017). The client, who is experiencing conflict, works with the counselor to reassess their options and choices. The counselor works as a partner in the reframing of the client's problem, providing options and encouragement but allowing the client to be ultimately responsible for the choices they choose to make or not.

Overview of Common Techniques

Congruency is a key concept of the humanistic approach. It is defined as the genuineness and realness of the therapist, or the ability of the therapist to be professional yet real with their client in their thoughts and reactions (Corey, 2017). This congruency allows for a professional therapeutic relationship to form, grounded in the honest reactions and perceptions of both the client and counselor, creating an open exchange of ideas. Unconditional positive regard is another often misinterpreted concept of humanism. Unconditional positive regard is the acceptance of the client for who they are and where they are in their development combined with care about the person and their well-being while challenging the client to become a healthier version of themselves. The counselor, through congruent conversation, supports the client in the here and now yet encourages change to fulfill their fundamental good while keeping in mind it is the free will of the client to make the choice or not, thus placing the responsibility of success or consequent failure firmly in the client's choices. Finally, the concept of **accurate empathetic understanding** rounds out the foundation of the humanistic approach. This is not only the counselor's ability to understand the subjective world of another but also a skill that should be developed in the client. By developing an appreciation and understanding of other's thoughts, feelings, and values, the client becomes more able to accurately assess their interpretation of the behaviors of others. For example, did the man who cut you off on your way to work this morning do it to be a controlling jerk? Perhaps, but perhaps they were in a hurry to respond to an emergency at home, or perhaps they had a sick family member in the car they were rushing to the doctor. By considering the possible motivations of others rather than simply assuming they are the same as our interpretation, we become more empathetic and understanding of the individual and their experience of the world around them.

Combining these techniques together in a humanistic approach allows for the client to develop a sense of responsibility for themselves balanced with a sense of trust in their own abilities and the feedback from others (Marlow, 1991).

Strengths for Use Online

The very nature of online counseling necessitates the integration of a humanistic approach to the client in developing a healthy therapeutic connection with the counselor while feeling understood, connected, and encouraged to make healthy changes (Anthony & Merz Nagel, 2010; Capuzzi, & Stauffer, 2017; Corey, 2004, 2009, 2017; Popoola & Adebowale, 2012). The assessment of the client's basic needs and treatment goals is something counselors sometimes take for granted, but in the online format these assessments become even more important and necessary on an ongoing basis, as online counselors do not see the client as a whole before them. The humanistic approach allows the online format to feel less separated and more connected and holistic in the assessment of the client, their needs, and goals.

Adaptions to Consider

The basic concepts of congruency, unconditional positive regard, and accurate empathetic understanding blend seamlessly into the online counseling format but do require some adaptions to ensure their use to their fullest potential. Where in a face-to-face session body language is more overt to express these concepts, the online format requires more thought into the verbal expression of these to the client. The minute details of hand gestures, head nods, and focus can be lost in translation online, and thus need to be more purposeful and highlighted by additional verbalizations. Checking with the client on their understanding, use of summarization and clarification, and other basic counseling skills more frequently is necessary to ensure that the client feels understood, accepted, and encouraged.

Cognitive Behavioral Therapy

Cognitive Behavioral Therapy focuses on the individual's perceptions and processing of information. This approach assists clients in understanding that they have the power to change their thinking, and thus their perceptions of available coping strategies. Cognitive Behavioral Therapy couples with online counseling easily as it is goal oriented, collaborative, and allows for monitoring of change.

Foundational Beliefs

Cognitive theories focus on a person's perceptions and how information is processed. In the mid-1950s, Albert Ellis connected the way we act and feel to irrational thinking, which leads to maladaptive interactions with the world (for example, we must rely on others for our happiness) (Rice, 2015). Ellis developed an approach to therapy, rational emotive behavioral therapy (first called rational emotive therapy), that utilized behavioral techniques and cognitive reframing to evoke change.

Aaron Beck, with a background in psychoanalysis, developed cognitive therapy as a short-term and person-centered approach to aid individuals with depression (Beck, 1979). Also known as cognitive behavioral therapy (CBT), Beck connected the way we think to core beliefs and schemas, which frame the way we view the world (Rice, 2015). With CBT, cognitions can be altered to produce a desired change in feelings and behavior (Corey, 2017). More recently Marsha Linehan incorporated CBT precepts with mindfulness and acceptance in order to evoke change, developing dialectical behavior therapy (DBT) to use with clients with borderline personality disorder, and using modified versions for individuals with substance abuse and depression (Rice, 2015).

Overview of Common Techniques

Cognitive behavioral therapy typically begins by helping the client identify differences between core beliefs, or **schema**, and untrue or unhelpful assumptions, or maladaptive thoughts (Sanders, 2016), and by developing self-awareness of what our behavioral response is to our thoughts and feelings. CBT is client centered and collaborative. The client is seen as capable of identifying what is needed and making the change and is the authority on their experience. The counselor respects the client's autonomy and works with the client to help them achieve their desired goals and level of change (Levitt et al., 2015). There are numerous CBT techniques for the counselor to draw from. Traditional CBT includes homework, which encourages growth in self-awareness of the client's thoughts, feelings, and behaviors and the ability to identify them. For example, using an ABC worksheet, clients are often asked to record an activating event (A), beliefs about the event (B), and consequences (C) (Anthony & Merz Nagel, 2010).

Socratic questioning is another cognitive technique. Socratic questioning facilitates guided discovery and can be used to help clients identify core beliefs and maladaptive behaviors and to explore alternative ways to perceive a situation and respond (Rice, 2015; Sanders, 2016). This form of questioning provides a safe space for clients to explore what they are thinking and feeling and how it connects to their behavior. The miracle question is a popular intervention utilized by CBT counselors. There are a multitude of other CBT techniques available for counselors to draw on to help clients identify maladaptive thoughts and replace them with thoughts that are more realistic. **Brainstorming** with clients, asking them to "picture in their mind" what something else could look like, or teaching reframing strategies are additional examples of CBT strategies. Helping the client identify irrational beliefs is another CBT technique. Ellis and Ellis (2011) identified three irrational beliefs that lead to self-defeat: (a) "I MUST do well and be loved and approved by others"; (b) "Other people MUST treat me fairly, kindly, and well"; and (c) "The world and my living conditions MUST be comfortable, gratifying, and just, providing me with all that I want in life" (as cited in Corey, 2017, p. 272).

Strengths for Use Online

There are multiple cognitive techniques available to assist clients in addressing and changing their identified unwanted thoughts and behaviors. CBT is goal oriented and collaborative, and the online synchronous format does not hinder this component. In fact, Anthony and Merz Nagel (2010) noted CBT is often seen as "ideally suited" for online therapy. Additionally, the online format is conducive to utilizing CBT techniques, such as psychoeducation materials, homework, and questioning, to help clients meet their goals, which can often be accomplished with fewer sessions if not addressing complex mental health issues. Clients learn practical tools that are applicable to everyday life once they complete counseling. Because it is goal oriented, counselors can monitor progress and effectiveness (ACA, 2014, Section C.2.d.) to gauge if CBT techniques are working and adapt different techniques if needed.

Adaptions to Consider

For online counseling, Nagel and Anthony (2011) suggest homework assignments that incorporated text-based material, utilizing psychoeducation and **bibliotherapy**. Counselors will want to be sensitive to the client's experience with technology, including the ability to copy, print, save, and upload materials. It is important to ensure materials are shared through the Health Insurance Portability and Accountability Act (HIPAA)-compliant portals. With many online therapy platforms, clients can directly upload worksheets, journal entries, exercises, and documents into their online client folder or email them before the session, giving the counselor time to review client progress and strategize for the next session. Additionally, narrative therapy or encouraging journaling and blogging are techniques conducive to the online format (Anthony & Merz Nagel, 2010). These may also be shared electronically with the counselor and aid in gauging the progress of the client.

Socratic questioning is another cognitive technique that can be utilized online. Reframing, asking "the miracle question," brainstorming with the client, and talking through the exercise of using the ABC worksheet are all seamlessly applicable online. Additionally, helping the client identify irrational beliefs can occur online without any adaptions. CBT is client centered and collaborative. Getting feedback from the client about their online counseling experience and showing sensitivity to what they need to move forward toward their goals further enriches the counseling relationship as well as ensures maintaining a collaborative process.

Modern Theories

Modern theories include an array of theoretic approaches, each with a unique focus. These include choice and reality theories, feminist theory, and the postmodern approaches of social construct theory, solution-focused brief therapy (SFBT), narrative therapy, family systems therapy, and multigenerational family therapy. Counselors are encouraged to gain an understanding of each of these and integrate them into their therapeutic approach as they best suit the client.

Foundational Beliefs

Choice theory is rooted in the belief that we can choose to feel, think, and act differently and that symptoms are the results of choices we have made (Corey, 2017). Reality therapy is based in choice theory, and both share the focus on personal responsibility, which Corey says (2017) occurs when we meet our needs without limiting others from doing the same. The therapist's role in choice/ reality theory is to assist the client in focusing on the present and not on the symptoms themselves.

Feminist theory views problems through a sociopolitical and cultural lens, which acknowledges the oppression experienced by women and minority groups (Corey, 2017). Goals for feminist theory include assisting clients in trusting themselves and their own voice while understanding the role oppression and dictation of beliefs has influenced their self-definition. The development of healthy relationships and trust in themselves allows clients to bring about social change in their communities and the systems they are involved with. Feminist theory does not focus on assessment and diagnoses, as it views them as labeling and limiting of a client. Both male and female therapists and clients can work from a feminist point of view, as it is one that supports equality, understanding, and appreciation of the individual.

Social constructivism is a postmodern theory that places the client in the expert role and the counselor in the role of providing optimism for change. It is rooted in the belief that there are multiple truths, that reality is subjective, and that language influences its perception (Corey, 2017). The therapeutic relationship is collaborative and supportive.

Solution-focused brief therapy (SFBT) assists clients in shifting from being focused on the problem and the past to being focused on solutions and the present and beyond (Corey, 2017). The counselor believes that clients are their own expert and that they are able to make small changes that lead to bigger ones. The past is not important as the client has the ability to develop multiple solutions to any problem, and the problem may not be important to finding the solution.

Narrative therapy is rooted in the belief that the problem is the problem (Corey, 2017). It involves the counselor listening without judgment or interruption to the client's story, allowing the client to separate themselves from the problem, explore possible exceptions and solutions, and recreate the story for themselves by taking an active role. This approach is outlined in detail in Chapter 9.

Family systems and multigenerational theories are focused on understanding the impact and influence of the systems people are born into and live in. Problems are viewed as symptomatic of a problem within the system, not the individual (Corey, 2017). Effective management of these issues involves an understanding and appreciation of the individual but also the family system in which they function. The techniques associated with these theories are explored more in-depth in Chapter 10.

Overview of Common Techniques

Choice/reality theory techniques include the WDEP system and planning for change. The WEDP system is an acronym for the steps that lead to change. Corey (2017) explains the steps to be W, which stands for wants, or understanding what you want be and do; D or doing and direction, which includes identifying what you need to do and where you are headed; E for evaluation, when the client evaluates their current behaviors and how they assist or hinder them in meeting their goals; and P for planning. Planning is explored through the SAMIC3 system, which encourages the client to take **s**imple, **a**ttainable, **m**easurable, and **i**mmediate and involved steps that are **c**ontrolled by the planner, **c**ommitted to, and **c**onsistently done to bring about change (Corey, 2017).

Feminist theory brings techniques for use in counseling, which include empowerment, self-disclosure, bibliotherapy, assertiveness training, advocacy, and reframing/relabeling. Empowering is defined by feminist theory as encouraging an individual to do something in their life and assisting them to identify their own authority and power to change. Clients are encouraged to think about their self-definition, consider limitations they perceive, and challenge those limitations while rewriting their self-definition. Empowerment supports autonomy and self-responsibility.

Therapist self-disclosure is intended to support understanding and normalize an experience. This technique needs to be used sparingly as a means of highlighting similarities in human experiences but not to sanitize an individual's experience as less than the unique thing that it is. Self-disclosure needs to be guided by the benefit it brings to the client not the counselor. Bibliotherapy is the use of books to bring about change. This may be accomplished by either assigning or having the client choose books they are willing to read or workbooks they complete. Discussion of these before and after completion allows the counselor and client to explore application of the material to their lives as well as assist in redefining their experiences.

Assertiveness training assists individuals in becoming more comfortable with their own boundaries and thoughts and expressing these to others without regret or compromise. Assertiveness needs to be clearly distinguished from aggression. The former is rooted in establishing a firm ground for the speaker, the latter with taking away the rights of another to disagree or have a different point of view. Assertiveness training needs to be a thorough and complete aspect of treatment, not simply a technique explained once and expected to be mastered.

Advocacy for self and others is a key technique used in feminist theory. Advocacy is leading your support to a cause of change. It may take the form of self-advocacy, in which an individual strives for change within themselves, their behaviors, or within a social group or take on a larger focus of change within the community and systems in which the individual lives and works. Reframing/relabeling is a technique in which a client is encouraged to reestablish a perception or label considering their own experiences as well as those of others. Challenging one's own viewpoint or that of another allows us to consider alternative reasoning for actions or definitions for words. By challenging our viewpoint to consider others, we find meaning in events and come to appreciate differences.

Solution-based brief therapy employs the skillful use of questions by the counselor, which allows the client to explore how things would be different if they opted to choose one solution over another, allowing the client to try on outcomes prior to committing to the implementation of the change. Corey (2017) identifies various forms of questions counselors may use, including exceptions, or asking the client to explain a time when the problem did not exist and what was different; scaling, or asking for a rating on a scale from 1–10 where the client is on an aspect of the problem or solution; and the miracle question, in which the client is asked to consider what would need to occur for the problem to cease to exist.

Strengths for Use Online

Choice/reality theory appears to be a match for online counseling in that it shares similar goals. Choice/reality theory emphasizes choices and personal responsibility, both of which are common traits of online counseling clients. The belief that the client knows what is best for themselves and what they need is fostered in an equitable therapeutic relationship between counselor and client.

Feminist theory brings with it many strengths, including its focus on empowerment and the ability of the client to rewrite their current role in society, making it one that they choose instead of were handed. Solution-focused brief therapy fits many managed care models and assists the client in developing an insight into possible solutions rooted in their strengths and abilities. Narrative therapy allows the client to express themselves free from judgment while learning to appreciate their role in rewriting and constructing their future. Both family-based and multigenerational theories bring into consideration the values and system into which the client was born while considering how they impact their current decision making and behaviors.

An understanding of the modern theories allows the counselor to develop an integrative approach to counseling. This allows the counselor to use evidence-based techniques in a combination that matches the client's preference, ability, and background. This personalization of theoretic approach and techniques provides effective problem solving tailored to the unique individual client.

Adaptions to Consider

The WDEP system and planning for change may be transformed into a worksheet, as is provided in this chapter, for use with online clients. The counselor may ask the client to complete these worksheets and bring them into the next session to discuss, thus providing a continuity between therapy and times the client is not in session, much like any homework assignment in the face-to-face format. This will assist clients in learning to assess for themselves what is needed to make a change and to be able to provide themselves feedback in the future of what has worked and what has not.

Bibliotherapy may involve the choosing of a fiction, nonfiction, or self-help book by either the counselor or client to read and discuss. The topic of the book would be discussed prior to reading, with both the counselor and client sharing their thoughts on the topic. Upon completion of reading the book, the conversation would be revisited, exploring what the client experienced during the reading, and what, if any, parts are applicable to their daily lives.

Assertiveness training is adaptable to online counseling. Education on assertiveness may occur through a combination of outside readings and in-session discussion. Role playing with the counselor during session may assist the client in practicing their assertiveness with feedback on healthy boundaries and alternative means of being assertive. Caution must be used in educating the client on the differences between assertiveness and aggression, with follow-up discussions in session about practices in the client's daily life.

Scaling questions may be used to assist clients in rating an aspect of the problem or solution on a scale from 1–10. This may be accomplished through in-session discussion as it would in face-to-face session, or it may be useful for the counselor to have a scale to share with the client for a more visual interpretation of the changes. Asking the client to distinguish the differences between ratings will help to facilitate further exploration of what will or will not work for them in any given situation. See Figure 5.1 for an example of a scaling visual presentation and the associated worksheet.

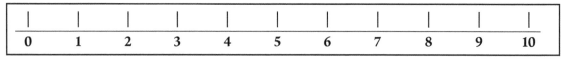

FIGURE 5.1. Sample scale to share with online clients to rate intensity of emotions, situations, etc.

Multicultural/Social Justice/Ethical Considerations

In any theoretic approach, a counselor needs to consider the multicultural, social justice, and ethical considerations of the chosen approach as well as the issues brought forth by the client. Consider not only the client's culture, socioeconomic status, traditions, and values, but their comfort with technology, age, and view of counseling. Social justice refers to the consideration of the client and their environment, social situation, and the counselor's ability to empower the client to access services and advocate for themselves. Ethics of counseling, according to the ACA standards, as well as the state the counselor is licensed in and those of applicable certification boards, apply to each client seen regardless of setting. As you will see explored more in-depth in coming chapters, the online counseling realm brings unique applications of these considerations to the client.

There are specific nuances that need to be considered regarding theory and treatment with diverse clients. Psychoanalytic theory may be culturally inappropriate, is highly subjective, and does not assist the client in identifying maladaptive behaviors. Humanistic approaches such as Adlerian therapy may be too individualistic for clients from a collective culture, do not account for the impact of oppression on the client, and may not be directive enough for those clients requiring more structure due to lack of insight or intellectual disability. Person-centered theory such as Jungian therapy, focuses on the individual, their experiences, and co-assessment with the counselor, all of which may be incongruent with clients from collective cultures and who are seeking a more active role from the therapist. Existential theory, with its emphasis on an individual's choice to change their life, may alienate clients who have experienced social injustices. It may also lack a sense of direction for some clients, feeling too abstract.

Cognitive behavioral therapy may be too confrontational for some clients and may overlook the influence of past experiences on current choices and behaviors. Choice theory may overlook the role of unconscious influences on client choices, fail to assist in the development of insight on behalf of the client, and is open for the counselor to impose their personal culture or definitions onto the client. Feminist theory's lack of neutrality on behalf of the counselor may lead to the imposition of the counselor's culture and alienate certain groups while lacking insight into the client's personal experience. Solution-focused brief therapy may seem to mechanical with its focus on techniques over the therapeutic relationship, and the counselor's lack of knowing may equate to a lack of under-standing and expertise for some clients. Narrative techniques may lead to counselors imposing their own definitions and summary of client experiences onto the client.

The integration of spirituality into any counseling session is best left to the client's discretion. Some clients may be very open discussing their beliefs, while others view it as a more intimate topic only shared with specific individuals in their life. Understanding and appreciation of spiri-tuality as a cultural variable will encourage the counselor to approach the topic with both respect and understanding.

Age is yet another variable to consider with clients. Age influences a client's perspective, is shaped by their experiences, and may influence a client's comfort with various forms of technology and specific aspects of any given theory. Consideration of this important variable is yet another dynamic in choosing a theory, its use in treatment, and any modification necessary to include it in online counseling.

Mastery of theories and their associated techniques takes specific training and years of practice under supervision. Counselors may misinterpret the simplicity of a technique to mean they have mastered it, which may lead to misuse of the technique minimally and abuse of power at the worst. Counselors are encouraged to obtain ongoing training and supervision in using any techniques or theoretic approach to ensure the best use and treatment for the client.

Whether online or face-to-face, theories that place the counselor in the role of expert or establish a dynamic with the counselor in the power position may even be triggering for some minority clients or clients who have experienced victimization. Understanding a client's worldview is vital to the treatment process and necessary to forming a therapeutic alliance with the online client. Integration of theory into treatment is a complex task that requires consistent diligence on behalf of the counselor to ensure its appropriate use and adaption to the client's needs and abilities.

Basic Counseling Theories and Adaption Summaries

Theory	Summary
Structuralism	Introspection, self-awareness, and mindfulness can be accomplished online via the written word through text for online counseling, much as journaling does in face-to-face counseling. Journaling can still be used but increase the use of technology and include creative means and comfort on behalf of the client.
Functionalism	Counselors will support the free will of the client while simultaneously holding them accountable for the logical consequences of their actions by personalizing the treatment plan to the goal of the client and their current abilities and resources.
Gestalt	Temper the use of these techniques as you would in face-to-face counseling. Journaling, blog, or text may assist the client in increasing their awareness of their use of the new skill while assessing the usefulness in various settings and situations as well as maintaining a running dialogue with their counselor. Empty chair, phantom letters, and role plays are appropriate and require very little modification for the online environment; however, they should only be used when the client is comfortable doing so. Modifications of these, as discussed in the chapter, are always appropriate, be it the talk with the empty car seat as you drive home or the phantom text that is deleted and never sent. Exaggeration of emotions and staying in the emotion are readily adapted to the online platform, using videoconferencing or other technological means such as sharing a screen shot of a picture representing an emotion or past person or event tied to the emotion to discuss.
Existential therapy	Counselors may choose to incorporate more concrete techniques when exploring topics such as death, anxiety, guilt, loneliness, and grief with clients; journaling, staying with the emotion, or cognitive restructuring may assist clients in exploring these topics while feeling more focused.
Behavioral therapy	This therapy requires more focused attention to minute changes in nonverbal cues and reading the body language of the client. Establishing reward-based incentives to reduce or change behavior may be tracked as efficiently online as in person, and the counselor may use modeling and behavioral rehearsal and engage in role playing with the client online. Using imaginative stimuli, or in vivo desensitization, may be practiced as a tool to reduce fear when triggered. Contingency contracts may be established and shared as easily online as in person as well.

Theory	Summary
Psychoanalysis	The counselor will pay attention to minute details of hand gestures, head nods, and focus, which can be lost in translation online, and thus need to be more purposeful and highlighted by additional verbalizations. Checking with the client on their understanding, use of summarization and clarification, and other basic counseling skills more frequently is necessary to ensure that the client feels understood, accepted, and encouraged.
Humanism	Use of congruency, unconditional positive regard, and accurate empathetic understanding blend seamlessly into the online counseling format but do require some adaptions to ensure their use to their fullest potential via more detailed explanation, where nonverbals may be lost due to technology. Nonverbals like head nodding may need to be slightly more dramatic to be conveyed in the computer screen. Checking with the client on their understanding, use of summarization and clarification, and other basic counseling skills are required more frequently.
Cognitive behavioral therapy	Homework assignments that incorporate text-based material, utilizing psychoeducation, and bibliotherapy are helpful. Counselors will want to be sensitive to the client's experience with technology, including the ability to copy, print, save, and upload materials and ensure these are only shared through HIPAA-compliant portals. Narrative therapy and journaling or blogging as well as use of Socratic questions and the "miracle question" are techniques conducive to the online format.
Choice/reality theory	The WDEP system may be created into a worksheet to provide to the client as homework and be reviewed in the following session. The SAMIC3 system can be utilized in much the same way. Explanation of autonomy and responsibility for logical consequences needs to occur frequently as it is in face-to-face sessions. Keeping a running log of choices and resulting consequences can also be helpful to provide feedback to the client from themselves regarding their choices and consider alternatives if a different outcome is desired.
Feminism	Techniques such as empowerment, self-disclosure, bibliotherapy, assertiveness training, advocacy, and reframing/relabeling are easily modified in the online realm, requiring slightly more introduction and explanation of their purpose and value. Self-disclosure needs to be monitored to remain professional despite the personal setting. Bibliotherapy and assertiveness training may be accomplished through homework or discussing or viewing videos together during session with an exploratory discussion following. As in face-to-face sessions, a discussion differentiating assertiveness and aggression is necessary.
Social construct theory	No significant modifications are required in using this theory online. Counselors may want to take extra time to explain their places as in this approach the client is in the expert role and the counselor in the role of providing optimism for change. This collaboration is achieved through open discussion as in face-to-face sessions.
Solution-focused brief therapy	Scaling questions may be used to assist clients in rating an aspect of the problem or solution on a scale from 1–10, accomplished through in-session discussion as it would in face-to-face session, or it may be useful for the counselor to have a scale to share with the client for a more visual interpretation of the changes. Asking the client to distinguish the differences between ratings will help to facilitate further exploration of what will or will not work for them in any given situation.

Theory	Summary
Narrative therapy	No significant modifications are necessary to successfully use this approach in the online environment. The counselor listens without judgment or interruption to the client's story, allowing the client to separate themselves from the problem, explore possible exceptions and solutions, and recreate the story for themselves by taking an active role.
Family systems and multigenerational theories	No significant modifications are necessary in these approaches as effective management of these issues involves understanding and appreciation of the individual but also the family system in which they function. Additional understanding of various family members' access and ability to use technology is required, as well as a firm establishment of rules of sharing in sessions involving different members of families, couples, or multigenerational households.

SUMMARY

The theoretic orientation according to Whitehead (1916) provides the counselor with a framework on which to build their counseling skills while creating knowledge. Understanding one's theoretical orientation is an important step in developing and building a professional counselor identity (Testa et al., 2015). Theories assist inexperienced counselors in navigating appropriate treatment interventions and assessments while being a channel for incorporating research into counseling. Rousseau (1968) commented on the use of theories by humans to understand their experiences and the world around them, much as Whitehead highlights its use to guide us through experiences others have dealt with before. Throughout career development your understanding and appreciation of theory will be changing and refining based on your clinical skills and experiences. Keeping an open mind to various theoretic approaches and techniques allows a clinician to remain well rounded, informed, and skilled in matching their approach to the needs and comfort level of the client. Understanding how to adapt your theoretic approach and interventions to meet the client's needs in the online realm will increase the effectiveness of those interventions while ensuring the treatment is rooted firmly in evidence-based practices.

CASE EXPLORATION

Consider the following case study:

Consider the fact that Pat is a transgender female and the life partner to Tristin, but they are not married. Raymond has some difficulty accepting Pat in a parental role for no other reason that Pat is not Juan and carries some resentments toward Juan and Tristin for breaking up and having to have two households. However, Raymond states he does not feel "ready" to discuss this with Pat or Juan yet and is afraid to discuss it with Tristin because he "doesn't want to make her cry." The counselor will introduce some Gestalt techniques to use online.

Katrina: So, Raymond, last week we talked about you feeling unsure of how to talk to your mom and dad about your feelings about them breaking up, and you shared you were having difficulty getting close to Pat because she's not your dad. Where are you at with that today?

Raymond: I'm feeling frustrated with all these feelings. I can't talk to my dad because he just gets angry, and I can't talk to my mom because she just cries and tells me she's sorry, but she had to leave if she was ever going to happy. My mom keeps asking me what the problem is with Pat, and I can't tell her that basically it's that she's not my dad and never will be. I just don't know.

Katrina: Well that's a lot to share, and I'm happy you're choosing to share it with me. What if we practiced you talking to your dad, your mom, or even Pat? Do you think that would help in any way? Say, maybe help you find the right words?

Raymond: I don't know; I mean I don't want to role play or stuff like that. I saw that in my psychology class at school, and there is no way I'm going to do that. It's weird.

Katrina: Okay, that's fair. How about we try something else? Have you ever had a conversation with yourself when no one else is around, you know like when you are walking home from school alone? Or have you ever written a text message to someone and decided after you read it again that you didn't want to send it?

Raymond: You're not going to think I'm crazy if I say yes are you?

Katrina: Absolutely not!

Raymond: Yep, I've talked to myself walking home. I've had a whole conversation with my teacher who wanted to see me the next day about a test I didn't do well on. I was answering any questions I thought he might have.

Katrina: And how did that work out?

Raymond: Well I felt better going in the next day because I felt like I was ready to talk to him and to explain myself no matter what he asked. And you know what, it turned out okay. I was ready for him to be cool or annoyed, and he was cool and I was ready for that. I didn't just go in looking for a fight, you know?

Katrina: I do. It sounds like you practiced it in your head and felt prepared even without having anyone else around. That's called a practice conversation. And it does exactly what you said: It makes you feel ready to deal with a conversation any direction it goes. You know what you will or won't say because you thought it through.

Raymond: Yep, it helped. And the text, I did the same with when my friend sent me one about some nonsense at school. I jumped in and wrote a response and when I read it, I thought hey, this isn't something I want to be involved in or say, so I deleted it.

Katrina: And how did that make you feel?

Raymond: Like I made a good choice, didn't take the bait you know?

Katrina: I do. That's called a phantom letter. It's something we write to get out our reactions and thoughts but don't actually send because it's either not worth it like you decided it to be or it wasn't possible to because either the other person wouldn't be open to talk about or isn't here with us anymore.

Raymond: Like my dad. He gets angry when I talk about him and mom breaking up like I'm blaming him, but I'm not; I just have so many questions and thoughts, so maybe the phantom letter would help me say what I have to without actually having to talk to him and watch him get cranky.

Katrina: So, what do you think might help with that?

Raymond: I think my practice talk might because maybe then I can be ready to talk to him and explain I'm not blaming him.

Katrina: Well why don't we think about it this week and try both and see which one fits. Next time we can figure out which one felt better and seems to fit you more and we can go from there. What do you think?

Raymond: Sounds fair, since I don't really have to deal with anyone else just yet but it might help me to get stuff off my chest. I'll try them and let you know.

Worksheets

CLIENT FEEDBACK ABOUT SATISFACTION WITH THERAPEUTIC APPROACH

Client satisfaction is closely related to the therapeutic relationship built between the client and the therapist. Checking in with your client to get feedback about their online counseling experience and their perception of the usefulness and effectiveness of the therapeutic approaches being utilized is important.

Use a scale from 1–10, with 10 being the most satisfied and 1 the least satisfied, gauge client satisfaction in the following areas:

1. How comfortable are you feeling using technology to attend your online counseling session?

   _____

   _____

   _____

2. How confident do you feel about our approach to therapy and the goals that have been identified?

   _____

   _____

   _____

3. How do you feel about growing in self-awareness?

   _____

   _____

   _____

4. How do you feel about being heard and that your concerns are being addressed?

_____

_____

_____

5. How do you feel about finding solutions to your concerns and problems?

_____

_____

_____

AM I INTEGRATING THEORIES AND TECHNIQUES THAT ARE APPROPRIATE FOR MY CLIENT IN AN ONLINE COUNSELING FORMAT?

PRACTICE BEING SELF-REFLECTIVE.

What counseling techniques do I normally draw on and feel comfortable with utilizing in session? Do these work well online?

_____

_____

_____

_____

Regardless of which theories and techniques I decide to incorporate into the client's online therapy, am I using my basic counseling skills (empathy, active listening, reflections, paraphrasing, challenging, and confronting)?

_____

_____

_____

_____

Am I integrating theory and techniques that I believe fit the client or that fit the client's situation and presenting problem? Or both?

_____

_____

_____

_____

_____

WDEP WORKSHEET

WDEP is a process to assist you in deciding to make a change:

> **W** stands for wants, or understanding what you want be and do
> **D** or doing and direction, which includes identifying what you need to do and where you are headed
> **E** for evaluation of your current behaviors and how they assist or hinder you in meeting your goals
> **P** for planning

For planning, remember the **SAMIC3** system, which encourages the client to take **simple, attainable, measurable, and immediate** and involved steps that are **controlled**, **committed** to, and **consistently** done to bring about change (Corey, 2017).

Step	Answer	Steps you need to add or things you need to overcome to succeed
W:		
D:		
E:		
P:		

Basic Counseling Forms

SCALING SKILLS

For this exercise consider the problem you are facing and the possible solutions. Please list at least three and explain why you chose that rating over the rating above and below it. What would need to happen for it to move to the higher number?

1	2	3	4	5	6	7	8	9	10

Topic you are rating	Reasoning for current rating	What would need to occur for this to be higher?

Online Resources

An in-depth review of online counseling certification programs and the use of theories online reveals a lack of specific information pertinent to the use of theories in online synchronous counseling. For this reason, the sources provided are theory specific with appropriate modification of the techniques discussed previously in this chapter.

- **American Counseling Association (ACA): Articles related to theories.** https://www.counseling.org/search/#/theories/page=1

- **American Psychological Association (APA): Overview of theories.** https://www.apa.org/topics/therapy/psychotherapy-approaches

- **National Institute of Health, Office of Behavioral and Social Science Research: Social and behavioral theories chapter.** http://www.esourceresearch.org/tabid/724/default.aspx

References

American Counseling Association. (2014). *ACA code of ethics.* https://www.counseling.org/resources/aca-code-of-ethics.pdf

Anthony, K., & Merz Nagel, D. (2010). *Therapy online: A practical guide.* SAGE.

Beck, A. T. (1979). *Cognitive therapy and the emotional disorders.* Meridian.

Capuzzi, D., & Stauffer, M. D. (2016). *Counseling and psychotherapy: Theories and interventions* (6th edition). American Counseling Association.

Corey, G. (2004). *Designing an integrative approach to counseling practice. VISTAS Online.* https://www.counseling.org/knowledge-center/vistas/by-year2/vistas-2004/docs/default-source/vistas/vistas_2004_29

Corey, G. (2009). *The art of integrative counseling (2nd edition).* Thomson Brooks/Cole.

Corey, G. (2017). *Theory and practice of counseling and psychotherapy (10th edition).* Cengage.

Corey, G., Corey, M., & Callanan, P. (2011). *Issues and ethics in the helping profession* (7th edition). Brooks/Cole.

Corsini, R. J., & Wedding, D. (2010). *Current psychotherapies (9th edition).* Brooks/Cole.

Derrig-Palumbo, K., & Zeine, F. (2005). *Online therapy: A therapist's guide to expanding your practice.* Norton.

Dewey, J. (1902). *The child and the curriculum.* University of Chicago Press.

Donnelly, D. (2015). Behavior therapies: Overview. In I E. Neukrug (Ed.), *The SAGE encyclopedia of theory in counseling and psychotherapy* (pp. 94–97). SAGE. http://dx.doi.org/10.4135/9781483346502.n40

Ellis, A., & Ellis, J. (2011). *Theories of psychotherapy. Rational emotive behavior therapy.* American Psychological Association.

Fancher, R. E., & Rutherford, A. (2017). *Pioneers of psychology: A history (5th edition).* Norton.

Foulds, M. L. (1971, April 4–8 and September 3–7). *Gestalt dreamwork as a method of self-discovery* [Paper presentation]. American Psychological Association Convention, Washington, DC, and the American Personnel and Guidance Association convention, Atlantic City, NJ. https://files.eric.ed.gov/fulltext/ED054474.pdf

Freud, S. (1900). *The interpretations of dreams*. Hogarth.

Hansen, J. (2000). Psychoanalysis and humanism: A review and critical examination of integrationist efforts with some proposed resolutions. *Journal of Counseling & Development, 78(1)*, 21–28. https://psycnet.apa.org/doi/10.1002/j.1556-6676.2000.tb02556.x

Hansen, J. (2005). The devaluation of inner subjective experiences by the counseling profession: A plea to reclaim the essence of the profession. *Journal of Counseling & Development, 83(4)*, 406–415. https://doi.org/10.1002/j.1556-6678.2005.tb00362.x

Lau, A., Barnett, M., Stadnick, N., Saifan, D., Regan, J., Wiltsey Stirman, S., Roesch, S., & Brookman-Frazee, L. (2017). Therapist report adaptions to delivery of evidence-based practices with a system-driven reform of publicly funded children's mental health services. *Journal of Consulting and Clinical Psychology, 85(7)*, 664–675. https://doi.org/10.1037/ccp0000215

Levitt, D., Darnell, A., Erford, B., & Vernon, A. (2015). Integrating theory into practice. In B. Erford (Ed.), *Clinical experiences in counseling*. Pearson.

Mangal, S. K. (2011). *Advanced educational psychology (2nd edition)*. PHI.

Marlow, E. (1991). Excellence in the counseling curriculum. *Viewpoints*. https://files.eric.ed.gov/fulltext/ED341910.pdf

Maslow, A. H. (1943). A theory of human motivation. *Psychological Review, 50(4)*, 370–396. https://doi.org/10.1037/h0054346

Mays, L. (2018). Psychoanalytic theory. In M. Borstein (Ed.), *The SAGE encyclopedia of lifespan human development* (pp. 1758–1760). SAGE. http://dx.doi.org/10.4135/9781506307633.n657

Milton, J., Polmear, C., & Fabricius, J. (2011). *A short introduction to psychoanalysis*. SAGE.

Min Shim, J. (2011). Structuralism's relevance in a post-structural era: Re-visiting research on multicultural curricular studies. *Journal of Curriculum Studies, 43(6)*, 739-758. https://doi.org/10.1080/00220272.2011.591435

Murphy, L., Mitchell, D., & Hallett, R. (2011). A comparison of client characteristics in cyber and in-person counseling. *Annual Review of CyberTherapy and Telemedicine, 9*, 121–124.

Nagel, D. M., & Anthony, K. (2011). Text-based Online Counseling: Chat. In R. Krause, G. Stricker & C. Speyer (Eds.), Online counseling: *A handbook for mental health counseling.* (pp. 169–182). Elsevier/Academic Press.

Popoola, B. I., & Adebowale, O. F. (2012). *Online guidance and counseling: Toward effectively applying technology*. IGI Global.

Poh Li, L., Jaladin, R., & Abdullah, H. (2013). Understanding the two sides of online counseling and their ethical and legal ramifications. *Porcedia: Social and Behavioral Sciences, 103*, 1243–1251. https://doi.org/10.1016/j.sbspro.2013.10.453

Puleo, S., Daughhetee, C., & Newell, J. (2015). Practicing professional responsibility. In B. Erford (Ed.), *Clinical experiences in counseling*. Peterson, Inc.

Rice, R. (2015). Cognitive-behavioral therapy. In E. Neukrug (Ed.), *The SAGE encyclopedia of theory in counseling and psychotherapy* (pp. 195-199). SAGE. http://dx.doi.org/10.4135/9781483346502.n77

Rousseau, H. J. (1968). The impact of educational theory on teachers. *British Journal of Education Studies, 16(1)*, 60–71. https://doi.org/10.1080/00071005.1968.9973208

Ryan, R. M., Lynch, M. F., Vansteenkiste, M., & Deci, E. L. (2010). Motivation and autonomy in counseling, psychotherapy and behavior change: A look at theory and practice. *The Counseling Psychologist, 39(2)*, 193–260. https://doi.org/10.1177/0011000009359313

Sanders, D. (2016). The evolving world of cognitive and mindfulness-based interventions. In B. Douglas, R. Woolfe, & S. Strawbridge (Eds.), *The handbook of counseling psychology* (pp. 297–316). SAGE.

Schneider, K. J., & Krug, O. T. (2010). *Existential-humanistic therapy*. American Psychological Association.

Seel, N. M. (2012). James, William (1842–1910). In N. M. Seel (Ed.) *Encyclopedia of the sciences of learning* Springer. https://link.springer.com/referenceworkentry/10.1007%2F978-1-4419-1428-6_1485

Speyer, C., & Zack, J. (2003). Online counselling: Beyond the pros and cons. *https://www.researchgate. net/profile/John_Suler/publication/273014254_Psychotherapy_in_Cyberspace_A_5-Dimensional_ Model_of_Online_and_Computer-Mediated_Psychotherapy/links/5553719508ae980ca60855dc/ Psychotherapy-in-Cyberspace-A-5-Dimensional-Model-of-Online-and-Computer-Mediated-Psychotherapy. pdf.*

Suler, J. (2000). Psychotherapy in cyberspace: A 5-dimensional model of online and computer-mediated psychotherapy. *CyberPsychology and Behavior, 3*, 151–160. https://www.researchgate.net/deref/ http%3A%2F%2Fdx.doi.org%2F10.1089%2F109493100315996

Testa, D., Headley, J., & Adamson, N. (2015). From envisioning to actualization: Marketing yourself in the 21st century. In B. Erford (Ed.), *Clinical experiences in counseling* (pp. 306–325). Pearson.

Whitehead, A. N. (1916). The organization of thought. *Proceedings of the Aristotelian Society, 17*, 58–76. https://doi.org/10.1126/science.44.1134.409

Wilks, D., & Ratheal, J. D. (2010). A historical review and contemporary reassessment of free will: Concepts in psychological humanism and counseling. *Journal of Humanistic Counseling, Education and Development, 49*(2), 147–162. https://doi.org/10.1002/j.2161-1939.2010.tb00094.x

Wiltsey Stirman, S., Garmarra, J. M., Bartlett, B. A., Calloway, A., & Gutner, C. A. (2017). Empirical examinations of modifications and adaptions of evidence-based psychotherapies: Methodologies, impact, and future directions. *Clinical Psychology Science and Practice, 24*(4), 396–420. https:// doi.org/10.1111/cpsp.12218

Assessment and Diagnosis

Debra M. Perez and Kristal James

Clinicians regularly engage in assessment and diagnosis, which are important responsibilities and need to be approached carefully. State regulations surrounding diagnosis and assessment are specific and need to be adhered to. Additionally, most professional organizations have strict rules and regulations regarding diagnosing and assessment, such as National Association for Social Workers (NASW), American Associaiton of Marriage and Family Therapists (AAMFT), National Board of Certified Counselors (NBCC), and American Counseling Association (ACA), to name a few. Each clinician is required to become familiar with their own professional organization's code of ethics. The ACA's Code of Ethics will be explored in more detail throughout this chapter and will guide our focus.

Assessment and diagnosis are generally embedded into the clinical counselor's daily responsibilities with each client. Clinicians are required to determine capacity to give informed consent prior to engaging in formal assessment, diagnosis, or even a counseling relationship (ACA, 2014). Assessment is often thought of as formal testing, but there are other components to assessment. Client welfare, general assessment, mental status, multicultural issues/diversity, confidentiality, treatment planning, and so on are all examples of assessments in which a clinician engages in each session (ACA, 2014) and may vary based on the platform and purpose of sessions. For the purpose of this chapter, we will focus on separating formal testing from other forms of assessment leading to diagnosis in an online format.

Online tests and assessments may be beneficial to the counselor in a number of ways. They free the counselor from administering time-intensive tests, results are available quickly and via the computer, automated interpretation is an option, archiving of scores keeps data safely stored, and updates are the responsibility of the test owner (Kraus et al., 2011). Clients can be referred to testing centers or complete tests from home. Testing can involve "personality inventories, career-interest questionnaires, or intellectual ability tests" (Kraus et al., 2011, p. 229), to mention a few.

Assessment

Assessment begins at the initial contact with the client and continues in some form, whether formally or informally, throughout the counseling process. The information gathered during a clinical interview is utilized to determine how best to serve the client, tailoring counseling to the client's needs as therapy progresses. ACA (2014) defines the purpose of assessment as gathering "information regarding the client for a variety of purposes, including, but not limited to, client decision making, treatment planning, and forensic proceedings. Assessment may include both qualitative and quantitative methodologies" (Standard E.1.a.). Therefore, a counseling assessment is used for a variety of tasks, including to collect client data necessary to identify problems, to inform a DSM diagnosis, and to guide the formation of a treatment plan with goals and measurable objectives. Further, the assessment may help the counselor understand and conceptualize what the client is experiencing.

Initially, the counselor completes an intake assessment through a clinical interview, gathering the client's personal history, information on their current situation, and circumstances that brought the client in for therapy. While this type of intake assessment can occur at the first appointment and lead to diagnosis, it must be clear that assessment is not just a strategy used to make a diagnosis or a one-time event, but rather an ongoing process the counselor utilizes to evaluate the client, their functioning, and progress. Assessment can either be structured or unstructured, depending on the needs of the client and the stage in the counseling process (Guo et al., 2012).

While completing an initial intake, Guo et al. (2012) stress the importance of assessing specific areas of the client's functioning. First, the authors recommend the potential legal and ethical issues the client may present with be addressed before continuing with the initial assessment, such as a refusal to sign paperwork. Second, the authors explain any areas requiring crisis intervention should be addressed, especially any indications of suicidal or homicidal thoughts. Crisis intervention will be discussed in detail in Chapter 8. Third, Guo et al. (2012) recommend the assessment evaluate whether the client is a good fit for counseling, requiring a referral and discharge if the client is not appropriate for the manner of therapy. Next, the authors suggest evaluating the client's medical conditions to understand the potential impact on their mental health as well as to determine if a referral for medical services is necessary. The fifth step in the process suggested by Guo et al. is to seek consultation and supervision for any concerning behaviors or statements made by the client, especially if the client is suicidal or homicidal. Supervision and consultation are also beneficial for support when the clinician is inexperienced or the information provided by the client does not lead to a clear diagnosis. Finally, the authors recommend a diagnosis be generated based on the information presented, which will lead to the last step, intervention and treatment planning.

Testing

Formal assessment could include the use of a testing instrument, which would follow specific procedures and would measure identifiable psychological areas that cannot be measured by direct observation. Therefore, testing may be part of an assessment, but not all assessments include testing. Prior to administration, an instrument or testing measure requires careful consideration to determine appropriateness and relevance, and the clinician must participate in specialized training. Sections E.6.

and E.7. of the ACA (2014) Code of Ethics discuss the importance of assessing the appropriateness of the instrument and administration conditions. Similarly, technologically administered assessments are not new and have also been addressed by the ACA Code of Ethics: "Counselors ensure that technologically administered assessments function properly and provide clients with accurate results" (Standard E.7.c). It is imperative that online tests are normed for online use and that the counselor does not administer a test normed for in-person administration in an online format. In addition to understanding and complying with ethical codes for a given professional organization, each state may have unique licensing board laws specific to telebehavioral health practices, which is covered in more detail in Chapter 3.

The ACA (2014) Code of Ethics clearly states that tests are to only be administered under conditions that align with their standardization. Standardized assessments have gone through extensive testing to ensure the results are valid and reliable. **Validity** indicates how well a test measures what it says it does (Salkind, 2017). **Reliability** indicates that the test is consistent (Salkind, 2017) and is an important component of assessment accuracy. Standardized tests have been **normed** or proven to show validity and reliability for a specific population when administered in a specific way, which will be clearly identified on each assessment. Some tests have been evaluated for reliability across multiple platforms and administrative means, called **parallel forms reliability** (Salkind, 2017). A test normed for face-to-face administration cannot transfer to online administration. It is a clinician's responsibility to ensure a test is normed for online administration prior to use, a process that is completed by reaching out to the test publisher for information about the test.

All assessments should be given with purpose and analyzed by the trained clinician to determine the effectiveness of the measurement tool (Suskie, 2018). Because of the advancements of technology, outcome measures are available and can provide consistent short-term measurements to treatment as frequently as every session if desired (Bauer & Moessner, 2012). Additionally, pre- and post-treatment assessments can assist in providing valuable data regarding clinical outcomes (Bauer & Moessner, 2012). It is imperative that counselors only use tests they are trained and qualified to administer and interpret.

Before beginning the first assessment, the clinician must be trained in administration and interpretation of the assessment. Then the counselor should practice administering the assessment in the format in which it will actually be administered (i.e., online or in person). Begin by identifying the appropriate candidate, preparing the examinee and examiner for administration, troubleshooting, and practicing repeatedly (Pearson, n.d.). Counselors should never administer a test without first receiving training and supervision. By proactively intervening before test administration, the counselor will be able to manage client worries or unease regarding the test being administered. Counselors must consider potential needs, plan for and provide breaks, ensure only authorized individuals have access to the instrument or measure, minimize distractions, and consider other special testing needs in advance (Pearson, n.d.). The Federal Education Rights and Privacy Act (FERPA) and Health Insurance Portability and Accountability Act (HIPAA) mandate that platforms used to administer telebehavioral health assessments are confidential and secure according to their standards. Clinicians need to be aware of which act they need to follow and ensure the online platform meets necessary confidentiality requirements, as well as the requirements of the ACA (2014) Code of Ethics and state and local laws and standards. These areas are addressed in more detail in Chapter 3.

Diagnosis

Diagnoses are generally required by third-party payers (i.e. insurance companies) to receive financial reimbursement for services. Section E.5. of the ACA (2014) Code of Ethics is dedicated to the diagnosis of mental health disorders and specifically covers the importance of obtaining a proper diagnosis, cultural sensitivity, historical and social prejudices in the diagnosis of pathology, and even refraining from a diagnosis when clinically relevant. Much research has been conducted on a variety of diagnoses on specific populations (Newsom et al., 2016), all of which show comparable results between online and face-to-face assessments.

Diagnosis takes specialized training and supervision. Counselors need to help clients understand that diagnoses are snapshots of their symptoms and a way to categorize symptom clusters to guide the treatment plan. A diagnosis is not a label or summary of who they are. Diagnosing needs to be done in partnership with the client. Assist the client in understanding the use of the diagnosis in describing their symptoms and developing their treatment plan.

Diagnosing is rooted in accurate assessment, which includes consideration of the subjective information provided by the client coupled with the objective assessment of the counselor. In the online format this may include consideration of the client's environment, behaviors, speech patterns, and overall presentation. The use of technology to increase the accuracy of assessment and diagnosis is a clear advantage to the field of counseling and applicable to the synchronous online format (Casper & Berger, 2005).

Transition to Telebehavioral Health

Synchronous assessments and diagnoses are achieved whenever the clinician and the client are engaged with each other at the same time. A great benefit to this approach is that it allows the client and clinician the opportunity to develop a relationship and can provide an opportunity for the clinician to ask clarifying questions if needed. This can be done face-to-face in person or virtually. **Asynchronous** simply means the opposite. Anytime a clinician is gathering information from a client not in real time, it is considered asynchronous. This often looks like completion of forms and providing information necessary for proper assessment and diagnosis. One great benefit to this approach is it allows the client the opportunity to gather necessary information and can provide adequate time for processing without pressure or needing to coordinate time with the clinician. **Hybrid** methods use a combination of the two. Many clinicians are already using a hybrid approach to diagnosis and assessment regardless of modality of treatment.

Despite concerns that online assessment and diagnosis may not be as effective as that completed in a face-to-face setting, research suggests otherwise. Juárez et al. (2018) found that children ages 20 and 34 months of age diagnosed with autism spectrum disorder (ASD) were able to be appropriately diagnosed through telebehavioral health diagnostic screening. None of the participants were misdiagnosed as having ASD when they actually did not have it, and 78% of the participants were accurately diagnosed online with ASD when compared to face-to-face diagnosis. Similarly, telebehavioral health has been shown to be beneficial in rural and larger hospitals when used to assist in emergency room evaluations, although more research is required (Donley, 2017).

Self-assessments using technology to identify the presence or absence of symptoms for personality disorder diagnosis indicate similar results for those using face-to-face methods of assessment (Ballester et al., 2019; Chakhssi et al., 2019; van Bebber et al., 2017). Individuals with developmental disabilities can also benefit from use of telebehavioral health assessments (Szeftel et al., 2012). Specific software to help increase validity and reliability in the ability to accurately diagnose using telebehavioral health platforms has undergone clinical trials and has been proven effective (Malhotra et al., 2017). Global recognition of the effectiveness of telebehavioral diagnosis is also available and not limited to the United States (Mazhari et al., 2019).

Telebehavioral Health Barriers

One of the biggest barriers to telebehavioral health is skepticism and resistance, coming primarily from the clinician (Kupczynski et al., 2017). Fear can limit the effectiveness of telebehavioral health assessment and diagnosis. This reluctance can be overcome with proper training and ongoing education. Clinicians must be competent in their practice area, which includes transitioning from face-to-face to an online platform, as online work can be seen as a specialty requiring competence and training (ACA, 2014). Ethically sound counselors must also identify and evaluate clinician bias prior to practicing in an online format (ACA, 2014). The COVID-19 pandemic has necessitated a transition to online assessment and diagnosis of mental health disorders. Knowledge and understanding can combat fear and help develop the needed skills. Many organizations provide ongoing training and board certification in telebehavioral health, which is addressed in various chapters throughout the book.

Access to technology, age, and gender may play a role in willingness to engage in telebehavioral health technologies (Abel et al., 2018). Rural communities may struggle with access to advanced technologies even though they often benefit significantly from this available resource (Chang et al., 2016). Caucasian clients have been shown to have more success at engaging in technology, while their clinician counterparts seem to struggle more with their willingness to implement technology into practice (Abel et al., 2018; Kupczynski et al., 2017). Younger clients seem to be more willing to engage in using online platforms, as are females (Abel et al., 2018). It is important to note that although these differences may be apparent in some research, it does not mean this will be true for all clients or that some of these barriers cannot be overcome. Determining the client's ability to access needed technology for successful intervention is a critical component to the accuracy of assessment and diagnosis.

Seminal work suggests the biggest identifier of treatment outcomes is the therapeutic relationship (Rogers, 1957). This appears consistent with emerging research that identifies client preference and connection to the counselor predicts treatment outcomes (Campbell et al., 2019), as well as their willingness to disclose needed information for accurate assessment (Bradford & Rickwood, 2015). Although research found that adolescents between ages 15 and 17 preferred e-assessment over talk assessment based on their perceived comfort level in taking them, other adolescents preferred synchronous assessments, feeling the clinician could better interpret their responses with consideration of their body language (Bradford & Rickwood, 2015).

Application

The quality of existing clinical skills is a good indicator of projected effectiveness in telebehavioral health assessment and diagnosis (Hilty, n.d.). A good clinical foundation is necessary, and telebehavioral health builds on top of excellent clinical skills for successful transition and implementation (Hilty, n.d.). Active listening, reflective practice, and unconditional positive regard are foundational components that transfer online, as addressed in Chapter 7. Awareness and compliance of the professional association's ethical codes is a requirement of all clinicians. If a clinician is already lacking in skills, the ability to successfully assess and diagnose will also suffer. Seeking supervision, self-assessing, and continuing to work on clinical skills will also determine the quality and effectiveness of telebehavioral health services. Skill modification is addressed in detail in Chapter 7.

Basic Adaptations

Barriers to telebehavioral health services can be overcome with creativity and planning. Aging individuals may struggle more with technology than their youthful counterparts; but telephone-based assessments have proven to be very effective with little to no difference between face-to-face modalities (Conwell et al., 2018). Adaptations in practice interventions are important when moving to an online setting for assessment and diagnosis.

Appropriate assessment equipment, including data analysis software for testing, proper internet speed, and computers or tablets appropriate for the assessment measure or software, is essential to effective administration of online assessments (Bauer & Moessner, 2012). Integration of technological use into assessment can greatly enhance the ability to track treatment progress and areas of deficit regardless of treatment modality (Bauer & Moessner, 2012). The effects and various functions of the placement of video technology should be experimented with prior to session and used with purpose (Hilty, n.d.). Wide versus narrow angles on a camera, for example, can serve different purposes. Sitting further away from the camera or using a wide angle allows for more of an individual to be seen but limits the clarity of the picture. Using different camera angles or asking a client to point their camera to specific things may be helpful when diagnosing or conducting telebehavioral health assessments (Hilty, n.d.). Centering the individual in the camera so the shoulders and head fill the majority of the screen is the most common practice (Hilty, n.d.).

Telebehavioral health interviewing for assessment and diagnosis generally takes more time (Hilty, n.d.). Clinicians should be patient with the added time needed and adapt by adding time or additional sessions as needed. Attention span may be more limited when working with specific populations like children in an online environment. Two half-hour sessions may be more effective than an hour-long session, for example. Enhanced gestures are recommended by Hilty (n.d.) to communicate online because subtle gestures may not be noticed. To test clinician capability and comfort level in the online format, recordings can be done alone in mock sessions, using a coworker or supervisor in a role-play scenario. Additionally, recordings using actual clients in live sessions can be evaluated for assessment competency and accuracy, but laws, policies, and ethical codes need to be followed when recording and all clients should be informed and give permission prior to recording.

Environment and setting for assessments require different planning for online counseling than those conducted face-to-face. Establishing ground rules, plans for disruptions in technology, and education on how to use technology are important factors when preparing for accurate assessment and diagnosis (Hilty, n.d.). Counselors have less control over the safety, security, and confidentiality of a clinical setting in an online environment and are advised to take extra time establishing ground rules regarding confidentiality, appropriate ways to manage their environment, and establishing code words or gestures to communicate breaches in security or safety as necessary. This is addressed in more detail in Chapter 3.

A clinician can see a client in an authentic way because they are in their own environment, with behaviors and symptoms evident more quickly as the client may be less inhibited in their own home or chosen environment. This is an important component of the online assessment. Respect and active listening are key factors in establishing an online presence and building telebehavioral health rapport and may assist in organization as well as assessment and diagnosis (Hilty, n.d.).

SUMMARY

Assessment and diagnosis in the online format are similar to face-to-face. Assessment in both settings involve collecting data from the client about their history and current experiences. Online assessment provides access to the client's environment, which is unseen in face-to-face settings. Formal testing can be part of an assessment and requires additional training and supervision. Any tests used for the telebehavioral health assessment will need to be normed for administration and evaluation online, which can be verified through the test publisher. Assessment and diagnosis online have been shown to be as accurate as face-to-face.

CASE EXPLORATION

Raymond, a 16-year-old boy, has been able to meet individually with Katrina, a supervised clinician working toward licensure, and express some of his personal feelings regarding the family dynamics. He has expressed feelings of frustration, sadness, and hesitation in openly discussing his emotions with his family. Katrina has been able to work individually with Raymond and has decided to assess for additional mental health concerns. She hopes to use this information to better ensure she is meeting Raymond's needs and taking care not to skip over them while addressing the family needs. Katrina has decided to have him take the DSM-5 Self-Rated Level 1 Cross-Cutting Symptom Measure-Child Age 11–17 (APA, 2019). This measure is a level 1 self-administered exam, which means a clinician could send it to the client for him to take on his own, so it would be an appropriate tool for both online and face-to-face counseling modalities. Additionally, these are available in the public domain and require no additional training beyond knowledge in the use of the DSM-5, making these assessments an appropriate option for her as a counseling intern (APA, 2019).

In the case of Raymond, he showed elevated scores for depression, anger, irritability, and anxiety. When scores are elevated on the level 1 assessment, the level 2 assessments can be given to further determine the level of need for a possible diagnosis and/or clinical focus in treatment interventions (APA, 2019). In this case, Raymond showed minimal outcomes in anxiety, irritability, depression, and anger. Katrina used this to help her determine that ongoing assessment and focus may be an area of desired clinical intervention. After reviewing the results with her supervisor, it was determined that there is a minimal chance that Raymond's emotional needs are more urgent than the family system needs. Additionally, it has been determined that assisting Raymond and his family with their communication and family dynamics will likely positively affect his emotional state. Additional assessment(s) can be done periodically to check in on Raymond's emotional state and ensure the symptoms are not elevating. Katrina has gathered a baseline assessment and can continue to assess from this point forward in their treatment of Raymond and his family.

Worksheets

CLIENT SYMPTOMS AND DIAGNOSIS WORKSHEET

To better assist you in understanding how your symptoms determine your diagnosis, please complete the following list of symptoms and rate their intensity using the scale. Please share this with your counselor in your next video session to guide your discussion of your symptoms and diagnosis.

Rating scale:

1: Minimal, occurs 1–2 times per month

2: Minimal but occurring weekly 1–3 times

3: Minimal but occurring daily

4: Moderate, occurring 1–4 times a month

5: Moderate, but occurring more frequently, 3–10 times a month

6: Moderate, but very frequent, 11-plus times a month

7: Moderate but occurring daily

8: Intense, but infrequent, occurring 1–2 times a month

9: Intense but more frequent, occurring 1–2 times a week

10: Intense and occurring daily

Symptoms (Feelings or difficulties you are experiencing that are disturbing or difficult to manage; what brings you to counseling and what you would like to change)	Frequency (Use scale)	Notes for Counselor (Note any specific details you want your counselor to be aware of; you will discuss these in detail in your next session)	Diagnosis (Leave blank, you will complete this with your counselor in session)

Symptoms (Feelings or difficulties you are experiencing that are disturbing or difficult to manage; what brings you to counseling and what you would like to change)	Frequency (Use scale)	Notes for Counselor (Note any specific details you want your counselor to be aware of; you will discuss these in detail in your next session)	Diagnosis (Leave blank, you will complete this with your counselor in session)

*Please use additional pages as needed to discuss each of your symptoms or notes for your counselor.

Basic Counseling Forms

CONSIDERATIONS FOR ASSESSMENT

You have trained well and are ready to begin doing assessments online. This checklist will help you determine and prepare for your upcoming assessment. This is not an exhaustive checklist, so please feel free to make your own to fit your needs.

ASSESSMENT CHECKLIST

☐ **Appropriate assessment**
Remember, your chosen assessment must be appropriate for your client needs, but also must be appropriate and permitted to be used in a virtual environment without diminishing accuracy.

☐ **All necessary technology is available**
Based on your chosen assessment, you have prepared and made the necessary technology available to the client or have verified their access to the needed technology.

☐ **Confidentiality**
Any transfer of documents or sensitive information (including an interview) must be done in a confidential environment. Ensure your method of gathering data is compliant with HIPAA rules and regulations.

☐ **Effective technology**
All users of technology have been properly trained on how to use the technology. This is important to ensure the information assessed is a true reflection of capabilities and not a limitation in technology capabilities.

☐ **Verify assessment**
Some diagnoses or assessments rely heavily on nonverbal cues. Be sure to have a backup option to verify deficits in nonverbal communication if being done by observation only.

☐ **Proper training**
You have properly trained and feel comfortable administering an assessment (formal or informal) in an online environment.

☐ **Practice**
You have practiced and/or received proper supervision conducting assessments in an online environment.

☐ **Plan B**
You have communicated with your client(s) what to do and how to manage challenges or unpredictability in technology.

☐ **Risk/benefit analysis**
Risk, limitations, and benefits of online assessments have been clearly communicated with your client(s). An informed consent has been signed.

☐ **Understanding**
Client(s) have been given proper support and an opportunity to ask questions before and throughout the online assessment process. Expectations for both client and clinician have been clearly communicated with others and will continue to be addressed as needed.

CONSIDERATIONS FOR INTAKE

You have trained well and are ready for your first online intake. Using a checklist can help you be prepared for your first intake. With proper preparation, your chances of initial success will increase. Use the checklist to help you prepare for your first intake. Adjust as needed for your own intake checklist for future sessions.

INTAKE CHECKLIST

☐ **Confidentiality**
You have created a confidential environment and discussed ways to ensure a confidential environment on clinician and client end in addition to the platform used to conduct the intake.

☐ **Informed consent**
An informed consent has been signed and clearly states the limitations and plans for how to minimize limitations associated with online platforms.

☐ **Risk assessment**
You have checked for appropriateness of conducting an online intake and have resources available near the client(s) in case of a high-risk situation and/or emergency.

☐ **Proper training/supervision**
You have proper training and/or supervision and feel comfortable conducting a virtual intake.

☐ **Practice**
You have practiced, in advance, conducting an intake. It is advised to record your practice and review your recording prior to engaging in a virtual intake for the first time with a client.

☐ **Technology is available**
You have prepared your own technology and verified it is working prior to the intake. You have also verified the availability of technology for your client(s).

☐ **Effective technology**
All users of technology have been properly trained on how to use the technology and a plan for how to navigate disruptions to technology is in place.

☐ **Accuracy**
You have verified that an online intake is an appropriate way to gather needed information and a follow-up plan is developed on how to obtain additional information as needed.

☐ **Understanding**
You have created a way to check for client understanding as well as options to navigate questions and technological support as needed.

☐ **Cultural/diagnosis and technology awareness**
You recognize that culture and technology may influence the way information is obtained and assessed. You have taken into consideration the variables culture, diagnosis, and technology create and feel comfortable navigating them in an online environment.

Online Resources

- **Pearson Assessments**: Houses many of the standardized tests. They offer training for test administration, authorization and licensing information, and specific information regarding telepractice/digital solutions to test administration. https://www.pearsonassessments.com/professional-assessments/digital-solutions/telepractice/about.html

- **Q-global**: A subsite of Pearson. It is the portal that houses all the standardized tests an individual or organization has purchased. Tests can be sent directly from Q-global to the client for completion. Scores and reports are easily stored, managed, and interpreted. https://www.pearsonassessments.com/professional-assessments/digital-solutions/q-global/about.html

- **American Psychiatric Association Publishing**: The DSM-5 has developed a list of online assessment measures. These are not standardized tests but are developed in partnership with the APA to assist clinicians in the assessment and diagnostic process. Additionally, they offer standardized assessments to help with standardized approaches to diagnosis. This is often used for research. https://www.psychiatry.org/psychiatrists/practice/dsm/educational-resources/assessment-measures. https://www.appi.org/products/structured-clinical-interview-for-dsm-5-scid-5

- **Unbound** Medicine: A downloadable DSM-5 guide with interactive decision-making trees for diagnosing. https://www.unboundmedicine.com/products/dsm-5_differential_diagnosis

- **Mind ReMake Project**: A list of online assessments for counselors to use. https://mindremakeproject.org/2018/07/21/free-online-assessment-and-screening-tools-for-mental-health/

References

Abel, E. A., Shimada, S. L., Wang, K., Ramsey, C., Skanderson, M., Erdos, J., Godleski, L., Houston, T. K., & Brandt, C. A. (2018). Dual use of a patient portal and clinical video telehealth by veterans with mental health diagnoses: Retrospective, cross-sectional analysis. *Journal of Medical Internet Research, 20*(11), 1–10. https://doi.org/10.2196/11350

American Counseling Association. (2014). *2014 ACA code of ethics.* https://www.counseling.org/docs/default-source/default-document-library/2014-code-of-ethics-finaladdress.pdf

American Psychiatric Association. (n.d.). *History of telepsychiatry.* https://www.psychiatry.org/psychiatrists/practice/telepsychiatry/toolkit/history-of-telepsychiatry

Ballester, L., Alayo, I., Vilagut, G., Almenara, J., Cebrià, A. I., Echeburúa, E., Gabilondo, A., Gili, M., Lagares, C., Piqueras, J. A., Roca, M., Soto-Sanz, V., Blasco, M. J., Castellví, P., Forero, C. G., Bruffaerts, R., Mortier, P., Auerbach, R. P., Nock, M. K., Sampson, N., Kessler, R. C., & Alonso, J. (2019). Accuracy of online survey assessment of mental disorders and suicidal thoughts and behaviors in Spanish university students. Results of the WHO World Mental Health-International College Student initiative. *PLoS ONE, 14*(9), 1–22. https://doi.org/10.1371/journal.pone.0221529

Bauer, S., & Moessner, M. (2012). Technology-enhanced monitoring in psychotherapy and e-mental health. *Journal of Mental Health, 21*(4), 355–363. https://doi.org/10.3109/09638237.2012.667886

Bradford, S., & Rickwood, D. (2015). Young people's views on electronic mental health assessment: Prefer to type than talk? *Journal of Child and Family Studies, 24*(5), 1213–1221. https://doi.org/10.1007/s10826-014-9929-0

Campbell, A., Ridout, B., Amon, K., Navarro, P., Collyer, B., & Dalgleish, J. (2019). A customized social network platform (kids helpline circles) for delivering group counseling to young people experiencing family discord that impacts their well-being: Exploratory study. *Journal of Medical Internet Research, 21*(12), 1–15. https://doi.org/10.2196/16176

Casper, F., & Berger, T. (2005). The future is bright: How can we optimize online counseling, and how can we know whether we have done so? *The Counseling Psychologist, 33*(6), 900–909. https://doi.org/10.1177/0011000005280183

Chakhssi, F., Dijksman, I., Velmans, M. L., Zoet, J. M., Oostendorp, J. M., Dinant, G. J., & Spigt, M. (2019). The concurrent validity of a web-based self-report assessment for personality disorders. *Personality and Mental Health, 13*(1), 53–62. https://doi.org/10.1002/pmh.1438

Chang, J. E., Sequeira, A., McCord, C. E., & Garney, W. R. (2016). Videoconference grief group counseling in rural Texas: Outcomes, challenges, and lessons learned. *Journal for Specialists in Group Work, 41*(2), 140–160. https://doi.org/10.1080/01933922.2016.1146376

Conwell, Y., Simning, A., Driffill, N., Xia, Y., Tu, X., Messing, S. P., & Oslin, D. (2018). Validation of telephone-based behavioral assessments in aging services clients. *International Psychogeriatrics, 30*(1), 95–102. https://doi.org/10.1017/S1041610217001752

Donley, E., McClaren, A., Jones, R., Katz, P., & Goh, J. (2017). Evaluation and implementation of a telepsychiatry trial in the emergency department of a metropolitan public hospital. *Journal of Technology in Human Services, 4*, 292-313. https://doi.org/10.1080/15228835.2017.1367351

Guo, Y-J., Wang, S-C., & Johnson, V. (2012). Clinical assessment in the counseling process: A teaching model. *VISTAS Online, 1*, 1–6. https://www.counseling.org/docs/default-source/vistas/vistas_2012_article_10.pdf?sfvrsn=1fe57056_14

Hilty, D. M. (n.d.). *Learning to do telemental health.* American Psychiatric Association. https://www.psychiatry.org/psychiatrists/practice/telepsychiatry/toolkit/learning-telemental-health

Juárez, A. P., Weitlauf, A. S., Nicholson, A., Pasternak, A., Broderick, N., Hine, J., Stainbrook, J. A., & Warren, Z. (2018). Early identification of ASD through telemedicine: Potential value for underserved populations. *Journal of Autism and Developmental Disorders, 48*, 2601–2610. https://doi.org/10.1007/s10803-018-3524-y

Kraus, R., Stricker, G., & Speyer, C. (Eds.) (2011). *Online counseling: A handbook for mental health professionals (2nd ed.).* Academic Press.

Kupczynski, L., Garza, K., & Mundy, M.-A. (2017). Counselors' perceptions of online and face-to-face counseling. *The Online Journal of Counseling and Education, 6*(1), 1–17.

Malhotra, S., Chakrabarti, S., Shah, R., Sharma, M., Sharma, K. P., Malhotra, A., Upadhyaya, S. K., Margoob, M. A., Maqbool, D., & Jassal, G. D. (2017). Telepsychiatry clinical decision support system used by non-psychiatrists in remote areas: Validity and reliability of diagnostic module. *Indian Journal of Medical Research, 146*(2), 196–204. https://doi.org/10.4103/ijmr.IJMR_757_15

Mazhari, S., Nejad, A. G., Mofakhami, O., Raaii, F., & Bahaadinbeigy, K. (2019). Evaluating the diagnostic agreement between telepsychiatry assessment and face-to-face visit: A preliminary study. *Iranian Journal of Psychiatry, 14*(3), 236–241.

Newsom, C., Schut, H., Stroebe, M., Birrell, J., & Wilson, S. (2016). Telephone versus in-person intake assessment for bereavement intervention: Does efficiency come at a cost? *Death Studies, 40*(2), 71–79. https://doi.org/10.1080/07481187.2015.1068244

Pearson (n.d.). *Staying connected through telepractice.* https://www.pearsonassessments.com/professional-assessments/digital-solutions/telepractice/about.html

Rogers, C. R. (1957). The necessary and sufficient conditions of therapeutic personality change. *The Journal of Consulting Psychology, 21*, 95–103. https://doi.org/10.1037/h0045357

Salkind, N. J. (2017). *Statistics for people who think they hate statistics* (6th ed.). SAGE.

Suskie, L. (2018). *Assessing student learning: A common sense guide* (3rd ed.). Jossey-Bass.

Szeftel, R., Federico, C., Hakak, R., Szeftel, Z., & Jacobson, M. (2012). Improved access to mental health evaluation for patients with developmental disabilities using telepsychiatry. *Journal of Telemedicine and Telecare, 18*(6), 317–321. https://doi.org/10.1258/jtt.2012.111113

van Bebber, J., Wigman, J. T. W., Wunderink, L., Tendeiro, J. N., Wichers, M., Broeksteeg, J., Schrieken, B., Sytema, S., Terluin, B., & Meijer, R. R. (2017). Identifying levels of general distress in first line mental health services: Can GP-and eHealth clients' scores be meaningfully compared? *BMC Psychiatry, 17*(1), 1–10. https://doi.org/10.1186/s12888-017-1552-3

Clinical Skills for Synchronous Counseling

Sarah Littlebear, Debra M. Perez, and Tricia M. Mikolon

Counseling skills are the foundation by which we provide treatment. Ultimately skills facilitate the therapeutic alliance and guide the change process. Understanding the nuances of clinical skills used in a synchronous online counseling environment and how they are similar or different from a face-to-face counseling environment is critical to the distance counselor. The skills utilized within each of these modalities look strikingly similar, but the use of camera and microphone bring the counselor and client together in a unique way. Micro skills are defined as the foundational skills required to be an effective counselor in order to support client change and require modification to fit the relationship from a distance. Due to the expansion of technology, the manner in which counseling skills are taught and practiced has changed. This chapter provides an overview of the utilization of counseling skills in a synchronous online counseling setting.

Differences Between Online and Face-to-Face Formats

The clinical skills required to successfully provide counseling are the same for both face-to-face and online modalities, though the skills are impacted by the differences in the environments. In a synchronous online counseling environment, clients are located in a known environment and are more likely to experience a disinhibition effect where they feel more likely to self-disclose (Lapidot-Lefler & Barak, 2015). With the utilization of videoconferencing, the counselor and client view one another's upper body and face, so the client's anonymity could increase, leading to the client letting their guard down. Appreciation of the client's tone and nonverbal cues are lacking in text-based communication and may be difficult to decipher in videoconferencing platforms due to limited visual field and audio distortions (Baker & Ray, 2011). Challenges in relationship building are created for the counselor, client, and supervisor when trying to navigate the virtual environment and are explored in Chapter 2.

Asynchronous counseling sessions often appear more task based, while synchronous sessions have a more reflective and purposeful focus (Li et al., 2013; Trepal et al., 2007). According to Trepal et al., clients report feeling favorably overall toward online counseling, but express more concern with certain risks such as suicide. Suicide and the specific counseling skills necessary for crisis intervention are covered more thoroughly in Chapter 8. Technology may work smoothly during synchronous video counseling, and counselors can see the visual cues, but clients may still report experiencing a limited sense of connection (Kinsley & Henning, 2015). Counselors need to use their skills to foster the therapeutic relationship while incorporating the technology rather than allowing it to become a barrier.

Counseling Skills

Counseling skills assist counselors in building the therapeutic relationship with the client and conveying both empathy and understanding. Counseling skills include both verbal and nonverbal skills and require both training and practice. The foundational counseling skills are explored in this section of the chapter.

Building the Relationship

Building the therapeutic relationship is similar in both face-to-face and online environments. Counselors can assist in the development of the therapeutic relationship through the use of basic counseling skills modified to fit the online counseling formats. Core counseling skills, such as building rapport, active listening, and attending to nonverbal cues, allow the counselor to listen empathetically to the client and better understand their experiences, regardless of counseling format. Relationship-building skills will be explored and necessary online modifications discussed. The dynamics of the therapeutic relationship are addressed in more detail in Chapter 2.

Empathy

Empathy is the counselor's ability to understand the client's lived experiences and reflect them back in a manner that conveys understanding. The therapeutic relationship is enhanced by the utilization of empathy. The ability to understand someone else's experience does not change in the online platform.

Genuineness

Genuineness is the counselor's ability to congruently be themselves. The way someone feels about a topic or situation remains consistent regardless of the setting. When a counselor's expressions match their nonverbal reactions, the client can trust the counselor and the therapeutic relationship grows. Genuineness remains consistent whether face-to-face or online modality is utilized.

Unconditional Positive Regard

Unconditional positive regard is an expression of warmth and shows that the counselor fully accepts the client as they are and respects them and their decisions without judgment. The level of acceptance furthers the therapeutic relationship and increases the client's comfort with disclosure. There are no online modifications necessary.

Nonverbal Skills

Developing the skills to attend to nonverbal communication enhances a counselor's understanding of the client. The 3 V's + B foundation can help guide the counselor in session (Blonna et al., 2011; Ivey & Ivey, 2007). These nonverbal skills include visuality (eye contact), vocal quality (tone, pitch, volume of voice), verbal tracking (remaining with client story), and body language. Using nonverbal skills increases the counselor's attention to the client's needs and provides important information about the client in addition to the words they are speaking. Some nonverbal skills require modification in the online format, while others do not.

Visual/Eye Contact

Visual or eye contact is a cardinal skill in counseling. In a face-to-face session, this entails the counselor keeping their eyes focused on the client's eyes, showing an interest in the client and what they are sharing. During a synchronous counseling session with video, direct eye contact is more challenging. The counselor will have to adjust how they look at the client to determine the best way to make eye contact. Breaks in eye contact are typical during any session, but in order to presently engage with clients, eye contact should look genuine. Breaking eye contact is often more noticeable online than in person. When counseling online, it is recommended to maintain eye contact much as you would in person. Many assume that looking into the camera is appropriate; however, this would lead to missing out on nonverbal communication from the client. Placement, or positional variety, of webcams or monitors can be inconsistent; thus, the observance of eye contact and other physical nonverbals can be difficult to measure (Chen et al., 2020). Including a discussion about eye contact in the initial session can bridge that gap and allow the counselor to explain that they look in the client's eyes but do not know what that looks like for the client. Directly addressing how the counselor handles eye contact, such as when something in the environment distracts the counselor or the counselor turns their eyes a different direction and the camera captures these seemingly subtle changes, can put the client at ease and help them understand what the counselor appears to be looking at on screen. Additionally, to avoid eye fatigue, it may be important for the counselor to occasionally look away from the screen, which should be used when collecting thoughts to speak, and not when the client is speaking. Positioning the monitor at eye level or slightly above can also alleviate some of the strain on the counselor's eyes as well as create a more natural view of the counselor on the screen.

Posture

Counselors should adopt an open and inviting posture that encourages client sharing. In a face-to-face environment that includes leaning toward the client, keeping arms and legs uncrossed. Forward-leaning posture, along with high eye contact, was found to enhance perceptions in the counseling relationship as well as display higher empathy from the counselor (Dowell & Berman, 2013). This enhances the therapeutic relationship and is an important consideration when providing online counseling. Leaning in toward the camera slightly will give the sense of a greater connection with the client. As with eye contact, adjustments may have to be made, as movements on camera can be quite noticeable or overwhelming. For example, leaning too far away from the camera could appear cold and distant, while leaning too close to the camera could make it difficult for the client to view the counselor and to see the counselor's body language or feel connected. Finding a comfortable, yet appropriate sitting position is important in the online environment, just as in person. If there is a need for regular shifting of positions, it can be mentioned to the client at the start of the session so that the client does not misinterpret the counselor's behavior.

Vocal Quality

Vocal quality includes the volume, speed, and tone of voice. The volume of the counselor's voice should be encouraging and nonthreatening. The speed should help pace the client, and the tone should convey empathy and match what the client is sharing. The vocal quality is different in the online format, as some of what is heard is controlled by the speakers on the computer. Ensuring you are audible through the speakers and that your speaker volume is at an appropriate level are keys to being able to attend properly. Most videoconferencing platforms include a microphone and speaker test, and completing one before each session is recommended. Generally, speaking at an average volume would be best, as some people feel the need to speak louder when videoconferencing. As you attend to the client, your volume may be altered to match the client's volume and content both face-to-face and virtually. Many clinicians find that utilizing quality headphones ensures they can hear the client without the distraction of outside noises. This may allow for a fuller immersion in the counseling experience. Use of headphones can help ensure confidentiality as well (Chen et al., 2020).

Body Language

Body language in the online environment looks differently than it does in person. In the online environment, the counselor is usually unable to see the client's entire body and use this information as feedback about the client's comfort with the topic or their emotional state. Body language is reduced to the subtle changes that are seen in the client's face, eye movements, shoulders, breathing changes, and slight shifts in positioning. While it is initially challenging to notice slight changes, overtime those slight changes become more magnified and will provide the same information that body language provides in person.

Attending

Micro skills, such as attending, or fully and actively listening to the client, allow the client to feel understood and accepted. Attending requires the counselor to orient their body toward the client and be free of distractions, focusing only on the client. Attending also includes eye contact, head nods, mirroring body positioning, leaning forward, and facial expressions. Some aspects of attending look differently in the online format than in face-to-face formats. Eye contact and leaning forward were previously discussed. Heads nods may need to be larger to make them more distinct in the online environment, as clients may not notice a subtle head nod they would notice in a face-to-face counseling session. Since only a portion of the face and body can be seen, the counselor should ensure the portion of them visible in the camera is oriented toward the screen. Facial expressions must be monitored to encourage rather than discourage communication from the client and are similar online as they are in face-to-face sessions.

Verbal Skills

In addition to attending to the client utilizing active listening and voice volume in responses, the counselor will also use **verbal tracking skills**, such as paraphrasing and summarizing, in similar ways as they are used in person. The main difference in the online environment is that these skills are used with greater care and more intentionality due to the potential delay in audio or video technology. In a face-to-face session, the counselor can see when the client is pausing to think and would not talk during that time. Online, this is not always as clear, so verbal skills would need to be limited to ensure the counselor does not talk over the client, especially when the client is processing. Congruency in verbal and nonverbal communication can be lost when engaging in counseling in the virtual environment. In a face-to-face session, counselors are trained to be present and in sync with their clients. However, in the synchronous online session, there is an obvious distance between counselor and client, as well as a potential delay in response times. Counselors must keep in mind verbal elements that may or may not be effective in the online environment. This will be discussed further in the following sections.

Rapport Building

Incorporating these skills into each counseling session was outlined by Ivy et al. (2018). Initially, rapport is built and structure is outlined according to the authors. The client is then encouraged to share their story with the counselor while identifying their strengths through questioning and clarifying. The authors discuss the next stage as the point in the session when a client determines what they want to happen or change, which then allows for exploration of the possible alternatives or inconsistencies the client is experiencing. The final stage allows for the client to begin to take chances to bring about change with encouragement from the counselor, transferring their learning and insight into their daily life (Ivy et al., 2018).

Cultural considerations are fundamental to any counseling session regardless of format. Counselors need to assess their own appreciation of attitudes and beliefs that differ from their own, as well as their own cultural knowledge prior to meeting with clients, and be open to learning and appreciation of those that vary from their own. Tomlinson-Clark (2013) identifies the strength of self-reflection to "combat cultural bias and ethnocentric assumptions" (p. 7) on behalf of the counselor. Counselor understanding and appreciation of cultural differences allow for rapport to begin forming within the therapeutic relationship. Distance may impact the degree of connectedness a client perceives with the counselor; therefore, providing the warmth and openness that comes with relationship building is exceptionally important in a synchronous online environment.

Reflection

Reflection is the ability to say back to the client what the counselor heard the client say, as well as summarizing their emotions. Reflecting back to the client is an additional skill that fosters the therapeutic alliance by conveying active listening and understanding. This skill is utilized similarly in face-to-face and online sessions. However, online usage requires intentionality to ensure the client is done speaking before the counselor reflects back what was heard. Delays due to technology will need to be kept in mind when using this skill.

Interpretation and Reframing

Interpretation and reframing skills allow the client to clarify for themselves both their motivation to change and contributing factors they can control (Strong et al., 1979). Interpretation and reframing help the counselor restate something that is bothering the client in a new manner, which allows the client to see how to move forward or how to look at something from a new perspective. Interpretation and reframing are used online similarly to the manner they are used in person.

Questioning and Focusing

A counselor's use of questions allows for the conversation to progress forward while providing clarification and prompts to further explore aspects of the experience. Coupled with focusing skills and summarizing, these micro skills forge the foundation of rapport and understanding between counselor and client, underpinning the therapeutic relationship. Questioning in a session must be carefully undertaken in a synchronous online session. Placing questions appropriately can be more challenging, and it is helpful for the counselor to consider if the questions make sense if a transcription of the session were completed. Additionally, due to potential delays in communication across the distance, questioning can be ill-timed and spoken on top of the client speaking, leading to client frustrations and choppy, seemingly confrontational sessions.

Focusing requires the counselor to understand the areas the client would like to address in counseling and help the client to stay on track. Focusing allows the issue to be zoomed in on and helps the client stay on one topic, rather than skipping around. Utilizing questioning can help the client and counselor focus on the areas that are important to the client. Focusing is used similarly online as in person.

Paraphrasing and Summarizing

Paraphrasing is used to repeat back to the client portions of what they have shared with the counselor. Summarizing is a brief statement of the main points shared by the client and is longer than paraphrasing, more like longer paraphrases. Both are used similarly online as they are used in person. However, as other verbal techniques, they must be used intentionally after it is determined the client is done speaking, not simply pausing to collect their thoughts. Also, paraphrasing and summarizing require more words from the counselor and should be kept to a minimum to prevent the counselor from talking more than the client, especially accounting for the potential connection delays that take up time during the online session.

Positive Asset Search

Throughout the counseling process, additional skills allow the relationship between counselor and client to deepen while further addressing current issues and goals the client is working toward. The use of a positive asset search, where the counselor and client explore the client's strengths, support system, and available resources, allows the exploration of possible avenues for change. The counselor accomplishes this by making prompt statements such as "Tell me about something you do well" or "What do others tell you that you do well?" There are no modifications necessary to utilize this skill in the online environment.

Confrontation

The use of confrontation, or the challenging of the client's thoughts, perceptions, or choices by means of highlighting incongruencies, allows the client to consider underlying emotions and conflicts they may have otherwise overlooked. Confrontation is an advanced skill and requires a good rapport with the client. Utilizing confrontation in online sessions requires careful consideration to ensure the client is open to what the counselor is saying and to ensure the timing of its use. Additionally, the counselor will need to consider the delays in technology to ensure proper use of this technique.

Silence

Counselors can convey a sense of connection and the willingness to listen, selectively attending to the client's stories and concerns, using **silence** appropriately and engaging in the right amount of talking time. The stillness, or lack of movement in the room, can benefit the counselor willing to listen, which enhances the counselor and client connection. Providing silence ensures the counselor is not talking over the client and that the message is being processed to its fullest extent. Use of silence is a skill that can be even more beneficial remotely than in person, but understanding delays in audio and video need to be considered and adjusted to. Everly and Lating (2017) caution that the excessive use of silence may imply a lack of interest and should be used sparingly. Acknowledging silence may require a more active approach in the online format as to not confuse it with technological interference. The counselor may incorporate the silence into the treatment more actively by acknowledging the need to stop and consider certain aspects of the topic of discussion.

Talk time, or the amount of time each person speaks during the verbal exchange between counselor and client, is similar in synchronous online counseling as it is during in-person sessions. Clients, particularly adults, will have enough to speak about and should be engaging in most of the dialogue. Again, high-speed internet is best to avoid delays in audio and video, but the counselor must be careful not to "talk over" or inadvertently interrupt the client due to delays. Additionally, the ability to help draw out strengths from the client is beneficial. Understanding the unique variables that influence a client's choice to use online counseling, the counselor has a powerful tool in helping the client find strengths and resources they can draw from and utilize for both the technology and the counseling sessions.

Wrapping Up

When ending the session, the counselor must be clear about the ending, similar to how clarity would occur surrounding the ending of a face-to-face session. An example of ending a session by the counselor may sound like, "I am glad we were able to meet today. It means a lot that we are able to share this space together even if we are not physically in the same place." It is important to discuss ahead of time how a session is ended, so clients do not feel that a disconnection due to a technical difficulty is the counselor negatively responding to something the client admitted to in session. Online clients will need to understand the difference between being disconnected due to a technical glitch and the actual end of the session. Making the end of the session similar each time will provide a clear indication to the client of the difference between technology glitches and the end of the session and can include a summary of anything the client chose to work on for the week and the next scheduled appointment time.

Conclusion

Verbal skills, such as responding, noting and reflecting, confrontation, focusing, using encouragers, paraphrasing, and summarizing are used online similarly to the manner they are used in person. However, similar to questioning, timing is vital, and the counselor will need to account for the potential delays in communication caused by the internet connection. Additionally, questioning, confrontation, and focusing require a stronger therapeutic relationship, whether being used online or in person, and should be used after the relationship is strongly established, a task that takes more intentionality in the online environment.

Asynchronous Skills

When utilizing chat-based services, verbal skills must translate into writing. Written communication skills are of utmost importance in live chat services. For example, the manner in which the client expresses themselves in writing (all caps, italics, spacing, etc.) or simplification of the language can be related to message content (Alleman, 2002). The absence of body language further hinders the therapeutic relationship. Mallen et al. (2005) recommend checking with the client to determine if empathy is being conveyed. Empathic messages can still be conveyed, particularly when a client is describing something difficult. A statement such as, "That sounds very difficult. I sense a lot of pain in your statement," could be a response to a text statement from a client who is trying to cope with a troublesome situation.

Crisis Counseling

When experiencing a crisis reaction, it is likely the client will need access to a counselor to address acute symptoms or help prevent further psychological distress. When working through a crisis from a distance, counselors have traditionally provided services via the telephone to address the crisis and provide support (Krysinska & De Leo, 2007). Online crisis counseling through videoconferencing has been used additionally to supplement the process of crisis intervention. With the increased need for distance counseling, particularly with the COVID-19 pandemic, synchronous crisis counseling has become more prevalent. In completing crisis and suicide interventions, advanced counseling skills are necessary in addition to the basic skills previously covered (Rigsbee & Goodrich, 2019). Rapport is to be built with the client very quickly, and validating the client's story is of utmost importance. Listening skills are critical in helping the client, as much of the assessment is conducted by allowing for "ventilation" of emotions. Utilizing the micro skills along with a structured process for addressing suicidality may help counselors provide effective crisis intervention. Ideally, the counselor will connect with the client online and be able to see them while waiting for emergency services or family to arrive to assist the client. This provides services similar to how the telephone is used except that it enhances the status evaluation with visual information that may not otherwise be evident. Because the intervention is completed in an online format, the counselor must use skills of engagement and those designed specifically for crisis response. A detailed discussion of online crisis counseling can be found in Chapter 8.

Termination

As in any counseling relationship, termination of services will occur at some time in online counseling. The termination of online counseling services may look different depending on the types of clients one sees and where those clients are located and requires some adjustment or creativity on behalf of the counselor. Since termination is a "goodbye" of sorts for the counseling relationship, the counselor begins termination with the first session. The goal of counseling is for the client to increase their coping skills and meet their therapeutic goals so that they are functioning at their full potential, thus moving beyond the counseling relationship. Keeping this in mind, termination should be discussed from the onset of the therapeutic relationship. Online counseling can be a long-term counseling option for some clients, and a short-term solution for others. By preparing for termination from the initial session, the counselor ensures best practices for either type of client, long term or short term.

Preparation for termination of counseling begins in the first session and is incorporated as a goal from the start, with evaluation of the process throughout the counseling process regardless of setting. Incorporation of ongoing support and additional services will be incorporated as they fit the client and regardless of treatment length, thus requiring the counselor to be aware of available services in the client's area. The counseling relationship for some clients acts as bridge to other services or different treatment in the future, so it is important for counselors to assist clients in developing goals, as this enhances the likelihood of services continuing at some point (Dowling & Rickwood, 2014). Therefore, ongoing goals post-termination must be consistent with the resources available to the client.

Supervision

When supervising counselors who are providing synchronous online counseling, it is important to highlight the special issues that can impede the skills of a counselor. According to Haberstroh and Duffey (2011), it is important for supervisors to assess online counselors in how empathy is communicated, that the client's story is understood, challenges are addressed and responded to, and their own effectiveness is evaluated. The consideration of transference and countertransference is critical in the online environment. Keeping in mind ethical considerations such as beneficence, nonmalfeasance, and fidelity are particularly critical to the online counseling experience and attended to by supervisors (Haberstroh & Duffey, 2011). Supervisors will need to evaluate the online supervisee on these areas, as well as on other counseling skills. These skills will be further explored in Chapter 14.

Multicultural Applications

The counselor in a synchronous online counseling session should maintain cultural competency while paying critical attention to the client. Making assumptions about a client's culture from a distance is a trap that counselors could fall into, particularly with the amount of information gathered synchronously, such as atmosphere in the client's home environment or a more casual appearance of the client. While it is important to gather information from the client, counselors must keep in mind that it is simply information. Utilizing clinical skills appropriately includes gathering information through observing nonverbal and verbal communication. Counselors must maintain the awareness that not only are they observing the individual on the screen, but they are interacting appropriately with clinical skills and techniques.

Zastrow and Krist-Ashman (2007) provided guidelines for "multicultural issues in verbal and nonverbal communication" (p. 81), citing the need for counselors to slow down their rate of speech with clients who have English as their second language as well as to be conscious of their nonverbal gestures and respect differences in personal space. The authors also suggest that counselors seek clarification and feedback from their clients about communication, be aware of their volume of speech, and be both "humble and respectful of cultural differences" (Zastrow & Krist-Ashman, 2007, p. 81), thus creating an environment of understanding and respect, which may enhance communication. Finally, counselors are encouraged to continue to seek learning opportunities to expand their cultural appreciation and use an interpreter as needed to assist the client's understanding and comfort level (Zastrow & Krist-Ashman, 2007).

Counselors take care not to impose their own culture, biases, or beliefs when gaining understanding about the client and their background while remaining flexible and attentive to the individual client's needs and cultural identity (Smaby & Maddux, 2010). Nickson et al. (2020) stress that counselors need to keep in mind that "we are all multicultural beings" (p. 120) and that culture is comprised of unique mixtures of variables. Keeping aware of these variables may assist counselors in modifying their approach to best fit the unique cultural aspects of their clients, thereby solidifying the therapeutic relationship in both mutual respect and understanding. The RESPECTFUL counseling cube (D'Andrea & Daniels, 2001; Nickson et al., 2020) may provide a positive lens for counselors to explore the numerous variables that constitute a client's culture:

(R) religion/spirituality
(E) economic class and background
(S) sexual identity
(P) psychological maturity
(E) ethnic/racial identity
(C) chronological stage
(T) trauma history/experiences
(F) family background/history
(U) unique physical characteristics
(L) geographical location

Socioeconomic class/background, sexual identity, family history, unique physical characteristics, and experiences of trauma may influence the client's world view as well as bring about social justice issues. Psychological maturity and biological age both influence an individual's perception of themselves and their abilities to face challenges. Clients from collective cultures who value unity of the community and selflessness may feel conflicted to pursue their own rights and concerns, although they will not confront the counselor on these goals, instead valuing the expertise of the counselor (Balkir Neftçi & Barnow, 2016). Those from collective cultures tend to avoid eye contact and readily accept feedback as a form of respect, even if they do not plan to follow up with the recommendations.

The Association for Multicultural Counseling and Development's (AMCD) multicultural counseling competencies state that culturally skilled counselors seek out consultation, ongoing training, and consultation rooted in their ability to identify their own skill limitations in working with diverse populations and refer to more qualified professionals as necessary to benefit the client (I.C.1.). Additionally, culturally skilled counselors will actively pursue personal understanding of their own biases, culture, and identity in the pursuit of a "non-racist identity" (I.C.2. para. 13). Further, the AMCD identifies culturally appropriate intervention strategies to include the counselor's ability to engage in both verbal and nonverbal communication with their clients, adjusting them as needed to meet the client's abilities/skills, with full appreciation of their own limitations and needs to avoid unfavorable outcomes ((II.C.1.).

Further to this point, culturally skilled counselors will, according to the AMCD guidelines, "exercise institutional interventions skills on behalf of their clients" while assisting clients in not personalizing problems rooted in racism or bias (II.C.2., para. 30), while incorporating "traditional healers and religious and spiritual leaders and practitioners in the treatment of culturally different clients when appropriate (II.C.3., para 31). Appreciation of spirituality as an intimate topic ensures that the client will determine the depth of discussion on this topic and its role in their daily life. Counselors will also utilize qualified translators or refer to a qualified bilingual counselor as needed (II.C.4.), gain appropriate training in assessment with understanding of cultural biases of instruments and their appropriate use (II.C.5.) while being "cognizant of sociopolitical contexts in conducting evaluation and providing interventions and should develop sensitivity to issues of oppression, sexism, elitism, and racism" (C.II.6., para. 34). Finally, as in any counseling relationship, the counselor is expected to inform and educate their client on the processes of counseling, including "goals, expectations, legal rights and the counselor's orientation" (II.C.7., para. 35).

To be a culturally competent counselor, one must commit themselves to consistent self-evaluation of their own cultural influences and biases while seeking to find both understanding and appreciation of those who differ from their own (Tomlinson-Clark, 2013). Expanding one's own worldview and the appreciation of the differences that make the client unique allow the counselor and client to work together in a stage of understanding and respect (LeBeauf et al., 2009; Tomlinson-Clark, 2013). Applications of this to specific populations will be covered in Chapter 9.

Discussion of Applicable Skills

Skill	Summary
Building the Relationship	
Empathy	May need to be expressed verbally and more frequently in the online environment.
Genuineness	Same as in face-to-face sessions but require more verbalization and a higher frequency.
Unconditional positive regard	Require more verbal expression and to be used more frequently in the online environment.
Nonverbal Skills	
Visuality/eye contact	Maintain eye contact as you would in person, focusing on the camera not the person on the screen. Position the camera at eye level. Discuss eye contact in the first session and as needed throughout the counseling process to clarify the difference between the online environment and face-to-face counseling. Clear your background of distracting or overly personal items and ask the client to do the same. Avoid eye fatigue by occasionally taking breaks between sessions.
Posture	Adopt an open and inviting posture. Lean forward toward the camera; do not cross legs or arms. Pay attention to eye contact as noted. Acknowledge position shifts to eliminate misunderstanding by the client; question their position shifts for clarification.
Vocal quality	Keep volume encouraging and nonthreatening. Check with the client regarding their volume on the computer and assist in modifying as needed. Speed needs to be upbeat but not rushed. Tone needs to be professional and inviting, and avoid being monotone.
Body language	Limited view provided by the camera requires more inquiry for clarification. Pay attention to changes in client's facial expression, posture, eye movements, shoulders, breathing and positioning; always ask for clarification; do not assume meaning or that there is no concern. Be sure to explain clarifications are due to the limited view provided by the screen and are for understanding and to encourage open communication between client and counselor.
Attending	Modifications are noted, as attending encompasses your eye contact, posture, vocal quality and body language.

Skill	Summary
Verbal Skills	
Rapport building	Easily adapted by having client share a picture or object to discuss its meaning or share a tradition they hold dear.
Reflection	Same as in face-to-face counseling, however the counselor needs to be more aware of when the client is done talking as technological delays may interfere.
Interpretation and reframing	Needs to be used more frequently to ensure understanding.
Questioning and focusing	Used more frequently for clarification and introduced prior to use to ensure client understands the purpose of the question.
Paraphrasing and summarizing	May need to be used more frequently to ensure understanding. Both require more complete and detailed explanation. Want to encourage the client to correct as needed to enhance understanding.
Positive asset search	An ongoing process. No modification is necessary for the online environment.
Confrontation	In the online environment the counselor needs to carefully consider its use and provide a clear lead in discussion of the purpose of the confrontation, be it for clarification or to consider alternatives. Consider delays in technology and allow for silence.
Silence	Same as in face-to-face counseling, however the counselor needs to be more aware of when the client is done talking as technological delays may interfere. Be sure to encourage the client to speak more than the counselor. Discuss remediation of technological issues should they occur.
Wrapping up	No modification necessary.
Conclusion	Same as face-to-face counseling, however the counselor may want to create concluding series of behaviors, such as the client logging off first to ensure mutual understanding and respect.
Asynchronous skills	Counselors need to pay attention to word choices, as well as font and text colors used. These require more words to clearly communicate thoughts as well as the use of more questions to ensure understanding.
Termination	As in face-to-face counseling, this needs to be discussed throughout the counseling process. As the termination date occurs the counselor and client may reduce the frequency of sessions and transition to a more consultive relationship. Both the counselor and client need to agree on a final session date and an explanation on how to re-enter counseling should it be necessary in the future provided. Review of the treatment plan goals and development of ongoing personal goals for the client is encouraged.

SUMMARY

There are many verbal and nonverbal skills needed to be an effective counselor. The skills learned for in-person sessions can be modified for use in the synchronous counseling environment, leading to successful outcomes for online clients. Some skills are easily transferable to the online environment and require little to no modification, whereas others require a greater amount of modification for successful use. The counselor transitioning to the synchronous online environment will need to understand how to modify and accurately use these necessary counseling skills. Counselors looking to work on an asynchronous counseling platform will require greater skill modification.

CASE EXPLORATION

Katrina seeks consultation from her supervisor Eugene regarding her inability to get Raymond to open up about his feelings about his parent's divorce and his mother's relationship with Pat.

Katrina: I just feel stuck; he says he has no feelings about any of it and is fine, but clearly he does as his tone of voice becomes more agitated his body language more closed when the topic comes up.

Eugene: Have you tried confronting his incongruency between his words and his body language?

Katrina: I don't want to argue with him about it and frustrate him more!

Eugene: Confrontation isn't arguing; it's highlighting the incongruencies you are seeing, perhaps something like "Gee Raymond I'm a bit confused. You say you don't have any feeling about your mother's relationship with Pat, but each time we mention it your head drops down and you cross yours arms and slump down in the chair. And your tone of voice seems a bit sharper than usual. Do you think there may be something else you are feeling other than "fine"?

Katrina: Oh, I see, I'm asking him to explain the inconsistencies, not arguing the point but exploring it more.

Eugene: Exactly. Confrontation isn't aggressive or about being right or wrong; it's about assisting the client with seeing when their body language and words don't match, thus allowing them to explore the underlying feelings more clearly.

Katrina: I'll have to try that in our next session and let you know how it goes.

Worksheets

HOW AM I FEELING RIGHT NOW?

On a separate piece of paper, please draw the first thing that comes to your mind. Use colors and shapes to represent anything you like.

When you have completed the activity, please explain in words what each part of the picture represents to your counselor.

_____

_____

_____

_____

_____

_____

_____

_____

_____

EMOTIONAL IDENTIFICATION WORKSHEET

Please draw or write three emotions you felt this week in column 1:

Emotion	What made me feel this way	What I can do about it

Emotion	What made me feel this way	What I can do about it

FEEDBACK FOR COUNSELOR'S ATTENDING BEHAVIOR: SYNCHRONOUS ONLINE COUNSELING

	Not demonstrated	Minimally demonstrated	Demonstrated competence	Comments and suggestions
Attending behavior				
Eye contact: Visual *Direct with client/toward camera, but with occasional breaks for client comfort; culturally appropriate*				
Body position *Open, attentive, facing client, body and head are positioned toward client and slightly leaning in May mirror client body language*				
Voice tone *Reflects client's, appropriate volume/rate, warm*				
Facial expressions *Shows concern/interest, genuine response to client's emotions*				
Verbal tracking *Restating or summarizing client statements*				
Minimal encouragers *Use of nonverbal or slight verbal encouragers to show counselor is listening (head nodding, "mmm-hmm," "uh-huh," etc.)*				

Basic Counseling Forms

COUNSELING SKILLS CHECKLIST

Engaging:

- [ ] 1. Introduce counselor and process

- [ ] 2. Introduce client and their reason for coming to counseling

- [ ] 3. Avoid using closed question; ask open-ended question

- [ ] 4. Attend to the client; pay attention and actively listen to what is being stated both verbally and nonverbally. Be aware of own body language

- [ ] 5. Silence: be comfortable with it. Allow the client time to consider answers, give yourself permission to do the same

- [ ] 6. Avoid being the expert or giving advice. Work with the client to find their goals, perceived abilities, and limitations and develop goals and interventions as a team.

- [ ] 7. Reflect and summarize. Repeating back your understanding in your own words of what the client has shared assist in developing trust and mutual understanding. This is also useful in helping the client and counselor to focus on topics being addressed.

- [ ] 8. Be real. Share your genuine self with the client; temper your reactions but don't sanitize your responses to lack true emotion and your own thoughts.

Online Resources

- **Counseling skills and techniques review**: This link provides an overview of counseling skills and techniques. https://teach.com/online-ed/counseling-degrees/counseling-techniques/

- **American Psychological Association**: This is a link to APA provided continued education entitled "Practice Makes Perfect: Strategies That Hone Practitioner's Skills." https://www.apa.org/monitor/2018/01/ce-corner

- **American Counseling Association**: This link connects the reader to the ACA resource entitled "Telebehavioral Health Information and Counselors in Health Care" https://www.counseling.org/knowledge-center/mental-health-resources/trauma-disaster/telehealth-information-and-counselors-in-health-care

- **Counseling Tutor**: This resource, entitled "Effective Counselling Skills" will help readers review counseling skills. https://counsellingtutor.com/basic-counselling-skills/

References

Alleman, J. R. (2002). Online counseling: The Internet and mental health treatment. *Psychotherapy: Theory, Research, Practice, Training, 39*(2), 199–209. https://doi.org/10.1037/0033-3204.39.2.199

Association for Multicultural Counseling and Development. (n.d). *AMCD multicultural counseling competencies.* https://www.counseling.org/Resources/Competencies/Cross-Cultural_Competencies_and_Objectives.pdf

Baker, K. D., & Ray, M. (2011). Online counseling: The good, the bad, and the possibilities. *Counselling Psychology Quarterly, 24* (4), 341–346. https://doi.org/10.1080/09515070.2011.632875

Balkir Neftçi, N., & Barnow, S. (2016). One size does not fit all in psychotherapy: Understanding depression among patients of Turkish origin in Europe. *Noro psychiatry archive, 53*(1), 72–79. https://doi.org/10.5152/npa.2016.12666

Blonna, R., Loschiava, J., & Watter, D. N. (2011) *Health counseling: A microskills approach for counselors, educators and school nurses* (2nd edition). Jones and Bartlett Learning.

Chen, S., Wathen, C., & Speciale, M. (2020). Online clinical training in the virtual remote environment: Challenges, opportunities, and solutions. *The Professional Counselor, 10* (1), 78–91. doi:10.15241/syc.10.1.78 https://files.eric.ed.gov/fulltext/EJ1250982.pdf

D'Andrea, M., & Daniels, J. (2001). RESPECTFUL counseling: An integrative model for counselors. In D. Pope- Davis & H. Coleman (Eds). *The interface of class, culture, and gender in counseling* (pp. 417–466). SAGE.

de Silva, J.A.M., Siegmund, G., & Bredemeier, J. (2015). Crisis intervention in online psychological counseling. *Trends in Psychiatry and Psychotherapy, 37* (4), 171-182. http://dx.doi.org/10.1590/2237-6089-2014-0026

Dowell, N. M., & Berman, J. S. (2013). Therapist nonverbal behavior and perceptions of empathy, alliance, and treatment credibility. *Journal of Psychotherapy Integration, 23*(2), 158–165. https://psycnet.apa.org/doi/10.1037/a0031421

Dowling, M., & Rickwood, D. (2014). Investigating individual online synchronous chat counselling processes and treatment outcomes for young people. *Advances in Mental Health, 12* (3), 216–224. https://www.researchgate.net/deref/http%3A%2F%2Fdx.doi.org%2F10.1080%2F18374905.2014.11081899

Everly, G. S., & Lating, J. M. (2017). The John Hopkins guide to psychological first aid. John Hopkins University Press.

Haberstroh, S., & Duffey, T. (2011). *Face-to-face supervision of online counselors: Supervisor perspectives.* https://www.counseling.org/Resources/Library/VISTAS/2011-V-Online/Article_66.pdf

Ivey, A. E. & Ivey, M. B. (2007). *Intentional interviewing and counseling: Facilitating client development in a multicultural society* (6th edition). Thomas Brooks/Cole.

Ivey, A. E., Ivey, M. B., & Zalaquett, C. P. (2018). *Intentional interviewing and counseling: facilitating client development in a multicultural society* (9th edition). Cengage.

Kingsley, A., & Henning, J.A. (2015). Online and Phone Therapy: Challenges and Opportunities. *The Journal of Individual Psychology 71*(2), 185-194. doi:10.1353/jip.2015.0010

Krysinska, K. E., & De Leo, D. (2007). Telecommunication and suicide prevention: Hopes and challenges for the new century. *Omega: Journal of Death and Dying, 55*(3), 237–253. https://doi.org/10.2190/OM.55.3.e

Lapidot-Lefler, N., & Barak, A. (2015). The benign online disinhibition effect: Could situational factors induce self-disclosure and prosocial behaviors? *Cyberpsychology: Journal of Psychosocial Research on Cyberspace, 9*(2). https://doi.org/10.5817/CP2015-2-3

LeBeauf, I., Smaby, M., & Maddux, C. (2009). Adapting counseling skills for multicultural and diverse clients. In G. R. Walz, J. C. Blaur & R. K. Yep (Eds.), *Compelling counseling interventions: VISTA 2009* (pp. 33–42). American Counseling Association. https://www.counseling.org/Resources/Library/VIS-TAS/2009-V-Print/Article%204%20LeBeaufSmabyMaddux.pdf

Li, L. P., Jaladin, R. A. M., & Abdullah, H. S. (2013) Understanding the two sides of online counseling and their ethical and legal ramifications. *Procedia Social and Behavioral Sciences, 103*, 12431–1251. https://doi.org/10.1016/j.sbspro.2013.10.453

Mallen, M. J., Vogel, D. L., & Rochlen, A. B. (2005). The practical aspects of online counseling: Ethics, training, technology, and competency. *The Counseling Psychologist, 33*(6), 776–818. https://doi.org/10.1177/0011000005278625

Nickson, A. M., Carter, M., & Francis, A. P. (2020). *Supervision and professional development in social work practice.* SAGE.

Rigsbee, N. P., & Goodrich, K. M. (2019). Exploring the efficacy of online suicide assessment training in counselor education. *Counseling Outcome Research and Evaluation, 10* (1), 34–48. https://doi.org/10.1080/21501378.2017.1409598

Smaby, M., & Maddux, C. (2010). *Basic and advanced counseling skills: Skilled counselor training model.* Cengage.

Strong, S. R., Wambach, C. A., Lopez, F. G., & Cooper, R. K. (1979). Motivational and equipping functions of interpretation in counseling. *Journal of Counseling Psychology, 26*(2), 98–107. https://doi.org/10.1037/0022-0167.26.2.98

Tomlinson-Clarke, S. (2013). Multicultural counseling competencies: Extending multicultural training paradigms toward globalization. *VISTAS Online.* https://www.counseling.org/docs/default-source/vistas/multicultural-counseling-competencies.pdf?sfvrsn=7&sfvrsn=7

Trepal, H., Haberstroh, S., Duffey, T., & Evans, M. (2007). Considerations and strategies for teaching online counseling skills: Establishing relationships in cyberspace. *Counselor Education and Supervision, 46*, 266–279. https://doi.org/10.1002/j.1556-6978.2007.tb00031.x

Zastrow, C., & Krist-Ashman, K. K. (2007). *Understanding human behavior and the social environment* (7th edition). Thompson.

8

Crisis Response From a Distance

Sherry Todd, Tina Pharr, and Andrea D. Josephs

Counseling is rarely sought when life is going well. Generally, some form of distress and quite often a crisis reaction is the impetus to seek counseling. More often than not, clients seek counseling services due to something in life creating a sense of disequilibrium, and if our resources are overwhelmed or ineffective in managing this imbalance, the result is a crisis reaction (Everly, 2015; Rosen et al., 2020). People seek help for these reactions and distress to regain a sense of stability and normalcy. The Crisis Text Line (n.d.) reported distress related to relationships, depression, suicidality, isolation/loneliness, and self-harm as the most frequently presented concerns. College counselors have noted similar findings with student distress related to anxiety, depression, and family and academic concerns being the most frequently reported problems (Pérez-Rojas et al., 2017). Additionally, college counselors have reported that 8.4% of students receiving counseling report suicidal ideation (Pérez-Rojas et al., 2017). According the Center for Collegiate Mental Health (CCMH, 2020), there has been a steady increase in suicidality and nonsuicidal self-injurious behaviors over the past 9 years. Finally, one projection reports that we are on the verge of a mental health crisis as calls to a U.S. helpline increased 891% since this time last year (Levine, 2020). The uncertainty and duration of the COVID-19 pandemic has created an urgency for telebehavioral health counselors to obtain postgraduate crisis-intervention and suicidality training.

Despite the alarming number of clients presenting with high levels of distress, many master's-level mental health professionals receive little to no practical crisis-intervention training through their graduate programs (Barrio-Minton & Pease-Carter, 2011; Guo et al., 2016). The American Counseling Association (ACA, 2014) ethical standards address ethical implication and best practices for providing distance counseling. However, there is little guidance in terms of providing crisis intervention via telebehavioral health platforms. Postgraduate training is highly recommended by the authors but not required by most credentialing entities (Lum, 2010; National Board for Certified Counselors [NBCC], 2020) and no standard training exists at the time of this book's development. A review of the current literature available on telebehavioral health reveals an absence of crisis or suicide intervention mentioned in any meaningful way. This chapter will explore crisis counseling and risk of lethality in-depth in an effort to fill the gap in training for master-level counselors and practicing clinicians. Further, the application and nuances of crisis counseling online, as well as the ethical, legal, and Council for Accreditation of Counseling and Related Educational Programs (CACREP) standards related to crisis counseling are discussed.

Historical Context of Crisis

Historically, the term *crisis* refers to a disruptive life event, usually categorized as emergencies, such as natural disasters driven by natural causality (hurricanes, tornado, floods, volcanic eruptions, etc.); technological disasters like explosions, fire, toxic leaks; and even situations caused directly by man, such as terrorist attacks, urban violence, mass shootings, and school shootings. Recently, global crises such as COVID-19 causing unexpected loss and disillusionment necessitate that counselors are properly trained in various methods of crisis response. Generally, crises occur when tension and stress in life exceed the capacity to cope. Crisis reactions can also be related to situations that involve threats to life, property, home, and well-being. Grief and loss, significant relational changes, being diagnosed with a terminal illness, suicidal thoughts, and so on (da Silva et al., 2015) may result in a crisis reaction.

The most important aspect of a psychological crisis is not the incident or event per se; rather it is the arrangement of circumstances in which an individual finds themselves, their perception of the event, their resources, and the ability to access those resources (Lopez Levers, 2012). In psychological terms, crisis can be better understood as a reaction to a situation that a person sees as a threat to their physical and/or mental well-being (Lopez Levers, 2012). In such cases, clients might experience psychological distress and clinical symptoms that require immediate psychological care. People who experience a critical or traumatic event often present with anxiety or depression. Depending on the severity of the event and crisis reaction, clients might develop trauma-related pathologies such as acute stress and posttraumatic stress disorder (PTSD) (da Silva et al., 2015).

Historical Synthesis of Crisis Intervention and Distance Counseling

Crisis intervention as we know it today dates back to the First World War and was influenced by "military psychiatry, community mental health, and suicide intervention initiatives" (Every, 2006, p. 17). An early provider of crisis intervention was the first suicide **prevention** organization, New York City's Save-A-Life League, founded by Henry Marsh Warren in 1906 (Miller & Gould, 2013). Early crisis-intervention theories surfaced in response to Boston's Coconut Grove Fire of 1942 (Smith, 2006). While working with the fire survivors, Eric Lindemann (1979) formulated a theory of normal grief patterns based on the commonalities in the survivors' emotional suffering and needs (Smith, 2006). Gerald Caplan (1964) combined his knowledge from working with the Coconut Grove survivors and families at the Harvard Public Health Family Guidance Center to identify factors that influence a family's crisis response (Parad & Caplan, 1960; Smith, 2006). Caplan introduced the idea that the crisis is the result of an event and is not the event itself (Jackson-Cherry & Erford, 2014). More recent disasters such as the September 11th terrorist attack, as well as hurricanes Katrina and Rita, have also contributed to the way we respond to crisis reactions caused by various critical incidents or traumatic events.

As mentioned in Chapter 1, distance counseling dates as far back as Sigmund Freud. The first crisis hotline was established at the Children's Hospital in Los Angeles in 1968 (Aguilera, 1998). As technology has improved the platforms for providing distance crisis intervention, services increased to include text and chat hotlines. Providing access to clients who may not otherwise seek assistance, removing barriers such as transportation, and reducing concerns about stigma are a few of the advantages. The disadvantages of anonymous hotlines are numerous, including not being able to actually see the person in crisis or know their physical location. One of the more serious problems with distance crisis intervention is that people experiencing a crisis reaction are potentially at risk of lethality, and may remain at risk due to the proximity of the counselor and emergency services. Synchronous online counseling provides the accessibility of a crisis hotline without many of the disadvantages or risks. Crisis hotline workers may be limited by anonymity, but synchronous online counselors are able to have eyes on their clients and provide a more informed level of crisis intervention than telephonically. According to Trepal et al. (2007), clients report feeling favorably overall toward online counseling, but with certain risks, such as suicidality, online platforms may not be appropriate or preferred. The authors agree that certain mental health problems such as suicide may be more challenging to address online; however, it has become necessary and counselors must find proven and well-tested means of meeting this increasing need generated by the pandemic.

In March of 2020, many counselors were suddenly forced to move their practices online during the onset of the coronavirus pandemic, creating a significant need for training competent telebehavioral health providers. This resulted in an actual parallel process, as opposed to a conceptual parallel process, for many counselors and supervisors as we are experiencing the event with our clients and supervisees. In addition to the change in the way services are delivered, there is the increased need for services due to clients experiencing crisis reactions due to loss of income, children out of school, exposure to the virus, inability to find usual grocery items, and so on. This event appears to have changed the way counseling is practiced, and time will tell if the change is the new norm or temporary. No matter the outcome, the need for and shift to telebehavioral health was exacerbated due to the COVID-19 pandemic. As many people experience crisis reactions related to the pandemic, there is a distinct move toward online counseling. This chapter seems particularly relevant as counselors transition to online formats and many of our clients experience crisis reactions due to the pandemic.

Crisis Conceptualization

A **crisis** is the *reaction* to an event; the crisis is not the event (Every, 2015; Jackson-Cherry & Erford, 2014). Critical incidents, traumatic experiences, and disasters are types of *events* that may or may not cause a crisis reaction. The term *crisis* is defined in most texts (Jackson-Cherry & Erford, 2014;

James & Gilliland, 2017; Kanel, 2019) as the response to an event. However, the word *crisis* is often used to describe an event, even in texts defining crisis as the reaction. The term *crisis response* causes even further confusion as it is used "inconsistently and interchangeably, or without specificity" (Jackson-Cherry & Erford, 2014, p. 12). Response is often used synonymously with reaction, as well as being used to describe the intervention. For the purposes of this book, the **crisis reaction** and **crisis response** are the experience of the individual after a traumatic event or critical incident. Reaction and response involve symptoms. The **crisis intervention** is the counseling service provided to reduce a crisis reaction or response. Crisis intervention involves providing a service.

A crisis reaction is based largely in perception (Jackson-Cherry & Erford, 2014). One event experienced by two different people may be perceived by one person as traumatic or critical and the other person may not perceive it as a problem. Perception will determine if a crisis reaction is experienced or not. Our perception is influenced by many factors such as age, life experiences (Jackson-Cherry & Erford, 2014), intellect, and personality. Critical incidents are traumatic experiences that include car accidents, animal bites, house fire, witnessing violence, and so on. Traumatic experiences are based on perception and influenced by numerous factors. What might seem traumatic to a 4-year-old may not seem traumatic to an adult. A person who experienced a violent environment as a child may be less likely to perceive a fight as a traumatic event, whereas another person could perceive the same fight as extremely distressing. Events that we typically think of as traumatic experiences may include sexual assault, robbery, physical assault, or any experience where a person might feel violated or their life was threatened. Disasters are a different type of event. Hurricanes, wild fires, earthquakes, tornados, mass violence, terrorism, and pandemics are some of the disaster events that may lead to a crisis reaction. The likelihood of a client having experienced one or more of these types of events is very strong, suggesting that many of our clients have experienced a crisis reaction at some point in life.

Crisis Reactions

Most individuals exposed to an adverse experience, traumatic event, critical incident, or disaster will not need any type of mental health intervention (Everly, 2015; Rosen et al., 2020). A crisis response is typically the result of an event being perceived as critical or traumatic, and this perception results in considerable distress, followed by the ineffectiveness of previously used coping mechanisms (Yeager & Roberts, 2005), and the distress is not resolved. According to MacDonald (2016), a negative event occurs, leading to a feeling of subjective distress. The distress leads to an impairment in functioning, because usual coping skills fail to improve functioning. The experience of the crisis reaction is multidimensional and experienced on all domains: cognitive, emotional, physical, behavioral, relational, and spiritual. Frequently, the crisis reaction begins in the cognitive and emotional domains, or in the thoughts and feelings. Interestingly, thoughts come before and strongly influence feelings. If the reaction is not mitigated at the cognitive-emotional level, it moves to the physical and behavioral domains. Symptoms such as gastrointestinal problems, trembling, headaches, profuse sweating, or weakness may be physical manifestations of a crisis reaction. Increased substance use, poor hygiene, and risk taking are some behavioral reactions. Again, if the symptoms are not mitigated at this level, relational (work, school, home) and spiritual (any change in norm) problems may intensify. Once distress is impacting our relationships and spirituality, dysfunction and disorders should be ruled out. Keep in mind dysfunction and disorders are treatment concerns rather than crisis reactions. Crisis intervention will not mitigate disorders, only the crisis reaction related to the disorder.

Crisis Response (Reaction) Phases

Caplan (1964) identified the following phases of crises (reaction) that still hold true today:

- Initial increase in stress resulting from the impact of the stimulus (event); the individual attempts to use their default problem-solving responses (coping strategies)
- Coping strategies are ineffective, allowing the stress and discomfort to increase as the stimulus (event) continues
- Further increased stress leads the individual to employ internal and external emergency problem-solving mechanisms

  - The use of emergency problem-solving mechanisms may lead to the problem being solved or the event ends and homeostasis is restored

- If the problem continues without resolution or avoidance, tension continues to rise and major disorganization occurs. There may be a shift from distress to dysfunction at this point.

Crisis Intervention

Crisis intervention is how we *respond* to a client's crisis reaction, or what we do to assist a person experiencing distress and who is unable to cope effectively. Crisis intervention is not psychotherapy or clinical counseling; rather it is psychological first aid (PFA) or early psychological intervention (EPI) (Everly, 2015). The goal of crisis intervention is stabilization and to assist the client in returning to their baseline level of functioning (Everly, 2015). If a person is not able to return to their baseline level of functioning, then we must facilitate a referral to the next level of care. This is the minimum goal, while the maximum goal is improvement in functioning above the pre-crisis level (Aguilera, 1998).

The National Volunteer Organizations Active in Disaster (NVOAD), in conjunction with American Red Cross, International Critical Incident Stress Foundation (ICISF), National Organization for Victim Assistance (NOVA), and the Salvation Army, released the following consensus points in reference to crisis intervention or early psychological intervention (Everly, 2015):

- Early Psychological Intervention (EPI) is valued.
- EPI is a multi-component system to meet the needs of those impacted.
- Specialized training in early psychological intervention is necessary.
- EPI is one point on a continuum of psychological care. This spectrum ranges from pre-incident preparedness to post-incident psychotherapy, when needed.
- Cooperation, communication, coordination and collaboration are essential to the delivery of EPI. (pp. 19–20)

One type of EPI is critical incident stress management (CISM). CISM is a comprehensive system of interventions developed to manage critical incident stress among first responders (Everly, 2015). CISM originated in the 198's with the critical incident stress debriefing (CISD) or "the debriefing" as the first intervention developed by Jeffery Mitchell in 1974. The CISD is one intervention of many under the CISM umbrella. CISM is introduced here because specific techniques from this system will be discussed later in the chapter, and it is easily applied at a distance. The six core elements of CISM include the following:

- Strategic planning (or prevention)
- Assessment/triage
- Individual/psychological first aid
- Informational groups
- Interactive groups
- Resilience (Everly, 2015)

Discussion of Applicable Skills

Crisis intervention is not counseling or psychotherapy, yet some of the basic skills we employ as counselors are crucial to assisting a person experiencing a crisis reaction. Counseling skills are discussed in greater depth in Chapter 7. This chapter will briefly discuss the specific skills related to crisis intervention. The skills mentioned here are the very "basic tools on which the success of the intervention may depend" (Jackson-Cherry & Erford, 2014, p. 67).

Rapport as it relates to crisis intervention can be understood as the healthy working relationship between the person in crisis and the intervener. Beginning from the initial contact, rapport continues to develop throughout the crisis-intervention process (Jackson-Cherry & Erford, 2014, p. 67). By using the client's name, the initial connection is strengthened. Call the person by name when you want to emphasize something you are saying or reinforce a genuine connection. Trust is foundational to any relationship and an ingredient in rapport building. Trust and rapport must be developed quickly in crisis work. Trust is based on similar values and beliefs and actions matching words. Look for opportunities to identify similar values or beliefs. If appropriate, notice things in the environment or clothing of the client to connect, such as ball teams, books, spiritual symbols, or artwork. Further this by showing that your words and actions align; say what you mean and mean what you say. This advanced skill will demonstrate authenticity. The counselor's ability to convey empathy, genuineness, and acceptance will significantly influence the success of the intervention (Jackson-Cherry & Erford, 2014). Building rapport in synchronous online counseling requires some intentionality and must happen quickly in crisis intervention. More about building rapport in a synchronous online environment is discussed in Chapter 7, including important multicultural considerations.

Attending skills are important to the counseling relationship and in crisis intervention. Clients report nonverbal skills are significant to the development of a healthy therapeutic relationship (Bedi, 2006). The attending skills include eye contact, body language, tone, and use of silence. Eye contact is important to counseling and has cultural implications that will be addressed later in this chapter. Eye contact in the online environment requires the counselor to look at the camera and alternate that with looking just below the camera, as explained further in Chapter 7. Positioning the camera and computer are important to avoid distortions. The client should be able to see the counselor's eyes, so avoid lighting problems making it difficult to see facial features or causing eyeglass glare.

Body language can be more difficult to read via video conferencing. The counselor should have the camera located far enough away to ensure the client is able to see the counselor's shoulders and not just a face or head. By sitting further away, the counselor can use leaning in when wanting to convey interest or concern. Tone and clarity are important aspects of crisis intervention in the online platform. Underestimating the power of tone is problematic as emotion is frequently expressed by the tone of voice (Jackson-Cherry & Erford, 2014). The crisis counselor should be very cognizant of pitch, pacing, and volume. Crisis intervention requires the counselor to be a little more directive and confident, and a calm tone will convey strength; however, be careful to ensure your tone is not bossy or punitive. It is important to have a good microphone so that you are not shouting at clients or people in crisis, as this could change the success of the intervention. Having quality equipment and a great broadband service are important to providing effective online crisis intervention, especially related to tone.

Finally, silence is very useful as a crisis-intervention skill. Often someone reacting to a traumatic event just needs a cathartic release, and allowing the client to express their distress while the counselor is present and supportive, yet silent, is providing a *compassionate presence*. The client experiencing crisis distress needs "space to think, to sort out their thoughts, and to process what is happening" (Jackson-Cherry & Erford, 2014, p. 71). Everly (2015) warns to use silence carefully, as too much silence may appear disengaged. Do not be afraid to use silence. If done correctly, silence is a powerful tool that will provide the counselor a chance to collect their thoughts. In distance crisis intervention, it may be helpful to acknowledge the silence by saying "I am here for you if you need me, yet I appreciate [respect] your need to [take your time with this] sit with this" (Jackson-Cherry & Erford, 2014, p. 71). Being intentional about the attending skills will be advantageous to the crisis-intervention process.

Listening skills and questioning are basic counseling skills necessary to providing effective crisis intervention. Clients experiencing a crisis reaction are often "freewheeling in an ideational flight of emotions or thoughts" (James & Gilliland, 2017, p. 75). The listening skills of summary, paraphrasing, and reflecting are vital in crisis intervention to achieve an understanding of the problem, to identify the most distressing aspect, and to identify the reactions the client is experiencing in the moment (Jackson-Cherry & Erford, 2014). Summarizing or paraphrasing what a person experiencing a crisis reaction is reporting is a means of gaining clarity and conveying understanding, as clear expression is often difficult for a person experiencing a crisis reaction. Prompts to summarize or paraphrase might start with "It sounds like you are saying…" or "What I am hearing you say is…" while focusing on key issues and feelings. Using client pauses to insert a summary or paraphrase is optimal (Everly, 2015).

Reflection builds empathy and rapport, helps to label what the person in crisis is experiencing, and can gain client buy-in (Everly, 2015; Jackson-Cherry & Erford, 2014). A reflective statement might start with "Katrina, you seem really angry about …" Reflecting is not telling someone how they feel; rather it is focusing in and identifying meaning. A skillful counselor will assess a client's body language, tone, and facial expression to infer what the client is experiencing (Jackson-Cherry & Erford, 2014). Keep in mind, crisis intervention is not psychotherapy. The goal of crisis intervention is to contain the reaction, while the goal of therapy is often to release and work on the emotion.

Questioning is a skill that involves the use of closed-ended and open-ended questions. Closed-ended questions, or yes-no questions, tend to cause people to stay in their heads or in the logical, cognitive domain. Closed-ended questions elicit factual information and aid in the assessment of what the client is experiencing (James & Gilliland, 2017). Closed-ended questions are instrumental for safety assessment and planning. James and Gilliland suggest the following guidelines in developing closed-ended questions: "Request specific information, obtain a commitment, increas[e] focus, and avoid negative interrogatives" such as "Don't you want to live?" (p. 75). The authors discuss that open-ended questions facilitate deeper meaning or thought and are used to gather information about thoughts, feelings, and behaviors. Open-ended questions tend to evoke more emotion, or the affective domain. James and Gilliland (2017) suggest using the following to develop open-ended questions: "Request description, focus on plans, expansion, assessment, and stay away from 'why' questions" (p. 74). Questioning is a skill important to guiding the client through the crisis reaction.

Jackson-Cherry and Erford (2014) refer to questioning skills as primary in crisis counseling. Questioning in crisis intervention should be focused and follow a structure to avoid becoming an interrogation or bombarding a client. Everly (2015) suggests using the "diamond technique" as a structure he created for crisis intervention that uses both questioning and listening skills. The diamond technique is applicable to telebehavioral health and face-to-face counseling and will be discussed in greater detail later in this chapter in an effort to address the gap in the literature around crisis intervention at a distance.

Intake and Assessment

Very specific protocols for crisis intervention should be established at the onset of treatment, whether the online counseling client is experiencing a crisis reaction or not. Suitability for online counseling should be the starting point. Of course, you may have to provide crisis intervention while determining suitability. Emergency planning must be discussed during the intake process. **Contact information** for emergency services in the immediate vicinity of the client could be very important if a client has a medical or a mental health emergency. In an emergency, it will be more difficult to gather the necessary information and may waste valuable time. The client should sign a **release of information** for three friends or family members who are willing to act as emergency contacts and support. Two phone numbers for each would offer the most coverage. Ensure that the contact is willing to check in with client or do a wellness check, if required. In an emergency situation, the counselor should be prepared to provide the following information to emergency personnel: client name, date of birth, address on file, "the situation details, the patient's diagnosis and how it could influence interactions with law enforcement officers, and the contact information for local mental health support" (Luxton et al., 2016, p. 69). That is in addition to the client's physical location if different from address on file, contact phone number and email, emergency contact, and other relevant information collected at intake and at the beginning of every session. High-risk situations may require that the emergency contact is in the same location, not necessarily the same room, and available by phone or text message in case of an emergency. All emergency plans must include the consent of the client and are arranged at the onset of treatment or as soon as risk is identified. This will be discussed in greater detail in the lethality section. Assessment and intake are important in crisis prevention work and are explored in detail in Chapter 6.

Crisis Assessment: Signs and Symptom Recognition at a Distance

Asking more questions during an online crisis assessment is necessary as we are unable to view all the body language we would in a face-to-face session. Be careful not to ask so many questions in rapid succession that it feels like an interrogation, as this can increase client distress. Signs of a crisis reaction, traumatic or disaster stress are multidimensional. Crisis reactions are natural human reactions to out of the ordinary events (Everly, 2015). That is not to say that crisis reactions are normal; they are not. Generally, the reaction would be viewed as abnormal on a typical day. However, as a reaction to an event that is significantly distressing, the resulting crisis response seems appropriate to the situation. Refer to the Signs and Symptoms of Traumatic Stress PDF. An additional factor to consider is distress versus dysfunction; both require identification and assessment. Distress requires monitoring, ongoing assessment, and the development of a safety plan while dysfunction requires action on the counselor's part (Everly, 2015). Action on the counselor's part might include contacting the client's emergency contact to physically be with the client, contacting emergency services, or obtaining a safety commitment to stay on the line or video meeting until help arrives. Lethality is a specific type of assessment and will be discussed later in this chapter.

Intervention

The goals of crisis intervention are to "foster natural resiliency" through stabilization, reduction in symptoms, facilitating a return to previous level of functioning, or a referral to the next level of care (Everly, 2015, p. 16). In conducting crisis invention, the counselor addresses a specific issue and attempts to assist the individual in resolving the issue. If there are numerous issues, ask for the worst one and focus the intervention on that problem. The client and counselor work collaboratively to reduce anxiety, manage disabling emotions, strengthen the individual's coping skills, and expand internal resources and external supports (Myer et al., 2013; Smith, 2006; Turley, 2013). The principles of crisis intervention are simplicity, brevity, innovation, pragmatism, proximity, immediacy, and expectancy (Everly, 2015) and are easily applied face-to-face or at a distance.

Structure is the antidote to chaos (Everly, 2015). The "diamond technique" structure, according to the author, simply begins with asking closed-ended questions, yes-no, at the onset of the intervention, such as "Will you speak with me?" or "Are you able to step over here?" Move to asking open-ended questions, such as "Tell me about what happened" (Everly, 2015). Eventually work toward summarizing and paraphrasing what you have heard (Everly, 2015). This may be a good time to ask, "What is the worst part?" Finally, end the intervention with closed-ended questions (Everly, 2015), such as "Will you be able to contact your pastor?" or "Are you okay to return to work?" This technique is applicable in face-to-face and distance interventions.

Numerous crisis-intervention models have been developed to assist both individuals experiencing a psychological emergency and individuals so overwhelmed that their ability to cope is significantly compromised. One intervention model is the SAFER-R model used in CISM individual crisis intervention (Everly, 2020). The SAFER-R acronym stands for

Stabilize: Introduce, meet basic needs, mitigate acute stressors.

Acknowledge the crisis: Provide an opportunity for clients to tell their stories.

Facilitate understanding: Provide normalization and reassurance as appropriate.

Encourage effective coping: Engage in mechanisms of action such as problem solving.

Reassess reentry or referral: Facilitate access to continued care (International Critical Incidents Stress Foundation [ICISF], 2020; Everly, 2015)

The SAFER-R model offers a format for the crisis intervention that will work online or face-to-face. The SAFER-R model works very well with the structure of the diamond technique. Ultimately, moving the client from the emotional reactive state of a crisis to a more logical and problem-solving state is the key to crisis intervention. Shift the client back into their head, to the logical domain, and out of the emotional domain. Keep in mind the key to therapy is to open the client up to work in the emotional realm. While the goal of crisis intervention is the opposite, closing the client up is the intent. Additional training in CISM and the SAFER-R model are strongly encouraged and available through the ICISF.

Lethality Risk at a Distance

Hipple and Beamish (2007) found that suicide was one of the most distressing critical incidents counselors face. Despite client denial of lethality during the assessment, clients may report experiencing suicidality during the course of treatment. Best practices include (a) "practicing within local regulations, (b) using clinical judgment in patient selection, (c) utilizing accepted suicide assessment parameters, and (d) addressing contingency plans" (Godleski et al., 2008, pp. 279–280). Even when following best practices, suicidal and homicidal clients pose a serious risk. No counselor or other mental health professional is able to predict with 100% accuracy if a client will complete a suicide (O'Brien & Hauser, 2016). A "thorough and comprehensive assessment of risk" will inform "interventions based on immediate suicide risk factors" (O'Brien & Hauser, 2016, p. 195). In-depth biopsychosocial assessments offer the counselor a comprehensive snapshot of the client's background, strengths, supports, stressors, and level of functioning and can alert counselors to lethality risk factors. During the assessment, it is essential that the counselor conduct an assessment of the environment. When a client is in our office, we are able to remove potential weapons and reduce other risk factors. This is not the case when a client is in their home or vehicle. Asking more direct questions about a plan and means is imperative in lethality assessment at a distance. In addition to the thorough assessment at the onset of treatment, continuous and comprehensive check-ins and follow-up services are necessary.

Screening tools such as the SAD PERSONS can be helpful when used as part of a comprehensive assessment. The SAD PERSONS is not a clinical assessment and was not designed as such; rather it is a quick tool or triage for gathering data used in determining the need for additional evaluation developed originally for medical students by Patterson et al. (1983). It is assessing *risk factors* only. Juhnke and Granello (1996) modified the SAD PERSONS scale as follows:

S: Male sex = 1

A: Age 15–25 or 59-plus years = 1

D: Depression or hopelessness = 2

P: Previous suicidal attempts or psychiatric care = 1

E: Excessive ethanol or drug use = 1

R: Rational thinking loss (psychotic or organic illness) = 2

S: Single, widowed, or divorced = 1

O: Organized or serious prior attempt = 2

N: No social support = 1

S: Stated future intent (determined to repeat or ambivalent) = 2

The client is assigned points based on the factors present. Scores of 3 or more are indicative of heightened risk and merit close monitoring. The SAD PERSONS scale has received criticism for not assessing for suicide plans and means, and studies have shown the scale has little to no validity in predicting suicide (Birnbaumer, 2013; Saunders et al., 2013). However, the scale can be a starting point and beneficial in assisting counselors to identify red flags. Counselors should also assess for suicide plans and means, always alerting the authorities if the client is in immediate or imminent danger. The same is applicable to a homicidal client as well: Assess risk, plan, and means and notify authorities when in doubt.

An assessment and treatment program that appears to be very effective is the Collaborative Assessment and Management of Suicidality (CAMS) Framework™.

CAMS Framework™ is first and foremost a clinical philosophy of care. It is a therapeutic framework for suicide-specific assessment and treatment of a patient's suicidal risk. It is a flexible approach that can be used across theoretical orientations and disciplines for a wide range of suicidal patients across treatment settings and different treatment modalities (CAMS-Cares, 2020).

Cams Suicide Status Form–4 (SSF-4) is a thorough assessment currently available in the CAMS book. CAMS is remarkably affordable and easy to learn. CAMS is applicable face-to-face or at a distance. CAMS provides the counselor a structure to openly discuss suicide with a client, encouraging the client to "coauthor" the treatment plan. This is powerful for both the client and the counselor, really reducing fear and anxiety for both.

This is a very basic overview of crisis intervention at a distance with potentially lethal clients. In no way is this exhaustive training. Risk of lethality can be assessed at a distance, and when prevention planning begins at intake, safety increases. All readers are encouraged to obtain additional training in suicide prevention, intervention, and postvention. In addition to training, become familiar with the emergency mental health commitment process in any state where you practice. Understanding the process of having clients assessed for lethality by a state or local authority can be priceless when an incident occurs.

Violence in the home and other higher-risk situations should be considered in the discussion of crisis counseling at a distance. Child abuse, intimate partner violence, and elder abuse pose serious challenges to counseling a client at a distance. The challenge increases exponentially if sessions take place in the home where the violence occurs. Creating a "safe space" for clients in the physical office is important and how to create this online is explored in chapter 9. Be hyperalert to changes in lighting, position in camera view, attire (turtlenecks, scarves, hats, etc.), and clients appearing hesitant to speak freely or making erratic or unusual eye movements. At the onset of treatment, when you are sure the client is alone, ask them to create a code word or hand sign to indicate the need for help in the form of law enforcement or emergency medical services. This can be embedded in the informed consent, with the client initialing beside the safety code. In such cases, it is wise to frequently check in, reminding the client that there is a safety protocol in place and ensure they remember it without speaking the plan out loud. Also, it is required to identify where the client is physically at the beginning of each session and is especially important if their environment is not their norm. With high-risk clients, it may also be beneficial to ask who else is present in the home and ensure the client can speak freely. Proper preplanning can make the difference to a client at risk.

Postvention

Postvention can be a form of prevention. Often the crisis intervention will end in hospitalization for the most serious suicidal cases. Clients are generally released from inpatient hospitalization with medication and little treatment to address the problem that sent them to the hospital; therefore many clients continue to experience suicidality. In general, counselors are not adequately prepared to work with suicidal clients (Morris & Minton, 2012) and this includes after the client is released from the hospital. Focusing treatment on the causal diagnosis rather than the symptoms is very effective in reducing suicidality. Although this is not a chapter on treatment, assess for underlying, unresolved trauma as the causal diagnosis as an effective means of treating suicidality long term. Chronic suicidality is a growing treatment concern, and counselors are encouraged to obtain post-graduate training in this area.

Technology can offer an added layer of prevention and intervention, after a critical incident. Text messaging can serve to augment care during the high-risk post-discharge period (Czyz et al., 2020) when a client returns to the community. Text messaging may be especially advantageous for adolescents who at times fail to follow their established safety plans (Czyz et al., 2020). Counselors can utilize customized daily text messaging to provide tips, reminders, check-ins, and encouragement to clients. It should be noted that text messaging is not a secure means of communicating with clients and should not be used to communicate any confidential information. Additionally, there are numerous coping and tracking apps available that can be incorporated into the treatment plan.

In reference to post-disaster counseling, "telemental health (TMH) has the capacity" to bring "evidence based best practices in mental health care to those in need" in remote and difficult to reach populations (Augusterfera et al., 2015, p. 541). "TMH can support much-needed mental health capacity building in low resource and post-disaster settings" (Augusterfera et al., 2015, p. 544) as we mention in the information on the pandemic. There is a scarcity of literature on the use of online counseling post-disaster (Augusterfera et al., 2015). Many areas experience a problem in locating mental health services following a disaster due to saturation and lack of long-term resources and funding. Telebehavioral health following a disaster would be advantageous for many reasons, including risk reduction for responders (medical, physical safety, etc.), travel expense, drain on community resources, and access to specialists. More research and investigation in the area of post-disaster counseling is suggested.

Pandemic

The pandemic of 2020 created a tremendous need for counselors to provide services via the internet. The need is twofold: First there are the stay-at-home orders and social distancing requirements. Then there is also the escalating stress and resulting distress increasing the demand for more telebehavioral health providers (Robbin, 2020; Rosen, 2020). The World Health Organization (WHO, 2019) reports that disorders such as depression and anxiety will more than double during a humanitarian crisis and the number only increases with those residing in conflict-ridden areas. The need for mental health services to be available to people quarantined or in a rural setting or without childcare is only going to increase as we face unprecedented challenges with the current pandemic (Robbins, 2020). The uncertainty and ambiguity of the pandemic are creating significant stress that is resulting in crisis reactions, with many telebehavioral health providers seeing a 50% increase in business (Robbins, 2020). Preparing counselors to provide crisis counseling services online seems pertinent. It is all together possible that mental health treatment has changed forever, creating a need for counselors to rapidly adopt distance counseling as a new platform.

CACREP

The Council for Accreditation of Counseling and Related Educational Programs (CACREP) first mandated the inclusion of crisis response education in the publication of the 2009 standards (CACREP, 2009). Crisis response continues to be mandated in the 2016 CACREP standards. Clinical mental health counseling programs with CACREP accreditation have little guidance and great freedom in how crisis response is taught. Morris and Minton (2012) conducted a study finding a serious deficiency in crisis response and suicide risk training in counselor education. Many counselor education programs minimally prepare counselors in training for assessing and intervening with suicidal clients, with treatment of suicidality nonexistent. Some programs offer a three–credit hour course while others offer a short seminar. This difference in training has created a vast range of skill in the field among graduate-level mental health counselors. The type of crisis intervention training a counselor received will also impact the counselor's ability to provide crisis intervention in the online format. Additional training in crisis intervention is strongly recommended.

ACA Code of Ethics

While crisis response is not specifically addressed in the 2014 ACA Code of Ethics, client welfare is the primary responsibility of all counselors. Counselors are required to include emergency procedures designed to address times that the counselor is not available in the informed consent and disclosure documentation when practicing online counseling (ACA, 2014, H.2.a.).

> The development of clinic policy and crisis protocols is important to appropriately manage both standard "everyday" delivery of telebehavioral health and to properly handle crisis situations. … Crisis protocols should be tailored to the individual needs and capacity of the organization and community partner providing telebehavioral health services, and all parties should have a clear understanding of the crisis protocol (Jones et al., 2014, para. 25).

Additionally, supervisors are mandated to "establish and communicate to supervisees procedures for contacting supervisors or, in their absence, alternative on-call supervisors to assist in handling crises" (ACA, 2014, F.4.b.). This is addressed more thoroughly in Chapter 13. The authors recommend training for supervisors specific to crisis-invention best practices.

Multicultural Competency in Crisis Intervention

Counselors are able to provide services at a greater distance due to the ever-changing technology. Therefore, crisis services are being provided to more diverse groups than historically possible. Telebehavioral health has increased access to underserved, marginalized, and vulnerable people. With the expanded access to clients from diverse cultures, telebehavioral health providers must "carefully question and assess their competence" with people different from themselves (Luxton et al., 2016, p. 109). Events that frequently trigger a crisis reaction in one culture may not have the same effect on members of another culture. Further, coping mechanisms vary significantly among cultures. A culturally appropriate reaction to a traumatic event may appear to be a breakdown of coping to members of another culture. This must be balanced with "not over-generalizing cultural information or stereotype groups" because most people are influenced by several cultural groups (Luxton et al., 2016, p. 111).

Language is one of the most important manifestations of culture. Some important cultural concepts cannot be satisfactorily translated from one language to another. The client's preferred language should be considered necessary to crisis intervention. It is better to have a trained interpreter rather than a family member as a translator (Luxton et al., 2016). The Red Cross and private organizations, as well as high school language departments, often have trained translators. It goes without saying that necessary releases and paperwork will need to be signed.

Attention to nonverbal communication is important in crisis intervention, along with an awareness of cultural nuances that impact crisis reactions. Counselors and supervisors must be aware of how behaviors including eye contact, physical contact, and proximity can be different among cultures (Sandoval et al., 2009). Eye contact is somewhat decreased when services are delivered via the computer, and camera placement is crucial. Luxton et al. (2016) report that Caucasians report decreased eye contact is somewhat problematic, while Native Americans and Asian people may prefer decreased direct eye contact. It is important to avoid misinterpretation during crisis intervention; therefore competence in cultural diversity is necessary.

Despite improved technology and access, the pandemic has drawn attention to the disparity in internet access across the nation. It appears that there continues to be an affluence attached to online counseling and internet access in general. Cost for distance counseling services may be affordable, yet if the internet is not available it diminishes the types of services available to all people. As counseling professionals, we must continue to advocate for expanded and inclusive access to the internet and counseling services at a distance. Chapter 3 explores the legal and ethical issues related to this topic.

Limitations

Limitations to online crisis intervention include lack of nonverbal cues, delayed response to text messages and emails, and technical difficulties (Luxton et al., 2016). To address the possibility of technical difficulties during crisis intervention, it is vital for the counselor to have alternative contact information and a back-up plan in place. Another limitation is the physical distance between the client in crisis and the counselor. The most effective resolution is to gather emergency contact information for more than one person who can be on scene quickly and a release of information to speak with and enlist help from those individuals in case of an emergency. The emergency contact can elicit help from others as needed, as they are not bound by confidentiality, and this should also be discussed with the client. Proper planning starting with policies and procedures clearly outlined for the client in the initial contact will significantly impact this limitation. A final limitation is the lack of available literature on crisis intervention or suicide assessment/intervention in telebehavioral health, although CAMS is looking very promising.

SUMMARY

Crisis prevention, intervention, and postvention are an area of weakness for many counselors. There is a lack of consistent training and no clear guidance from the accrediting body. This is true for counseling in general and counseling at a distance. Because clients tend to experience crisis reactions at the onset or during the course of treatment, it is important for counselors to seek postgraduate training in crisis and suicide prevention, intervention, and postvention. This chapter introduces the history of crisis intervention and briefly reviews the history of online treatment. Crisis reaction and response are terms that have multiple meanings and can be confusing. Crisis is clearly defined as a response to an event and not the event itself. Responding to the event "can easily lead to over intervention, and the potential to interfere with the natural recovery mechanism" (Everly, 2006, p. 121). Responding to the crisis reaction is more appropriate and effective. Crisis reactions and symptoms of crisis will inform interventions. Specific skills needed for effective crisis intervention are imperative to the success of the intervention. The limitations of distance crisis counseling and suggestions for change must be explored. This chapter is not an exhaustive resource for crisis intervention or suicide assessment, but it is a starting point with a consistent message to pursue more training in crisis and suicide assessment and intervention.

CASE EXPLORATION

Katrina is a provisionally licensed counselor, under supervision. Katrina is working with Raymond Levai, a 16-year-old male. Raymond sent Katrina a text making an indirect suicidal statement. Katrina responds to Raymond's text and also alerts her supervisor Eugene.

Katrina: [text message] Hi Raymond. It's Katrina. I received your text message and would like to meet with by video conference if you are open to that. I will send you a confidential link. Are you willing to meet with me now? [Note: yes/no question]

Raymond: Yes.

A few minutes later Katrina and Raymond are meeting in Katrina's secure telehealth office. Katrina also ran through the SAD PERSONS risk assessment:

S: Male sex = 1 ✓

A: Age 15–25 or 59-plus years = 1 ✓

D: Depression or hopelessness = 2   Raymond has no hx

P: Previous suicidal attempts or psychiatric care = 1   Raymond has no hx

E: Excessive ethanol or drug use = 1   Raymond has no hx

R: Rational thinking loss (psychotic or organic illness) = 2   Raymond has no hx

S: Single, widowed, or divorced = 1 ✓

O: Organized or serious prior attempt = 2   Raymond has no hx

N: No social support = 1   Raymond has supportive family and several good friends

S: Stated future intent (determined to repeat or ambivalent) = 2   plans to get the license

Raymond scored a 3, which is relatively low risk, but he does have a plan and the plan is feasible with means. Katrina will meet with Raymond via video conference to further assess intent and develop a safety plan with Raymond.

Katrina: Thanks for meeting with me. Are you in a safe place where you can speak freely and privately?

Raymond: Yes.

Katrina: Will you tell me where you are, the physical address? For our records, you know that is required. That will also help me keep you safe.

Raymond: I am at my mom's the address is 2540 Summerville Rd. ... [Although this is not a yes/no question, it is a cognitive question requiring thinking rather than emoting] [steps up to this point are S stabilization from SAFER-R].

Katrina: Thanks. In your text you said you wanted to drive the car into a wall because you failed the written driving exam. Did I understand that correctly? [Yes/no, but leaves room for more detail; an acknowledging part of SAFER-R]

Raymond: I am sorry for this. It's really not a big deal. I was just upset.

Katrina: Well it sounded like a big deal when you sent the text. You were really looking forward to having your driver's license by the junior prom this spring, right? [acknowledging and encouraging telling the story].

Raymond: Yes.

Katrina: Can you tell me what happened? [open-ended question, more emotional or affective; F facilitate understanding part of SAFER-R].

Raymond: My mom was supposed to take to the exam this morning, but as usual she had things to do with her job and was running late. My dad said he would take me but he would not be home until later in the afternoon. Nothing ever goes right for me.

Katrina: That sounds really disappointing, but your dad made it home in time to get there?

Raymond: We barely made it to the test site in time and I was so stressed out that I couldn't even think about the test. I forgot everything I read last night when I studied. My parents have screwed everything up since they got divorced. Now I will never be able to get my license.

Katrina: Wow, that sounds like a lot. The reason your parents asked you to meet with me was because of the divorce, so let's talk about that when we meet Tuesday. Right now, let's focus on what happened today to make you feel so bad [noting that there are some significant feelings about the divorce that are surfacing and need to be discussed in the next session, but staying focused on the current problem]. What is the worst part of what happened today [narrowing the focus]?

Raymond: Yeah, I guess the worst part is not passing the test. I really thought I would be driving this weekend. My friends are never gonna let it go [he laments a little more].

Katrina: So, it sounds like you are really disappointed that you did not pass the test and won't be able to drive this weekend [paraphrase and summarize]. When can you take the test again [future plans = safety factor against suicide, assessing readiness to move forward in SAFER-R]?

Raymond: Disappointed is understating it … not worth driving the car into a wall though. I think the guy said I can take it again in 30 days. That is like a lifetime.

Katrina: It is not a lifetime [gentle contradiction], although I do believe it will feel like it [validation]. And what can you do to ensure you pass next time [problem solving]?

Raymond: Make sure my parents don't let their work stress me out [he's 16]?

Katrina: Well that is one way, but it will be more difficult to control that aspect. What about studying? You said you studied last night, but did you study any other time [working toward closure with yes/no questions again]?

Raymond: No.

Katrina: How much would you study for a major history exam? The night before? You hate history and you would have studied more than a night. The driving exam is really important, so do you think it deserves more time than you gave it [problem solving, encouraging adaptive coping of the SAFER-R]?

Raymond: I guess if you look at it like that …

Katrina: Sounds like you have 30 days to really get to know the information and nail that test. Does that sound like something you can do [reassess of the SAFER-R]?

Raymond: Yes.

Katrina: How are you feeling you feeling right now [looking for hope, resilience, coping]?

Raymond: I feel a lot better. Studying will probably really help. My mom said I should study but I thought I had it.

Katrina: Sounds like you know what you need to do. Before we go, remember I mentioned that I would have to tell your parents about our meeting today. It is important that we let all the adults who care about you know what is going on. And because I am under supervision, I will have to inform my supervisor. You managed this situation well by reaching out and using your resources. Feel proud of yourself. I want you to feel safe in being honest with me about feeling like you want to hurt yourself or anything else. Can you commit to reaching out again if anything comes up before our session Tuesday [re-entry of the SAFER-R]?

Raymond: This went way better than I thought it would. Thank you, Miss Katrina. I will text you if anything is wrong, but I really need to get studying.

Katrina: I will see you Tuesday at the usual time [re-entry].

Raymond: See you then.

Sessions ends. Katrina contacts both parents and her supervisor. She completes her documentation. Katrina reflects and realizes that this was a low-risk suicide situation and her crisis-intervention skills were applied fairly well, but she needs more training in suicide intervention. Katrina signs up for a CAMS training to start improving her skill and competence in this area.

Exercise Questions

1. Would Raymond be considered high risk for suicide?
2. List Raymond's risk factors.
3. In what phase of the SAFER-R model would you encourage narrative expression?
4. What are other ways you might help normalize the situation and offer reassurance?
5. How might suicide risk in a virtual platform differ from face-to-face intervention?
6. Can the SFF-4 be conducted in telehealth sessions?

Worksheets

SIGNS AND SYMPTOMS OF TRAUMATIC STRESS

Highlight or circle any symptoms that you have experienced in the past 30 days, indicating *only* the items that you have experienced more often than not. For example, do not circle headache if you had five headaches in a month, but do circle headaches if you had a headache 20 days out of 30.

Physical	Cognitive	Behavioral	Emotional	Relational	Spiritual
fatigue/tiredness	confusion	repetitive actions	fear	change in relations	questions about faith
nausea	nightmares	antisocial acts	guilt	parents/grandparents	change in interactions with faith community
fainting	uncertainty	inability to rest	grief	brothers/sisters	guilt, survivor guilt
twitches	super alert or watchful	pacing	panic	spouse	anger at God
vomiting	not trustful of others	erratic movements	denial	friends	searching for meaning and hope
dizziness	pictures randomly pop up in your head	change in social activity	anxiety/nervousness	teachers/employers	questions about good and evil
weakness	blaming someone	eating less than usual	irritability/crankiness	neighbors	concern about vengeance, justice, or payback
chest pain	difficulty problem solving	change in speech patterns/communication	depression	legal problems	
headache	difficulty focusing	eating more than usual	intense anger or rage	educational issues	changes in spiritual practices
high blood pressure	difficulty making decisions	super aware of surroundings	feeling uneasy	family problems	rumination on forgiveness/payback
rapid heart rate	difficulty with math	alcohol or marijuana use	no feeling/feeling numb	aggression in relationships	over-relying on faith and prayer
muscle shaking/twitching	difficulty with language	missing work/school	snapping quickly/hitting a 10 and not calming quickly	social media/community problems	realization of vulnerability and mortality
grinding teeth	difficulty remembering	other substance use	feeling overwhelmed	isolation	overly concerned about hereafter
difficulty seeing	difficulty identifying objects or people	other addictive behavior	losing it for no reason	unemployment or underemployment	questioning God
jumpy	poor abstract thinking	change in unusual activity	serious anger over little stuff	stigma, racism, sexism	comfort in knowing deceased is with God

Adapted from ICISF material (2010). icisf.org

Sherry Todd, PhD, LPC, ATR-BC, CTTS 2017

Basic Counseling Forms

TELEHEALTH INDIVIDUAL SUICIDE SCREEN

Establish client safety prior to screening. Contact POLICE if client is not safe.

CLIENT: _____   SCREENER: _____   Date: _____

AGE: _____   M / F   RACE/ETHNICITY: _____

LOCATION OF CLIENT & CONTACT: _____   INFORMANTS: _____

SAD PERSON RISK FACTORS: S A **D** P E **R** S **O** N S (circle the letter of all risk factors–see scale in chapter
***RED** letters indicate greater risk)*

→ **DISCUSSION SUMMARY:**

   1. Depression. Based on your understanding of depression, do you think you are depressed?   **Y / N**
       IF YES: What percentage of the time do you think you are depressed?
       30% or less   31–60%   more than 60%

     ○ ***Alternate Question:*** How many days a week? 0–1   2–3   4 or more
       How long have you felt this way?   less than 2 wks   2–4 wks more than 1 mo   6 mo or more
       Did something cause the depression? **Y / N**   If yes, what? _____
                                            (describe on back of page)

   2. Change in eating habits?   Eating More   Eating Less   explanation _____

   3. Change in sleeping habits?   Sleeping More   Sleeping Less   explanation _____

   4. Do you have less energy than usual? **Y / N**   explanation _____

   5. Not interested in normal activities (the things that you usually like to do)?   **Y / N**
     Do you attribute that to anything? _____

   6. Treatment. Have you ever seen a counselor or therapist? **Y / N** Who? _____
     ○ Currently in treatment?   **Y / N** Who? _____

   7. Medications. History of taking medication?   **Y / N**   if yes, what? _____
     ○ Currently taken medication?   **Y / N**   if yes, what? _____

   8. Suicide.   Have you ever thought about committing suicide? **Y / N** Did you think of a plan? **Y / N**
                                                              How? _____

     ○ Have you ever made a suicide attempt?   **Y / N** How many times? _____ When? _____
       Does anyone know about this (did you tell anyone?) **Y / N** Who? _____
       What happened afterwards? _____

     How suicidal do you feel **right now**, on a scale of 1-10, where **1** is **not suicidal** at all and **10** is
     suicidal with a plan? _____
       Why would you say that number today? _____
       What is the highest number you have been on that scale at any given time? _____

9. Does anyone in your family have a history of problems with depression/suicide?   **Y / N**
Who? _____

10. What prevents/ has prevented you from killing yourself? (ie: What keeps you from committing suicide?)
Y / N _____

11. Have you ever engaged in self mutilating behavior (cutting, branding, eraser burns)?   **Y / N**
What self-mutilation have you done? _____

12. Trauma. Have you ever experienced or witnessed any of the following: NOTE: if yes to anything please go through CISM steps
☐ Natural Disaster (earthquake, hurricane, tornado, fire)
☐ Assault (physical or sexual)
☐ Medical Trauma (sudden/chronic illness, surgical procedure)
☐ Sudden or Violent Death of a loved one
☐ Community Violence (robbery, mugging, banking)
☐ Child Abuse (physical, emotional, sexual)
☐ Witness Violence against someone else (domestic or community)
☐ Terrorist Incident (9/11 loss, experience)
☐ Been shot, shot at, seen someone shot
☐ Know someone who committed suicide
☐ Car Accident where you or someone else was seriously hurt
☐ Other _____

IF YES, do you ever think about it when you are not trying to? Have dreams about it? Think it is happening again?   **Y / N**
Do you ever try not to think about it, avoid the places or people who remind you of it?   **Y / N**
Do you think that experience interferes with your ability to perform in school or with your relationships?   **Y / N**

STOP! If client disclosed traumatic experience go to Page 3 of screen and follow the questions there before continuing.

13. Symptoms. Please highlight **all** of the **Signs & Symptoms** on the **List** that you experience more days than you don't experience.

14. Coping. How do you deal/cope with the things listed on the signs and symptom you identified? _____

15. What activities do you do to reduce stress? (ex: read, work out, ride a bike, etc.) _____

16. Who do you consider to be included in your support group? _____

17. Who can you talk to about stress/feelings? _____

18. Would you go to this person to talk if you felt like you wanted to hurt yourself?   **Y / N**

19. What are your plans for your future? (college, trade school, marriage, military, etc.) _____

20. If there were someone to talk to like me, would you be willing to talk to them or participate in a group?
Y / N

CLIENT INITIALS [   ]   **Date:** _____

Additional Screener Comments: _____

_____

_____

_____

_____

_____

_____

_____

_____

_____

_____

_____

_____

RECOMMENDATION:

_____

_____

_____

_____

_____

_____

REFERRAL: ☐ **HOSPITAL**   ☐ **OUTPT**   ☐ **IN-HOME**   ☐ **Detox**   ☐ **Police/CIT**
          ☐ **MD**   ☐ **ER**   ☐ **Community Services**   ☐ **OTHER** _____

CALL(S):   ☐ **PARENT:** _____   **PHONE:** _____

Parent Comments: _____

_____

_____

_____

_____

_____

☐ **CPS**   **Time:** _____   **Worker taking call** _____   **Comments:** _____
☐ **POLICE**   **Time:** _____   **Officer taking call** _____   **Comments:** _____
☐ **OTHER** _____

FOLLOW UP: ☐ **10 DAYS** ☐ **20 DAYS** ☐ **30 DAYS**

PERSON TO FOLLOW UP: _____

COMMENTS: _____

_____

_____

_____

_____

_____

_____

Date FOLLOW UP Conducted: _____ **Screener:** _____ **Recommendations Followed?** Y / N

COMMENTS: _____

_____

_____

_____

_____

_____

_____

_____

_____

_____

_____

_____

ACTION: _____

_____

_____

_____

_____

_____

_____

_____

_____

_____

_____

CLIENT INITIALS [   ]   **Date:** _____

Modified critical incident stress process to use if client discloses trauma. Stop and do this before continuing with screen. Critical Incident Stress Management (CISM) is a comprehensive system of crisis intervention techniques developed by George Everly, PhD and Jeff Mitchell, PhD. The questions below were adapted from the International Critical Incident Stress Foundation's (ICISF) CISM techniques and interventions.

FACTS: Please tell me what happened (if they already have then do not redo, just summarize what they have said.

What was your reaction to that? What were you thinking and feeling?

What kinds of feelings do you have when you think about that now?

Will you highlight the things on this list that you experience more days of the week than not? (provide the student with symptom sheet on the backside of this sheet and a highlighter)   →

How are you dealing or coping with those symptoms you have identified?

Return to Page 1 of Individual Screening and begin with the Coping Section #14. You should have completed the symptoms checklist during the previous page of questions.

Online Resources

- **Psychological First Aid and Skills for Psychological Recovery (FREE COURSES):** Free courses available to assist in using Psychological First Aid skills. https://learn.nctsn.org/course/index.php?categoryid=11

- The **CAMS Suicide Prevention Assessment, Intervention & Treatment:** Provides training and certification for mental health professionals for working with suicidal clients. https://cams-care.com/

- The **National Suicide Prevention Lifeline:** A national network of local crisis centers that provides free and confidential emotional support to people in suicidal crisis or emotional distress 24 hours a day, 7 days a week. https://suicidepreventionlifeline.org/chat/

- **Mental Health & Suicide Prevention Glossary:** Counselors must be familiar with the language and words used when talking about suicide prevention. This site offers a glossary of terms associated to mental health and suicide. https://suicidepreventionlifeline.org/mental-health-suicide-prevention-glossary/

- **Resources to Support Mental Health and Coping with the Coronavirus (COVID-19):** Resources for coping skills and mental health issues related to the coronavirus. https://www.sprc.org/covid19

- **Designating 988 for the National Suicide Prevention Lifeline**: The rules require all phone service providers to direct all 988 calls to the existing National Suicide Prevention Lifeline by July 16, 2022. During the transition to 988, Americans who need help should continue to contact the National Suicide Prevention Lifeline by calling 1-800-273-8255 (1-800-273-TALK) and through online chats. Veterans and Service members may reach the Veterans Crisis Line by pressing 1 after dialing, texting 838255, or chatting online.www.veteranscrisisline.net.

References

Aguilera, D. C. (1998). *Crisis intervention: Theory and methodology* (8th ed.). Mosby.

American Counseling Association. (2014). *2014 ACA code of ethics.* https://www.counseling.org/knowledge-center

Augusterfer, E. F., Mollica, R. F., & Lavelle, J. (2015). A review of telemental health in international and post-disaster settings. *International Review of Psychiatry, 27*(6), 540–546. https://doi.org/10.3109/09540261.2015.1082985

Barrio-Minton, C. A., & Pease-Carter, C. (2011). Status of crisis preparation. *Journal of Professional Counseling, 38*(2), 5–17. https://doi.org/10.1080/15566382.2011.12033868

Bedi, R. P. (2006). Concept mapping the client's perspective on counseling alliance formation. *Journal of Counseling Psychology, 53*, 26–35. https://psycnet.apa.org/doi/10.1037/0022-0167.53.1.26

Birnbaumer, D. M. (2013, August 2). *A sad performance by the SADPERSONS scale.* NEJM Journal Watch. http://www.jwatch.org/na31829/2013/08/02/sad-performance-sadpersonsscale

Caplan, G. (1964). *Principles of preventive psychiatry.* Basic Books.

Center for Collegiate Mental Health. (2020, January). *2019 annual report* (Publication no. STA 20-244). https://files.eric.ed.gov/fulltext/ED602859.pdf

Collaborative Assessment and Management of Suicidality (CAMS). Frequently Ask Questions. What is CAMS? https://cams-care.com/faqs/

Council for Accreditation of Counseling and Related Educational Programs. (2009). *2009 CACREP standards.* https://www.cacrep.org/wp-content/uploads/2017/07/2009-Standards.pdf

Council for Accreditation of Counseling and Related Educational Programs. (2016). *2016 CACREP standards.* http://www.cacrep.org/wp-content/uploads/2018/05/2016-Standards-with-Glossary-5.3.2018. pdf

Crisis Text Line. (n.d.). *How does crisis text line work?* [Text HOME to 741741]. https://www.crisistextline. org/

Czyz, E. K., Arango, A., Healy, N., King, C. A., & Walton, M. (2020). Augmenting safety planning with text messaging support for adolescents at elevated suicide risk: Development and acceptability study. *JMIR Mental Health, 7*(5), e17345. https://doi.org/10.2196/17345

da Silva, J. A., Siegmund, G., & Bredemeier, J. (2015). Crisis interventions in online psychological counseling. *Trends in psychiatry and psychotherapy, 37*(4), 171–182. https://doi.org/10.1590/ 2237-6089-2014-0026

Everly, G. (2006). *Assisting individuals in crisis* (4th ed.). International Critical Incident Stress Foundation.

Everly, G. (2015). *Assisting individuals in crisis* (5th ed.). International Critical Incident Stress Foundation.

Everly, G. S., Jr. (2020). Psychological first aid (PFA) to expand mental expand mental health support and foster resiliency in underserved and access-compromised areas. *Crisis, Stress, and Human Resilience: An International Journal, 1*(4), 227–232. https://www.crisisjournal.org/ article/12297-psychological-first-aid-pfa-to-expand-mental-health-support-and-foster-resiliency-in-underserved-and-access-compromised-areas

Godleski, L., Nieves, J. E., Darkins, A., & Lehmann, L. (2008). VA telemental health: Suicide assessment. *Behavioral Sciences & the Law, 26*(3), 271–286. https://doi.org/10.1002/bsl.811

Guo, Y., Wang, S., Lok, H. K., Phillips, A., & Statz, S. (2016). Crisis counseling courses in counselor preparation. *VISTAS Online.* https://www.counseling.org/knowledge-center/vistas/by-year2/ vistas-2016/docs/default-source/vistas/article_458bfd25f16116603abcacff0000bee5e7

Hipple, J., & Beamish, P. M. (2007). Supervision of counselor trainees with clients in crisis. *Journal of Professional Counseling: Practice, Theory, & Research, 35*(2), 1–16. https://doi.org/10.1080/15566382.2007. 12033834

International Critical Incidents Stress Foundation. (2020). *SAFER-R revised model of individual crisis intervention.* https://icisf.org/wp-content/uploads/2020/04/SAFER-Revised-Model.pdf

Jackson-Cherry, L. R., & Erford, B. T. (2014). *Crisis assessment, intervention, and prevention* (2nd ed.). Pearson.

James, R. K., & Gilliland B. E. (2017). *Crisis intervention strategies* (8th ed). Cengage.

Jones, A. M., Shealy, K. M., Reid-Quiñones, K., Moreland, A. D., Davidson, T. M., López, C. M., Barr, S. C., & de Arellano, M. A. (2014). Guidelines for establishing a telemental health program to provide evidence-based therapy for trauma-exposed children and families. *Psychological Services, 11*(4), 398–409. https://doi.org/10.1037/a0034963

Juhnke, G. A., & Granello, P. F. (2005). Shattered dreams of professional competence: The impact of client suicides on mental health practitioners and how to prepare for it. *Journal of Creativity in Mental Health, 1*(3/4), 205–223. https://doi.org/10.1300/J456v01n03_12

Kanel, A. (2019). *A guide to crisis intervention* (6th ed). Cengage.

Levine, M. (2020, April 7). *Calls to US helpline jump 891%, as White House is warned of mental health crisis.* ABC News. https://abcnews.go.com/Politics/calls-us-helpline-jump-891-white-house-warned/story?id=70010113

Lindemann, E. (1979). *Beyond grief: Studies in crisis intervention.* Jason Aronson.

Lopez Levers, L. (2012). *Trauma counseling: Theories and interventions.* Springer.

Lum, C. (2010). *Licensure requirements for professional counselors – 2010.* American Counseling Association. https://www.counseling.org/docs/licensure/72903_excerpt_for_web.pdf

Luxton, D. D., Nelson, E., & Maheu, M. M. (2016). *A practitioner's guide to telemental health: How to conduct legal, ethical, and evidence-based telepractice.* American Psychological Association.

MacDonald, D. K. (2016). *Crisis theory and types of crisis.* http://dustinkmacdonald.com/crisis-theory-types-crisis/

Miller, D. N., & Gould, K. (2013). Forgotten founder: Harry Marsh Warren and the history and legacy of the Save-A-Life League. *Suicidology Online, 4,* 12–15. http://www.suicidology-online.com/pdf/SOL-2013-4-12-15.pdf

Morris, C. A., & Minton, C. A. (2012). Crisis in the curriculum? New counselors' crisis preparation, experiences, and self-efficacy. *Counselor Education & Supervision, 51*(4), 256–269. http://dx.doi.org/10.1002/j.1556-6978.2012.00019.x

Myer, R. A., Lewis, J. S., & James, R. K. (2013). The introduction of a task model for crisis intervention. *Journal of Mental Health Counseling, 35*(2), 95–107. https://doi.org/10.17744/mehc.35.2.nh322x3547475154

National Board for Certified Counselors. (2020). *National certified counselor* (NCC). www.nbcc.org/certification/ncc

O'Brien, E., & Hauser, M. (2016). *Supervision and agency management for counselors.* Springer.

Parad, H. J., & Caplan, G. (1960). A framework for studying families in crisis. *Social Work, 5*(3), 3–15. https://doi.org/10.1093/sw/5.3.3

Patterson, W. M., Dohn, H. H., Patterson, J., Patterson, G. A. (1983). Evaluation of Suicidal Patients: The SAD PERSONS scale. *Psychometrics, 24*(4), 343-349. Dio:10.1016/S0033-3182(83)73213-5.

Pérez-Rojas, A. E., Lockard, A. J., Bartholomew, T. T., Janis, R. A., Carney, D. M., Xiao, H., Youn, S. J., Scofield, B. E., Locke, B. D., Castonguay, L. G., & Hayes, J. A. (2017). Presenting concerns in counseling centers: The view from clinicians on the ground. *Psychological Services, 14*(4), 416–427. https://doi.org/10.1037/ser0000122

Robbins, R. (2020). *Coronavirus pandemic sets up potential breakout moment for virtual mental health care.* STAT. https://www.statnews.com/2020/04/13/remote-mental-health-livongo-omada/

Rosen, C. S., Glassman, L. H., & Morland, L. A. (2020). Telepsychotherapy during a pandemic: A traumatic stress perspective. *Journal of Psychotherapy Integration, 30*(2), 174–187. http://dx.doi.org/10.1037/int0000221

Sandoval, J., Scott, A. N., & Padilla, I. (2009). Crisis counseling: An overview. *Psychology in the Schools, 46*(3), 246–256. https://doi.org/10.1002/pits.20370

Saunders, K., Brand, F., Lascelles, K., & Hawton, K. (2013). The sad truth about the SADPERSONS scale: An evaluation of its clinical utility in self-harm patients. *Emergency Medicine Journal.* https://doi.org/10.1136/emermed-2013-202781

Smith, H. B. (2006). Providing mental health services to clients in crisis or disaster situations. *VISTAS Online, 3,* 13–15. https://www.counseling.org/docs/default-source/vistas/providing-mental-health-services-to-clients-in-crisis-or-disaster-situations.pdf?sfvrsn=17dd7e2c_10

Trepal, H., Haberstroh, S., Duffey, T., & Evans, M. (2007). Considerations and strategies for teaching online counseling skills: Establishing relationships in cyberspace. *Counselor Education & Supervision, 46*(4), 266–279. https://doi.org/10.1002/j.1556-6978.2007.tb00031.x

Turley, B. (2013). Crisis support: The legacy and future of Helplines. *Australia: Lifelines.* https://www.lifeline.org.au/media/j12j5jmt/crisis-support-the-legacy-and-future-of-helplines-2013.pdf

World Health Organization. (2019). *Mental health in emergencies.* https://www.who.int/news-room/fact-sheets/detail/mental-health-in-emergencies

Yeager, K. R., & Roberts, A. R. (2005). Crisis intervention for persons diagnosed with clinical disorders based on the stress-crisis continuum. In A. R. Roberts (Ed.), *Crisis intervention handbook: Assessment, treatment, and research* (3rd ed.) (pp. 90–119). Oxford University Press.

Special Groups, Populations, and Considerations

Counseling for Diverse and Vulnerable Populations

Michelle Harrision, Erin Lofties, and Shara Goudreau

All people deserve equal access to and use of professional counseling services. The recent expansion and use of telebehavioral health have magnified the opportunities for individuals, who traditionally experienced numerous obstacles, to receive quality and specialized mental health services. Current research indicates the use of telebehavioral health helps to fill a gap in treatment among underserved communities and individuals when seeking counseling. Studies have been conducted that reflect the benefits of telebehavioral health in rural communities (Mahmoud et al., 2018; Sorocco et al., 2013; Turvey, 2018) and with veterans (Goss et al., 2017; Shore et al., 2014), both populations benefiting greatly from distance counseling. Multiple benefits of telebehavioral health have been identified, including improved access, decreased stigma, improved client outcomes, convenience, and economic benefits (Luxton et al., 2016), all notably relevant for the diverse populations discussed in this chapter. **Stigma** is the experience of prejudice, discrimination, or social shame associated with having a negatively perceived identity, status, or attribute. Clients can experience **stigmatizing** behavior, or the process of becoming disgrace or inviting blame.

Understanding the unique needs of each client, as well as the multicultural, ethical, and social justice responsibilities that apply, remains constant regardless of the format of the counseling, but those working online need to be proficient with the necessary modifications to best address considerations consistently and effectively. One of the exciting aspects of utilizing telebehavioral health for these unique populations is that many of the evidence-based techniques and theories recommended for use in treatment are easily transferable and adaptable for use with the online format. The diverse populations explored include individuals with attention deficit hyperactivity disorder (ADHD), those living in rural communities, veterans, the LGBTQIA+ population, and other vulnerable populations, such as those who have experienced trauma through human trafficking, sexual assault, and intimate partner violence. Each of these populations faces barriers when pursing counseling, many of which may be overcome through online synchronous counseling. Counselors can learn to modify their fundamental skills and apply best therapeutic practices specific to these diverse populations in order to serve these clients in the online synchronous format.

Serving Diverse Populations Using Telebehavioral Health

Luxton et al. (2016) described numerous benefits of telebehavioral health applicable to serving diverse populations, including easily assessable services, increasing privacy and decreasing stigma, improved client outcomes, convenience of services, and economic benefits. Telebehavioral health offers mental health services in real time (Luxton et al., 2016) without requiring counselor and client to be in the same office (Turvey, 2018). Telebehavioral health allows clients who may not otherwise have access or who fear stigma in their community to bypass the traditional clinical setting (Luxton et al., 2016). In a review of the effectiveness of telebehavioral health, Hilty et al. (2013) concluded telebehavioral health services are "unquestionably effective in most regards" (p. 451), not only for client outcomes but also for diagnosis and assessment, for a variety of populations, and in multiple settings, quelling concerns that it is inferior to traditional, face-to-face counseling. Additionally, Hilty et al. found telebehavioral health to be equivalent to in-person care and to enhance primary care services.

Telebehavioral health offers multiple conveniences for diverse populations, including increased hours of available services, opportunities to check in with clients, collaborative opportunities with families, and creating an environment that supports treatment (Luxton et al., 2016). Other benefits and conveniences for diverse and vulnerable populations may decrease travel expenses and lost wages, may remove the cost of child or elder care, and may reduce expenses associated with seeking specialty services (Luxton et al., 2016). Nonmonetary costs, such as stress navigating unfamiliar cities and health care facilities, are also reduced (Luxton et al., 2016).

Multicultural, Social Justice, and Ethical Considerations

Counselors are required by the code of ethics (American Counseling Association [ACA], 2014) to practice cultural sensitivity and carefully consider how "clients' problems are defined and experienced" (Standard E.5.b.). The impact of their "socioeconomic and cultural experiences" when developing treatment plans (Standard E.5.b.) should also be considered. When working with diverse populations, it is especially important to be cognizant of multiple ethical and cultural considerations respectful of client diversity, and to not impose personal values (ACA, 2014, Standard A.4.b.). Additionally, it is essential to understand the impact of the client's culture on the meaning of confidentiality and privacy when working with any population, especially veterans, the LGBTQIA+ population, and vulnerable populations (ACA, 2014, Standard B.1.a.). Standard A.7.a. states that counselors advocate and address barriers that prevent access for clients, while Section C.5 identifies that counselors are ethically obligated to ensure accessible and competent counseling for marginalized populations and not "condone or engage in discrimination" (ACA, 2014, p. 9).

Counselors consider cultural and educational barriers and ensure the informed consent, which communicates the purpose, benefits, limitations, and scope of confidentiality of counseling, is clear and understandable (ACA, 2014, Standard A.2.a) and specifically addresses online considerations. Informed consent is explored in detail in Chapter 3. Clients may process the consent form more efficiently when it matches their preferred learning style, such as visual, auditory, and tactile (Fatahi et al., 2018), so different learning styles should be taken into consideration when discussing the informed consent. "Most people prefer an identifiable method of interacting with, taking in, and processing stimuli or information" (Abbas, 2012, p. 51).

In choosing to work with unique populations, the counselor may need additional training and supervision that ensures the counselor is able to address the client's individual needs (ACA, 2014, Standard C.2.a; Standard C.2.f). The counselor needs to be aware of how their own personal cultural background, experiences, values, and attitudes, may bias or influence ethical practices with clients. Practicing telebehavioral health may introduce a wider variety of clientele for counselors, potentially necessitating additional training. For example, counselors may lack the knowledge to properly work with clients' specific needs and experiences (Luxton et al., 2016) and lack advanced training to understand the needs of clients from various cultural and ethnic groups. For instance, trafficked individuals or people with complex trauma may require the counselor to receive specialized training to address very specific treatment needs. For example, many providers gain certifications, like certified trauma treatment specialist (CTTS) or eye movement desensitization and reprocessing (EMDR), when working with individuals from these populations. Counselors may lack the knowledge to properly work with clients' specific needs and experiences in a telebehavioral health setting and be beyond their scope of expertise (Luxton et al., 2016). Therefore, additional training in diversity and working with especially vulnerable populations is strongly encouraged.

Counseling Services for Diverse Populations

Special populations require additional considerations when counseling in the online platform. Clients diagnosed with ADHD, living in rural areas, identifying with the LGBTQIA+ population, or those who are military veterans will be addressed, identifying the areas that will need to be addressed for online counseling.

Telebehavioral Health and Clients With ADHD

Access to mental health care providers with specialty training in ADHD is limited for individuals outside of metropolitan areas (Vander Stoep et al., 2017). According to the researchers, this gap is filled by primary care physicians (PCPs) who diagnose and prescribe medications and by community therapists who provide psychotherapy. Research indicates that most PCPs are not providing pharmacological treatments consistent with best-practice guidelines (McCarty et al., 2015; Vander Stoep et al., 2017) and most therapists are not providing evidence-based behavioral interventions recommended for ADHD treatment (Vander Stoep et al., 2017). Furthermore, PCPs still need assistance in treating children with ADHD, especially with more severe or comorbid conditions (McCarty et al., 2015). Vander Stoep et al. (2017) state, "New models of care are needed to bring child mental health expertise to underserved communities and to promote the delivery of evidence-based mental health treatments" (p. 28). Telebehavioral health offers greater access to counselors with expertise in ADHD, expanding the reach into previously underserved and remote areas.

Telebehavioral health provides equal access to treatment by helping to "redistribute the workforce and to correct disparities in children's access to needed mental health care" (Myers et al., 2013, p. 372). Systemic barriers, including distance to services, access to transportation, scheduling conflicts, childcare needs, and limited specialty services, can be overcome with telebehavioral health services (Sibley et al., 2017). Logistical challenges associated with face-to-face meetings among various professionals, the client, and family can be reduced and removed, allowing for easier collaboration in developing individualized education plans (IEPs) and behavioral plans for ADHD youth (Palmer et al., 2010). Furthermore, telebehavioral health provides access to correctional facilities where ADHD youth make up a large percentage of incarcerated individuals (Palmer et al., 2010).

Another benefit of telebehavioral health is providing treatment within real-world settings where the ADHD impairment occurs, thus improving the "ecological validity of care" (Sibley et al., 2017, p. 469), and could include symptoms related to ADHD or family and relational issues. This modality reduces "reported stigma associated with physical visits to mental health services" (Hollis et al., 2017, p. 474), allowing the individual to receive needed services while eliminating psychosocial barriers to treatment. Videoconferencing is the preferred way to provide telebehavioral health services. This delivery modality for teens with ADHD has shown to be as effective as face-to-face delivery in reducing symptoms of ADHD in participants as acknowledged by parents and teachers (Sibley et al., 2017). This study noted additional benefits of videoconferencing such as fewer cancellations, a better fit for the family schedule, removing the distance, and beginning sessions on time. Considering the various benefits and access to empirically supported mental health care support, telebehavioral health may remove many barriers to treatment for individuals with ADHD. Traditional face-to-face approaches commonly used with individuals with ADHD are easily transferable to the online environment. A discussion of these modalities is included in discussions of therapeutic approaches and techniques in this chapter.

Telebehavioral Health in Rural Communities

Research indicates multiple barriers often prevent individuals living in remote and rural areas from accessing and receiving mental health services (Luxton et al., 2016; Mahmoud et al., 2018; Simms et al., 2011; Turvey, 2018). A significant barrier is the known shortage of psychiatrists, psychologists, and specialty mental health providers for patients who live in a rural community (Lambert et al., 2015; Luxton et al., 2016; Mahmoud et al., 2018). Mahmoud et al. (2018) reported "up to 75% of the rural population of the United States does not have access to mental health clinicians" (p. 1). Higher rates of unemployment and poverty, the loss of wages when missing work, and the extra cost and stress of traveling out of town for services (Mahmoud et al., 2018; Simms et al., 2011), as well as lack of mental health insurance and limitations on transportation (Luxton et al., 2016), are additional barriers. Luxton et al. and Mahmoud et al. also identify a concern for confidentiality and being stigmatized for seeking services as barriers in rural and small communities.

Telebehavioral health removes several barriers that prevent patients in remote and rural areas from seeking mental health services. By providing services to patients in their homes by way of technology, geographical deterrents are eliminated (Turvey, 2018). As such, patients in rural communities have increased accessibility to a variety of providers and services. Examples include access to specialty services that offer multilingual practitioners (Mahmoud et al., 2018; Turvey, 2018), and Luxton et al. (2016) note the ability to connect with professionals who provide services for specific cultures such as military personnel and veterans, the elderly, or specific ethnic groups isolated by location. Remaining within a familiar, comfortable environment may relieve inhibitions, reduce stress, and improve treatment outcomes (Luxton et al., 2016). Staying within the home for counseling increases a sense of privacy and provides protection from stigma (Luxton et al., 2016; Mahmoud et al., 2018; Simms et al., 2011), a fear often felt by individuals in rural communities. Additionally, growing literature indicates the quality of telebehavioral health services and client satisfaction equals in-person services (Lambert et al., 2015; Zeren, 2015). Counselors may need, however, to advocate for high-speed internet action in their state's rural communities.

Telebehavioral Health and the LGBTQIA+ Populations

There is a significant need for mental health counseling for **LGBTQIA+** individuals and families, as LGBTQIA+ clients experience a higher rate of trauma, mood disorders, anxiety, and substance use disorders than the cisgender or heterosexual populations (Pachankis et al., 2020; Scheer et al., 2020; Yule et al., 2013). The stigma-related stressors often experienced by individuals may explain the disparity in mental health and wellness compared to the **cisgender** or heterosexual populations (Pachankis et al., 2020). **Transgender** individuals experience self-harm, disordered eating, and suicidal ideation at higher rates than cisgender individuals (Lefevor et al., 2019), while facing the additional barrier of finding competent, accepting medical and mental health providers. Sexual minorities report higher incidences of childhood sexual and physical abuse (Scheer et al., 2020). This is likely due to LGBTQ children being more vulnerable as a marginalized group and more likely to be homeless, discriminated against, and lacking a healthy support system. **Asexual** individuals, according to some studies, report higher levels of social withdrawal and interpersonal difficulties, perhaps due to society's expectation that all humans are innately interested in sex (Yule et al., 2013). **Bisexual** individuals are more likely to live at or below the federal poverty rate than other sexual orientations (Vencill et al., 2018), which not only carries its own stressors but in turn makes traditional counseling potentially prohibitive. Bisexual individuals are also more likely to hide their orientation from providers or receive negative evaluations from medical providers in cases in which they have disclosed sexual orientation (Vencill et al., 2018). Unfortunately, research is still lacking in some areas, particularly in nonbinary gender identity (Lefevor et al., 2019), and thus practitioners who are lacking firsthand knowledge and experience may initially struggle to understand their client's world. LGBTQIA+ individuals of color may experience a toxic combination of challenges including racism within the LGBTQIA+ community, **cissexism** (discrimination against transgender people), and heterosexism in communities of color, and sexism-driven interpersonal abuse (Scheer et al., 2020).

Some of the challenges linked to LGBTQIA+ mental health issues, such as poverty, unstable housing, lack of family support, and discrimination, may also make seeking counseling, online or face-to-face, more difficult. LGBTQIA+ youths are at an increased risk for homelessness, for example (Rusow et al., 2018). This is magnified for LGBTQIA+ individuals who are also members of other marginalized communities, such as communities of color or rural communities. LGBTQIA+ individuals may also hesitate to seek any services due to internalized stigma and phobia, as well as fear of being outed (Veltman & La Rose, 2019). Furthermore, there are still few interventions specifically designed for LGBTQIA+ individuals and the unique challenges they face (Pachankis et al., 2020).

Online counseling provides LGBTQIA+ individuals greater access to trained professionals outside their local community. Clients may fear being "outed" to their family, job, or church (Derrig-Palumbo & Zeine, 2005), and thus having a counselor in another city or part of the state may provide the client an extra sense of privacy. Similarly, seeking a counselor within a small community could be especially uncomfortable if the client is nervous about having to see their counselor outside the office (Luxton et al., 2016). Online counseling provides a sense of professional boundaries and autonomy so that the client does not feel compelled to come out before they are ready.

Despite the requirements of the ACA code of ethics, clients may still come across counselors in traditional settings who are unable or unwilling to treat them, often due to religious beliefs (Minnix, 2018). Online counseling allows clients to work with counselors who are willing, trained, and understanding of the cultural components of the LGBTQIA+ population. Online counseling increases access to affirmative counseling. **Affirmative counseling** embraces a scientific perspective that LGBTQIA+ relationships are normal and healthy expressions of affection and human relationships (Robertson & Avent, 2016). Affirmative counseling is an essential component of counselor competence (Minnix, 2018), though this is not always put into practice.

The online platform may also allow counselors to share resources such as websites, articles, and online support groups with clients. While a counselor in a small community may only be familiar with local resources, the telehealth professional can help the client search for clinics, shelters, and specialists, such as voice coaches who assist transgender clients in modifying their vocalizations to match their gender identity. Screen sharing, available through some platforms, can allow both parties to look at the resource together and explore the client's thoughts and feelings during the session.

Telebehavioral Health and Veterans

Veterans often struggle to access mental health services, and the challenges increase if living in rural communities (Shore et al., 2014). Of all veterans, 23% reside in rural communities, (U.S. Department of Veterans Affairs [VA], Office of Rural Health [ORH], 2015). Shore et al. (2014) reports a disparity in health-related quality-of-life scores amongst rural veterans compared to urban veterans, which may be related to access to mental health care. In a study focusing on rural American Indian (AI) and Alaska Native (AN) veterans, Goss et al. (2017) noted a distrust of the Veteran Association and the complexities and impact of the veteran's culture as barriers.

Another significant barrier for veterans is convenient access to veteran clinics (Shore et al., 2014; Sorocco et al., 2013). Like those in rural communities, the cost of traveling out of town to access specialized care and feeling stigmatized for seeking services (Shore et al., 2014) are additional barriers. Veterans often suffer from mood disorders, anxiety disorders, and substance use, as well as posttraumatic stress syndrome (PTSS) (Chen et al., 2019). Finding a local Veteran Health Administration (VHA) facility with qualified mental health providers can be a challenge (Chen et al., 2019).

Shore et al. (2014) acknowledge veterans' perceptions of safety are an important component for care and may be another barrier to seeking mental health services.

Telebehavioral health addresses the geographical barrier and relieves the burden of traveling in order to seek mental health services (Chen et al., 2019). In a survey of 34 veterans who experienced home-based telebehavioral health, 91% reported preferring using telebehavioral health versus traveling to see a provider (Shore et al., 2014). These veterans also reported feeling safe while using telebehavioral health. Goss et al. (2017) discuss a model for patient care that benefits AI and AN veterans by increasing opportunity and continuity of care, as well as incorporating cultural and spiritual components into treatment. A pilot study conducted by Sorocco et al. (2013) incorporated telebehavioral health into a comprehensive service for rural veterans who were previously ineligible for home-based primary care. In this study, veterans met psychotherapeutic goals via telebehavioral health services and the authors concluded "telemental health works" (Sorocco et al., 2013, p. 352).

The VA endorses online counseling, or telebehavioral health, for its veterans. In fact, the VA has a separate website dedicated to assisting veterans in exploring telehealth options (see Additional Online Resources at the end of the chapter), describing what it is, the types of telehealth available to them, and how it works. Growing research indicates an array of treatments to address veteran mental health needs can be effective via the telebehavioral health platform (Chen et al., 2019). Evidence-based therapeutic practices such as trauma-informed care, motivational interviewing, and solution-focused therapy often used to treat veterans are adaptable to the online format. Applications of these practices online to specific populations are discussed later in this chapter.

Vulnerable Populations

Human trafficking, sexual assault, and intimate partner violence survivors require additional considerations in the online platform. Human trafficking survivors may face language and economic barriers. When working with a survivor of intimate partner violence, safety will need to be addressed.

Telebehavioral Health and Human Trafficking Survivors

Human trafficking is defined as the intentional and illegal transporting of a person from one country or one area to another for the purpose of forced labor or sexual exploitation. Research that focuses on the barriers for human trafficking survivors to access mental health services is limited, but those identified are similar to what rural communities, veterans, and the LGBTQIA+ populations encounter. Just as these populations face limited access to qualified mental health providers and resources, it is difficult for survivors to connect with specialized providers and resources (Bocinski, 2017). Access to multilingual providers and specialty services sensitive to ethnic and cultural needs is an identified barrier for trafficked individuals (Bosinski, 2017). Survivors, like many veterans, struggle finding and maintaining employment according to the authors, limiting economic resources to access providers. Stress from traveling for services, loss of work, cost of providing childcare, and navigating new and unfamiliar places in order to receive services are additional obstacles for survivors (Bocinski, 2017).

Like veterans, PTSD is a prevalent diagnosis for human trafficking survivors (Hemmings et al., 2016; Levine, 2017) and because of the trauma incurred, feeling safe is important. While veterans distrust the VA, survivors similarly struggle to trust service providers and individuals in authority (Litam, 2017; Ross-Sheriff & Orme, 2015). Similar to individuals in rural communities, survivors are concerned about protecting their privacy (sometimes related to their safety) and being stigmatized (Litam, 2017). Additionally, victims of trafficking and intimate partner violence may be forced or coerced by a family member or a partner to engage in sexual acts for the family member or partner's financial gain (Verhoeven et al., 2015). Counselors are currently undertrained and equipped to assess, identify, and meet the needs of human trafficking survivors (Thompson & Haley, 2018), making access to those who are trained even more difficult. Online counseling offers access to counselors trained to address the special needs of persons who have experienced trafficking.

Telebehavioral health counselors need to also consider how vulnerable populations may face language barriers and advocate for the client to have the resources to ensure the client is able to understand the informed consent. Human trafficking survivors often face language barriers and educational disadvantages (Clawson et al., 2008). Research indicates that among minors who have been trafficked, schooling is often interrupted or denied, and the impact of trauma deters their learning (Bocinski, 2017). Advocating for online educational services may be necessary and part of the treatment plan.

Though the research is expanding, there is a recognized lack of evidence-based research on accessing and attending to the mental health needs of this population (Domoney et al., 2015; Levine, 2017; Litam, 2017). Human trafficking is a complex and complicated social justice issue. The potential benefits of online telebehavioral health for trafficking survivors seeking aid in recovery seem similar to the benefits identified in the research for online counseling with rural populations and veterans discussed earlier in this chapter. Online therapy may provide survivors more access to counselors who have specialty training in understanding how to address mental health issues specific to survivors.

Utilizing the online format may increase the survivor's sense of control over their environment and increase feelings of safety because they are in their own home during the counseling session. It also provides a layer of privacy important to survivors. Building and creating trust and safety are key components of trauma-informed care, essential for providing care to this population (Litam, 2017; Ross-Sheriff & Orme, 2015). Telebehavioral health provides the client unique autonomy in the counseling relationship and may relieve fear of stigmatization and self-disclosure (Zeren, 2015). Additionally, online counseling removes the cost and the potential inconveniences involved with travel, navigating large cities or care facilities, hiring childcare, and sometimes loss of work involved with an office appointment (Luxton et al., 2016; Zeren, 2015).

Telebehavioral Health and Intimate Partner Violence and Sexual Assault Survivors

The Centers for Disease Control and Prevention (CDC) estimates that one in three women and one in four men will experience physical violence and/or sexual violence by a partner and sexual violence by someone who is not a partner, and the numbers are higher when psychological abuse is included (Berry et al., 2020). Women are at a higher risk for experiencing severe violence and thus for mental health consequences (Clark et al., 2018). Young people are at an especially high risk. One study found approximately 80% of college students report experiencing psychological abuse in at least one relationship (Ross et al., 2019). Approximately 25% of rural women experience intimate partner violence, a higher rate than suburban and urban women (Gray et al., 2015). People in abusive relationships with children may be reluctant to leave for a number of reasons, including financial dependence and fear of putting their children in unknown situations (Clark et al., 2018).

Intimate partner violence (IPV), sometimes a form of **domestic violence**, has been linked to anxiety, depression, and dysfunctional attachments (Ross et al., 2019). Sexual violence within the domestic relationship is associated with increased prevalence of PTSD and comorbid conditions such as anxiety, depression and substance abuse (Hamrick & Owens, 2018). Children exposed to intimate partner violence are 25% more likely develop PTSD than their peers (Paul, 2019). The chronic nature of intimate partner violence impacts survivors differently than other trauma, such as natural disasters, and it has an effect on development (Paul, 2019). Adult survivors of adverse childhood experiences are more likely to develop risky health behaviors and chronic disease (Hargreaves et al., 2019).

Technology allows abusers to track victims in new ways, including spending, phone and text records, and location (Berry et al., 2020). Counselors may want to go over additional confidentiality considerations with clients, including having a private space to meet and how to navigate potential concerns such as a partner seeing appointment reminder texts, teletherapy apps, and log-ins. If a victim is unable to leave the house or has to leave the house under the guise of running other errands, telebehavioral health could provide a new avenue to treatment. Counselors working online may also be more easily able to provide sessions outside of typical office hours, which in turn may help clients who need to talk when their partner is not present. Clients and counselor will need to confirm privacy to ensure the client's partner is not present, eavesdropping, or likely to suddenly intrude during the session, by asking the client to use a code word if they are not able to talk openly. For example, the client may ask the counselor how their dog is, when both parties know the counselor does not have a dog. Counselors may also provide case management and quickly link the clients to resources such as psychoeducational articles, advocacy organizations, or legal help.

Through this online format, counselors can provide psychoeducation about relationship red flags and equality in relationships, as well as referrals to local domestic violence organizations for shelter or advocacy. Counselors can assess for relationship dynamics in session if they are unclear about the nature of the client's family life. Because many women from this population suffer from lowered self-esteem (Tutty et al., 2016), counselors can explore how clients feel about themselves, as well as explore thoughts and feelings about future relationships. Of course, counselors will need to be aware and make clear the duty to report violence toward, or in the presence of, a minor based on local laws. The counselor will need to have a protocol ready for such situations. This is discussed and outlined in detail in Chapter 3.

Therapeutic Approaches and Techniques

There are a number of therapeutic approaches and techniques adaptable to use online with individuals in rural communities, with veterans, individuals with ADHD, and the LBGTQIA+ and vulnerable populations. For instance, psychoeducation can be used to assist any of these populations.

Adaptable online, counselors can share worksheets and review diagrams and psychoeducational materials, such as identifying PTSD symptoms, providing coping skills, identifying cycles of abuse, or teaching calming techniques in session. Face-to-face group therapy is sometimes utilized for these populations, especially trauma survivors (van der Kolk, 2014). While the use of online groups is still developing, many online platforms are not secure and group counseling must be conducted in a secure and safe environment. Group counseling at a distance is covered in detail in Chapter 12.

Though not limited to the approaches discussed in this section, the following therapies and techniques are known evidence-based approaches that could be utilized and adapted online to use with clients in these vulnerable populations. These therapeutic approaches include trauma-informed care, cognitive behavioral therapy (CBT), solution-focused brief therapy (SFBT), motivational interviewing (MI), narrative therapy and other creative approaches. Eye movement desensitization reprocessing (EMDR) has been adapted for use online and dialectic behavioral therapy (DBT) techniques are easily applied at a distance. Treatment protocols for ADHD include a combination of psychosocial treatments and pharmacotherapy (Rockhill, et al., 2013; Usami, 2016). While pharmacotherapy is outside the scope of this chapter, various psychosocial treatments will be explored.

Trauma-Informed Care

The impact of trauma is prevalent among the populations discussed in this chapter. Violence, abuse, neglect, loss, war, disasters, and other emotionally damaging experiences cause trauma (Substance Abuse and Mental Health Services Administration [SAMHSA], 2014). SAMHSA defines trauma as a result of "an event, series of events, or set of circumstances that is experienced by an individual as physically or emotionally harmful or life threatening and that has lasting adverse effects on the individual's functioning and mental, physical, social, emotional, or spiritual well-being" (p. 7). SAMHSA describes a trauma-informed approach that operates from four assumptions and six key principles, from which both the counselor and the organization the counselor works for can use as a framework for assessing and treating an individual. The core assumptions of **trauma-informed care** include *realizing* the possibility of trauma impacting the client; being trained to recognize the signs and symptoms of trauma; *responding* by integrating trauma-informed assessments and policies into the whole culture of the organization and treatment provision; and actively resisting re-traumatizing the client. The trauma-informed approach builds on resiliency in recovery and is culturally sensitive. SAMHSA (2014) identifies six key principles of trauma-informed care to be safety; trustworthiness and transparency; peer support; collaboration and mutuality; empowerment, voice and choice; and cultural, historical and gender issues. Trauma-informed care can be implemented through telebehavioral health as easily as it is face-to-face.

The Adverse Childhood Experience (ACE) screening is becoming known as an integral part of trauma-informed care (Schulman & Maul, 2019). Counselors must be trained in the screening process with the intention of incorporating information gained in a useful and positive manner into the client's overall therapeutic plan. Cultural sensitivity is also important when using the ACE screening tool or any trauma screen with a client. As in person, adapting a trauma-informed approach to counseling and using the ACE screening tool are all easily utilized online with clients. Trauma-informed care also means being able to refer to multiple services and collaborate with other providers in order to address multiple adverse effects trauma has on the client (Schulman

& Maul, 2019), such as referring the client for EMDR or to a 12-step group in the community or online for support with recovery. Having a trauma-informed approach means the counselor understands that something happened to the client that had an adverse impact, and not seeing the client as having something wrong that needs to be fixed. Telebehavioral health does not prevent the counselor from having this trauma framework to work from with clients described in this chapter. Adaptions include ensuring the client feels safe and can develop a trusting and transparent relationship with the counselor in the online format. Rapport-building skills are discussed in Chapter 2. The counselor should be able to connect the client with other peers in their local community for support, either through online groups or in person. Safety is a tremendous factor and can be established through various techniques such as turning cameras around so that everyone knows the meeting is private, establishing code words, and having excellent crisis plans in place, as discussed in Chapter 8. Clients who have experienced trauma must establish safety, develop coping skills, and understand dysregulation. The skills utilized to accomplish these goals are applicable face-to-face and at a distance.

Cognitive Behavioral Therapy

Research highlights the successful adaptation of cognitive behavioral strategies to the telebehavioral health format, possibly because of its skill-focused approach and practicality (Luxton et al., 2016), sometimes involving apps that the client can use outside of the session, rather than pen-and-paper homework. Cognitive trauma therapy, sometimes known as cognitive trauma therapy for battered women (CTT-BW) was developed specifically for survivors of IPV and includes psychoeducation, exposure, and cognitive restructuring (Allard et al., 2018). As a treatment, it has been shown to be highly effective at decreasing PTSD symptoms (Beck et al., 2016).

Cognitive behavioral therapy (CBT) has also proven effective in the treatment of PTSD in interpersonal violence survivors (Iverson et al., 2011) and decreasing PTSD symptoms (Tambling, 2012), though literature covering the application of CBT to sexual assault and intimate partner violence survivors is still limited. The literature supports the use of CBT and behavioral therapy with children and adults with ADHD. CBT that focuses on planning skills with adolescents has been shown to reduce behavioral symptoms of ADHD 1 year after treatment has ended (Boyer et al., 2016). Various skills training included in CBT and behavioral approaches such as organization, planning and time management, cognitive reappraisal strategies, mindfulness meditation (Knouse et al., 2017), and social skills training (Sinacola et al., 2020) are effective in reducing behavioral symptoms of ADHD in adults (Nimmo-Smith et al., 2020). Interventions, including cognitive remediation therapy, problem solving, cognitive restructuring, and behavioral change, have also been associated in reducing symptoms of ADHD in adults (Nimmo-Smith et al., 2020). Third-wave therapies, such as mindfulness-based cognitive therapy (MBCT) and dialectical behavioral therapy (DBT) that teach mindful awareness help redirect attention to the present and help regulate emotion in adults (Nimmo-Smith et al., 2020) and children (Evans et al., 2018). Additionally, involving parents of children with ADHD in mindfulness practices can increase awareness and acceptance of their child's needs that may allow for more enjoyment and satisfaction in the parent-child relationship and less externalizing behaviors of the child (Evans et al., 2018). CBT was developed from theories of memory and learning and utilizes systematic procedures (Lee & Edget, 2012).

Traditional cognitive behavioral therapy has the client identify, question, and replace unhelpful thoughts (Geschwind et al., 2020).

Trauma-focused CBT (TF-CBT) is a structured, phase-based model designed for children and adolescents as well as their caregivers (Cohen et al., 2018), though it may be modified for adult survivors. CBT is an effective treatment for a variety of mental health concerns including depression, anxiety, and suicidal ideation, but it is important that CBT be modified to address minority stressors such as those faced by the LGBTQIA+ community (Austin & Craig, 2015).

Online CBT, or internet-based CBT, is also known as iCBT. Internet-based CBT is efficacious for many diverse clients (Lawlor-Savage & Prentice, 2014). Online messaging can reduce client discomfort around awkward or deeply personal questions (Lawlor-Savage & Prentice, 2014) as clients explore their thought patterns and behaviors. Some iCBT programs provide automated steps and interactions, giving the client a chance to work at their own pace and gain additional help outside time with the counselor.

Solution-Focused Brief Therapy

The solution-focused brief therapy (SFBT) approach assumes that the client is the expert and a resourceful person (Winbolt, 2011). Solution-focused therapists pay attention to word usage and focus on ways to use supportive language (Tambling, 2012). Additionally, SFBT focuses on three components of the client's life: abilities and strengths, the present and future, and successes (Winbolt, 2011). The counselor and client identify baby steps that the client can take to reach their goals (Geschwind et al., 2020). Rather than focusing on the problem, the counselor helps the client look at the successes and strengths, which in turn may help the client find new approaches and ways to tackle a situation (Winbolt, 2011). At this time, very little literature exists related to the application of SFBT online. Modifications to SFBT via telehealth could include sharing journals, checklists, and psychoeducational resources with clients. This information can be shared through a secured connection between the counselor and client in real time or in advance of a scheduled session. While traditional SFBT works with many populations, it may not be appropriate for sexual assault and DV/IPV survivors as this may lead to re-traumatization or triggering (Yoshimura & Campbell, 2016). Counselors should use a trauma-informed approach and be mindful that the SFBT may not be a good fit for these individuals.

Motivational Interviewing

Miller and Rollnick (2013) define motivational interviewing (MI) as "a collaborative conversation style for strengthening a person's own motivation and commitment to change" (p. 12). In MI, **ambivalence** is seen as the central barrier to change and is explored with the client. There are several key components of MI that work well with the special populations described in this chapter. These are described in what Miller and Rollnick call the "MI Spirit" (p. 13) and include acceptance, collaboration, evocation, and compassion. The overall style of MI is *guiding,* but also integrates directing and following the client. The counselor respectfully meets the client where they are and fosters an environment for change. MI is client centered and the counselor values acceptance, which includes unconditional positive regard, empathy, autonomy, and affirmation. Further, MI is nonjudgmental and nonauthoritarian. The client is considered the expert about their experiences and self. The counselor explores what is important to the client and does not make assumptions. In MI, the client welfare and needs are prioritized. These elements communicate honoring the independence of the client, an important factor for each of the populations identified in this chapter. Respecting client autonomy and being client centered build a sense of safety and trust in the relationship, central to trauma-informed care and a component of TF-CBT.

The VA (n.d.) endorses MI as a brief, evidence-based, goal-directed therapeutic approach that helps veterans to build on personal strengths to improve their lives. MI helps clients change or adapt behavior and has been successful treating a variety of health and behavioral issues, such as gambling, substance use, quality of life, and approach to change and treatment (Frost et al., 2018; Hettema et al., 2005; Yakovenko et al., 2015). MI may help determine whether a client is ready to leave a DV or IPV situation. Motivational interviewing can decrease ambivalence and increase confidence, which can help IPV survivors make changes such as leaving an abusive relationship (Hughes & Rasmussen, 2010). A recent study by Gerassi and Esbenson (2020) noted providers who work with sex trafficking victims should be trained in using MI. The techniques used for MI are easy to implement with the client online. Asking open-ended questions, setting goals, practicing empathy, and developing the client's self-efficacy can all be accomplished in the online setting. Motivational interviewing allows the client to do problem solving and self-reflecting with the counselor (Hughes & Rasmussen, 2010). Online counseling with a shared screen option or secure messaging can allow clients to look at questions and pros and cons lists and process questions and possibilities with the counselor. MI is a transtheoretical approach that can easily be used online and integrated with many theories.

Narrative Therapy and Other Creative Approaches

Narrative therapy allows clients to give voice to their trauma, reconsider identity conclusions, and place hope in the present (Augusta-Scott & Brown, 2007). Narrative therapists help clients to explore the stories they tell themselves about their lives and, when needed, change the stories to be more helpful (Abels & Abels, 2001). One of the major components of narrative therapy is the conversational map. **The conversational map** is comprised of five components: inquiry, the backstory, pivotal events, evaluation of effects, and the summary (Augusta-Scott & Brown, 2007). The process of re-authoring in narrative therapy allows clients to reconstruct unhelpful stories into more useful ones (Augusta-Scott & Brown, 2007). Narrative therapy for telehealth is still largely unresearched, but the format may allow the counselor and client to look over text versions of client narrative and explore key words, ideas, and themes together.

Eye Movement Desensitization Reprocessing (EMDR)

The American Psychiatric Association (APA), U.S. Department of Defense, and World Health Organization (WHO) all endorse **eye movement desensitization reprocessing** (EMDR) as a therapeutic approach for treating PTSD and traumatized victims (Shapiro, 2014); while research supporting the use of EMDR online is only beginning, it has been positive. Similar to TF-CBT, EMDR seeks to help the client experience reduced subjective distressing perceptions and increase positive cognitions connected to the traumatic experience (Shaprio, 2014). Although EMDR requires specific training and certification, an EMDR-trained therapist will weave the basic counseling skills used to address trauma into the online therapeutic plan, such as teaching mindfulness exercises for grounding and identifying cognitive perceptions of a traumatic event. The **floatback technique** (Shapiro, 1996) is adaptable to the online setting when the counselor helps the client identify and associate earlier events with a current disturbing event. Additionally, helping the client to recognize and become aware of how they are feeling in their body is another component of EMDR that is adaptable to online counseling. Similar to educating the client to identify feelings, identifying somatic sensations connected to thoughts can be a tool that helps the client understand and recognize triggers related to their trauma (van der Kolk, 2014). Although there are many providers utilizing the full EMDR protocol via telehealth and even automated EMDR apps, research about the efficacy of online EMDR and the appropriateness for online use is still in its infancy yet shows great preliminary results.

Expressive Writing and Homework

Online counselors may assign expressive writing interventions specifically related to client experiences and perceptions. Research has shown such homework can decrease depression symptoms (Pachankis et al., 2020). Online formats may allow counselors to easily provide writing prompts, and if the client chooses, review the content of the client's writing. Numerous journaling apps are available but should be vetted for security and privacy prior to use with clients.

SUMMARY

Telebehavioral health providers have a unique opportunity to serve diverse populations with specific needs who may not otherwise have to access to quality mental health care. When considering the barriers individuals in these special populations face, telebehavioral health is a beneficial solution. Telebehavioral health allows counselors to provide specialized services, referrals, psychoeducation, and resources not easily available to diverse populations. For example, it may be difficult for individuals to find counselors who understand the complexities and can adequately address the treatment needs of specialized populations such as veterans, individuals who have been trafficked, LGBTQIA+, victims of domestic violence, victims of sexual assault, individuals with ADHD, and other diverse populations. Telebehavioral health may assist these groups by increasing accessibility to competent clinicians, may reduce financial burdens due to transportation needs and having to miss work to travel far for appointments, and decrease the fear and stigma of receiving counseling services, among those living in rural communities. Therefore, online telehealth opens doors and expands access for diverse populations to have equal opportunity for quality mental health services. Research continues to grow reflecting the efficacy of online counseling, including research that telebehavioral health has been useful helping traumatized populations, women veterans, and survivors of intimate partner violence (Luxton et al., 2016), populations included in this chapter. Because some individuals in these populations are more vulnerable, the counselor should have safety plans and utilize online assessment tools, as discussed in Chapter 6.

CASE EXPLORATION

Tristin is battling depression. She is feeling isolated in her small town and struggling to make new friendships. Counseling options in her rural community are limited, and it is a struggle to find one that she feels comfortable with and is within her insurance network. Through a Google search, she found a counselor, Katrina, who provided online counseling. She liked the counselor's approach and background described on the website and the practice took her insurance. She has been seeing the Katrina for a couple of weeks. From prior sessions, the counselor wondered if Tristin could have been victim of IPV and uses a trauma-informed approach in session and provides psychoeducation material to review.

Katrina: Tell me more about your relationship with and marriage to Juan.

Tristin: Juan was very controlling. He had to know where I was every minute of the day. If I came home 5 minutes late from picking up the kids at school—just because we stopped for ice cream—he would totally freak out. Like I had done something wrong for getting them an afterschool treat. I literally had to give him a report of how I spent my time every day. It got so tiring.

Katrina: How is your current relationship with Pat different?

Tristin: Pat doesn't have to know what I am doing every day or where I am at all times. But it does bother me if I am late, and he asks me where I have been. It's like he doesn't trust me. I usually end up saying something about it, and then he gets mad and says he doesn't really care. That hurts too.

Katrina: Any other similarities or differences that you notice between your relationship with Juan and Pat?

Tristin: Juan also had a problem with my family. I couldn't see them very much. He was convinced they were all against him, and they were unhealthy for our relationship. They really did try to like Juan, but they didn't like the way he treated me all the time. Before our marriage, it seemed like we were pretty social. We had a lot of friends who we would hang out and do, you know, normal stuff. After we got married, he wanted to go out with them less and less. It seemed like my world just kept getting smaller and smaller—like it was only Juan and me and then the kids. No one else was allowed.

Katrina: That had to be difficult. To have less contact with family and friends who cared about you.

Tristin: Yeah. It got pretty lonely, but I was just focused on trying to make Juan happy, you know? Pat isn't like that. He doesn't have a problem with my family.

Katrina: Do you see your friends or family very often now?

Tristin: Pat and I see my family at the holidays. I talk on the phone with my mom every week. Things are pretty good there. I don't talk to my old friends as much though. I feel like things have been different. I put them at distance, and I don't know how to get close to them again. And I don't know many people where I live now. It's almost like I don't know how to make friends anymore.

Katrina: How would you rate your self-esteem now? It sounds like a lot changed during your relationship with Juan.

Tristin: I'm definitely not as confident as I used to be. Juan used to put me down a lot. He liked to tell me I was stupid or that I don't think whenever we would have a disagreement.

Katrina: How did that impact your ability to speak up for yourself?

Tristin: I'm still having a hard time with that. Pat is really understanding and supportive, but I still get scared to say something when I disagree. He's never insulted me or anything, but I still question myself all the time. I get really anxious when he's upset about something, even though he doesn't take it out on me. I'm really skittish around people in general when they seem mad or frustrated.

Katrina: What was Juan like when he was angry?

Tristin: Sometimes he would throw stuff or bang his fist on the table. He would yell, but mostly he would say a lot of mean stuff. He would threaten me and guilt trip me. But then he could also be so nice to me. When we first got together, he offered to pay the bills so I could finish school, but eventually that changed. And he would say such nice things to me. He would be so encouraging, tell me how beautiful and talented I am, then something would set him off, and suddenly, I was the worst person in the world.

Katrina: Thank you for sharing with me today. It sounds like your previous relationship was really tumultuous and had a lasting impact on you. I'm going to attach these worksheets, including these illustrations of healthy versus controlling relationships.

Worksheets

CULTURAL SENSITIVITY SELF-ASSESSMENT

Am I aware of how my own culture affects me?

_____

_____

_____

_____

_____

_____

_____

Does my cultural background encourage respect of diverse populations and the values held in different cultures?

_____

_____

_____

_____

_____

Do I find myself being sensitive to differences in diverse populations, including those of different social class, race, sexual orientation, and gender?

_____

_____

_____

_____

_____

Do I have a sincere interest in the well-being of the client? Do I hold respect, value, and care for the individual and believe I am appropriately trained and equipped to effectively honor the welfare of the client?

_____

_____

_____

_____

_____

How can I seek training to better serve diverse populations?

_____

_____

_____

_____

If I am honest, do I find that I have a bias regarding certain populations? How can I process that to better serve diverse populations?

_____

_____

_____

_____

How can I distinguish between what I am considering good for me and what I value, and what the client deems good for them and what they value, ensuring that I am not imparting my goals and values on the client and incorporating them into the treatment plan?

_____

_____

_____

_____

_____

INTIMATE PARTNER/DOMESTIC VIOLENCE AND TRAFFICKING QUESTIONNAIRE

Does the client describe feelings of powerlessness in a relationship?

_____

_____

_____

_____

Does the client describe frequent fighting?

_____

_____

_____

_____

_____

Does the client describe feeling put down or degraded by a family member or partner?

_____

_____

_____

_____

Is the client afraid of their partner or family member?

_____

_____

_____

_____

_____

Does the client feel safe at home? If not, does the client have somewhere safe to go?

_____

_____

_____

_____

_____

Does the client's partner or family members know that they are meeting with a counselor?

_____

_____

_____

_____

_____

Does one partner in the client's relationship seem to earn the majority of the income? Do both partners have input into how the money is spent?

_____

_____

_____

_____

_____

When the client discusses their relationship, do they mention their partner tracking their whereabouts with an app? Are they expected to check in with their partner frequently?

_____

_____

_____

_____

Has the client described doing things they do not want to do sexually?

_____

_____

_____

_____

_____

Are there mentions of performing sexual acts in exchange for money, drugs, or other material gain? Does the client receive these, or does someone else?

_____

_____

_____

_____

_____

Does the client feel pushed to use drugs or alcohol by their partner or family member?

_____

_____

_____

_____

_____

Is a minor present in the home? Does the concern for abuse necessitate reporting based on local law?

_____

_____

_____

_____

_____

_____

SAFETY PLAN

STEP 1: _Know When to Get Help_

What are triggers or warning signs that alert you to your problem? Thoughts, feelings, or behaviors?

STEP 2: _Understand How You Cope_

What are healthy things that you can turn to that bring relief from the problem?

STEP 3: _Identify Your Support_

Who are the friends or family that you can contact if you are not able to cope with problem yourself? List them with contact information.

STEP 4: *Seek Professional Help*

If the problem persists or you have self-harming or suicidal thoughts, reach out to a professional support system.

Local emergency number:

Local counselor or agency:

VA hotline: 855-948-2311

Domestic Violence hotline: 1-800-799-SAFE (7233)

National Human Trafficking hotline: 1-888-373-7888 or text 233733

Suicide hotline: 1-800-SUICIDE

1-800-TALK

Online Resources

- **ADHD Resource Guide:** Outlines available resources for those with ADHD symptoms.: https://www.healthline.com/health/adhd/resource-guide

- **Centers for Disease Control and Prevention ADHD Resource Guide:** Provides useful information regarding ADHD prevention and management: https://www.cdc.gov/ncbddd/adhd/

- **Children and Adults With Attention-Deficit/Hyperactivity Disorder (CHADD):** Useful resources for child and adults in managing symptoms of ADHD: https://chadd.org/

- **Journal for Rural Mental Health:** Provides articles on rural mental health treatment, research and policies: https://www.narmh.org/

- **National Domestic Violence Hotline:** Resources for domestic violence victims and survivors: https://www.thehotline.org

- **National Human Trafficking Hotline:** Resources for human trafficking victims and survivors: https://humantraffickinghotline.org/

- **Rape and Incest National Network (RAINN):** Resources for rape and incest victims and survivors: https://www.rainn.org/about-national-sexual-assault-telephone-hotline

- **Therapist Aid:** Worksheets, tools and handouts to assist clients with various issues and skill development: https://www.therapistaid.com

- **U.S. Department of Veteran Affairs, VA telehealth services:** Available resources and contacts for veterans: https://telehealth.va.gov/

- **World Professional Association of Transgender Health (WPATH):** Professional and educational services for transgender health: https://www.wpath.org

References

Abbas, P. G. (2012). A match or mismatch between learning styles of the learners and teaching styles of the teachers. *International Journal of Modern Education and Computer Science, 4*(11), 51–60. https://doi.org/10.5815/ijmecs.2012.11.05

Abels, P., & Abels, S. L. (2001). *Understanding narrative therapy: A guidebook for the social worker.* Springer.

Allard, C. B., Norman, S. B., Thorp, S. R., Browne, K. C., & Stein, M. B. (2018). Mid-treatment reduction in trauma-related guilt predicts PTSD and functioning following cognitive trauma therapy for survivors of intimate partner violence. *Journal of Interpersonal Violence, 33*(23), 3610–3629. https://doi.org/10.1177/0886260516636068

American Counseling Association. (2014). 2014 *ACA code of ethics.* https://www.counseling.org/Resources/aca-code-of-ethics.pdf.

Augusta-Scott, T., & Brown, C. (2007). *Narrative therapy: Making meaning, making lives.* SAGE.

Austin, A., & Craig, S. L. (2015). Transgender affirmative cognitive behavioral therapy: Clinical considerations and applications. *Professional Psychology: Research and Practice, 46*(1), 21–29. https://doi.org/10.1037/a0038642

Beck, J. G., Tran, H. N., Dodson, T. S., Henschel, A. V., Woodward, M. J., & Eddinger, J. (2016). Cognitive trauma therapy for battered women: Replication and extension. *Psychology of Violence, 6*(3), 368–377. https://doi.org/10.1037/vio0000024

Berry, O. O., Fitelson, E., & Monk, C. (2020). Recognizing and addressing domestic violence: Issues for psychiatrists. *Psychiatric Times, 37*(2) https://www.psychiatrictimes.com/view/recognizing-and-addressing-domestic-violence-issues-psychiatrists

Bocinski, S. G. (2017, September 27). *The economic drivers and consequences of sex trafficking in the United States* [Briefing paper, IWPR #B369]. https://iwpr.org/wp-content/uploads/2020/09/B369_Economic-Impacts-of-Sex-Trafficking-BP-3.pdf

Boyer, B. E., Geurts, H. M., Prins, P. J. M., & Van der Oord, S. (2016). One-year follow-up of two novel CBTs for adolescents with ADHD. *European Child & Adolescent Psychiatry, 25*(3), 333–337. https://doi.org/10.1007/s00787-015-0776-3

Cheesmond, N. E., Davies, K., & Inder, K. J. (2019). Exploring the role of rurality and rural identity in mental health help-seeking behavior: A systematic qualitative review. *Journal of Rural Mental Health, 43*(1), 45–59. https://doi.org/10.1037/rmh0000109

Chen, C., Palfrey, A., Shreck, E., Silvestri, B., Wash, L., Nehrig, N., Baer, A., Schneider, J., Ashkenazi, S., Sherman, S., & Chodosh, J. (2019). Implementation of telemental health (TMH) psychological service for rural veterans at the VA New York Harbor healthcare system. *Psychological Services,* 1–7. https://doi.org/10.1037/ser0000323

Clark, H. M., Grogan-Kaylor, A., Galano, M. M., Stein, S. F., Montalvo-Liendo, N., & Graham-Bermann, S. (2018). Reducing intimate partner violence among Latinas through the Moms' Empowerment program: An efficacy trial. *Journal of Family Violence, 33*(4), 257–268. https://doi.org/10.1007/s10896-018-9957-4

Clawson, H. J., Salomon, A., & Grace, L. G. (2008). *Treating the hidden wounds: Trauma treatment and mental health recovery for victims of human trafficking.* https://aspe.hhs.gov/system/files/pdf/75356/ib.pdf

Cohen, J. A., Deblinger, E., & Mannarino, A. P. (2018). Trauma-focused cognitive behavioral therapy for children and families. *Psychotherapy Research, 28*(1), 47–57. https://doi.org/10.1080/10503307.2016.1208375

Derrig-Palumbo, K., & Zeine, F. (2005). *Online therapy: A therapist's guide to expanding your practice.* Norton.

Domoney, J., Howard, M., Abas, M., Broadbent, M., & Oram, S. (2015). Mental health service responses to human trafficking: A qualitative study of professionals' experiences of providing care. *BMC Psychiatry, 15*(289), 1–9. https://doi.org/10.1186/s12888-015-0679-3

Evans, S., Ling, M., Hill, B., Rinehart, N., Austin, D., & Sciberras, E. (2018). Systematic review of meditation-based interventions for children with ADHD. *European Child & Adolescent Psychiatry, 27*(1), 9–27. https://doi.org/10.1007/s00787-017-1008-9

Fatahi, S., Shabanali-Fami, F., & Moradi, H. (2018). An empirical study of using sequential behavior pattern mining approach to predict learning styles. *Education and Information Technologies, 23*(4), 1427–1445. https://doi.org/10.1007/s10639-017-9667-1

Frost, H., Campbell, P., Maxwell, M., O'Carroll, R. E., Dombrowski, S. U., Williams, B., Cheyne, H., Coles, E., & Pollock, A. (2018). Effectiveness of motivational interviewing on adult behaviour change in health and social care settings: A systematic review of reviews. *PloS one, 13*(10), e0204890. https://doi.org/10.1371/journal.pone.0204890

Gerassi, L. B., & Esbensen, K. (2020). Motivational interviewing with individuals at risk of sex trafficking. *Journal of Social Work, 32*, 43–57. https://doi.org/10.1177/1468017320919856

Geschwind, N., Bosgraaf, E., Bannink, F., & Peeters, F. (2020). Positivity pays off: Clients' perspectives on positive compared with traditional cognitive behavioral therapy for depression. *Psychotherapy, 57*(3), 366–378. https://doi.org/10.1037/pst0000288

Goss, C., Richardson, W. J., Dailey, N., Bair, B., Nagamoto, H., Manson, S., & Shore, J. (2017). Rural American Indian and Alaska Native veterans' telemental health: A model of culturally centered care. *Psychological Services, 14*(3), 270–278. https://doi.org/10.1037/ser0000149

Gray, M. J., Hassija, C. M., Jaconis, M., Barrett, C., Zheng, P., Steinmetz, S., & James, T. (2015). Provision of evidence-based therapies to rural survivors of domestic violence and sexual assault via telehealth: Treatment outcomes and clinical training benefits. *Training and Education in Professional Psychology, 9*(3), 235–241. https://doi.org/10.1037/tep0000083

Hamrick, L. A., & Owens, G. P. (2019). Exploring the mediating role of self-blame and coping in the relationships between self-compassion and distress in females following the sexual assault. *Journal of Clinical Psychology, 75*(4), 766–779. https://doi.org/10.1002/jclp.22730

Hargreaves, M. K., Mouton, C. P., Liu, J., Zhou, Y. E., & Blot, W. J. (2019). Adverse childhood experiences and health care utilization in a low-income population. *Journal of Health Care for the Poor & Underserved, 30*(2), 749–767. https://doi.org/10.1353/hpu.2019.0054

Hemmings, S., Jakobowitz, S., Abas, M., Bick, D., Howard, L. M., Stanley, N., Zimmerman, C., & Oram, S. (2016). Responding to the health needs of survivors of human trafficking: A systematic review. *BMC Health Services Research, 320*. https://doi.org/10.1186/s12913-016-1538-8

Hettema, J., Steele, J., & Miller, W. (2005). Motivational interviewing. *Annual Review Clinical Psychology, 1*, 91–111. https://doi.org/10.1146/annurev.clinpsy.1.102803.143833

Hollis, C., Falconer, C. J., Martin, J. L., Whittington, C., Stockton, S., Glazebrook, C., & Davies, E. B. (2017). Annual research review: Digital health interventions for children and young people with mental health problems—A systematic and meta-review. *Journal of Child Psychology and Psychiatry and Allied Disciplines, 58*(4), 474–503. https://doi.org/10.1111/jcpp.12663

Hughes, M., & Rasmussen, L. (2010). The utility of motivational interviewing in domestic violence shelters: A qualitative exploration. *Journal of Aggression, Maltreatment & Trauma, 19*(3), 300–322. https://doi.org/10.1080/10926771003705213

Iverson, K. M., Gradus, J. L., Resick, P. A., Suvak, M. K., Smith, K. F., & Monson, C. M. (2011). Cognitive-behavioral therapy for PTSD and depression symptoms reduces risk for future intimate partner violence among interpersonal trauma survivors. *Journal of Consulting and Clinical Psychology, 79*(2), 193–202. https://doi.org/10.1037/a0022512

Knouse, L. E., Teller, J., & Brooks, M. A. (2017). Meta-analysis of cognitive-behavioral treatments for adult ADHD. *Journal of Consulting and Clinical Psychology, 85*(7), 737–750. https://doi.org/10.1037/ccp0000216

Lambert, D., Gale, J., Hartley, D., Croll, Z., & Hansen, A. (2015). Understanding the business case for telemental health in rural communities. *Journal of Behavioral Health Services & Research, 43*, 1–13. https://doi.org/10.1007/s11414-015-9490-7

Lawlor-Savage, L., & Prentice, J. L. (2014). Digital cognitive behaviour therapy (CBT) in Canada: Ethical considerations. *Canadian Psychology, 55*(4), 231–239. https://doi.org/10.1037/a0037861

Lee, S. A., & Edget, D. M. (2012). *Cognitive behavioral therapy: Applications, methods and outcomes.* Nova Science.

Lefevor, G. T., Boyd-Rogers, C. C., Sprague, B. M., & Janis, R. A. (2019). Health disparities between genderqueer, transgender, and cisgender individuals: An extension of minority stress theory. *Journal of Counseling Psychology, 66*(4), 385–395. https://doi.org/10.1037/cou0000339

Levine, J. A. (2017). Mental health issues in survivors of sex trafficking. *Cogent Medicine, 13*(1), 1–13. https://doi.org/10.1080/2331205X.2017.1278841

Litam, S. D. (2017). Human sex trafficking in America: What counselors need to know. *The Professional Counselor, 7*(1), 45–61. https://doi.org/10.15241/sdal.7.1.45

Luxton, D. D., Nelson, E. L., & Maheu, M. M. (2016). *A practitioner's guide to telemental health: How to conduct legal, ethical, and evidence-based telepractice.* American Psychological Association. https://doi.org/10.1037/14938-000

Mahmoud, H., Sers, M., & Tuite, J. (2018, January 4). *Enhancing telemental health for rural and remote communities.* https://www.beckershospitalreview.com/healthcare-information-technology/enhancing-telemental-health-for-rural-and-remote-communities.html%C2%A0

McCarty, C. A., Vander Stoep, A., Violette, H., & Myers, K. (2015). Interventions developed for psychiatric and behavioral treatment in the children's ADHD telemental health treatment study. *Journal of Child and Family Studies, 24*(6), 1735–1743. https://doi.org/10.1007/s10826-014-9977-5

Miller, W., & Rollnick, S. (2013). *Motivational interviewing: Helping people change.* Guilford.

Minnix, G. M. (2018). Reconciling counselors' Christian beliefs and lesbian, gay, bisexual, and transgender affirmation: A grounded theory. *Counseling & Values, 63*(1), 110–128. https://doi.org/10.1002/cvj.12076

Myers, K., Vander Stoep, A., & Lobdell, C. (2013). Feasibility of conducting a randomized controlled trial of telemental health with children diagnosed with attention-deficit/hyperactivity disorder in underserved communities. *Journal of Child and Adolescent Psychopharmacology, 23*(6), 372–378. https://doi.org/10.1089/cap.2013.0020

Nimmo-Smith, V., Merwood, A., Hank, D., Brandling, J., Greenwood, R., Skinner, L., Law, S., Patel, V., & Rai, D. (2020). Non-pharmacological interventions for adult ADHD: A systematic review. *Psychological Medicine, 50*(4), 529–541. https://doi.org/10.1017/S0033291720000069

Pachankis, J. E., Williams, S. L., Behari, K., Job, S., McConocha, E. M., & Chaudoir, S. R. (2020). Brief online interventions for LGBTQ young adult mental and behavioral health: A randomized controlled trial in a high-stigma, low-resource context. *Journal of Consulting & Clinical Psychology, 88*(5), 429–444. https://doi.org/10.1037/ccp0000497

Palmer, N. B., Myers, K. M., Vander Stoep, A., McCarty, C. A., Geyer, J. R., & DeSalvo, A. (2010). Attention-deficit/hyperactivity disorder and telemental health. *Current Psychiatry Reports, 12*(5), 409–417. https://doi.org/10.1007/s11920-010-0132-8

Paul, O. (2019). Perceptions of family relationships and post-traumatic stress symptoms of children exposed to domestic violence. *Journal of Family Violence, 34*(4), 331–343. https://doi.org/10.1007/s10896-018-00033-z

Robertson, D. L., & Avent, J. R. (2016). African American counselors-in-training, the Black church, and lesbian-, gay-, and bisexual-affirmative counseling: Considerations for counselor education programs. *Counseling & Values, 61*(2), 223–238. https://doi.org/10.1002/cvj.12039

Rockhill, C., Violette, H., Vander Stoep, A., Grover, S., & Myers, K. (2013). Caregivers' distress: Youth with attention-deficit/hyperactivity disorder and comorbid disorders assessed via telemental health. *Journal of Child and Adolescent Psychopharmacology, 23*(6), 379–385. https://doi.org/10.1089/cap.2013.0019

Ross, J. M., Drouin, M., & Coupe, A. (2019). Sexting coercion as a component of intimate partner polyvictimization. *Journal of Interpersonal Violence, 34*(11), 2269–2291. https://doi.org/10.1177/0886260516660300

Ross-Sheriff, F., & Orme, J. (2015, February 2). Human trafficking: Overview. *Encyclopedia of Social Work*, 1–19. https://doi.org/10.1093/acrefore/9780199975839.013.945

Rusow, J. A., Goldbach, J. T., Rhoades, H., Bond, D., Lanteigne, A., & Fulginiti, A. (2018). Homelessness, mental health and suicidality among LGBTQ youth accessing crisis services. *Child Psychiatry & Human Development, 49*(4), 643–651. https://doi.org/10.1007/s10578-018-0780-1

Scheer, J. R., Harney, P., Esposito, J., & Woulfe, J. M. (2020). Self-reported mental and physical health symptoms and potentially traumatic events among lesbian, gay, bisexual, transgender, and queer individuals: The role of shame. *Psychology of Violence, 10*(2), 131–142. https://doi.org/10.1037/vio0000241

Schmidt, I. D. (2014). Addressing PTSD in low-income victims of intimate partner violence: Moving toward a comprehensive intervention. *Social Work, 59*(3), 253–260. https://doi.org/10.1093/sw/swu016

Schulman, M., & Maul, A. (2019). *Screening for adverse childhood experiences (ACES) and trauma.* Center for Health Care Strategies, 1–8. https://www.chcs.org/media/TA-Tool-Screening-for-ACEs-and-Trauma_020619.pdf

Shapiro, F. (1996). *Eye movement desensitization and reprocessing level II training manual.* EMDR Institute.

Shapiro F. (2014). The role of eye movement desensitization and reprocessing (EMDR) therapy in medicine: Addressing the psychological and physical symptoms stemming from adverse life experiences. *The Permanente Journal, 18*(1), 71–77. https://doi.org/10.7812/TPP/13-098

Shore, P., Goranson, A., Ward, M., & Lu, M. (2014). Meeting veterans where they're @: A VA home-based telemental health (HBTMH) pilot program. *International Journal Psychiatry in Medicine, 48*(1), 5–17. https://doi.org/10.2190/PM.48.1.b

Sibley, M. H., Comer, J. S., & Gonzalez, J. (2017). Delivering parent-teen therapy for ADHD through videoconferencing: A preliminary investigation. *Journal of Psychopathology and Behavioral Assessment, 39*(3), 467–485. https://doi.org/10.1007/s10862-017-9598-6

Simms, D. C., Gibson, K., O'Donnell, S., & Hunsley, J. (2011). To use or not to use: Clinicians' perceptions of telemental health. *Canadian Psychology, 52*(1), 41-51. http://dx.doi.org/10.1037/a0022275

Sinacola, R., Peters-Strickland, T., & Wyner, J. D. (2020). *Basic psychopharmacology for mental health professionals.* Pearson.

Sorocco, K., Bratkovick, K., Wingo, R., Qureshi, S., & Mason, P. (2013). Integrating care coordination home telehealth and home based primary care in rural Oklahoma: A pilot study. *Psychological Services, 10*(3), 350–352. https://doi.org/10.1037/a0032785

Substance Abuse and Mental Health Services Administratiaon. (2014*). SAMHSA's concept of trauma and guidance for a trauma-informed approach.* https://store.samhsa.gov/product/SAMHSA-s-Concept-of-Trauma-and-Guidance-for-a-Trauma-Informed-Approach/SMA14-4884

Tambling, R. (2012). Solution-oriented therapy for survivors of sexual assault and their partners. *Contemporary Family Therapy: An International Journal, 34*(3), 391–401. https://doi.org/10.1007/s10591-012-9200-z

Thompson, J., & Haley, M. (2018). Human trafficking: Preparing counselors to work with survivors. *International Journal for the Advancement of Counseling, 40*(3). https://doi.org/10.1007/s10447-018-9327-1

Turvey, C. (2018). Telemental health care delivery. In J. J. Magnavita (Ed.), *Using technology in mental health practice* (pp. 25–42). American Psychological Association.

Tutty, L., Babins-Wagner, R., & Rothery, M. (2016). You're not alone: Mental health outcomes in therapy groups for abused women. *Journal of Family Violence, 31*(4), 489–497. https://doi.org/10.1007/s10896-015-9779-6

U.S. Department of Veteran Affairs. (n.d.). *Motivational interviewing and motivational enhancement therapy.* https://www.mentalhealth.va.gov/substanceuse/met-sud.asp

U.S. Department of Veteran Affairs, Office of Rural Health. (2015). *Annual Report 2015.* https://www.ruralhealth.va.gov/docs/ORH_Annual_Report_2015_FINAL.pdf

Usami, M. (2016). Functional consequences of attention-deficit hyperactivity disorder on children and their families. *Psychiatry and Clinical Neurosciences, 70*(8), 303–317. https://doi.org/10.1111/pcn.12393

van der Kolk, B. A. (2014). *The body keeps the score: Brain, mind, and body in the healing of trauma.* Viking.

Vander Stoep, A., McCarty, C. A., Zhou, C, Rockhill, C., Schoenfelder, E. N., & Myers, K. (2017). The children's attention-deficit hyperactivity disorder telemental health treatment study: Caregiver outcomes. *Journal of Abnormal Psychology, 45*(1), 27–43. https://doi.org/10.1007/s10802-016-0155-7

Veltman, A., & La Rose, T. (2019). LGBTQ mental health: What every clinician needs to know. *Psychiatric Times, 36*(12), 21–23. https://www.psychiatrictimes.com/view/lgbtq-mental-health-what-every-clinician-needs-know

Vencill, J. A., Carlson, S., Iantaffi, A., & Miner, M. (2018). Mental health, relationships, and sex: Exploring patterns among bisexual individuals in mixed orientation relationships. *Sexual & Relationship Therapy, 33*(1–2), 14–33. https://doi.org/10.1080/14681994.2017.1419570

Verhoeven, M., van Gestel, B., de Jong, D., & Kleemans, E. (2015). Relationships between suspects and victims of sex trafficking. Exploitation of prostitutes and domestic violence parallels in Dutch trafficking cases. *European Journal on Criminal Policy and Research, 21,* 49–64. https://doi.org/10.1007/s10610-013-9226-2

Winbolt, B. (2011). *Solution focused therapy for the helping professions.* Jessica Kingsley.

Yakovenko, I., Quigley, L., Hemmelgarn, B., Hodgins, D., & Ronksley, P. (2015). The efficacy of motivational interviewing for disordered gambling: Systematic review and meta-analysis. *Addictive Behaviors, 43,* 72–82. https://doi.org/10.1016/j.addbeh.2014.12.011

Yoshimura, C. G., & Campbell, K. B. (2016). Interpersonal violence and sexual assault: Trauma-informed communication approaches in university counseling centers. *Journal of College Student Psychotherapy, 30*(4), 300–312. http://dx.doi.org/10.1080/87568225.2016.1221720

Yule, M., Brotto, L., & Gorzalka, B. (2013). Mental health and interpersonal functioning in self-identified asexual men and women. *Psychology & Sexuality, 4*(2), 136–151. https://doi.org/10.1080/19419899.2013.774162

Zeren. S. (2015). Face-to-face and online counseling: Client problems and satisfaction. *Education and Science, 40*(182), 127–141. https://doi.org/10.15390/EB.2015.4696

Online Marriage, Couple, and Family Counseling

Colleen Grunhaus and Jeremiah Peck

Marriage, couples, and family counseling (MCFC) is a growing specialization in the counseling field and has transitioned to the online format. Traditional in-office marriage, couple, and family counseling (MCFC) entails unique theoretical, practical, ethical, and logistic considerations. Each of these facets are influenced by the theoretical orientation of the clinician, the goal of counseling, family composition, how many people are in the room, and a variety of other factors. When pairing the intricacies of MCFC with telebehavioral health or an online mode of delivery, these considerations have profound implications for both the logistical and therapeutic processes.

This chapter explores the research that delineates the best practices associated with utilizing telebehavioral health in MCFC. The practical, logistical, ethical, and multicultural considerations required to navigate the implementation and preparation of MCFC, the different approaches to integrating online interventions in the therapeutic process, and how family counseling skills may translate to the online delivery format are discussed. Additionally, both the benefits of online MCFC as it related to overcoming barriers and objections to treatments, as well as common drawbacks to implementing this approach to care, are outlined. The chapter concludes with a case exploration to demonstrate how all these considerations come together in a simulated scenario. Worksheets, forms, and resources to further equip you to successfully provide online MCFC are also provided.

Fundamentals of Marriage, Couple, and Family Counseling

MCFC emphasizes interpersonal approaches and thinking to address the family as a social system rather than a collection of individuals. MCFC is a paradigm shift from individual therapy, as client symptoms emerge from relational rather than intrapsychic origins. Counselors engaged in relational work understand that problematic interactions have circular rather than linear causes, and intervention requires engagement with the whole system. The **family system** is a theoretical approach to conceptualizing and understanding each individual within the family as having a unique role and function, which operates within and constitutes the collaborative system.

This comprehensive counseling treatment was founded in the 1950s, gained research momentum in the 1960s, saw a proliferation of family-based applications and technique experimentation in the 1970s, and became a dynamic worldwide endeavor by the 1980s (Goldenberg et al., 2017). A pattern of greater integration and the sharing of family therapy models emerged in the 1990s (Goldenberg et al., 2017); and in the 21st century, MCFC therapists adapted and developed theories to better account for cultural and compositional differences (Goldenberg et al., 2017). These foundational stages of growth and change established MCFC as a substantial force in the field of counseling.

Unfortunately, there are barriers for couples and families to initiate and maintain involvement in MCFC, and online counseling may ease some of these barriers. Couples and families may decline to initiate services due to stigma related to help seeking. Online counseling increases confidentiality by keeping services within the home and eliminating the crowded waiting room or the need to interface with front desk staff (Cicila et al., 2014).

In addition, some multistressed families may struggle with childcare concerns, lack of access to transportation, and financial burdens that could possibly be alleviated with the convenience of online counseling (Cicila et al., 2014). Many families today also struggle with arranging multiple schedules and may not realistically be able to have the entire family system attend each counseling session, which could limit the effectiveness of treatment. Telebehavioral health counseling may reduce this burden for families by engaging the family at a time and place that best suits everyone's availability (Gassova & Werner-Wilson, 2018).

Online Marriage, Couples, and Family Counseling

Technology developments have multiplied the mediums for counselors to maintain engagement with clients. The research for telebehavioral health counseling is overwhelmingly focused on individual services. However, emerging research has begun analyzing the current state of MCFC online services and the effectiveness.

In a review of marriage and family therapists listed on counseling websites, Gassova and Werner-Wilson (2018) found that 64% of marriage and family therapists provided audio or phone counseling services. About half of the marriage and family therapists provided counseling through synchronous videoconferencing; and written communication through email or chat was provided by 43% of MCFC providers (Gassova & Werner-Wilson, 2018). Disparate practices were found related to offering services to clients in certain states or abroad, and the inclusion or exclusion of minors (Gassova and Werner-Wilson, 2018). This study highlighted the prolific practice of online MCFC and also the lack of uniformity in the delivery of these services among various providers.

Online services are currently being provided to couples and families in conjunction with face-to-face services or solely through online means. Both methods are gaining popularity and show promising results. In addition, online MCFC resources may decrease time in therapy, decrease stigma related to accessing services, and increase therapy attendance (e.g., Cicila et al., 2014; Doss et al., 2017; Gassova & Werner-Wilson, 2018).

Telebehavioral Health Interventions Adjunct to Face-to-Face Services

MCFC providers express greater comfort in utilizing online interventions as an adjunct to traditional face-to-face services rather than implementing services completely online (Hertlein et al., 2014). There are a variety of **adjunct online interventions**, or educational material accessed over the internet that can be used as ancillary to in-person or online counseling, currently targeted to couples and families. For example, educational websites that are monitored and initiated by MCFC experts can be utilized in conjunction with traditional in-office sessions, alongside videoconferencing or other synchronous online counseling mediums, or as a precursor to therapy when on a waitlist. Expert-run informational websites have been shown to provide increased education for couples, to assist in pinpointing problem areas and to prompt a referral to counseling (Cicila et al., 2014).

Online assessment tools aimed at determining couples' relationship problem areas can be a helpful addition to face-to-face therapy alone. One such instrument, the Relationship Evaluation Questionnaire (RELATE; Busby et al., 2001), is an in-depth online questionnaire that assesses many pertinent variables impacting couples (e.g., personality, preferences, values, support systems, etc.). Larson et al. (2007) found that couples who completed this questionnaire online and received a brief interpretation with a therapist showed greater relationship satisfaction than the control group. In addition, Larson et al. determined that even if the couple completed the online survey and then self-interpreted, participants still experienced greater relationship satisfaction than the control group, although results were not as greatly improved as the intervention group that included the therapist interpretation.

Other online interventions that may be utilized in conjunction with synchronous in-person services include apps that provide reminders of therapy homework, track moods, or administer guided meditation (e.g., Doss et al., 2017). These online interventions keep clients engaged in between sessions and may be administered to clients on a waitlist to possibly shorten time in therapy. Online programming can be implemented in conjunction with face-to-face MCFC or completely online MCFC.

Telebehavioral Health Marriage, Couples, and Family Counseling

Telebehavioral health MCFC is conducted by a counselor utilizing videoconferencing, audio or phone communication, and/or written communication such as email or instant messenger. Services provided through synchronous video conferencing have equally effective outcomes when compared to outcomes of therapy conducted in person (Dunstan & Tooth, 2012). MCFC offered completely online can increase the likelihood that all family members can attend sessions and can provide unique interventions in the family's home environment. Comer et al. (2015) found that implementing internet-delivered parent–child interaction therapy (I-PCIT) allowed therapists to provide parent coaching in the family's natural environment during real-life problematic interactions. This online intervention provided in the family's home environment was more effective than PCIT provided in a traditional clinic setting (Comer et al., 2017).

MCFC offered completely online may also help couples who have **long-distance relationships**, or a romantic relationship where involved parties live at a geographical distance, which limits the frequency of their physical contact and interactions), such as deployed active-duty service members. Active-duty service members and their spouses experience substantial stress during the entire deployment cycle (Farero et al., 2015). Online MCFC during a long-distance deployment can assist the marital couple in addressing problems early, increasing communication, and decreasing stigma related to help seeking (Farero et al., 2015).

Telebehavioral health MCFC expands potential clientele by removing barriers impeding underserved populations. For example, videoconferencing can be implemented with the prison population or families that struggle to attend an office visit with an emotionally disturbed child (Mallen & Vogel, 2005). Although online MCFC offered through videoconferencing, phone, or written communication decreases barriers to services and can produce comparable outcomes to in-person counseling, some counselors continue to experience discomfort with the online medium. Hertlein et al. (2014) found that 42% of marriage, couples, and family counselors were very uncomfortable with treating individuals online, 50% were very uncomfortable treating couples online, and 54% were very uncomfortable treating families online. This discomfort may be related to ethical concerns, perceived barriers to therapeutic alliance, or a lack of training (Hertlein et al., 2014). In the spring of 2020 counselors had to face this discomfort as the pandemic made the transition to online necessary. Some aspects of therapy may not easily translate to an online platform, as explored in this chapter, and further research is needed to determine what MCFC theories are most adaptable to the medium.

Ethical Concerns Related to Telebehavioral Health Marriage, Couple, and Family Counseling

Telebehavioral health MCFC, such as videoconferencing, audio or phone calls, or asynchronous or synchronous written communication such as email or instant messaging, entail unique ethical considerations. Couples and family counselors may experience hesitancy with the medium, particularly due to questions regarding privacy and confidentiality, safety, competency, and geographical limitations of licensure. Ethical codes have expanded to govern the delivery of online MCFC and address these concerns. Chapter 3 explores ethical considerations in more detail.

Initiating Telebehavioral Health Marriage, Couple, and Family Counseling

Prior to initiating telebehavioral health MCFC, counselors ensure that technology-assisted counseling is appropriate for each member of the couple or family by considering "professional, intellectual, emotional, and physical needs" (American Association for Marriage and Family Therapists [AAMFT], 2015, Standard VI, 6.1). Counselors can have an initial consultation with clients to assess for technology literacy and connectivity (Doss et al., 2017), and for the appropriateness of online MCFC for the family. If clients present with acute safety concerns, online MCFC may not be appropriate (Doss et al., 2017).

Prior to initiating services, counselors choose technology they are comfortable with and ensure that their chosen technology platform meets appropriate ethical and legal standards (International Association of Marriage and Family Counselors [IAMFC], Section I.4). Counselors also inform clients in writing of the risks and benefits to online counseling and both parties' responsibility in mitigating these risks (AAMFT, 2015, Standard VI.6.2). Further, counselors do not engage in online MCFC without appropriate training (AAMFT, 2015, Standard VI.6.6). Ethical and legal standards are addressed in Chapter 3.

Confidentiality and Privacy

Confidentiality is often an ethical dilemma in MCFC. Counselors "respect and guard the confidences of each individual client" and disclose limits of confidentiality that may occur due to multiple individuals engaged in counseling (AAMFT, 2015, Standard II). Online MCFC adds another dimension to confidentiality concerns. If members of a couple or family seeking videoconferencing services are at the same location (i.e., their residence) and the counselor is conferencing remotely, privacy of the communication can be more reasonably expected; whereas if multiple clients are joining from different locations, the privacy of the communication is less certain for each participant as additional parties may be present off screen without the others' knowledge (Wrape & McGinn, 2019). Counselors also can verify the identity of each family member every session through the use of code words or other identifiers when utilizing a form of technology that may obscure identity (i.e., written communication; American Counseling Association [ACA], 2014, Standard H.3).

Any form of distance counseling also introduces privacy difficulties in that the communications must be secure. Counselors must ensure the hardware, software, platforms, and practices used feature secure **end-to-end encryption** for all participants, which is a method of secure telecommunication that encrypts and decrypts communication between parties and prevents unauthorized third-parties from accessing the communication (Caldwell et al., 2017). Counselors utilize online mediums that meet "legal requirements related to protected health information" (IAMFC, 2017, Section I.4) and satisfy laws related to the confidential storage of documentation (AAMFT, 2015, Standard VI.6.4; IAMFC, 2017, Section I.1). All clients must be informed in writing of both the protections and limitations of the technology utilized for documentation and the provision of services (AAMFT, 2015 Standard VI.6.3, Standard VI.6.4). For additional information on security and technology, see Chapter 4.

Counselors may consider conducting the initial assessment in person to discuss confidentiality concerns and risk mitigation (Wrape & McGinn, 2019). This may ensure clients' understanding of expectations and personal responsibility (i.e., attending in a private setting, utilizing headphones if necessary, etc.) in preparation for implementing online MCFC. Further, clients will have the opportunity to ask questions and provide informed consent prior to engaging in the medium to which they are consenting.

Safety

Counselors ensure that safety precautions and logistics are implemented and communicated prior to commencing telebehavioral health MCFC; these procedures may be revisited at the beginning of each session. Clients should be informed ahead of time what to do in the case of an emergency and if the counselor is unavailable or how to reconnect with the counselor if connectivity is lost (ACA, 2014, Standard H.2.a.). When conducting counseling with multiple participants at various locations, online couples and family counselors can confirm the exact location of each client at the beginning of each session to ensure the counselor will be able to direct emergency services to the appropriate location if crisis intervention becomes necessary (Caldwell et al., 2017).

Counselors may experience a diminished ability to facilitate de-escalation if clients experience intense emotions and the counselor is conferencing remotely (Wrape & McGinn, 2019). Counselors can teach and practice calming or grounding techniques early in treatment and ask clients to utilize agreed-on hand signals or passwords to indicate when a family member is becoming **flooded**, defined as the time when an individual becomes unable to process further without de-escalation due to an overwhelming experience of intense emotions. At this point, counselors could facilitate verbal de-escalation in order to take a break from the provoking topic. This intervention is an important part of couples and family self-monitoring of physiological symptoms and conflict resolution and is a method of de-escalation that could be implemented remotely. Individuals who have higher safety risk (i.e., acute self-injury, active suicidal ideation, aggressive behavior, etc.) may not be appropriate for online MCFC. An initial in-person intake would allow the counselors to screen for safety concerns and determine the appropriateness of online counseling. Crisis management is discussed in detail in Chapter 8.

Competence and Training

Some counselors are hesitant to utilize telebehavioral health MCFC due to a lack of technological training or competence, or uncertainty regarding how to adapt counseling practices and interventions to the online setting (Hertlein et al., 2015). ACA (2014) recommends that counselors providing online services "develop knowledge and skills regarding related technical, ethical and legal considerations" and even complete additional coursework or certification programs (Standard H.1.a.). Similarly, AAMFT (2015) advises counselors to obtain competency in the variety of online modalities or platforms in order to select the format that is current, advanced, and best suited to clients (Standard VI.6.6). The National Board of Certified Counselors (NBCC) offers a board-certified-telemental health provider credential that licensed counselors can earn through the completion of a minimum of nine continuing education credits on telebehavioral health topics and successful passing of a final examination (NBCC, n.d.).

Professional Boundaries

Boundary-related concerns are a perceived ethical issue when conducting telebehavioral health MCFC. Some marriage, couples, and family counselors indicated that clients engaging through email may blur professional boundaries if the client perceives the counselor is always available (Hertlein et al., 2015). **Boundaries** are professional limitations to the nature, purpose, and occurrence of the clinical relationship between the client and the counselor. Engaging with clients over social media may also obscure boundaries or create dual relationships (Hertlein et al., 2015). ACA (2014) advises counselors to include social media policies within their informed consent that identify professional boundaries when using social media (Standard H.6.b.). Boundary confusion may be prevented if counselors have direct communication with couples and families at the start of telebehavioral health MCFC services. Counselors can communicate clear boundaries around digital interaction in between sessions and what to do when the counselor is not available (Caldwell et al., 2017). Couples and families that have difficulty respecting boundaries may not be suited for telebehavioral health MCFC. See Chapter 3 for more information on social media and communication.

State Licensure

Counseling occurs at both the counselor's and the clients' location; therefore, it is pertinent the counselor ensures legal and ethical compliance with the laws and rules governing both locations. As previously discussed, one of the benefits of telebehavioral health MCFC is overcoming potential geographical barriers related to receiving services. However, in cases of providing couples counseling for a long-distance relationship, or family counseling where members of the family reside in different locations, the counselor must ensure they are not practicing outside of the state in which they are licensed (Caldwell et al., 2017). It is important for counselors to check with their state's licensing board to determine the laws governing telebehavioral health conducted across state lines (see Chapter 3).

Multicultural Implications

Marriage, couple, and family counselors recognize the client's culture and identity factors have a profound influence on symptom presentation, family membership, family hierarchy and organization, gender roles, and a wide range of family functioning. Culturally competent counselors consider factors such as race and ethnicity, spirituality and religion, age, education, gender identity, sexual orientation, and other factors when delivering and determining the appropriateness of telebehavioral health MCFC (Goldenberg et al., 2017; Hilty et al., 2019). Counselors ensure that they continuously develop cultural awareness, strengthen cultural competency, and address personal biases or stereotyping (IAMFC, 2017, Section A). In addition, counselors contextualize family factors by identifying patterns that are common to many families, specific to the family's culture, or unique to a particular family in order to distinguish when cultural issues are relevant contributors to a family's presentation and functioning (Goldenberg et al., 2017). This avoids applying broad stroke cultural dynamics that may not pertain to every family in a particular group.

Currently, there is a paucity of research regarding the efficacy of telebehavioral health MCFC for specific populations. As such, counselors must embody cultural humility to foster personal awareness, knowledge, and the application of specific skills when working with various populations in a telebehavioral health MCFC setting (Blumer et al., 2015; Sue et al., 2019). Online psychiatry has been shown to have similar effectiveness as in-person care for a variety of cultures to include Latinx, Native American, and Asian populations (e.g., Mucic, 2010; Shore et al., 2006; Weiner et al., 2011). Telebehavioral MCFC may benefit clients if the counselor utilizes online interpreting services to address linguistic barriers; and clients can access culturally sensitive services in their language through online methods if these are not present in their local environment (Hilty et al., 2019). Online MCFC may also assist a family caring for an individual with a disability as the counselor can facilitate the family's creative problem solving in their home while eliminating the burden of travel (Sue et al., 2019).

Telebehavioral health MCFC may also create barriers. Body language, facial expressions, and eye contact (or lack of) are often culturally nuanced. Channeling this nonverbal communication through technological means may result in miscommunication or missed salient therapeutic data. It is pertinent for counselors to address this potential and to check in throughout sessions to ensure important messages are not being overlooked. It should not be assumed that participants are unable or unwilling to utilize technology or an online platform simply due to an age or ability stereotype; and MCFC counselors can assess every individual, couple, and family to determine if all parties are comfortable with the utilization and operation of the platforms employed (Caldwell et al., 2017).

Social Justice

Social justice is the advocacy and efforts to provide equitable access to counseling services for underserved populations. Counselors implement MCFC as a conduit of social justice to increase counseling access to underserved populations, address and discuss issues of oppression and privilege, and advocate for societal transformation (Goldenberg et al., 2017). Telebehavioral health MCFC can provide access to services for populations that might not otherwise have access due to several barriers such as finances, distance, lack of local resources, and social or religious stigma. Low-income racial and ethnic minorities experience an increased risk of relational distress and divorce and also encounter barriers to seeking treatment such as finances, transportation, and distance (Roddy et al., 2018). Among rural populations, which have diminished access to counselors who specialize in working with couples and families (Doss et al., 2017), Hispanic families are experiencing rapid population growth (Hilty et al., 2019). Those seeking couple or family counseling may have to travel greater distances to receive MCFC, which entails an increased financial burden of transportation costs such as fuel, longer childcare, and potentially more time off work to travel to and from appointments (Cicila et al., 2014). Completely online MCFC may relieve this financial burden and increase consistent access for all members of the family. Asynchronous online resources can be recommended as ancillary to in-person counseling depending on the clients' willingness and the presenting problems as a means of reducing the overall time and cost associated with counseling (Roddy et al., 2018). Multilingual counselors can serve language-diverse families through an online format who may not have access to these services locally. Asynchronous materials in different languages can also be utilized as ancillary to synchronous counseling.

Telebehavioral health MCFC can also increase access to services for couples and families experiencing social stigma as a barrier to seeking services. High numbers of couples seeking help online report concerns regarding trust and infidelity as reasons for seeking help (Roddy et al., 2018). Because telebehavioral health MCFC allows for couples to access services from the privacy of their home, this may counter the social stigma related to traveling in person to a counselors' office and sitting in a public waiting room (Cecila et al., 2014). This can also alleviate feelings of stigma related to help seeking present in specific populations, such as various religious groups (e.g., Muslim, Christian, etc.) or military culture (Farero et al., 2015). In addition, multiple barriers exist for immigrant families accessing mental health services in the United States (Sue et al., 2019). Telebehavioral health MCFC can specifically address multiple barriers that often prevent immigrant families from accessing services such as lack of transportation, irregular schedules, and language barriers. (Sue et al., 2019).

Adaptation of Counseling Interventions

Counselors should thoughtfully translate counseling interventions to the online platform. Some interventions may seamlessly convert, whereas other interventions may need to be adjusted. The informed consent, therapeutic relationship, and basic counseling skills are foundational to the practice of counseling and will be elaborated here. The application and adjustment of a MCFC approach will be addressed in the case study that follows.

Informed Consent

Due to the unique considerations of telebehavioral health MCFC, counselors should clearly communicate and establish with the clients the specific expectations, boundaries, and contingencies related to receiving services through the agreed-on platforms. The informed consent provided to all parties involved in the counseling process clearly delineates the expectations of ensuring the environment and surroundings are most conducive to navigating personal matters, including actively engaging in session and minimizing outside distractions to the best of each participants' ability, which may approximate an in-office clinical experience (Wrape & McGinn, 2019). In MCFC, this is particularly pertinent when counseling multiple participants when individuals may be conferencing from multiple locations.

The counselor should include a disclosure statement for clients regarding the potential risks and benefits of therapy, particularly related to online MCFC. As there is a scarcity of research for online MCFC specifically, it is presently regarded as somewhat experimental in nature, and clients must be informed of both this as well as potential alternatives to online MCFC (Caldwell et al., 2017). For examples of elements to include in an online MCFC informed consent, see the Online MCFC informed consent sample statements at the end of the chapter.

Therapeutic Relationship and Counseling Skills

Effective communication in the therapeutic process includes understanding nonverbal cues and expressions such as facial expressions and body language. The counselor may have a more difficult time observing these expressions in videoconferencing, especially when multiple family members are sitting farther away from the camera in order to all fit on a single screen (Wrape & McGinn, 2019). This will further diminish the counselor's ability to accurately perceive nonverbal cues and facial expressions, and thus necessitate the counselor relying more heavily on verbal cues and direct questions (Wrape & McGinn, 2019). Counselors can ask clarifying questions and verbally check in with the family member about thoughts and feelings and remind the family that this is one of the barriers for telebehavioral health MCFC. Similarly, counselors will not be able to rely on eye contact or posturing to indicate which family member they are addressing while conducting online MCFC. A telebehavioral health MCFC counselor will need to employ a more frequent use of first names when addressing specific family members in order to clearly indicate whom they are addressing to avoid miscommunications (Wrape & McGinn, 2019).

In addition, during the course of conducting MCFC, it is not uncommon for the counselor to recommend the utilization of individual services concurrently with a family's treatment. A best practice is to conduct additional research pertaining to the local resources available to the family for individual counseling or additional services local to their community (Wrape & McGinn, 2019). Similarly, if at some point it is determined that online MCFC is no longer a viable option for the family, the counselor can assist the family in finding appropriate in-person counseling services accessible to the family.

SUMMARY

Telebehavioral health counseling provides unique benefits and challenges to traditional MCFC. For some multistressed families, the online environment may relieve childcare obstacles, financial burdens, and transportation stresses. Telebehavioral health MCFC increases the likelihood more family members will be able to regularly attend sessions and thereby increase the effectiveness of system-oriented counseling. Counselors implementing telebehavioral health MCFC should be aware of and abide by the ethical standards and laws guiding the practice of technology-assisted MCFC and identify interventions that may need to be adapted. The illustrated case example demonstrates how telebehavioral health MCFC may be utilized to treat a diverse family with complex needs through a theory-based, culturally sensitive, and technologically informed approach.

CASE EXPLORATION

The Levai family decided to initiate MCFC due to frequent verbal altercations between Amy and Raymond. Amy was recently diagnosed with attention-deficit hyperactivity disorder (ADHD) and her impulsive and hyperactive behavior often provokes an irritated reaction from Raymond. Raymond also demonstrates flat affect and depressive symptoms. Tristin discovered superficial cuts on Raymond's arm 30 days ago. Raymond stated the cuts were self-inflicted and, out of concern for Raymond's safety, Tristin took him to an in-patient facility at that time to be evaluated, but he did not meet criteria for in-patient care.

Various issues present in the parental subsystem. Pat is unsure of her role within the family and how much parental authority she should hold. Pat prefers to defer to Tristin for parenting intervention and decisions, but Tristin would like additional help with enforcing rules in the home. The children have substantially less rules and expectations when they are at Juan's house. The transition back to Tristin and Pat's home is often tumultuous. Tristin shared that Juan is open to attending some counseling sessions.

Initial Family Assessment
Katrina initiates an in-person assessment to gain further information and orient the family to counseling. During this initial assessment, Katrina requests copies of court orders that grant joint custody of Amy and Raymond to Juan and Tristin (IAMFC, 2017, Standard B.6.). After a thorough risk assessment, Katrina discovers that since the self-injury was identified, Tristin and Juan have increased their supervision and removed sharp objects from his access at both homes. Raymond

has some self-injury ideation on a weekly basis and depressive symptoms to include feelings of worthlessness, fatigue, irritable mood, and some sleep disturbance.

The Levai family requests that Raymond receive individual therapy as he seems to be the "root of the problems." As a systems-oriented counselor, Katrina identifies that it would be most beneficial for all members of the family to be engaged in therapy. Katrina determines that the family may benefit from technology-assisted MCFC in order to diminish barriers to accessing family services and maximize participation of all family members. She assesses that Raymond's self-harm risk is not acute as he has substantial supervision and support from his parents, and the family is open to having additional individual counseling with Raymond.

Tristin, Pat, and Juan also indicate that they often use videoconferencing in their jobs and are sufficiently technologically savvy to navigate online counseling. The family accepts Katrina's suggestion to enroll Raymond in individual counseling with another counselor and utilize videoconferencing for family therapy so the entire family can attend sessions together weekly. Katrina will provide weekly family counseling sessions with Tristin, Pat, Raymond, and Amy, with sporadic coparenting sessions that involve Tristin, Pat, and/or Juan.

Online Marriage, Couple, and Family Counseling Informed Consent

Katrina reviews in writing necessary informed consent topics related to the risks and benefits of online MCFC and shares with the family that she is provisionally licensed and under the supervision of a licensed professional counselor. Katrina informs the family of the limits to confidentiality in family counseling and reviews her chosen technology platform that meets legal and ethical standards for encryption and security. She also recruits the family's help in ensuring a confidential environment by not sharing their family's confidences outside of session and making sure they are meeting with the therapist in a private location.

In order to establish boundaries around communication, Katrina shares that forms of communication such as email or phone calls can be utilized to confirm appointments, but it is not a venue for additional counseling. Katrina recommends weekly videoconferencing for the family and provides crisis numbers that can be utilized in the event of an emergency in between sessions. In addition, Katrina tells the family that if connection is ever lost in the middle of the session, she will attempt to reconnect the videoconference, and, if this fails, she will call the family to complete the session by phone. If this becomes a recurrent problem, the appropriateness of online MCFC will be reevaluated.

Cultural and Compositional Considerations

The Levai family consists of Juan, a second-generation Cuban American man who is divorced from Tristin, a Caucasian American woman who is recoupled with Pat. Pat is a Caucasian American transgender woman. Cuban American families tend to value hierarchy in family interactions and prefer present-oriented problem solving (Garcia-Preto, 2005). Therapy will incorporate a focus on the family hierarchy, utilize interventions that engage the here and now, and recruit participation from all family members (Garcia-Preto, 2005).

The family is a blended, binuclear family. Raymond and Amy shift weekly between Tristin's home and Juan's home to visit both custodial parents. Tristin's relationship with a transgender woman after being married to her children's father is impactful to Raymond and Amy. Tristin's sexuality and

Pat's gender identity will be a topic of discussion throughout family therapy to include assisting the family in developing a language to discuss sexual fluidity and gender expansiveness.

Conflict among the parental triad (Tristin, Pat, and Juan) is a salient part of the therapeutic work. Katrina discovers that Juan has used disparaging language when talking about Tristin and derogatory and degrading speech when referring to Pat in the presence of Amy and Raymond. During divorce and recoupling, children often experience competing loyalties and an array of emotions (anger, guilt, betrayal, etc.; McGoldrick & Carter, 2016). The ex-spouses will likely need to continue to resolve their post-divorce emotional residue and eliminate negative talk about each other in the presence of the children. In addition, the parents will need to develop and enforce consistent expectations for the children and both homes. Mothers often call on their new partners (stepparents) to intervene and discipline children; however, stepparents have the greatest success when they attempt to befriend the children prior to acting as a disciplinarian (McGoldrick & Carter, 2016). Strengthening Pat's relationship with the children and further delineating her role in the family system will also be important.

The family is navigating two life cycle stages: Raymond is an adolescent and Amy is still a young child but approaching adolescence. Adolescents who have a parent who comes out often experience confusion in the midst of their own sexual identity emergence (Welsh, 2008). Young children may struggle to reconcile competing perspectives of homophobia (e.g., Juan's comments) and their parent's sexual identity (Welsh, 2008). Verbal altercations between the siblings are likely influenced by the stress of the divorce and recoupling, Raymond's depressive symptoms (i.e., irritability), Amy's impulsivity and hyperactivity, and dissonance within the parental subsystem (e.g., lack of agreed-on rules, inconsistent enforcement of consequences).

Implementing Online Marriage, Couple, and Family Counseling

A few days before the family's initial session, Tristin and Pat agree to meet with Katrina briefly through videoconferencing. This meeting allows Katrina to confirm the family understands how to navigate the technology and to check connectivity. The four-member family then meets with Katrina through videoconferencing for their first online MCFC session.

At the beginning of the session, Katrina notes the exact location of the family so that in case of an emergency, Katrina would know where to direct emergency services. Katrina also reminds the family of the need to be in a private location to ensure confidentiality and their back-up plan for what do if the connection is disrupted. Katrina decides to implement a structural family therapy (SFT) approach with the Levai family because the family goals relate to boundaries, alignments, and hierarchy. These treatment goals include strengthening and delineating the family hierarchy, determining boundaries with Pat and the children, clarifying family rules, improving communication, and increasing connection and support between family members. In order to implement SFT effectively in an online environment, a few adjustments to interventions are necessary.

Family Therapy Techniques

In the beginning phase of therapy, Structural family therapists identify important family dynamics through tracking of process and join with the family by building rapport and emulating family interactions through mimesis (Goldenberg et al., 2017). Knowing that technology makes reading facial expressions and body language more difficult with multiple people sitting some distance away from the screen, Katrina reflects her observations of family interactions more frequently and checks for understanding. She relies on verbal reflection of content and feeling to build rapport rather than nonverbal interactions that may not always be clearly translated through videoconferencing. Katrina also utilizes circular questioning as a tool to understand the family's process and repetitive transactional patterns. This method does not depend on accurate assessment of body language and facial expressions but requires family members to reflect on and verbalize family processes.

Structural family therapists often regulate the intensity of a session by directing the family to salient and problematic family dynamics in order to disrupt homeostasis. Regulating intensity is also utilized to de-escalate interactions that are becoming too intense. This can be accomplished by directing the family to utilize calming strategies or by taking a break from the provocative topic. Katrina notices that Amy and Raymond can easily escalate into shouting matches during session. Katrina decides to engage the whole family in mindfulness and grounding techniques and discussions related to physiological signals they are becoming angry. The family agrees to monitor themselves in session and to indicate when they are becoming overwhelmed and need to take a break from the topic and circle back when they can engage relatively calmly. The family also chooses a code word they will say when they need to take a break. Katrina utilizes the password to direct Amy and Raymond to calm down in future sessions, and then directs Tristin to remind the children about these grounding techniques when they appear escalated in session. Eventually, Amy and Raymond begin to show signs of self-monitoring and are able to better tolerate distress when discussing difficult topics for longer periods of time. By creating a de-escalation plan that the whole family agrees to and practices, Katrina is better able to regulate intensity and de-escalate even through videoconferencing.

An enactment is a common SFT intervention that requires family members to act out a common family conflict in session as it occurs in daily life (Goldenberg et al., 2017). Katrina identifies that an enactment of family interactions particularly related to parenting, rule enforcement, or conflicts between Pat and the children would be helpful. After explaining the purpose of the intervention and providing guidance on the interaction to be enacted, Katrina indicates to the family the boundaries of the camera angle and asks them to ensure they can still be seen if they need to get up to demonstrate the enactment. Katrina also knows that this intervention at times is paired with regulating intensity interventions as enactments can bring up strong emotions. Katrina reminds them of their code word and thoroughly processes the experience of the intervention afterward from each family members' perspective.

Katrina also implements the intervention of boundary making by inviting Pat and Tristin to have a videoconferencing session alone to discuss partnership conflicts and to negotiate a parental strategy. Through negotiation, Tristin, Pat, and Katrina agree that Pat should have delegated authority to enforce the rules Tristin and Juan create. Katrina also includes coparenting sessions with Tristin and Juan to negotiate consistent rules for both homes and to discuss positive communication about the other parents in front of the children.

An unbalancing intervention often upsets homeostasis, empowers a disempowered family member, or reduces excessive power of a family member. Unbalancing occurs when a counselor uses their position of power as the family counselor to join with a family member and thereby increasing that family member's relative power. This could be accomplished by agreeing with one side of an argument or focusing on a family member who needs extra support in communicating something important. Raymond indicates to his individual therapist that he would like more support and intentional listening from his mother, Tristin. Katrina would like to have a session with Raymond and Tristin so that he can communicate his need for support. Katrina wishes she could use unbalancing to sit next to Raymond in session as this is a difficult conversation for Raymond to initiate. Since technology does not allow for this, Katrina chooses to use verbal encouragers while Raymond speaks and compliments Raymond on his courage to share. This verbal validation of Raymond is still an implementation of unbalancing as it serves to increase Raymond's power. Unbalancing can be used to split up coalitions within families who are present in the same room by asking family members to rearrange their seating, or to give the impression of unification by asking parents to sit next to each other. As always, after implementing this intervention, the counselor would process the family's experience.

Worksheets

WORKSHEET: DECISION TREE

Do the clients have concerns or goals that can be reasonably addressed through telebehaviroal health MCFC?

    If no, consider the best form of service to recommend based on the clients concerns or goals.

    If yes …

Do the clients present a level of severity of distress appropriate for online MCFC?

    If no, the severity of the issues or concerns may be too high and necessitate a recommendation to another form of treatment.

    If yes …

Do the clients have access to adequate, secure, and confidential means to engage in online MCFC?

    If no, determine what form of care is most appropriate based on the resources available to the clients.

    If yes …

Do the clients present the willingness and ability to use the relevant technology?

    If no, determine what form of care is most appropriate based on the willingness and ability of the clients.

    If yes, the clients may be a good fit for online MCFC.

Adapted from Caldwell et al. (2017).

Basic Counseling Forms

ONLINE MCFC INFORMED CONSENT SAMPLE STATEMENTS

Client Location

In order to ensure best practices regarding client safety and security, the location of participants engaging in online marriage, couples, and family counseling will be documented. In the instance where multiple participants are conferencing from different locations, the location of each participant will be documented at the beginning of each session.

Privacy and Confidentiality

While receiving online marriage, couples, and family counseling, the privacy of all participants is of high importance. Each person must attend counseling in a private setting. Although rare, there may be instances where the counselor will request to speak with or ask assessment questions of one or more participants individually while other participants are not present. The counselor will request one or more individuals to briefly leave the room until invited to return; the remaining family member(s) will pan the camera to show that the room is now otherwise cleared of any other persons and utilize headphones with the counselor to optimize private communication. Individual sessions with the counselor will be very rare as the goal of therapy is to focus on the marriage, couple, or family relationships. If individual therapy is desired or recommended, the counselor can assist with finding appropriate resources.

Safety and Crisis Protocol

Receiving distance counseling (telehealth) for relational or familial concerns can at times prompt intense feelings, including that of conflict or distress. All participants receiving telehealth services understand and agree that in the event of the escalation of such feelings, that the counselor will attempt to apply therapeutic interventions in order to calm and de-escalate the immediate situation. This may include asking one or more individuals to take a break from a topic or apply a previously discussed coping strategy. Further, it is understood and agreed on by all participating parties that should the aforementioned interventions or recommendations not be followed, or if at the counselor's discretion there is a reasonable concern for the immediate safety of any individual participating in counseling, the counselor will attempt to contact the emergency contact listed on the intake form or local emergency services. If the conference is terminated or is otherwise disconnected at a point where the counselor has concern for the safety of any individual participating in counseling, the counselor will attempt to reestablish connection at least once and no more than two times prior to contacting a listed emergency contact or local emergency services.

Alternate Treatment Options

Online marriage, couples, and family counseling is understood to be one treatment option among many, and as such may not be the best fit for every couple, family, or situation. The counselor will assess for the appropriateness of online services and may recommend alternative treatment options. The clients are also informed that in addition to online counseling, alternative treatment options may be available, including but not limited to in-person couples or family counseling, individual counseling, print and online self-help, educational and assessment resources, and local workshops (webinars) or groups.

Online Resources

- **The International Association of Marriage and Family Counseling (IAMFC):** A division of the American Counseling Association that provides a Code of Ethics that explicates right conduct in the practice of MCFC. Guidance on technology-assisted couples and family counseling is provided. The IAMFC Code of Ethics can be found here: http://www.iamfconline.org/public/IAMFC-Ethical-Code-Final.pdf

- **The American Association of Marriage and Family Therapy (AAMFT):** Provides standards for ethical practice when working with couples and families. The AAMFT Code of Ethics can be found here: https://www.aamft.org/Legal_Ethics/Code_of_Ethics.aspx

- **The National Board of Certified Counselors (NBCC):** Offers credentialing as a board certified-telemental health provider (BC-TMH). Information regarding attaining this credential can be found here: https://www.cce-global.org/credentialing/bctmh

References

American Association for Marriage and Family Therapy. (2015). *AAMFT code of ethics.* https://www.aamft.org/Legal_Ethics/Code_of_Ethics.aspx

American Counseling Association. (2014). *ACA code of ethics.* Author. https://www.counseling.org/resources/aca-code-of-ethics.pdf

Blumer, M., Hertlein, K., & VandenBosch, M. (2015). Towards the development of educational core competencies for couple and family therapy technology practices. *Contemporary Family Therapy: An International Journal, 37*(2), 113–121. https://doi.org/10.1007/s10591-015-9330-1

Busby, D. M., Holman, T. B., & Taniguchi, N. (2001). RELATE: Relationship evaluation of the individual, family, cultural, and couple contexts. *Family Relations, 50*(4), 308–316. https://doi.org/10.1111/j.1741-3729.2001.00308.x

Caldwell, B. E., Bischoff, R. J., Derigg-Palumbo, K. A., & Liebert, J. D. (2017). *Best practices in the online practice of couple and family therapy: Report of the online therapy workgroup.* American Association for Marriage and Family Therapy (AAMFT).

Cicila, L. N., Georgia, E. J., & Doss, B. D. (2014). Incorporating internet-based interventions into couple therapy: Available resources and recommended uses. *Australian & New Zealand Journal of Family Therapy, 35*, 414–430. https://doi.org/10.1002/anzf.1077

Comer, J. S., Furr, J. M., Cooper-Vince, C., Madigan, R. J., Chow, C., Chan, P., Idrobo, F., Chase, R. M., NcNeil, C. B., & Eyberg, S. M. (2015). Rationale and considerations for the internet-based delivery of parent-child interaction therapy, *Journal of Cognitive Behavioral Practice, 22*(3), 302–316. https://doi.org/10.1016/j.cbpra.2014.07.003

Comer, J. S., Furr, J. M., Miguel, E. M., Cooper-Vince, C. E., Carpenter, A. L., Elkins, R. M., Kerns, C. E., Cornacchio, D., Chou, T., Coxe, S., DeSerisy, M., Sanchez, A. L., Golik, A., Martin, J., Myers, K. M., & Chase, R. (2017). Remotely delivering real-time parent training to the home: An initial randomized trial of internet-delivered parent-child interaction therapy (I-PCIT). *Journal of Consulting and Clinical Psychology, 85*(9), 909–917. https://doi.org/10.1037/ccp0000230

Doss, B. D., Feinberg, L. K., Rothman, K., Roddy, M. K., & Comer, J. S. (2017). Using technology to enhance and expand interventions for couples and families: Conceptual and methodological considerations. *Journal of Family Psychology, 31*(8), 983–993. https://doi.org/10.1037/fam0000349

Dunstan, D. A., & Tooth, S. M. (2012). Treatment via videoconferencing: A pilot study of delivery by clinical psychology. *Australian Journal of Rural Health, 20*(2), 88–94. https://doi.org/10.1111/j.1440-1584.2012.01260.x

Farero, A., Springer, P., Hollist, C., & Bischoff, R. (2015). Crisis management and conflict resolution: Using technology to support couples throughout deployment. *Contemporary Family Therapy: An International Journal, 37*(3), 281–290. https://doi.org/10.1007/s10591-015-9343-9

Garcia-Preto, N. (2005). Latino families: An overview. In M. McGoldrick, J. Giordano, & J, K. Pearce (Eds.), *Ethnicity & family therapy* (3rd ed.) (pp.141–154). Guilford.

Gassova, Z., & Werner-Wilson, R. J. (2018). Characteristics of e-therapy websites involving marriage and family therapists. *The American Journal of Family Therapy, 46*(1), 27–43. https://doi.org/10.1080/01926187.2018.1428127

Goldenberg, I., Stanton, M., & Goldenberg, H. (2017). *Family therapy: An overview* (9th ed.). Cengage.

Hertlein, K. M., Blumer, M. L. C., & Mihaloliakos, J. H. (2015). Marriage and family counselors' perceived ethical issues related to online therapy. *Family Journal, 23*(1), 5–12. https://doi.org/10.1177/1066480714547184

Hertlein, K. M., Blumer, M. L., & Smith, J. M. (2014). Marriage and family therapists' use and comfort with online communication with clients. *Contemporary Family Therapy, 36*, 58–69. https://doi.org/10.1007/s10591-013-9284-0

Hilty, D., Gentry, M., McKean, A., Cowan, K., Lim, R., & Lu, F. (2019). Telehealth for rural diverse populations: Telebehavioral and cultural competencies, clinical outcomes and administrative approaches. *MHealth, 6*(20), 1–9. https://doi.org/10.21037/mhealth.2019.10.04

International Association of Marriage and Family Counselors. (2017). *IAMFC code of ethics.* Author.

Larson, J. H., Vatter, R. S., Galbraith, R. C., Holman, T. B., & Stahmann, R. F. (2007). The relationship evaluation (RELATE) with therapist-assisted interpretation: Short term effects on premarital relationships. *Journal of Marital and Family Therapy, 33*, 364–374. https://doi.org/10.1111/j.1752-0606.2007.00036.x

Mallen, M. J., & Vogel, D. L. (2005). Online counseling: A need for discovery. *The Counseling Psychologist, 33*(6), 910–921. https://doi.org/10.1177/0011000005280182

McCoy, M., Hjelmstad, L. R., & Stinson, M. (2013). The role of tele-mental health in therapy for couples in long-distance relationships. *Journal of Couple & Relationship Therapy, 12*(4), 339–358. https://doi.org/10.1080/15332691.2013.836053

McGoldrick, M. & Carter, B. (2016). The remarriage cycle: Divorced, multi-nuclear and recoupled families. In M. McGoldrick, N. Garcia Preto, & B. Carter (Eds.), The expanding family life cycle: Individual, family, and social perspectives (5th ed., pp. 408-427). Pearson.

Mucic, D. (2010). Transcultural telepsychiatry and its impact on patient satisfaction. *Journal Telemedical Telecare, 16*, 237–242. https://doi.org/10.1258/jtt.2009.090811

National Board of Certified Counselors. (n.d.). The board certified-telemental health provider (BC-TMH) credential. https://www.nbcc.org/resources/nccs/newsletter/the-board-certified-telemental-health-provider-bc-tmh-credential

Roddy, M. K., Georgia, E. J., & Doss, B. D. (2018). Couples with intimate partner violence seeking relationship help: Associations and implications for self-help and online interventions. *Family Process*, 57(2), 293–307. https://doi.org/10.1111/famp.12291

Roddy, M. K., Rothman, K., Cicila, L. N., & Doss, B. D. (2018). *Why do couples seek relationship help online? Description and comparison to in-person interventions.* Journal of Marital & Family Therapy, 45(3), 369–379. https://doi.org/10.1111/jmft.12329

Shore, J. H., Savin, D. M., Novins, D., & Manson, S. M. (2006). Cultural aspects of telepsychiatry. *Journal of Telemedicine and Telecare, 12*, 116–121. https://doi.org/10.1258/135763306776738602

Sue, D. W., Sue, D., Neville, H. A., & Smith, L. (2019). *Counseling the culturally diverse: theory and practice.* Wiley.

Weiner, M. F., Rossetti, H. C., & Harrah, K. (2011). Videoconference diagnosis and management of Choctaw Indian dementia patients. *Alzheimer's & Dementia, 7*, 562–566. https://doi.org/10.1016/j.jalz.2011.02.006

Welsh, M. (2008). Aphenomenological exploration of adolescents raised by same-sex parents. Unpublished doctoral dissertation, Massachusetts School of Professional Psychology, Boston, MA.

Wrape, E. R., & McGinn, M. M. (2019). Clinical and ethical considerations for delivering couple and family therapy via telehealth. *Journal of Marital & Family Therapy, 45*(2), 296–308. https://doi.org/10.1111/jmft.12319

Counseling for Students

K–COLLEGE

Rachel McRoberts and Anita M. Pool

Counseling is a unique professional relationship in which counselors help individuals of all ages address the difficulties in their lives (Remley & Herlihy, 2016). When working specifically with children and adolescents, counselors have numerous considerations to make: the age and developmental level of the child or adolescent; the youth's interests and personality; the systems in which the young person lives and functions; familial and cultural factors; presenting and underlying issues; goals for treatment; and the setting in which counseling takes place. These considerations are made within the context of the counselor's theoretical orientation and influence the choice of interventions and techniques.

Historically, counseling with young people has taken place primarily in traditional in-office settings such as agencies, schools, private practice offices, and hospitals. Research indicates youth in need face many access barriers to services (Grové & Reupert, 2017; National Center for Health Workforce Analysis, 2015). Despite the increase in youth mental health diagnoses and deaths by suicide in recent years, there continues to be a vast shortage of specialized mental health providers and barriers to access to treatment (Centers for Disease Control and Prevention [CDC], 2019; Collishaw, 2015; Curtin & Heron, 2019; Health Resources & Services Administration, 2018). Online counseling, also known as telebehavioral health, may provide the solution to such problems.

The growing need for telebehavioral health services became an immediate necessity in early 2020. The COVID-19 pandemic called for social distancing practices, which quickly and unexpectedly escorted therapists out of their offices. This led to the immediate incorporation of telebehavioral health with loosened federal and state guidelines (Medicare.gov, 2020). The current pandemic led to a surge of interest in counseling online, which included counseling of young people.

Advantages to Online Counseling With Young People

The benefits of offering telebehavioral health services for youth are numerous. First, systemic barriers, including access to culturally aligned and accessible care, can be addressed through telebehavioral health (Bhugra, 2016; Sibley et al., 2017). With more than 85% of households in the United States possessing Internet access (Ryan, 2018), telebehavioral health may improve access to treatment by removing barriers. Further, new and developing online technology allows portable access to counseling services for underserved children and families in the community. Additionally, online technology increases opportunities for collaboration with caregivers and teachers to develop **individualized education plans (IEPs)** in schools and residential treatment teams (Palmer et al., 2010). Increased access to counseling may also help lessen the stigma of receiving treatment (Hollis et al., 2017). The removal of barriers, increased opportunities for collaboration, and decrease in the stigma associated with receiving counseling may influence preventative care outcomes.

Telebehavioral health has also been found to increase access to services by fitting more conveniently into families' schedules and lifestyle (Hilty et al., 2013; Rockhill et al., 2013). When services are accessible, outcomes are more likely to improve. Telebehavioral health may also work better than traditional therapy due to novelty and preferential level of interaction for some, and it is just as effective for obtaining accurate diagnosis for children and families (Hilty et al., 2013; Sibley et al., 2017). Adolescents with depression, anxiety, and body image and eating disorders (Hollis et al., 2016; Kass et al., 2014; Schlegl et al., 2015) may appreciate the increased sense of privacy and autonomy that telebehavioral health may bring.

Online counseling may provide more power to the client and provide a space in which tensions and identity may be explored slightly differently than in person. Through the screen, a unique relationship of "interactive imagination" may be cultivated, which invites playing with "proximity and distance, of presence and absence, of reality and fantasy" (Roesler, 2017, p. 376). Online counseling may be particularly helpful for those who experience anxiety and shame, or are processing trauma, due to increased perceptual safety with the physical distance, reducing inhibition (Knaevelsrud et al., 2015; Roesler, 2017). Intensified self-disclosure (Barak & Gluck-Ofri, 2007), disinhibition (Minear et al., 2013), and a focus on one's inner life has been observed more greatly in intimate online interactions, which may also show to be an advantage in psychotherapy (Roesler, 2017).

Finally, young people are increasingly socializing and seeking services online (Johnson et al., 2015). Research has shown that young people who seek telebehavioral health services have low levels of hope but high levels of distress reduction and treatment outcome expectations (Dowling & Rickwood, 2016). Further, they tend to experience an increased sense of well-being afterward (Fukkink & Hermanns, 2009; Stephenson et al., 2019).

Challenges to Online Counseling With Young People

Although evidence continues to show that telebehavioral health can be as effective as traditional therapy (Cook & Doyle, 2002; Hilty et al., 2013), many unique ethical and practical challenges exist with this format (National Board for Certified Counselors [NBCC], 2016), particularly when working with young people. These include issues of privacy and confidentiality, mandatory reporting, and the management of emergency or crisis situations. These and other practical challenges need to be considered by the counselor prior to starting telebehavioral health counseling.

Privacy and Confidentiality

A primary ethical concern with online counseling is related to privacy and confidentiality. Because the counselor is unable to see who else is in the room with the client, ensuring privacy can be challenging. The limits to confidentiality in an online setting should be clearly stated in the consent and discussed with the parent/guardian and youth (American Counseling Association [ACA], 2014, H.2.c.). A plan can be developed in conjunction with the young client to alert the counselor if someone enters the room during a session, such as a code word.

It is important to foster an individual's autonomy and to provide a safe, confidential space to share, process, and be heard, no matter the client's age. Developing this skill when working with children is a nuanced process because children's privacy and sense of autonomy is often violated in many daily contexts. This may include the child having items taken away, confinement, or adults placing their hands on the child as punishment or coercion to modify behavior. Maintaining a safe, trusting therapeutic relationship with a child involves keeping much of the detail of sessions private. However, counselors should explain how, when, and why caregivers may be involved. The age of consent for treatment, which varies by state, needs to be considered for each case. Additional information on this topic is explored in Chapter 3.

Emergency or Crisis Situations

As part of informed consent, counselors should clearly establish a protocol for how emergency or crisis situations will be handled. For example, the steps to be taken if an adolescent expresses suicidal thoughts or ways the counselor can ensure that the adolescent is safe should be clearly outlined. A client-specific plan should be developed for emergencies, including but not limited to dialing 9-1-1. Emergency contact information for the client should be obtained during the intake and updated regularly in the event that the counselor needs to contact an adult. Additionally, emergency resources in the client's geographic area, such as crisis numbers and hospital locations, should be easily accessible. Finally, the counselor should confirm the address of the client at the beginning of the session in case an emergency situation arises that may warrant calling 9-1-1.

Mandatory Reporting

As mandatory reporters, counselors have an ethical and legal obligation to report known or suspected child abuse or neglect (Remley & Herlihy, 2016). Providing telebehavioral health services to a young person in their home may present unique situations for counselors that may not otherwise occur in traditional in-office sessions. For example, the counselor may witness an unsafe event or dangerous environment, such as overhearing language or seeing behavior that may be considered abusive. Parents/guardians and young clients should be made aware of the counselor's mandatory reporting obligations at the time of consent. It is imperative for counselors to be familiar with the mandatory reporting laws and procedures in their state.

Practical Challenges

Practical challenges may also be encountered with telebehavioral health, particularly with young children. Some challenges include difficulty engaging young people through a screen, the ability of little children to sustain attention, and the adaptation of interventions and techniques for use online, thus causing sessions to look different than in-person sessions. For example, counselors who are theoretically nondirective may find themselves being more directive in telebehavioral health sessions with their young clients. Also, the length of sessions may be shorter than traditional in-person sessions in a playroom, as young children may have difficulty sustaining attention in an online format. Finally, parents or guardians may be more involved in telebehavioral health sessions than they otherwise would be during traditional in-person counseling sessions. Some of the challenges require the further adaptations of treatment approaches and intervention, which will be discussed in the upcoming sections.

Additional potential issues involve the use of technology. Such issues may include the counselor's or client's loss of an internet connection or a weak internet connection, the client experiencing difficulty navigating the counseling platform, or a lost link for the client to sign into the session. According to the ACA (2014) Code of Ethics, the issues associated with using technology are addressed through informed consent. An alternate plan for handling technological issues should be discussed during the intake. Further consideration should be made for the use of technology with very young children, such as logistical issues and technological assistance during the session, which may require a parent to be present for the duration of the telebehavioral health session.

Training and Supervision

Online supervision is increasingly popular (Inman et al., 2019), and may be a "convenient and cost-effective" solution for play therapists to feel like "part of a team" (Paulson et al., 2015, p. 131) while encouraging continuing education and reflective practices. Supervisors have a duty to be aware of the cultural, technological, legal, and ethical implications of issues that may arise in our practice, including the use of videoconferencing and other technologies that may increase the risk of breaching confidentiality (ACA, 2014; Carlisle et al., 2017) and compliance with ongoing health insurance literacy (Brown, 2018). Greater access to theoretically aligned training and supervision via interactive online platforms could directly and easily address these needs (McRoberts, 2019).

Modification of Approaches and Techniques for Children and Adolescents

Delivering counseling services via telebehavioral health does not change a counselor's theoretical orientation; however, basic counseling skills, the approach to counseling, and some interventions may need to be modified to account for the online delivery of counseling services. The ability to be **telepresent** (Circle of Security International, n.d.), or emotionally engaged and regulated online, is a developmental skill for both the client and the therapist. The length of the telebehavioral health session may need to be shorter than an office session due the child's age or developmental level and attention span.

Basic Counseling Skills and Adaptations

Counselors are trained in basic counseling skills. These include the development of the therapeutic alliance, use of verbal and non-verbal skills, and assessment of current needs. The adaption of these and other counseling techniques to the online synchronous format are explored in this section.

Therapeutic Alliance

Safe, nurturing, responsive relationships in childhood not only build healthy brain architecture (Center on the Developing Child at Harvard University, 2011), but also help to protect and repair it (Blaustein & Kinniburgh, 2019; Wass et al., 2018). A strong therapeutic alliance can be established online in the same manner as traditional in-office settings. Through nonverbal body language, such as eye contact and facial expressions, as well as through verbal communication, counselors can express genuine interest, engagement, and connection with a young person. Additionally, therapeutic alliance is established when counselors meet their young clients where they are developmentally. The power of the therapeutic relationship, even when it is established online, should not be underestimated. As in traditional counseling, it is still the engagement within a supportive relationship itself that is identified as key to successful therapeutic outcomes with young people (Hollis et al., 2016; Kass et al., 2014; Schlegl et al., 2015).

The Use of Silence and Nonverbal Body Language

Although silence may feel awkward in everyday conversations, it is valuable in a therapeutic setting. Silence can allow young people the needed time to process, reflect, and respond to a tough topic or difficult question. However, silence may be experienced differently in an online setting than in a traditional in-office session. Without the ability to see the client's entire body and read the client's body language, counselors must rely on other cues to determine if the silence is occurring in a therapeutic manner. For example, is an adolescent being silent because she is processing the question just asked, or is she looking at social media on her phone outside of the view of the camera? Counselors who provide online counseling should be aware of the possibilities of other causes of silence. Expectations, such as not using a cell phone or tablet while in a telebehavioral health session, can be established with the child or adolescent early in the counseling relationship to reduce distractions, and thus the possibility of misunderstanding the silence.

Counselor's Theoretical Orientation and Treatment Modality

Many theoretical orientations recognize from a developmental perspective that routine and ritual is especially important for children to create consistency, predictability, and, therefore, emotional safety. Thus, continuing to hold the space with a focus on the emotional needs of the client and inviting creative expression during telebehavioral health is an important consideration for therapists (Freedle, 2020). The common theoretical orientations and treatment modalities of counselors who work with children and adolescents are presented with adaptations for telebehavioral health.

Expressive/Art Therapy

The expressive arts are as old as recorded humanity, with deep roots in relaying personal and cultural history, myth, ritual, as well as healing the mind and body. The power of creation has long been recognized in the field of mental health as assisting with emotional expression, insight, and positive mood enhancement (Jung, 1921/1971). The client's own imagination, symbolic language, and trusting innate healing potential are at the center of the expressive arts. The medium may change along with client need and interest, as well as in accordance with therapist training and expertise (Kossak, 2015). Clients are encouraged to explore, take risks, and engage in the embodiment of the creative process before imposing meaning on the work. Play, painting, drawing, sculpting, creative writing, music making, and movement are all considered aspects of the expressive arts, though there are areas of specialization.

Literature on how to modify expressive arts interventions for telebehavioral health is emerging (Brooke, 2017). Counselors may need to assist clients in adjusting their camera to frame the entire creative process so that both the client and the work are in view. While kinesthetic interaction with physical mediums is often preferable, a variety of digital applications (apps) and media exists to individually and interactively create works. These apps are increasingly accessible with the use of smartphones and tablets, popular with youth, and range from finger painting, coloring, and drawing, to sand trays with miniatures, to sound mixing and video recording. Screen-sharing applications through telebehavioral health software allows the therapeutic dyad to continue to connect while also viewing digital work. Interactive journals (Capacchione, 2001) may be used on secure platforms for digitally archiving portfolios of clients' work.

Bibliotherapy

Bibliotherapy involves the use of books in a therapeutic manner to help children and adolescents address a variety of issues, such as grief, divorce, trauma, and many others. Bibliotherapy can be used at any point during the counseling process as a way to introduce a tough topic and encourage discussion. In a traditional in-person session, the counselor and young person may sit side by side while the counselor reads the book and the child turns the pages. In a telebehavioral health session, the counselor may read the book and show the pictures to the child, or an electronic version of the book may be used via screen sharing. For very young children, the parent may check the book out from the library so the child can actually hold the book during the session while it is being read.

Play Therapy

Play therapy recognizes that children may have difficulty putting their thoughts and feelings into words. By offering toys and a safe, responsive relationship, play therapy allows children the space to communicate through the use of symbolic interactions (Kottman, 2014). Many children have toys or items that could easily be used as toys in the home for online play therapy. A basic list may include small baskets or totes with a manageable number of items such as the following:

- Art materials: Paper, crayons, washable markers, panned watercolors, Play-doh (store bought or homemade). Some materials may require greater supervision or space preparation and may depend on the developmental level of the youth, due to potential regression and messes, such as with wet paints, or safety considerations, such as pencils and scissors.

- Miniatures/action figures: Consider safety for younger children who may put items in their mouths. Items may include families of people, animals, magical creatures and items, household items such as furniture and food, vehicles, characters from stories/movies.
- Items from nature: Children may create various scenes through constructing and enacting with leaves, flowers, sticks, and stones.
- Soothers: Slow-rise squishies, stress balls, fidget spinners, bubble wrap, stuffed animals, and blankets at hand may be chosen by or offered to children if they feel overwhelmed.

Therapists may ask caregivers to assist in preparing a designated play space for virtual sessions, depending on treatment plan goals and the therapist's theoretical orientation. Nondirective therapists may encourage the use of the same items each week or invite the child to freely explore their play space. More directive therapists may ask for certain items to be collected for session depending on the intervention. Therapists may provide online support for parents by encouraging and coaching them through nondirective play time (Bratton & Landreth, 2020). More formally, the online-filial model of child parent relationship therapy (Hicks & Baggerly, 2017), teaching parents to engage in nondirective play with their children, has been proven efficacious.

Play therapists have expressed many barriers to training and supervision in their specialty area (Donald et al., 2015; Fall et al., 2007; Felton, 2016; Fountain, 2015; VanderGast et al., 2010), including a lack of local training and support. The national shortage of child mental health providers in the United States (National Center for Health Workforce Analysis, 2015) may professionally isolate play therapists while necessitating their engagement in practices beyond their competencies, resulting in a higher risk of burnout and ethical violations (Paulson et al., 2015). There is good evidence that play therapy techniques can be effectively taught through an exclusively online format (Hicks & Baggerly, 2017) despite documented barriers (Deane et al., 2015). Graduate programs in play therapy that use flipped classrooms, incorporating reading, watching videos, and taking quizzes online are being utilized with great success (Counselman-Carpenter, 2018), promoting active engagement in the classroom, reducing lecture time, and improving grades (Rathner & Schier, 2020). Research suggests that motivation, as well, can be influenced by the experience of learning at a higher level with increased levels of autonomy and reflective practices (Burton, 2020).

Sandplay

In sandplay, a room filled with often hundreds of miniatures, sand, and water is carefully prepared as sacred space. A nondirective, largely nonverbal modality, sandplay integrates Jungian psychology, play therapy, the expressive arts, and Eastern mindfulness practices (Kalff, 2020); clients are invited to use items in the room however they like to create a picture or world, suspending judgment and interpretation. Growing in international recognition as rooted in evidenced-based and trauma-informed practices for a variety of populations (Freedle & Slagle, 2018; Roesler, 2017), sandplay is also a supplemental therapeutic intervention especially when traditional verbal interventions have failed (Freedle et al., 2020) and is being adapted for an online format (Freedle, 2020).

While many families cannot designate a specific area in their home to sandplay, there are modifications that have been used by therapists for years that may be applicable. Ready-made sand tray kits are available online; therapists may encourage families to purchase their own or have their own stock for families to borrow for the duration of treatment.

Cognitive Behavioral Therapy

Cognitive behavioral therapy (CBT) focuses on the "interactive relationship between cognitions, emotions, and behaviors," and the importance of changing thinking patterns to create behavioral and emotional changes (Kress et al., 2019, p. 138). CBT has been found to be an effective modality for adolescents; however, additional modifications with high levels of caregiver involvement are needed to be effective for younger children (Minde et al., 2010) because young children have not yet developed the ability to think about their thinking, or conceptualize and then verbalize thoughts, feelings, and behaviors with insight. Research demonstrates the effectiveness of CBT for treating most psychosocial problems in childhood and adolescence (Smith-Adcock & Tucker, 2017). According to Vigerland et al. (2016), the use of internet-delivered CBT has become more popular in the past few years. Computerized cognitive behavioral therapy may be more effective for older adolescents with mild depression, anxiety, body image, and eating disorders when provided with additional support (Hollis et al., 2016; Kass et al., 2014; Schlegl et al., 2015).

CBT approaches use a variety of interventions, and it is common for counselors to use worksheets, handouts, games, or other visuals to help young people understand the relationship between their thoughts, feelings, and behaviors. Adapting the interventions for an online setting may include the use of screen sharing or the whiteboard function, or the use of online games in which both client and counselor can participate. Another adaptation may involve sending a worksheet or handout via email to be printed out prior to the session.

Mindfulness-Based Interventions

With roots in ancient Eastern meditation traditions, gaining popularity in the West since the 1970s, mindfulness is increasingly being recognized as a wellness strategy for preventing the negative effects of chronic stress for families and youth (Benton et al., 2019; Borquist-Conlon et al., 2019; Prenoveau et al., 2018). Mindfulness-based interventions are used to promote self-compassion and awareness, as well as acceptance, nonjudgment, and attention to the present moment (Kress et al., 2019) and can target a variety of concerns, including stress, depression, and anxiety (Cook-Cattone et al., 2019).

Mindfulness activities and interventions bring awareness to the person's body and focus attention on the present moment and can be taught in a variety of settings, including online. Because practice is required for skill mastery, the use of accessible technology may assist in promoting mindfulness for youth (Lucas-Thompson et al., 2019). Mindfulness activities may be selected from other digital media and shared with clients to practice before, during, or after session. Activities may integrate one or more senses, such as quietly observing the color, texture, smell, and then taste of a small food item, or the imagination, as in a guided meditation for physical and emotional relaxation.

Family Therapy

Involving parents, caregivers, and support systems through online counseling may be especially important to provide guidance on how to set up a therapeutic space, including access to toys and other supplies, providing ongoing encouragement and support, and help ensuring client safety (Bratton & Landreth, 2020; Usami, 2016). Young children may need additional supervision or more family-based interventions. As with office-based interventions, counselors are encouraged to navigate and protect an emotionally safe space for the child, nurturing the therapeutic relationship. Caregivers may assist the younger child with affect regulation, ensure safety, and support technical aspects of interventions, which may be, in and of themselves, therapeutic actions (Franklin, 2010). This also includes modulating how much the child is talked about as the identified client in their presence, determining if a family session without the client present is more appropriate. Parents may be asked to record their own play sessions with their children, outside of counseling, to be reviewed later, or use the bug-in ear technique to be coached through session, when using modalities such as child–parent relationship/filial therapy (Landreth & Bratton, 2020).

Needs Assessment

Like all counseling, it is important to start and address the needs of the person when moving onto an online platform (Slone et al., 2012). This includes adapting to environmental and social needs of the client and their family, such as access to the internet and connection with other community resources (Duncan et al., 2014). With preparation and flexibility on behalf of the counselor, the transition to telebehavioral health counseling can be made easier for the client.

SUMMARY

Counseling with children and adolescents has historically taken place in person; however, telebehavioral mental health services for young people has increased greatly in recent years. Technological advances and societal changes have resulted in an increase in accessibility and use of online counseling. Although online counseling is not without challenges, such as ensuring privacy and safety, such issues can be mitigated through proper training and planning. With modifications to basic counseling skills and adaptations to treatment approaches, mental health professionals can successfully meet the counseling needs of young people and their families by providing telebehavioral mental health.

CASE EXPLORATION

Amy Levai, 9 years old, has been referred to her elementary school counselor for engaging in distracting behaviors during class. She has been attending sessions at school, but meeting with the parents has been difficult due to scheduling and transportation issues, as well as relationship dynamics. The school counselor discusses with Amy the possibility, purpose, and benefit of meeting with her parents and asks if there is anything specific that Amy wants her to say, or not say. The school counselor initiates contact with the parents individually for online video sessions, respecting Amy's requests.

Considering the family as it has been provided:

The Levai family consists of Juan, the biological father of Amy and Raymond, and their biological mother, Tristin. Tristin and Juan divorced several years ago. Amy is a 9-year-old female and Raymond is a 16-year-old male. Tristin is currently in a long-term relationship with Pat and sharing custody of Amy and Raymond with Juan. The family system as a whole has numerous challenges and is seeking online counseling because they live in a remote area several hours from any counseling services. Katrina is a provisionally licensed mental health counselor in her state and is currently under the supervision of Eugene, a licensed professional counselor certified in telebehavioral health who resides 2 hours away from Katrina in the same state.

Facts that may surface throughout Katrina's work with the family: Pat is a transgender female; Pat and Tristin are life partners but are not married; and Katrina is pursuing her LPC and is not currently independently licensed.

In this case, what would be important information for the counselor to discuss with Amy before meeting with her parents?

What family dynamics would need to be taken into consideration when scheduling a family session?

What techniques might the counselor employ to assist Amy in feeling more open to sharing her feelings and motivations for her behaviors with her family?

Worksheets

WORKSHEET #1: PREPARATION

Regarding the Therapist

- What specific training in telehealth has the counselor received? Is it specific to children and adolescents and/or a particular modality?
- What platform is planning to be used? Does the counselor have training, supervision, and ongoing support in the medium?
- Billing: Some insurance companies do not cover telebehavioral health, shorter sessions, or family therapy and violate the parity laws that protect mental as well as physical health or demand individual providers use cost-prohibitive HIPAA-compliant platforms inaccessible to independent providers and clients (Center for Connected Health Policy, 2018).

Regarding the Client

- What factors indicate that online is the best medium for this young person to receive counseling?
- Are there any perceived barriers to providing online counseling?

- How comfortable is the client utilizing online mediums? What sites, apps, and games does the client use online?
- For the hyperactive client: Handheld or mobile devices may assist, try to create a low stimulating environment and to limit distractions, be sure to invite breaks and create shorter sessions, allow for standing/walking during session as needed.
- For clients with low energy: Interventions may be timed during periods where it is tough to get motivated (out of bed, homework, etc.)
- For clients with anxiety: Online counseling can provide real-time skill coaching

Regarding the Environment

- Does the family have secure and reliable access to videoconference technology (smartphone, iPad, computer, internet access, etc.)?
- How safe is the home, and is everyone in it supportive of the client being in counseling? If not, is there an alternate location that can be considered?
- Is there a safe adult who is willing and able to spend a session with the client and be available should an emergency occur?

WORKSHEET #2: CHECKLIST

- Age
- Does the young person have difficulty sustaining attention or focus?

  - Counselor: Limit distractions such as clutter, a busy wall or pattern or picture, tone of voice, delivery of materials over a secure connection (won't lose documents). Language should be clear, concise, and instructions brief.
  - Client: Find a space that is quiet and not highly trafficked.

- Does the young person have difficulty with sitting quietly for long periods?

  - Counselor: Limit activities to a set amount of time that works for the client, allow for breaks, encourage the client to stand, walk, march, clap, etc. Consider Kinesthetic needs.
  - Client: Standing during session, use of a stress ball

- Does the young person have access to a quiet, distraction-free environment?
- Does the child need assistance to stay on task?

  - Using the family to assist

- Include the family to support the child, learn skills, and accommodations
- Does the child have a space where they may speak freely?

  - Code words for not alone, someone is listening

- Does the young person have difficulty with eye contact?

  - Some challenges using videoconferencing include eye contact that may be difficult to detect because of camera placement.

- o Recommendations include collecting collateral information from teachers, family, and child to assess this behavior (Palmer et al., 2010).
- o Letting the child know where to look whether in the camera or on the therapist
- Are there other learning disorders or disabilities that might hinder their ability to access the session?
  - o Technology accessibility, accommodations such as recording the session and closed captioning.

Basic Counseling Forms

ONLINE INFORMED ASSCENT/CONSENT FOR MINORS (EXAMPLE)

Today's date: _____

Client name, date of birth:

Client physical address: _____

Primary contact name: _____ Phone number: _____ Email: _____

Names/ages/relationship of others living in the home: _____

Parent/guardian name: _____ Parent/guardian date of birth: _____

Does this caregiver live with client yes/no?

Address: _____ Email: _____ Phone: _____

Parent/guardian name: _____ Parent/guardian date of birth: _____

Does this caregiver live with client yes/no?

Address: _____ Email: _____ Phone: _____

Any current or history of involvement with Child Protective Services/DCS? (copy on file):
Any orders of protection? (copy on file)
Any custody arrangement or other active court orders? (copy on file)
Photo ID/passport (if available)

School name and contact information:

PCP contact information:

Emergency contact:

Name: _____ Relationship to client: _____

Primary phone: _____ Email address: _____

Does this person live with the client? If no, please provide address: _____

While online counseling may not be ideal for all children and adolescents, it may in many cases be a beneficial modality of accessing therapy.

The following conditions must be maintained for the safety of the child:

A caregiver must remain in the home during counseling sessions but should honor the confidentiality of the child and not remain in the room during counseling sessions. A check-in at the beginning or end of session is required.

A caregiver must remain accessible via phone during sessions in case of emergencies.

Should there be concern for the safety of the child, a caregiver will be contacted immediately. Should the caregiver not appear in the video promptly, emergency services will be contacted.

As with face-to-face counseling, if at any time you think your child is in crisis you must first ensure that safety of your child by contacting 9-1-1 or bringing your child to the emergency department. Only after the child is safe should you attempt to contact the therapist.

Your counselor has a responsibility to safeguard your confidentiality to the extent possible through adherence to industry standards for storage and protection of your health information.

Please be advised, however, that, in addition to the security issues outlined previously in this document, there are also specific instances in which therapists are either required by law or are permitted to breach confidentiality in order to protect client safety or public safety. These exceptions include situations in which child, elder, and dependent adult abuse are suspected, threats of harm to self or others, or in the event that a court compels disclosure through official order.

MY INVOLVEMENT WITH CLIENT'S SUPPORT TEAM MEMBERS

In my practice, an individual is my client. However, I do often work with nonoffending support system members, too, if my clients request or agree to it, it is determined to be in their best interest, and it is relevant to their treatment. These are standardly recorded as "family sessions" and may involve trusted partners, spouses, parents, other caregivers or relatives, foster parents, state or county child protective workers, case managers, or friends, with my client's permission and full knowledge. (See Notice of Privacy Policy for more information)

Family sessions are held with my client's goals and emotional well-being at the forefront.
I have a separate protocol for working with treatment teams of juveniles who have offended.

An important aspect of counseling is to foster an individual's autonomy and to provide a safe, confidential space to share, process, and be heard, no matter their age.

_____-year-old clients may sign for and consent to their own treatment, in accordance with
_____ state law.

At the onset of treatment, I discuss with both the minor and caregiver how and what information may be shared, with whom, and when, in a manner appropriate to the minor's age and understanding. It is my policy for minors to be aware if I plan to talk to, or meet with, a member of their support system.

Caregiver involvement in child treatment is often very important; a working therapeutic alliance between caregivers and therapist, as well as the child and therapist, is key. The options for family sessions with or without the child client present are determined on a case-by-case basis, at my discretion. Caregivers are encouraged to schedule family sessions without the client present to discuss sensitive matters that may compromise the child's healing process. I reserve the right to require family sessions without the client present should I perceive a need in the best interest of my child client.

I often do not share the specific content of a child's sessions with caregivers without input from the child, unless the content must be shared for safety reasons or if my professional judgment warrants sharing content for the welfare and health of those involved. I may maintain contact, as necessary, with the referring or subcontracted agency, unless otherwise requested, especially in the case of state or county childcare services involvement with foster care agencies. Release of child's state/county childcare services will not be granted to those accused of abuse or neglect, as outlined by _____ (state code).

Therapy is often nonlinear and is based on a trusting relationship, which is why I ask all caregivers not to overly inquire or otherwise investigate into the content of children's individual sessions (questioning the child, requesting progress notes, etc.). I am more than happy to provide confirmation of attendance and scheduled updates, with proper authorization, but I ask for us all to respect the child's privacy as much as possible. Children are told that what they say to me will remain private unless we discuss details first, or I have reason to believe that someone has been or could be harmed. I want us to honor that to preserve the integrity of the child's healing process, and for children who've been harmed to be able to develop trusting relationships.

Because my practice is trauma informed and attachment based, I ask that should a parent/legal guardian choose for a child in their care to work with me, they agree to avoid corporal, isolating, and overly restrictive punishments, as well as other practices that may be contributing to power struggles or emotional dysregulation, assist their child in coregulating, and commit to problem solving with new and developmentally appropriate skill development. Parenting philosophies encouraged are "gentle," "peaceful," "respectful," "attachment based," and "trauma informed."

Client signature _____ Parent/guardian signature _____

Online Resources

- **Association for Play Therapy:** Provides information and resources regarding the use of play therapy, links professionals to pertinent trainings and a link to assist in finding a qualified play therapist. https://www.a4pt.org/page/PTMakesADifference/Play-Therapy-Makes-a-Difference. htm Bratton, S. C., Landreth, G. L., & Bennett, M. (2020). Special parent-child play time handout. https://cdn.ymaws.com/www.a4pt.org/resource/resmgr/telehealth/4_-_Special_Parent-Child_ Pla.pdf

- **Healthline.com:** Discussion of 6 common eating disorders and their symptoms. https://www.healthline.com/nutrition/common-eating-disorders

- **Nationaleatingdisorders.com:** Resources available regarding eating disorders including information, screening tool and both a helpline and chat area. https://www.nationaleatingdisorders.org/help-support/contact-helpline

- **National Suicide Prevention Lifeline:** Provides information and resources for suicide prevention, including a special link for youth. https://suicidepreventionlifeline.org/

- **Connect Safely.org:** Provides resources youth in crisis including suicide prevention, mental health needs, dating abuse, cyberstalking, and domestic violence, as well as substance use. https://www.connectsafely.org/resources-for-youth-in-crisis/

- **Child Help USA National Hotline:** *Available 24/7, in over 170 languages Helps youth who are suffering child abuse;* 1-800-4-A-CHILD (1-800-422-4453) http://www.childhelpusa.org/

- **Crisis Textline:** *Support to all individuals in crisis;* text "HELLO" to 741741. Connects the user to a crisis counselor via text. www.crisistextline.org

- **Boys Town National Hotline: Provides services for parents and youth, as well as available resources.** *Available 24/7 Serving all at-risk teens and children;* http://www.boystown.org/hotline/

- **Trevor Project Lifeline:** *Confidential suicide hotline for LGBT youth;* 866-488-7386 http://www.thertrevorproject.org

- **Trans Lifeline:** hotline staffed by volunteers who are all trans-identified and educated in the range of difficulties transgender people experience. http://www.translifeline.org

- **National Teen Dating Violence Hotline:** Provides resources and answers to questions or concerns about dating relationships. http://www.loveisrespect.org

- **National Runaway Switchboard:** Provides confidential hotline supports runaway youth for safety. www.1800RUNAWAY.org

- **National Sexual Assault Hotline:** supports victims of sexual assault; LGBT-inclusive, via online counseling. www.rainn.org

- **Human Trafficking Hotline.org:** Information on human trafficking, as well as support for those in need of referrals and assistance. https://humantraffickinghotline.org/

  Available 24/7, confidential hotline; call 1-888-373-7888 24/7; text "HELP" or "INFO" to 233733

- **SMART Recovery Teen and Youth Program:** Provides information on the SMART program, substance recovery resources, and a link to the youth outreach program. https://www.smartrecovery.org/teens

- **Center for Disease Control and Prevention:** Sex education materials for youth and parents, provides information to assist individuals in making healthy informed decision regarding their sexuality. https://www.cdc.gov/healthyyouth/whatworks/what-works-sexual-health-education.htm

References

American Counseling Association. (2014). *ACA code of ethics.* https://www.counseling.org/resources/aca-code-of-ethics.pdf

Barak, A., & Gluck-Ofri, O. (2007). Degree and reciprocity of self-disclosure in online forums. *Cyberpsychology & Behavior, 10*(3), 407–417. https://doi.org/10.1089/cpb.2006.9938

Benton, J., Coatsworth, D., & Biringen, Z. (2019). Examining the association between emotional availability and mindful parenting. *Journal of Child and Family Studies, 28*(6), 1650–1663. https://doi.org/10.1007/s10826-019-01384-x

Bhugra, D. (2016). Social discrimination and social justice. *International Review of Psychiatry, 28*(4), 336–341. https://doi.org/10.1080/09540261.2016.1210359

Blaustein, M., & Kinniburgh, K. (2019). *Treating traumatic stress in children and adolescents: How to foster resilience through attachment, self-regulation, and competency.* Guilford.

Borquist-Conlon, D. S., Maynard, B. R., Brendel, K. E., & Farina, A. S. J. (2019). Mindfulness-based interventions for youth with anxiety: A systematic review and meta-analysis. *Research on Social Work Practice, 29*(2), 195–205. https://doi.org/10.1177/1049731516684961

Bratton, S. C., & Landreth, G. L. (2020). *Provide emotional support to play therapy clients through working with parents.* https://cdn.ymaws.com/www.a4pt.org/resource/resmgr/telehealth/2_-_Provide_Emotional_Suppor.pdf

Brooke, S. L. (2017). *Combining the creative therapies with technology: Using social media and online counseling to treat clients.* Charles C Thomas.

Brown, V. (2018). Infusing adult education principles into a health insurance literacy program. *Health Promotion Practice, 19*(2), 240–245. https://doi.org/10.1177/1524839917700369

Burton, E. (2020). Factors leading educators to pursue a doctorate degree to meet professional development needs. *International Journal of Doctoral Studies, 15*, 75–87. https://doi.org/10.28945/4476

Capacchione, L. (2001). *Interactive journal.* http://www.luciac.com/index.php/interactive-journal

Carlisle, R. M., Hays, D.G., Pribesh, S. L., & Wood, C. T. (2017). Educational technology and distance supervision in counselor education. *Counselor Education & Supervision, 56*, 33–49. https://doi.org/10.1002/ceas.12058

Center for Connected Health Policy. (2018). *State telehealth laws and reimbursement policies: A comprehensive scan for the 50 states and District of Columbia.* National Telehealth Policy Resource Center. https://www.cchpca.org/telehealth-policy/state-telehealth-laws-and-reimbursement-policies-report

Center for Diseases Control and Prevention. (2019). *Data and statistics on children's mental health.* https://www.cdc.gov/childrensmentalhealth/data.html

Center on the Developing Child at Harvard University. (2011, September 29). *2. Serve & return interaction shapes brain circuitry.* [Video file]. https://youtu.be/m_5u8-QSh6A

Circle of Security International. (n.d.). *Home page.* https://www.circleofsecurityinternational.com

Collishaw, S. (2015). Annual research review: Secular trends in child and adolescent mental health. *Journal of Child Psychology and Psychiatry, 56*, 370–393. doi: 10.1111/jcpp.12372.

Cook-Cattone, C. P., Anderson, L. M., & Kane, L. S. (2019). *The elements of counseling children and adolescents* (2nd ed.). Springer.

Cook, J. E., & Doyle, C. (2002). Working alliance in online therapy as compared to face-to-face therapy: preliminary results. *Cyberpsychology & Behavior, 5*, 95–105. https://doi.org/10.1089/109493102753770480

Counselman-Carpenter, E. A. (2018). Efficacy of the flipped classroom to teach play therapy: A mixed-methods study. *International Journal of Play Therapy, 27*(3), 146–156. https://doi.org/10.1037/pla0000076

Curtin, S. C., & Heron, M. (2019). *Death rates due to suicide and homicide among persons aged 10-24: United States, 2000-20017.* National Center for Health Statistics. https://www.cdc.gov/nchs/products/index.htm

Deane, F. P., Gonsalvez, C., Blackman, R., Saffioti, D., & Andresen, R. (2015). Issues in the development of e-supervision in professional psychology: A review. *Australian Psychologist, 50*(3), 241–247. https://doi.org/10.1111/ap.12107

Donald, E. J., Culbreth, J. R., & Carter, A. W. (2015). Play therapy supervision: A review of the literature. *International Journal of Play Therapy, 24,* 59–77. http://dx.doi.org/10.1037/a0039104

Dowling, M., & Rickwood, D. (2016). Exploring hope and expectations in the youth mental health online counselling environment. *Computers in Human Behavior, 55*(Part A), 62–68. https://doi.org/10.1016/j.chb.2015.08.009

Duncan, A. B., Velasquez, S. E., & Nelson, E. L. (2014). Using videoconferencing to provide psychological services to rural children and adolescents: A review and case example. *Journal of Clinical Child & Adolescent Psychology, 43,* 115–127. doi: 10.1080/15374416.2013.836452

Fall, M., Drew, D., Chute, A., & More, A. (2007). The voices of registered play therapists as supervisors. *International Journal of Play Therapy, 16,* 133–146. http://dx.doi.org/10.1037/1555-6824.16.2.133

Felton, A. D. (2016). *Identity in the sand: The exploration of counselor educators'-in-training professional identity development through sandtray* (10113665) [Doctoral dissertation]. ProQuest Dissertations and Theses database.

Fountain, Y. N. (2015). *Important factors that contribute to the professional quality of life for registered play therapists and supervisors* (3662757) [Doctoral dissertation]. ProQuest Dissertations and Theses database. (3662757)

Franklin, M. (2010). Affect regulation, mirror neurons, and the third hand: Formulating mindful empathic art interventions. *Art Therapy: Journal of the American Art Therapy Association, 27*(4), 160–167. https://doi.org/10.1080/07421656.2010.10129385

Freedle, L. R. (2020). Peppermint tea: The essence of sandplay in a time of crisis. *STA Regional Newsletter.* https://mailchi.mp/12ff6523a6ec/regional-news-3841393?e=d202244547

Freedle, L. R., Goodwin-Downs, D., Souza, J., & Cipponeri, A. (2020). The added value of sandplay therapy with emerging adults in an outdoor behavioral healthcare program. *Journal of Sandplay Therapy, 29*(1), 129–144. https://www.sandplay.org/journal/research-articles/the-added-value-of-sandplay-therapy-with-emerging-adults-in-an-outdoor-behavioral-healthcare-program/

Freedle, L. R., & Slagle, T. (2018). Application of the neurosequential model of therapeutics (NMT) in an integrative outdoor behavioral healthcare program for adolescents and young adults. In E. Perry, G. Griffin, M. Maikoetter, S. Graner, J. Rosenfelt, & B. Perry (Eds.), *Proceedings of the 2nd International Neurosequential Model Symposium: Banff, Alberta Canada, 2016* (pp. 20–26). The Child Trauma Academy Press.

Fukkink, R. G., & Hermanns, J. M. A. (2009). Children's experiences with chat support and telephone support. *Journal of Child Psychology and Psychiatry, 50*(6), 759–766. https://doi.org/10.1111/j.1469-7610.2008.02024.x

Grové, C., & Reupert, A. (2017). Moving the field forward: Developing online interventions for children of parents with a mental illness. *Children and Youth Services Review, 82,* 354–358. https://doi.org/10.1016/j.childyouth.2017.10.003

Health Resources & Services Administration. (2018). *Behavioral health workforce projections 2016-2030.* https://bhw.hrsa.gov/sites/default/files/bhw/health-workforce-analysis/research/projections/Behavioral-Health-Workforce-Projections.pdf

Hicks, B., & Baggerly, J. (2017). The effectiveness of child parent relationship therapy in an online format. *International Journal of Play Therapy, 26*(3), 138–150. https://doi.org/10.1037/pla0000033

Hilty, D. M., Ferrer, D. C., Parish, M. B., Johnston, B., Callahan, E. J., Yellowlees, P. M. (2013). The effectiveness of telemental health: A 2013 review. *Telemed Journal and E-Health, 19*(6), 444–454. https://doi.org/10.1089/tmj.2013.0075

Hollis, C., Falconer, C. J., Martin, J. L., Whittington, C., Stockton, S., Glazebrook, C., & Davies, E.B. (2017). Annual research review: Digital health interventions for children and young people with mental health problems—A systematic and meta-review. *Journal of Child Psychology and Psychiatry and Allied Disciplines, 58*(4), 474–503. https://doi.org/10.1111/jcpp.12663

Inman, A. G., Soheilian, S. S., & Luu, L. P. (2019). Telesupervision: Building bridges in a digital era. *Journal of Clinical Psychology, 75,* 292–301. https://doi.org/10.1002/jclp.22722

Johnson, K. R., Fuchs, E., Horvath, K. J., & Scal, P. (2015). Distressed and looking for help: Internet intervention support for arthritis self-management. *Journal of Adolescent Health, 56,* 666–671. doi: 10.1016/j.jadohealth.2015.02.019.

Jung, C. G. (1921/1971). The relativity of the symbol (R. F. C. Hull, Trans.). In H. Read, M. Fordam, G. Adler, & W. McGuire (Eds.), *The collected works of C.G. Jung: Psychological types,* Vol.6 (pp. 319–371). Princeton University Press.

Kalff, D. (2020). Sandplay: *A psychotherapeutic approach to the psyche.* Temenos Press.

Kass, A. E., Trockel, M., Safer, D. L., Sinton, M. M., Cunning, D., Rizk, M. T., Genkin, B. H., Weisman, H. L., O'Bailey, J., Jacobi, C., Wilfley, C., & Taylor, C. B. (2014). Internet-based preventive intervention for reducing eating disorder risk: A randomized controlled trial comparing guided with unguided self-help. *Behaviour Research and Therapy, 63,* 90–98. doi: 10.1016/j.brat.2014.09.010

Kauer, S. D., Reid, S. C., Sanci, L., & Patton, G. C. (2009). Investigating the utility of mobile phones for collecting data about adolescent alcohol use and related mood, stress and coping behaviours: Lessons and recommendations. *Drug and Alcohol Review, 28,* 25–30. https://doi.org/10.1111/j.1465-3362.2008.00002.x

Knaevelsrud, C., Brand, J., Lange, A., Ruwaard, J., & Wagner, B. (2015). Web-based psychotherapy for posttraumatic stress disorder in war-traumatized Arab patients: Randomized controlled trial. *Journal of Medical Internet Research, 17*(3), 73–87. https://doi.org/10.2196/jmir.3582

Kossak, M. (2015). *Attunement in expressive arts therapy: Toward an understanding of embodied empathy.* Charles C. Thomas.

Kottman, T. (2014). *Play therapy: Basics and beyond.* Wiley.

Kress, V. E., Paylo, M. J., & Stargell, N. A. (2019). *Counseling children and adolescents.* Pearson.

Landreth, G. L., & Bratton, S. C. (2020). *Child-parent relationship therapy (CPRT): An evidence-based 10-session filial therapy model* (2nd ed.). Routledge.

Lucas-Thompson, R. G., Broderick, P. C., Coatsworth, J. D., & Smyth, J. M. (2019). New avenues for promoting mindfulness in adolescence using mHealth. *Journal of Child and Family Studies, 28*(1), 131–139. https://doi.org/10.1007/s10826-018-1256-4

McRoberts, R. (2019). Theoretically matched play therapy supervision: Community considerations. *Play Therapy Magazine, 14*(3), 28–29. http://www.modernpubsonline.com/Play-Therapy/PlayTherapy-Sept2019/html/index.html

Minde, K., Roy, J., Bezonsky, R., & Hashemi, A. (2010). The effectiveness of CBT in 3-7 year old anxious children: Preliminary data. *Journal of the Canadian Academy of Child and Adolescent Psychiatry, 19*(2), 109–115. https://www.ncbi.nlm.nih.gov/pmc/articles/PMC2868557/

Minear, M., Brasher, F., McCurdy, M., Lewis, J., & Younggren, A. (2013). Working memory, fluid intelligence, and impulsiveness in heavy media multitaskers. *Psychonomic Bulletin & Review, 20*(6), 1274–1281. https://doi.org/10.3758/s13423-013-0456-6

National Board for Certified Counselors. (2017). *National Board for Certified Counselors (NBCC) policy regarding the provision of distance professional services.* https://www.nbcc.org/Assets/Ethics/NBCCPolicyRegardingPracticeofDistanceCounselingBoard.pdf

National Center for Health Workforce Analysis. (2015). *National projections of supply and demand for behavioral health practitioners: 2013-2025.* https://bhw.hrsa.gov/sites/default/files/bhw/health-workforce-analysis/research/projections/behavioral-health2013-2025.pdf

Palmer, N. B., Myers, K. M., Vander Stoep, A., McCarty, C. A., Geyer, J. R., & DeSalvo, A. (2010). Attention-deficit/hyperactivity disorder and telemental health. *Current Psychiatry Reports, 12*(5), 409–417. https://doi.org/10.1007/s11920-010-0132-8

Paulson, L. R., Casile, W. J., & Jones, D. (2015). Tech it out: Implementing an online peer consultation network for rural mental health professionals. *Journal of Rural Mental Health, 39*(3–4), 125–136. https://doi.org/10.1037/rmh0000034

Prenoveau, J. M., Papadakis, A. A., Schmitz, J. C. S., Hirsch, E. L., Dariotis, J. K., & Mendelson, T. (2018). Psychometric properties of the Child and Adolescent Mindfulness Measure (CAMM) in racial minority adolescents from low-income environments. *Psychological Assessment, 30*(10), 1395–1400. https://doi.org/10.1037/pas0000630

Rathner, J. A., & Schier, M. A. (2020). The impact of flipped classroom andragogy on student assessment performance and perception of learning experience in two advanced physiology subjects. *Advances in Physiology Education, 44*(1), 80–92. https://doi.org/10.1152/advan.00125.2019

Remley, T. P, & Herlihy, B. (2016). *Legal, ethical, and professional issues in counseling* (6th edition). Pearson.

Rickwood, D., & Bradford, S. (2012). The role of self-help in the treatment of mild anxiety disorders in young people: An evidence-based review. *Psychology Research and Behavior Management, 5*, 25–36. https://dx.doi.org/10.2147%2FPRBM.S23357

Rockhill, C. M, Violette, H., Vander Stoep, A., Grover, S., & Myers, K. (2013). Caregivers' distress: Youth with attention-deficit/hyperactivity disorder and comorbid disorders assessed via telemental health. *Journal of Child and Adolescent Psychopharmacology, 23*(6), 379–385. https://doi.org/10.1089/cap.2013.0019

Roesler, C. (2017). Tele-analysis: The use of media technology in psychotherapy and its impact on the therapeutic relationship. *Journal of Analytical Psychology, 62*(3), 372–394. https://doi.org/10.1111/1468-5922.12317

Ryan, C. (2018). Computer and internet use in the United States: 2016. *American Community Survey Reports*, ACS-39, U.S. Census Bureau. https://www.census.gov/content/dam/Census/library/publications/2018/acs/ACS-39.pdf

Schlegl, S., Burger, C., Schmidt, L., Herbst, N., & Voderholzer, U. (2015). The potential of technology-based psychological interventions for anorexia and bulimia nervosa: A systematic review and recommendations for future research. *Journal of Medical Internet Research, 17*, e85. doi: 10.2196/jmir.3554.

Sibley, M. H., Comer, J. S., & Gonzalez, J. (2017). Delivering parent-teen therapy for ADHD through videoconferencing: A preliminary investigation. *Journal of Psychopathology and Behavioral Assessment, 39*(3), 467–485. https://doi.org/10.1007/s10862-017-9598-6

Slone, N. C., Reese, R. J., & McClellan, M. J. (2012). Telepsychology outcome research with children and adolescents: A review of the literature. *Psychological Services, 9*, 272–292. doi: 10.1037/a0027607.

Stephenson, R., Todd, K., Kahle, E., Sullivan, S. P., Miller-Perusse, M., Sharma, A., & Horvath, K. J. (2019). Project moxie: Results of a feasibility study of a telehealth intervention to increase HIV testing among binary and nonbinary transgender youth. *AIDS and Behavior, 24*(5), 1517–1530. https://doi.org/10.1007/s10461-019-02741-z

Usami, M. (2016). Functional consequences of attention-deficit hyperactivity disorder on children and their families. *Psychiatry and Clinical Neurosciences, 70*(8), 303–317. https://doi.org/10.1111/pcn.12393

VanderGast, T. S., Culbreth, J. R., & Flowers, C. (2010). An exploration of experiences and preferences in clinical supervision with play therapists. *International Journal of Play Therapy, 19*(3), 174–185. https://psycnet.apa.org/doi/10.1037/a0018882

Vigerland, S., Ljotsson, B., Thulin, U., Ost, L., Andersson, G., & Serlachius, E. (2016). Internet-delivered cognitive behavioural therapy for children with anxiety disorders: A randomised controlled trial. *Behaviour Research and Therapy, 76*, 47–56. doi:j.brat.2015.11.006http://dx.doi.org/10.1037/a0018882

Wass, S. V., Noreika, V., Georgieva, S., Clackson, K., Brightman, L., Nutbrown, R., Santamaria Covarrubias, L., & Leong, V. (2018). Parental neural responsivity to infants' visual attention: How mature brains influence immature brains during social interaction. *PLoS Biology, 16*(12). https://doi.org/10.1371/journal.pbio.2006328

Group Work

Sherry Todd, Kristal James, and Debra M. Perez

Group counseling is a well-researched, effective, and efficient means of providing mental health treatment. In a meta-analysis conducted by Burlingame et al. (2016), group therapy was determined to be as effective as individual treatment. There are many benefits associated with group counseling, such as the group representing "a **microcosm**" of the real world, offering a supportive environment, and opportunities to practice new skills, and in general groups are cost effective (Corey, 2015, p. 6). Group counseling can be adapted to a variety of populations, and diversity in the group itself can offer a very rich experience for participants. Because geographic proximity is not a factor, online group counseling allows for more diversity than face-to-face groups. Familiarity with diverse populations is important to ethical and best practices. This chapter will review the basic group types, using them in various online counseling delivery modes. A solid foundation of group work is important, and additional training is recommended, as this chapter will only offer an overview of group types, process, skills, and techniques. Maintaining relationships, group cohesion, and unique considerations for online counseling will be addressed in this chapter. Cultural competency and ethical guidelines are explored and resources included. Group counseling offers opportunities that cannot be achieved through individual treatment, and distance delivery should be considered a viable and effective option for service delivery.

Brief History of Group Counseling

A group is a collaborative gathering with the purpose of achieving a specified goal regardless of modality, whether face-to-face, virtually, or other (Gladding, 2020). Group therapy originated in the medical field with physicians studying tuberculosis patients in the early 1900s (DeLucia-Waack et al., 2014). Prior to the 1960s, however, most counseling took place in dyads and did not include group counseling as a regular form of practice (Rosenthal, 2017). Associations now help clinicians understand and implement unique ethical and best practices in group work (American Group Psychotherapy Association [AGPA], n.d.; Association for Specialists in Group Work [ASGW], 2020). Associations advocate for, provide resources and training, as well as provide opportunities to connect with other group counselors. Group counseling is used in a variety of settings as common practice to obtain specific treatment goals.

ASGW (2020) has separated groups into four categories: task/work, psychoeducational, counseling, and psychotherapy, with best practices guiding each of these domains. Corey (2015) also includes support groups as a category. The various types of groups share some components but differ in the goals and purpose, leadership roles, and membership. There is ongoing debate regarding the differences between psychotherapy and counseling as the counseling profession continues to solidify its identity, hence the separation of counseling and psychotherapy groups. The difference between the two groups is deep rooted in the debate about the counseling professions' mission and the mission of psychotherapy. Counseling groups have been considered shorter in nature with a less deep dive into psychological issues than a psychotherapy group. The authors believe this is a minimization of the nature of counseling, as many counselors practice and follow theories associated with psychotherapy. Therefore, for the purposes of this chapter, counseling and psychotherapy groups will be combined and termed therapeutic or process groups.

Group Counseling

Most research associated with group development and progression in a virtual setting relates to academic performance in learning teams (Wang et al., 2019; Yoon & Johnson, 2008). Both traditional therapeutic groups and virtual academic learning team modalities suggest a need for the group to develop collaborative responsibility for group outcomes. Counselors providing online group services may benefit from recognizing the need for group cohesiveness and may need to demonstrate intentional flexibility in achieving the development of group ownership and responsibility. This may look like purposefully calling on group members by name to share their thoughts, allowing longer therapeutic silence, and even more intentionality behind encouraging one group member to share their thoughts or challenge another group member. Group dynamics is a three-credit course, required by the Council for Accreditation of Counseling and Related Educational Programs (CACREP) in master-level counseling programs; therefore it cannot be fully explored in this chapter. A thorough understanding of group dynamics and process is important prior to facilitating a group at a distance. In addition to a solid foundation in group counseling, it is important to have specific training in distance group counseling as there are subtle differences between online and in-person groups. Finally, readers are encouraged to research group counseling techniques with specific populations prior to reading and implementing information from this chapter.

The structure and types of group are also important to understand. Groups can be designed to be open or closed. An **open group** means anyone can attend a group session at any time with no specified start or end date requirement, whereas a **closed group** requires the participants to be screened for group participation with a clear start and stop date (Gladding, 2020). The types of groups identified in this book are task/work groups, support, psychoeducational, and therapeutic. **Task/work groups** are developed generally to address social or community problems, such as sex trafficking or food insecurity. **Support groups** are typically open groups, led by someone who shares the problems who may or may not be a professional. Support groups include Emotions Anonymous (AA, NA, GA), Recovery International, the Balanced Mind Foundation, and the National Alliance on Mental Illness. **Psychoeducational groups** are informative with a focus on leader-facilitated education and less interaction amongst members. Goal focus and skill building are important premises in psychoeducational groups. Psychoeducational groups may focus on almost any topic such as caring for elderly parents, creating a suitable learning environment for home schooling, coping skills for staying at home during a pandemic, mental health self-care, and any topic that information is provided with little interaction amongst group members. **Therapeutic** or process **groups** may include components of the other types of groups, such as support or psychoeducation, and offer participants opportunities to explore with other group members the root causes and current impact of problems, offering divergent perspectives, valuable feedback, and collective correction or encouragement. Grief and loss, survivors of abuse, anxiety/depression/anger management, as well as traumatic experiences are all types of therapeutic or process groups. Psychoeducational and therapeutic groups are the focus of this chapter, with the other types of groups being viewed as supplemental services. Psychoeducational and therapeutic groups will be associated with the different distance counseling delivery modalities introduced in the next section.

Modalities for Online Group Counseling

Online group counseling is available in several formats and modalities. Synchronous options for conducting counseling are recommended as the preferred method, yet other options for group counseling should be explored as viable based on client need and desired clinical outcome. Asynchronous, hybrid, and synchronous approaches are all appropriate modes for conducting group counseling and are discussed in more detail, applying each to the two types of groups mentioned, psychoeducational and therapeutic. Finally, subtle changes in skills necessary for facilitating distance group counseling are included in each section.

Asynchronous Group Counseling

Asynchronous group counseling allows the client and counselor the option to engage at their convenience, whether as an addition to scheduled sessions or as counseling on the fly. An Australian study conducted with youth ages 13–25 years experiencing family discord and exhibiting mild to moderate depression and anxiety, who engaged in a peer counseling support group at their convenience, suggests more effort is needed to achieve connectedness and maintain engagement (Campbell et al., 2019). Asynchronous counseling may require even more effort and training for older clients and people who have less experience with technology. Outcomes for those who remained engaged indicate there was perceived value in online group counseling by both counselors and participants (Campbell et al., 2019). Initial participation and engagement from students were very high the 1st week but saw a drastic decline by the second of 8 weeks (Campbell et al., 2019). Utilizing that initial engagement and maintaining the momentum are key components to the long-term success of a group, especially asynchronously. The skilled group counselor will be able to create a sense of intimate connection between group members and the group as a whole, an entity in and of itself, rather than developing individual connections between members. Open groups and larger process groups tend to create the sense of connection to the group; further investigation in this area will strengthen the asynchronous group experience.

The ability to connect both day and night is an important feature of the asynchronous environment that requires a more concerted effort to engage clients, and establishing ground rules and boundaries is imperative. In addition to general consent to treat, group rules concerning confidentiality and contact outside the group between group members and with the counselor must be established and enforced (Luxton et al., 2016). This is applicable to all types of groups and will be discussed further in the section on administrative tasks.

Weinberg and Rolnick (2020) discuss the physical presence of the counselor and group members aiding in the regulation of emotion in the group and contributing to the group connectedness. To compensate for the lack of physical presence, the counselor should increase their online presence. An online presence can be what is on the web about the counselor, as well as what your physical visible environment says about you as a professional counselor. Online group counselors should carefully design what is available through social media and a professional website as this will create a place for group members to learn more about your professional interests, style, and vision. The physical visible environment is viewed in the backgrounds of still pictures and images chosen.

Encouraging group participants to post pictures and the use of chat room avatars can be helpful, especially in asynchronous counseling. Putting a face with a name helps to create a connection. Video introductions can be encouraged but may require more technical skill and knowledge. Video, even if done asynchronously, allows members of the group to learn nonverbal styles from participants, which can help increase understanding when reading written communication in group. Video also reduces ambiguity but could compromise confidentiality, which makes it a less desirable option for some populations or settings. Some clients may be seeking asynchronous counseling for the autonomy offered, which should also be considered when asking for pictures or video to be posted. Careful screening of all group participants to assess goals and needs is recommended, in addition to assessing for suitability for online treatment.

Asynchronous Psychoeducational Groups

Psychoeducational groups are well suited to asynchronous counseling service delivery. In addition to the adaptions mentioned, there are a few nuances to encourage group member engagement and satisfaction. Psychoeducational groups tend to have less interaction and more information coming from the leader or other member. For that reason, psychoeducational groups can accommodate a larger number of participants. Enabling and monitoring the chat feature for larger psychoeducational groups is important. Being familiar with uploading documents and the availability of using graphics is helpful and adds an additional layer of interest to keep participants engaged. If possible, the leader or speaker should be visible to offer a human connection as that connection is often lost in asynchronous groups.

Asynchronous Process or Therapeutic Groups

A more focused and hands-on approach by group leaders is necessary to engage participants in asynchronous group counseling. One recommendation is to use brackets to verbalize nonverbal cues (Telehealth Certification Institute, n.d.) and embed them into verbal communication. For example, if you are trying to demonstrate empathy, group leaders could write something like "Carrie, it must be difficult to feel rejected [reflected pause and slightly leaning forward]. I'm curious if any of the rest of you have felt rejected too." At times, group participants may need group leaders to grant permission and provide encouragement to engage with each other. Asking a follow-up question to the group and even following up with asking participants what they would like to ask or say to each other is an appropriate way to model engagement. It may be necessary to redirect comments and questions to group members so it does not just end up being an individual discussion with a group leader and a participant with an audience observing. Although this is true for face-to-face groups too, it takes more effort for asynchronous groups to encourage this dialogue among group members. Rather than creating a discussion between the group member and leader, the leader should encourage responses and feedback from other group members, with the leader guiding the interactions.

Group leaders working in an online asynchronous environment need to become even more aware of subtle evidence of social injustice and exploitation to safeguard participants. Group buy-in to the ground rules, adherence to the rules, and careful screening will assist in the development of a safe asynchronous group environment. Creating an atmosphere of transparency and consequences for rule violations that are clearly outlined and enforced will encourage reporting without fear. Limitations in visibility mean that nonverbal body language will be missed. This could also increase unintended microaggressions and bias-based assumptions. This is addressed further in the social justice section of this chapter.

Keeping a confidential spreadsheet is a helpful tool that can help organize key points and participation from week to week. This helps the group leader recognize changes and patterns of activity. Sometimes this is the most obvious nonverbal communication offered by participants. If group leaders are not tracking participation, they may miss this important nonverbal message from group members. Weekly summaries and individual engagement with each participant are useful ways to summarize what is being heard and offer individualized recommendations. This can help ensure participants are feeling connected and understood. It also allows an opportunity to correct any misunderstandings, if present. Weekly summaries can be done using the same platform if private chat is available or through any other confidential method. Sometimes changing the method of contact can reengage clients, while other times it may not be appropriate, available, or helpful for clients. Clinical judgment is vital in making such decisions.

Hybrid Approach to Psychoeducation or Therapeutic Group Counseling

Hybrid approaches to group counseling consist of two or more modalities to engage in a group. Often, this is done with face-to-face and online participation. Another hybrid approach integrates asynchronous counseling services with synchronous counseling. A weekly or monthly synchronous group may be supported through a variety of asynchronous activities. Asynchronous activities may include apps, electronic journaling, and support group meetings. Apps for teaching coping such as breathing techniques, guided visual imagery, progressive muscle relaxation, and meditation are readily available and often free. There are also apps that track and change behaviors such as sleep, healthy eating, and exercise. Some apps are even more therapeutic as they address more emotional-based problems such as depression, anxiety, and a variety of addictions. Psychoeducational groups can be enhanced by having participants practice and track specific behaviors prior to the completion of an asynchronous or synchronous session. During a therapeutic group session, participants can be directed to other sites to complete assessments and surveys before returning to the synchronous or asynchronous group. Hybrid asynchronous and synchronous therapeutic group therapy is one means of providing services, while either can be combined with a variety of apps to complement or augment services being provided. This combination has the potential to significantly accelerate treatment.

Synchronous Group Counseling

Synchronous groups have group members who are actively engaged and participate at the same time. This is the preferred method of group counseling as it offers participants the opportunity to actually see other group members while providing real-time interaction within the group. One study done with students in a CACREP-accredited Master of Counseling program compared synchronous group counseling cohesion with a face-to-face method of group counseling and found the online participants reported less connection and more hesitation in authenticity than their face-to-face counterparts (Holmes & Kozlowski, 2015). This does not mean connectivity cannot be achieved and is in contrast to the idea of disinhibition with counseling online (Weinberg & Rolnick, 2020). Holmes and Kozlowski identified the key factor to online group success is contingent on the depth of social connectedness. Group leaders must create ways to enhance the group connectedness in synchronous sessions, just as in face-to-face group sessions.

Synchronous Psychoeducational Groups

Psychoeducational groups are intended to provide information with little interaction among the participants. Psychoeducational groups generally push information about a mental health or related topic. It may be less important for participants to see each other in a psychoeducational group because participant interaction is not necessary. Muting all participants is important when working with larger numbers of participants to reduce audio feedback, participant background noise, and other disruptions. However, the chat feature is vital for questions or comments from the participants. It may be best, especially in larger groups, to set the meeting up so the participants can only message the host rather than the whole group. Private messages and side conversations are very distracting for other participants. Synchronous online group therapy allows the group facilitator to share documents or other graphics such as PowerPoints, images, or videos in real time, facilitating opportunities for questions, comments, or discussions while the content is fresh. Platforms that offer webinars can provide psychoeducational group therapy for very large groups. This is not recommended for therapeutic groups where group interaction is more important. The larger the group the more restrictions, such as chat control, muting upon entering, and participant interaction, are required to keep the group moving and effective.

Synchronous Process or Therapeutic Groups

Process or therapeutic groups in the synchronous environment require more counselor skill and training. In addition to understanding group dynamics, the counselor must also be competent in the basic counseling skills and able to apply those skills at a distance. Not all skills are easily converted from face-to-face to telebehavioral health. Building rapport in the virtual environment is discussed in Chapter 2. Eye contact is important to building rapport and somewhat difficult online, even in synchronous counseling. The appearance of eye contact is best achieved by alternating between looking at the camera and a spot just below the camera. However, this view can lead to the counselor missing vital information provided through slight eye shifts, changes in breathing, shifts in position, and other nonverbal cues. A more effective option is to address the counselor's eye placement as making eye contact with each member as they speak and allowing the group to experience what that looks like. Additionally, it is important to explain to the group that the counselor will scan the screen to see all group members from time to time to assess comfort level with the topic being discussed. Verbal and nonverbal attending skills are similar for group and individual counseling, with adaptions for the online counseling delivery, and are discussed in more detail in Chapter 7.

Similar values and beliefs may facilitate trust in a group, ultimately developing stronger connections. Platforms that offer the poll feature are great for identifying group similarities. Generally, you have the option to make the poll anonymous, and that can help to develop trust in the beginning of group process. Later, polls and the chat box features can be beneficial in making more personal identifications of similar values and beliefs. Breakout rooms are another feature that can be used to conduct smaller groups or dyads for ice breakers or other activities to build relationships and develop group cohesion. Group efficacy is dependent on the cohesion of the group and ability of group members to form relationships with the group facilitator as well as each other (Holmes & Kozlowski, 2015). Remember that it will likely take longer to develop group cohesion in the online environment. Increasing the number of sessions to allow more time to develop trust may be very beneficial and necessary.

Silence is a powerful counseling skill that should be used with caution and intentionally. Although the use of therapeutic silence is applicable in all settings, counselors must be aware that additional time should be allotted for online engagement. From personal experience, it takes more time for group participants to unmute their microphones to collaborate with one another, or they may wait longer before speaking because they do not want to speak over someone else. One great feature available in an online setting not available in the face-to-face modalities is the use of chat. Participants may be more willing to chat than to speak. Group facilitators can increase connectedness by encouraging participation and encouraging people to use the microphone for speaking. Monitor the chat and do not allow it to be a distraction. It is possible to disable the chat feature in many platforms and this may be necessary if the chat feature is abused, creates a distraction, or takes away from the verbal interaction.

Group Modality and Technology Resources

When determining what modality to use, assessing resources is important. Careful consideration of the client's need is also important. Do group leaders already have a relationship with clients? What is the age of the clients? How important is control of the client environment? Does the information and purpose of the group change with limited control over the environment in an online setting? Will your agency be providing technology resources? Group participants should be provided with a quick FAQ and tips for technology when it fails. Technology problems will increase anxiety and should be avoided. Providing help desk contact information for the platform you are using is important to include in the FAQ, as well as any help provided by you or your agency. Deciding if groups will be conducted synchronously, asynchronously, or using a hybrid approach is a key initial consideration. Ongoing assessment of the purpose and/or reason is important and can help prioritize the need for group counseling. For example, if telebehavioral health is the only available option due to a disaster like the COVID-19 global pandemic, telebehavioral health modality becomes the most important, so the resources necessary to operate at a distance become critical to obtain. Using the worksheet at the end of this chapter can help group leaders determine best-fit group modalities and resources.

Administrative Online Group Counseling Tasks

As with all counseling services, administrative tasks are involved with conducting group counseling in an online format. Preparation and screening for group suitability are vital administrative tasks that may mitigate potential problems. Ensuring the participant has the right technology is also necessary. Initial paperwork, documentation and evaluation are also important administrative tasks discussed in more detail.

Group Member Preparation/Screening

Although screening is an important part for all groups, it can be an especially useful opportunity to assess individual fit before the group begins and offer some preparation. In addition to assessing appropriateness for group participation, screening can be used to troubleshoot technology, emphasize identifying a confidential location, and get the informed consent signed. Internet speed, use of pins/passwords to secure group meetings, and ensuring all necessary equipment like cameras and microphones are working become essential additions to traditional screening procedures when transitioning to an online environment. Participant operator error causes frustration and anxiety and will disrupt the group cohesion and flow.

Professional Disclosure Statement

A professional disclosure statement should include purpose, modality, length of group, attendance expectations, payment methods, and limits to confidentiality (Gladding, 2020). One thing to emphasize in group disclosure statements is the limited ability to safeguard confidential information due to multiple participants and also train participants how to maintain confidentiality (Gladding, 2020). Emphasizing participant ability to share their personal experiences without sharing other group members' experiences or identifying information is important (Gladding, 2020). One of the unique challenges to online groups is that extra discussion and training are necessary regarding the privacy of each participant's environment. In face-to-face groups, the clinician can control the privacy of each group session. This cannot be done online. Limitations to confidentiality need to be included in the professional disclosure statement. Additionally, voice assistants available on mobile phones, tablets, laptops, and home speakers have the ability to record full time in order to respond to users on demand and to provide feedback data to the manufacturer. Addressing this potential data breach is important in any counseling setting but is increased exponentially as more members are added to the synchronous group. A recommendation for increasing privacy includes having each participant use noise-canceling headphones. Gaming headphones are often an inexpensive and comfortable option. Discussing the need for participation in private locations during the screening process and identifying a code word for the group to use if confidentiality is being compromised to notify the group could all be useful strategies to help minimize confidentiality breaches (Telehealth Certification Institute, n.d.). Safety within the group is vital for a therapeutic and process group to be effective. Smaller groups than would be typical in face-to-face group counseling may be necessary to ensure confidentiality and participant safety.

Evaluation

Evaluation is an ongoing process in counseling. Group leaders should be evaluating efficacy, safety, client well-being, competence, and other unique needs as they arise but within each session at a minimum (American Counseling Association [ACA], 2014). Evaluations can be done formally or informally and are discussed in more detail in Chapter 6. Group work requires the ability to assess multiple people at the same time. Co-facilitators can be an effective way to enhance the ability to evaluate using different perspectives (Gladding, 2020). Additionally, self-esteem is developed through positive self-evaluation. The authors of this book suggest that group member self-evaluation with member checking for validation or redirection can be a very powerful group tool. Finally, group member evaluation of the group process provides vital feedback.

Multicultural/Social Justice Applications

Group counseling is often a "concrete representation of society" (Weinberg & Rolnick, 2020, p. 176) providing the opportunity to interact with people different from ourselves. Each member of the group brings their own religion, race, age, socioeconomic status, gender, sexual orientation, abilities, experiences, and more. Understanding, accepting, and respecting each individual in the group is paramount to group cohesion and safety. Never assume how a person identifies, and encourage the same of all group members. It is far better and more culturally sensitive to inquire. Values and beliefs are important to the development of group trust and cohesion, and the group provides an opportunity to practice new social skills. Group counseling provides the opportunity for group members to connect with and share ideas with those group members similar as well as different from themselves.

Multicultural Group Counseling
Multiculturalism is defined as "the belief systems" of members of various groups that can "ensure a more vibrant, dynamic, and empowered society" when the needs and values of diverse groups are

addressed (Singh et al., 2012, p. 2). Groupwork requires careful consideration of multicultural needs and exploration of how to navigate and adapt to these needs. Anderson (2007) defines multicultural group counseling as a procedure "that includes screening, assessing, and diagnosing dynamics of group social systems, members, and leadership for the purpose of establishing goals, outcomes, processes, and interventions that are informed by multicultural counseling knowledge, skills and abilities" as well as "a process of planning, implementing, and evaluating group work strategies from a socio-cultural context of human variability, group, and individual identity, worldviews, statuses, power, and other salient demographic factors to facilitate human and organizational development" (Anderson, 2007, p. 225).

Anderson (2007) states the importance of attending to multicultural considerations within groups is to prevent harm to group members. He explains multicultural group counseling focuses on the goal

> to promote human development and to enhance interpersonal relationships, promote task achievement, and prevent or identify and remediate mental, emotional, or behavioral disorders and associated distress that interfere with mental health, and to lessen the risk of distress, disability, or loss of human dignity, autonomy, and freedom. (Anderson, 2007, p. 226)

Counselors leading groups will need to evaluate the dynamics and perspectives between members and within the entire group, focusing on individuals' cultures, unique identities, and statuses (Anderson, 2007). It is important to consider how each interaction in the group is influenced by the counselor's multiple identities as well as the multiple identities of each group member.

Social Justice in Group Counseling

Social justice in group counseling is the awareness of how privilege and oppression influence group work (Singh et al., 2012). Group leaders must be aware of how social privilege and oppression affect the group dynamics and how to take action. Additionally, leaders must develop competence in recognizing power, privilege, and exploitation that can exist in various systems (Singh et al., 2012). Operating from a social justice perspective, group leaders evaluate their own internalized privilege and oppression, as well as evaluate the group dynamics for oppressive interactions (Singh et al., 2012). The group evaluation should include the leader working as an agent for social change, the observed information leading to changes made within the group, and the identification of oppression and privilege that affect group members (Singh et al., 2012). Individual success and healing can be impacted by misinterpreted cultural influences, insensitive comments, or overt marginalization within the group. The counselor will need to balance their power as group leader with the power afforded them by their places of privilege, while simultaneously balancing power differentials among group members. By leading through example, counselors can demonstrate to group members empathic understanding of the lived experiences of marginalization and oppression. This example can lead to greater awareness of individual members' privilege and power and the influence on others. By becoming aware of these areas, group members develop an empathic perspective and marginalized members are given the space to heal (Anderson, 2007).

Ethics and Best Practices

In addition to all the other ethical concerns when working in an online environment, groups create unique circumstances requiring careful consideration and planning. Assessment of group leader competency and group member/community need, program/group development and evaluation, group resources and modality, professional disclosure statement, group member preparation, evaluation, and technology advancement assessments are all areas needed to appropriately conduct best practices in group counseling (Valorie Thomas & Pender, 2008). Additional ethical considerations are mandated reporting, threats to safety between group members, internet abuse, and scope of practice. Finally, the laws for the state where you are licensed must be followed. Laws and regulations governing counseling vary from state to state, and ignorance is no excuse for violating regulations or laws.

Competency and Need

It is important for clinicians to be qualified to not only conduct group therapy, but online counseling. Not all states require specialty certifications (Center for Connected Health Policy, n.d.), but all counselors are required to maintain competency in their area of practice and maintain qualifications in these areas (ACA, 2014). Additionally, assessing community need and feasibility of the specific group having access to technology and broadband is also important. For example, just because there is a need for a service that online counseling can meet in rural communities does not mean that clients are able to access internet, have appropriate technology and equipment, and so on (Simms et al., 2011), or even enough physical space to ensure privacy. A domestic violence group online from a home where the group member and offender resides is not safe or ethical. There are many factors that must be considered prior to a client participating in an online counseling group.

Advancements in Technology

Group leaders in an online environment must not only maintain competence in the group topic and purpose, but technology advancements. Annual continuing education is required by regulatory agencies but may not be enough to securely and effectively ensure best practices in session (Board Certified-TeleMental Health, n.d.). For example, during the COVID-19 2020 pandemic, government officials waived HIPAA compliance requirements; however, it is still a clinician's job to maintain confidentiality (ACA, 2014; U.S. Department of Health and Human Services, 2020). Additionally, news reports were announcing a new phenomenon called "zoombombing" where uninvited participants would jump into online platforms and share inappropriate images and messages. Clinicians must be aware of breaches of confidentiality, cyber insecurities, and how to navigate changes in maintaining security without waiting for the certification cycle to renew. Platforms develop updates to protect users from problems like "zoombombing," but it is the counselor's ethical duty to maintain current and secure technology.

Another area of concern in online group work is confidentiality. While this is an issue for any form of group therapy, online groups pose another layer of confidentiality concern with unknown individuals able to listen off camera and the susceptibility of wireless signal hijacking. Additionally, with wireless devices, like Alexa and Siri, able to record even without user request, the potential for confidentiality violations increases exponentially in online group work. The counselor must make a concerted effort to protect group member confidentiality, including requiring passwords and headsets, room checking, and removing potential threats from the group meetings. Ensuring client confidentiality will facilitate richer group processes.

Commonalities and Patterns

Maintaining consistent and accurate research on technology-enhanced counseling can be difficult. Advancements in technology occur at such a rapid rate that it makes it difficult to obtain and maintain current research. Credentialing organizations recognize this limitation and therefore require annual recertification cycles to maintain board credentials instead of lengthier recertification/licensure cycles expected in other certifications (Center for Credentialing and Education, 2018). Rapidly changing technology does not limit our ability to learn from existing research. Even early research suggests efficacy of group work can be transferred to online platforms (Barak & Grohol, 2011). Emerging patterns identify the need to increase connections with group participants to achieve efficacy of online group counseling. Focusing on ways to connect with group participants while moving from in-person to online counseling, ongoing research in online group counseling, and considering multicultural and ethical applications will need ongoing focus and critical analysis in application.

Unique Online Group Challenges

Group counseling online offers a few unique challenges. The challenges include who and what types of problems are appropriate to treat with online group counseling. Determining service delivery is a consideration that is not necessary with face-to-face groups. The role of the group counselor and converting skills to the online delivery mode also present some challenges. Finally, technology will inevitably pose problems that do not occur in the face-to-face group.

Certain clinical syndromes and disorders are especially well suited for the online group counseling experience, while other disorders are not suitable for group counseling and some clients are not the best fit for telehealth services. Careful screening is remarkably important to a successful group experience. Once a treatment population and need have been identified, transitioning group skills to the online environment becomes necessary. The group counselor will have to determine the type of group offered: task, support, psychoeducational, or therapeutic; and the modality of the group: synchronous, asynchronous, or hybrid. Hybrid groups offer rich holistic experiences but the numerous components that need to be managed offer some challenges.

Group counselors must model for the group members the ability to increase awareness and sensitivity, effective communication styles, and leadership skills while recognizing obstacles and conducting ongoing self-reflection (Singh et al., 2012). Providing effective feedback and gentle confrontation are skills that should be modeled for the group. Asking for assistance when needed and good self-care are also important for the group members to emulate. Transparency and genuineness are excellent characteristics to model in a counseling group and will facilitate trust within the group. Specific skills and tips for online adjustments are covered earlier in this chapter. Intentionality will aid in modeling behaviors that will establish a healthy group environment.

Eliminating the barrier of distance is powerful, yet it presents some challenges for the group counselor. Increasing the geographic area to be used in group participant selection allows populations requiring specific group treatment to work with specialist. Diagnosis specific, language services, cultural connections, and topic specific groups are also more accessible when the geographic boundaries are expanded (Greenberg, 2019; McGraw et al., 2019; Yakunina et al., 2011). In fact, research suggests that the more social stigma exists, the more likely adults are to seek online counseling services (DeAndrea, 2015) to avoid the stigma. Group counseling presents both challenges and opportunities to interact with those like us and different. This unique facet is not able to be replicated in face-to-face groups as easily.

The challenge to manage numerous variables offers the opportunity to be creative within the framework of the chosen platform. Caregivers for children or elderly persons may benefit from group counseling but find it difficult to go into an office for face-to-face group sessions. By offering group therapy online, caregivers can have access to services without leaving the home. Additionally, the variety of online group topics and types is a challenge in that each topic or type may require additional accommodations or preplanning. For example, social skills groups for children on the autism spectrum will look entirely different than grief groups for adults who have lost a child. A support group in a hybrid format will look considerably different from a psychoeducational synchronous group to improve sleep hygiene, which will be different from a synchronous process group for batterers. The challenge to create effective groups online offers the counselor many options and the opportunity to customize treatment to the telehealth client.

SUMMARY

Although there are challenges to providing counseling groups from a distance, there are enormous benefits. Group counseling in its traditional form offers different perspectives, connection to others generally with a shared goal or purpose, and support. Groups may be task/work focused, support, psychoeducational, or therapeutic/process in nature. The accessibility of group counseling services via the internet has increased opportunities for many people who would not have the option for group treatment otherwise. Distance group counseling may be offered asynchronously, synchronously, or as a hybrid of the two. This chapter reviews the types of counseling groups offered in the various online modalities, specifically focusing on psychoeducational and therapeutic groups. The adaptions, accommodations, and nuances of the shift to distance group counseling are included. Administrative tasks such as confidentiality and basic forms are mentioned. Multicultural, social justice, and ethical considerations are discussed as well. The chapter concludes with a case scenario, resources, and worksheets.

CASE EXPLORATION

Katrina has been counseling Raymond, one of the two Levai children, on his anxiety regarding his family changes. During case consultation with her agency, a peer reports she has a group for adolescent males dealing with family changes, including those caused by divorce and remarriage.

This ongoing group provides support as well as psychoeducation on healthy relationships and emotional expression skills. Katrina decides to discuss this option with Raymond, highlighting the scheduled group times, group confidentiality, and how he would use their current synchronous platform to attend group. Katrina and Raymond review the chat function and breakout rooms, as well as how to raise your hand and agree or disagree via the system controls. Raymond agrees to try the group for the minimum six sessions and discuss his group experience with Katrina, with the updated treatment goal included in his treatment plan to work on concerns regarding group technology and emotional expression skills.

Worksheets

PERSONAL GOALS/GROUP FEEDBACK WORKSHEET

Your participation in group has shown your motivation to change as well as your openness to feedback from your peers and facilitator. In order to ensure your personal goals are being addressed, please complete the following worksheet to outline your goals (at least three) and actions steps (at least three for each goal) you plan to take to reach them. Bring this to your next group to review with your peers and note the group feedback in the corresponding column at that time.

Personal Goal (Be specific in what you want to accomplish or change)	Action Steps to Achieve This (List specific actions steps—at least three—that you can reasonably take to achieve your goal)	Group Feedback to Help You Obtain Your Goals

Personal Goal (Be specific in what you want to accomplish or change)	Action Steps to Achieve This (List specific actions steps—at least three—that you can reasonably take to achieve your goal)	Group Feedback to Help You Obtain Your Goals

*Please feel free to add additional goals and steps on the back of this worksheet or add additional sheets as you see necessary.

Basic Counseling Forms

CONFIDENTIALITY IN GROUPS

As you know, groups provide additional challenges to confidentiality. Using the ideas that follow, continue to develop your own checklist to use when reviewing confidentiality with clients. According the APA ethics code 10.03, clinicians must "describe at the onset the roles and responsibilities of all parties and the limits of confidentiality." Although video allows for more engagement and collaboration, it also creates additional concerns and potential breaches.

LIMITATIONS OR CONCERNS SURROUNDING ONLINE GROUP CONFIDENTIALITY

☐ **Security**
Group members should attend in a secure location. This should be free from distractions and potential for nongroup members to see or hear all or part of the group or its members.

☐ **Recordings/screen shot**
Even if recording features in the group platform are disabled, technology may allow outside recording or screenshots to be taken. Rules around this should be established.

☐ **Blackmail or sharing identity**
Group members may use information obtained as part of the group as blackmail. Seek legal consultation to determine how to address potential for blackmail and ways to provide security around it before engaging in online group.

☐ **Proper training/supervision**
Group leaders are prepared for groups and have a plan. Appropriate supervision is in place as needed.

☐ **Avatar/disguise**
Consider the possibility or need for some group members to block their identity, change their online name, or otherwise maintain anonymity. Please know that insurance companies may not provide reimbursement if a client's camera is blocked as it would be considered a telephone therapy.

CONSIDERATIONS FOR GROUP

You have trained well and are ready for your first online group. Using a checklist can help you be prepared for your first group. With proper preparation, your chances of initial success will increase. Use the checklist that follows to help you prepare for your first group. Adjust as needed for your own intake checklist for future sessions.

GROUP CHECKLIST

☐ **Confidentiality**
Client can provide a confidential environment consistently. Limitations to confidentiality have been discussed. Client is aware that ability to continue group participation is dependent on ability to maintain confidentiality.

☐ **Informed consent**
An informed consent has been signed and clearly states the limitations and plans for how to minimize limitations associated with online platforms as they relate to group.

☐ **Risk assessment**
You have checked for appropriateness of online group in general and for this group specifically. You have resources available near the client(s) in case of a high-risk situation and/or emergency. You feel your group members are appropriate for this setting.

☐ **Technology is available**
You have prepared your own technology and verified it is working prior to the intake. You have also verified the availability of technology for your client(s).

☐ **Effective technology**
All users of technology have been properly trained on how to use the technology and a plan for how to navigate disruptions to technology is in place. Rules regarding group chat use, screen sharing, and camera use have been clearly defined.

☐ **Accuracy**
You have verified that an online group is appropriate for each group member and their needs. You have also done a screening to determine all group members are appropriate for interaction together.

☐ **Proper training/supervision**
Group leaders are prepared for groups and have a plan. Appropriate supervision is in place as needed.

☐ **Practice**
You have practiced, in advance, conducting a group. It is advised to record your practice and review your recording prior to engaging in a virtual intake for the first time with a client. Be sure to practice with all leaders together and discuss the roles/responsibilities of each leader (i.e., will both leaders screen share? Who will manage the chat? etc.).

☐ **Understanding**
You have created a way to check for client understanding as well as options to navigate questions and technological support as needed.

☐ **Cultural/diagnosis and technology awareness**
You recognize that culture and technology may influence the way information is obtained and assessed. You have taken into consideration the variables culture, diagnosis, and technology create and feel comfortable navigating them in an online environment.

ONLINE GROUP COUNSELING INFORMED CONSENT

General Information

I, _____, hereby give permission for _____ to participate in online group counseling with _____. All signed informed consent and releases of information will remain active unless either party is notified in writing. The following information is supplemental information unique to groups and will remain active throughout the duration of participation in group counseling.

1. Online group therapy sessions will take place weekly or bimonthly and will be set for a time that is most convenient for group members.
2. All meetings will be held via a HIPAA compliant platform.
3. Groups will be limited to five clients and will be grouped by grade level and therapeutic goals.
4. If your child is unable to attend a group session, please contact your therapist 24 hours prior to their absence. Groups are significantly affected when group members are absent. Therefore, attendance is strongly encouraged and expected.

Confidentiality

Communication between your child and their therapist is privileged and confidential. The information shared in group counseling is treated with the deepest respect. Additionally, confidentiality is strongly encouraged among group members. This means all group members are asked the following:

1. Please do not discuss anything about any other group member outside of the group.
2. Group members must be able to participate in a private location free from distractions and/or the potential for nongroup members to overhear.
3. Recordings of any kind are not permitted of any part of group therapy.

Although, for the most part the information discussed in group therapy will not be shared by their therapist, there is an ethical and legal responsibility to share information in the following situations:

1. Client threatens to harm themself.
2. Suspected child abuse, neglect, and/or threats to harm others.
3. Records that are subpoenaed by a court of law.

_____ has access to all session summaries, goals, dates of service, progress, and other information as it pertains to services rendered under their jurisdiction.

Please know that although your therapist is doing all they can to provide a HIPAA-compliant environment, conducting sessions online can prove to be a bit challenging. It is important that you do what you can on your end to make sure your environment stays confidential. Things to consider are the location of your computer, who has access to it, who is in the room during sessions, malware, spyware, or other virtual challenges outside of the control of the counselor, and so on. If for any reason group counseling is not a good fit, I may discuss this with my counselor and/or _____ and an alternative modality of treatment may be offered.

Informed Consent to Online Group Therapy

I have read, understood, and discussed these things with my student. I have also had the opportunity to ask questions. I agree to these conditions and policies. I agree and consent for my child to participate in online group therapy provided by any counselor associated with _____.

I attest that I have legal custody of this individual and am authorized to initiate and consent for treatment and/or legally authorized to initiate and consent to treatment on behalf of this individual.

You have the right to withdraw your consent at any time by notifying this therapist and/or

_____.

I confirm that my therapist has explained the purpose of this form to me and I understand its content. My signature indicates my consent.

_____

Client printed name

_____

Signature of parent/legal representative   Print name   Date   Date signed

_____

Signature of therapist   Print name   Date signed

Online Resources

- **Center for Connected Health Policy:**
  The National Policy Resource Center is a website that discusses state laws and regulations according to state requirements. Counselors can quickly learn information regarding insurance, and other regulations by state: https://www.cchpca.org/

- **Mental Health America (MHA):**
  "Founded in 1909 is the nation's leading community-based nonprofit dedicated to addressing the needs of those living with mental illness and to promoting the overall mental health of all Americans. Our work is driven by our commitment to promote mental health as a critical part of overall wellness, including prevention services for all; early identification and intervention for those at risk; integrated care, services, and supports for those who need it; with recovery as the goal." The link is to numerous online support groups for a variety of problems: https://www.mhanational.org/find-support-groups

- **National Board for Certified Counselors: Board Certified Telemental-Health Provider:**
  A website where all licensed mental health professionals can obtain and maintain board certification in telemental health: https://www.cce-global.org/credentialing/bctmh

- **Substance Abuse and Mental Health Service Administration (SAMHSA):**
  Offers telebehavioral health specific information and training for mental health counselors: https://www.integration.samhsa.gov/operations-administration/telebehavioral-health

- **Association for Specialists in Group Work is a division of the American Counseling Association (ACA):**
  Offers professional membership in their organization independent of membership in ACA: https://www.asgw.org/

- **American Group Psychotherapy Association (AGPA):**
  Offers connection, education, and leadership training specific to group work: https://www.agpa.org/

References

American Counseling Association. (2014). *2014 ACA code of ethics.* https://www.counseling.org/resources/aca-code-of-ethics.pdf

Anderson, D. (2007). Multicultural group work: A force for developing and healing. *The Journal for Specialists in Group Work, 32*(3), 224–244. https://doi.org/10.1080/01933920701431537

Association for Specialists in Group Work. (2020). ASGW: A division of the American counseling association. Retrieved: https://www.asgw.org/

Barak, A., & Grohol, J. M. (2011). Current and future trends in internet-supported mental health interventions. *Journal of Technology in Human Services, 29*(3), 155–196. https://doi.org/10.1080/15228835.2011.616939

Board Certified-TeleMental Health. (n.d.). *Required training.* https://www.cce-global.org/credentialing/bctmh/training

Burlingame, G., Gleave, R., Erekson, D., Nelson, P., Olsen, J., Thayer, S., & Beecher, M. (2016). Differential effectiveness of group, individual, and conjoint treatments: An archival analysis of OQ-45 change trajectories. *Psychotherapy Research*, 26 (5), 556–572. 17p. 3 https://doi.org/10.1080/10503307.2015.1044583

Campbell, A., Ridout, B., Amon, K., Navarro, P., Collyer, B., & Dalgleish, J. (2019). A customized social network platform (kids helpline circles) for delivering group counseling to young people experiencing family discord that impacts their well-being: Exploratory study. Journal of Medical Internet Research, 21(12), 1–15. https://doi.org/10.2196/16176

Center for Connected Health Policy. (n.d.). *Home page.* https://www.cchpca.org/

Center for Credentialing and Education. (2018). *Telemental health professional training series: Module 5 Best Practices in Video Telemental Health.* https://www.cce-global.org/credentialing/bctmh/training

Corey, G. (2015). *Theory and practice of group counseling* (9th edition). Cengage.

DeAndrea, D. C. (2015). Testing the proclaimed affordances of online support groups in a nationally representative sample of adults seeking mental health assistance. *Journal of Health Communication*, 20(2), 147–156. https://doi.org/10.1080/10810730.2014.914606

DeLucia-Waack, J.L., Kalodner, C.R., Riva, M. (2014). *Handbook of Group Counseling and Psychotherapy* (2nd ed.). Sage.

Gladding, S. (2020). *Groups: A counseling specialty* (8th ed.). Pearson.

Greenberg, E. (2019). Group therapy with borderline, narcissistic, and schizoid adaptations. *Gestalt Review*, 23(2), 129. https://doi.org/10.5325/gestaltreview.23.2.0129

Holmes, C. M., & Kozlowski, K. A. (2015). A preliminary comparison of online and face-to-face process groups. *Journal of Technology in Human Services*, 33(3), 241–262. https://doi.org/10.1080/15228835.2015.1038376

Luxton, D., Nelson, E., & Maheu, M. (2016). *A Practitioner's Guide to Telemental Health: How to conduct legal, ethical, and evidence-based telepractice.* APA.

McGraw, K., Adler, J., Andersen, S. B., Bailey, S., Bennett, C., Blasko, K., Blatt, A. D., Greenberg, N., Hodson, S., Pittman, D., Ruscio, A. C., Stoltenberg, C. D. G., Tate, K. E., & Kuruganti, K. (2019). Mental health care for service members and their families across the globe. *Military Medicine, 184,* 418–425. https://doi.org/10.1093/milmed/usy324

Rosenthal, H. (2017). Encyclopedia of counseling (4th ed.). Routledge.

Ruffolo, M. C., Kuhn, M. T., & Evans, M. E. (2006). Developing a parent-professional team leadership model in group work: Work with families with children experiencing behavioral and emotional problems. *Social Work, 51*(1), 39–47. Retrieved from https://doi.org/10.1093/sw/51.1.39

Simms, D. C., Gibson, K., & O'Donnell, S. (2011). To use or not to use: Clinicians' perceptions of telemental health. *Canadian Psychology, 52*(1), 41–51. https://doi.org/10.1037/a0022275

Singh, A. A., Merchant, N., Skudrzyk, B., & Ingene, D. (2012). Multicultural and social justice competence principles for group workers. *The Journal for Specialists in Group Work, 37*(4,) 312–325, https://doi.org/10.1080/01933922.2012.721482

Telehealth Certification Institute. (n.d.). *TeleMental Health Training Certificate (THTC) program, online self-study.* https://telementalhealthtraining.com/products-listing/product/telemental-health-training-program-online-self-study

U.S. Department of Health and Human Services. (2020). *COVID-19 & HIPAA bulletin limited waiver of HIPAA sanctions and penalties during a national health emergency.* https://www.hhs.gov/sites/default/files/hipaa-and-covid-19-limited-hipaa-waiver-bulletin-508.pdf

Valorie Thomas, R., & Pender, D. A. (2008). Association for specialists in group work: Best practice guidelines 2007 revisions. *Journal for Specialists in Group Work, 33*(2), 111–117. https://doi.org/10.1080/01933920801971184

Wang, C., Fang, T., & Gu, Y. (2019). Learning performance and behavioral patterns of online collaborative learning: Impact of cognitive load and affordance of different multimedia. *Elsevier, 143*(2020). https://reader.elsevier.com/reader/sd/pii/S0360131519302362?token=96F07BFD-CA97B1D83882C265749D2414A41A4941FA491042DFB43EBFB993897893E47D189A9FC9B-45B6A507B0D176D8F

Weinberg, H. & Rolnick, A. (2020). *Theory and Practice off Online Therapy: Internet-delivered interventions for individuals, groups, families, and organizations.* Routledge.

Yakunina, E. S., Weigold, I. K., & McCarthy, A. S. (2011). Group counseling with international students: Practical, ethical, and cultural considerations. *Journal of College Student Psychotherapy, 25*(1), 67–78. https://doi.org/10.1080/87568225.2011.532672

Yoon, S. W., & Johnson, S. D. (2008). Phases and patterns of group development in virtual learning teams. *Educational Technology Research and Development, 56*(5–6), 595–618. https://doi.org/10.1007/s11423-007-9078-x

Synchronous Supervision

13 Foundations of Online Clinical Supervision

Elizabeth Brokamp and Tina Pharr

Clinical supervision, which "includes the supportive and educative activities of the supervisor designed to improve the application of counseling theory and technique directly with clients" (Association for Counselor Education and Supervision [ACES], 2011, p. 1), is a cornerstone of counselor education. The counseling profession is skill based and knowledge based, so formalized mentoring is a critical means to ensure emerging counselors meet minimum clinical standards. Supervision's importance to the field of counseling is evident in its inclusion the standards of the field, including those issued by the American Counseling Association (ACA), the American Mental Health Counselors Association (AMHCA), and the Council for Accreditation of Counseling and Related Educational Programs (CACREP).

A Foundation: Background and Models of Online Supervision

Distance supervision, which encompasses both synchronous and asynchronous modalities such as telephone, email, and videoconferencing, has been on the rise for many years (Brandoff & Lombardi, 2012). In the second decade of the millennium, many states' licensure laws were updated to allow clinical supervision by video, paving the way for the 2017 founding of the company Motivo, which touted itself as the first HIPAA-compliant platform exclusively for online clinical supervision. In May 2019, the ACA announced a partnership with Motivo, a move that signaled the embrace of online platforms for the delivery of supervisory services. More recently, the coronavirus pandemic of 2020, which involved public health admonitions to "socially distance" and resulted in massive closures of schools and businesses, meant a greater reliance on technology across most professional sectors, including counseling and counselor education. Finally, the substantial growth in the number of CACREP-accredited online programs in counseling indicates that distance supervision is likely here to stay (CACREP, n.d.; Carlisle et al., 2016).

Benefits of Online Supervision

While clinical supervision is professionally mandated, the specifics of how, when, and by what method of delivery are typically the purview of the state licensing entity, academic program, or individual clinical supervisor. The advent of digital and electronic means of communication added a new dimension to these supervision considerations, allowing counseling professionals to supervise trainees without needing to meet in person. The ability to supervise from a distance has had numerous benefits, including increasing trainees' access to supervision (Jordan & Shearer, 2019; McAdams &Wyatt, 2010), increasing flexibility in scheduling (Nelson et al., 2010), and lowering costs and time related to travel for trainees (Vaccaro & Lambie, 2007). Distance supervision is also critical for increasing access for counselors in rural and underserved communities (Belsak & Simonič, 2018), those for whom mobility may be an impediment, and counselors who are caretakers of children or the elderly for whom additional time away from home may be a hardship. Finally, distance supervision allows counselors access to supervisors who are subject matter experts (such as a supervisor who specializes in trauma or Adlerian play therapy) and/or who may reflect greater diversity in terms of social identities than those in the counselor's immediate area.

Increased accessibility is a compelling benefit of online supervision, providing both sociopolitical and pragmatic reasons to embrace distance modalities. However, the increased popularity of distance supervision is also likely due to its acceptance as valid and efficacious. Research suggests that supervision quality is linked more closely to individual supervisor skills than to the delivery platform (Jordan & Shearer, 2019). In fact, despite past concerns about the comparative efficacy of distance versus in-person supervision, the two modalities are now "perceived to be equitable in overall quality from the trainee perspective" (Jordan & Shearer, 2019, p. 327). Increased acceptance of distance modalities has also allowed for hybrid options, in which distance methods "can be used to enhance in-person supervision" (Belsak & Simonič, 2018, p. 241).

Pitfalls of Online Supervision

At the same time, the growth of distance supervision has raised important questions about its effectiveness compared to face-to-face interactions. Critics point out that it is difficult to pick up on body language in an online forum (Mallen et al., 2005), which may adversely impact the quality of the supervisory relationship, as well as impinge on the supervisor's observation of trainee micro skills. Finally, a less-referenced pitfall involves the relational, career, and practical ramifications of physical distance. In distance supervision, the supervisor and trainee may not work within the same community, making it less likely that the supervisor can recommend community resources, share networking contacts, or render help on site should the trainee experience an emergency with a client.

Other potential drawbacks to online interactions involve technological issues (Nelson et al., 2010), including that technology can be unreliable (problems with connectivity) and transmission delays may impact communication. Disconnects in communication due to technological limitations could be misconstrued as issues of competence, incorrectly attributed to multicultural difference, or viewed as a relational challenge between supervisor and supervisee. Both supervisor and trainee must also possess a base-level of skill and familiarity with the programs, devices, and machines utilized in distance supervision (Carlisle et al., 2017). Of utmost concern, the online modality can also make it difficult to ensure privacy, confidentiality, and security of data, as required by Health Insurance Portability and Accountability Act (HIPAA, 1996), the Family Educational Rights and Privacy Act (FERPA, 1974), and the American Counseling Association (ACA, 2014) Code of Ethics. While the upsides of distance supervision are numerous, the potential downsides highlight the importance of having a well-developed supervision plan to guide the supervisor's work.

Embracing a Model of Supervision

Prior to developing a plan, a supervisor must consider which model of supervision best captures their conception of the supervisory role, as well as how they view the growth and development of trainees. A model offers a conceptual framework (Bernard & Goodyear, 2019) that serves as a touchstone when the supervisor determines what content to cover in supervision sessions, how to address knowledge or skills deficits, and how to assess trainee competence. In the adoption of a model, however, it is important that supervisors remain open and adaptable; trainees enter supervision at different levels of knowledge and skill, make progress at varying rates, and respond differently to interventions. Accordingly, supervisors need to re-assess their own assumptions, teaching strategies, and methods throughout the supervision process.

Supervision Models

Supervision models have been the subject of entire books, which is evidence of both their importance in the supervision process, as well as the proliferation of the supervision theories on which the models rest. What follows is not a comprehensive overview but a sampling, with the intent of showing how distance supervisors may apply a conceptual model to the online practice of their craft. The four supervision models addressed here include developmental, multicultural, orientation specific, and process. Many more models exist that merit supervisor consideration, however. Readers interested in a more in-depth treatment of supervision models will find sources in this chapter's Online Resource section.

Developmental

Developmental theories of supervision are based on the premise that supervisees move through stages during the supervisory process, progressing from novice to autonomous professional. Developmental levels are considered fluid and are impacted by cognitive complexity, experience under supervision, and familiarity with a particular type of client (Bernard & Goodyear, 2019). Each of the stages has potential implications for the clinical supervisor's work with the supervisee and may influence the supervisor's expectations, the content of sessions, the assessment and evaluation of the trainee, and more.

The **integrated developmental model of supervision (IDM)**, a well-researched and widely utilized model, categorizes supervisees into one of four developmental levels based on experience, skill, and disposition (Bernard & Goodyear, 2019). As experience increases, supervisees are expected to gain self-awareness, competence, and autonomy. The IDM cites eight domains in which supervisees should be evaluated, including intervention skills, assessment techniques, interpersonal assessment, client conceptualization, individual differences, theoretical orientation, treatment plans and goals, and professional ethics (Bernard & Goodyear, 2019).

A clinical supervisor who adopts the IDM may be particularly interested in related research that pairs the model with specific interventions. Broadly classified as facilitative or authoritative (Heron, 1989) suggested interventions may include such actions as asking open-ended questions to aid in problem solving, offering validation to the supervisee, giving advice, providing information, or linking theory to practice. In utilizing the IDM or other developmental models, supervisors should consider how best to tailor these interventions to the online environment.

Multicultural

Multicultural models of supervision consider culture and context central to understanding human interactions. The goal of multicultural models is the integration of cultural awareness into every aspect of counselor development, which has numerous implications for supervision. For example, in multicultural models, the supervisory relationship itself is viewed as a "cultural encounter" (Falicov, 2014, p. 32) in which the social identities of the supervisor and supervisee, how they perceive and interact with one another, and how their biases and assumptions shape their work together, are considered critical areas of exploration.

One example of a multicultural model of supervision is the multidimensional ecological comparative approach (MECA) (Falicov, 2014). Rather than relying on generalizations about social identities, MECA asserts that culture is a complex, multidimensional concept that deserves careful and thoughtful ongoing consideration. Supervisors and supervisees must maintain "an ability to see the universal human similarities that unite people beyond color, class, ethnicity, and gender, while recognizing and respecting culture-specific differences that exist because of color, class, ethnicity, and gender" (Falicov, 2014, p. 43). The MECA posits that supervision relationships represent encounters between the supervisor's and the supervisees' cultural maps as they relate to theory, family, personal views, values, and preferences (Falicov, 2014). In addition to cultural diversity, another central construct of the MECA is social justice, which requires the supervisory dyad to consider the impact of power differentials attributable to differing social identities (such as social class, race, gender, religion, and sexuality) on their own interactions, as well as on their clients.

In addition to offering a theoretical framework for understanding clients and their contexts, the MECA offers specific tools and strategies that the supervisor can use in supervision sessions. A sample of suggested supervisory activities includes comparing the cultural maps of supervisor and supervisee for discussion of similarities and differences, engaging in periodic examination of the supervisory relationship and surrounding systems, incorporating readings on issues such as power and oppression, and developing cultural genograms for clients. These types of interventions provide "a continuous structure of awareness" (Falicov, 2014, p. 54) that can help the emerging counselor effectively address issues of diversity, power, authority, oppression, and discrimination in their therapeutic work.

Translating the MECA into an online environment takes care and attention, especially related to the establishment of trust between supervisor and supervisee. Many of the suggested activities related to cultural and sociopolitical awareness require self-examination and self-disclosure, for example, which requires a degree of vulnerability. Supervisors must understand the risks they are asking supervisees to take and acknowledge them, model an appropriate level of disclosure, discuss the potential tensions around revealing biases or assumptions, and help create a climate of open dialogue. Supervisors must also take special care to discuss the privacy and confidentiality of the supervisee's communications and what level of detail regarding supervision may be shared with academic institutions, accrediting bodies, and license-granting entities.

Orientation Specific

A variety of counseling theories are used as frameworks for clinical supervision, including psychodynamic, cognitive behavioral, client centered, and solution focused. For many counseling professionals, it is a natural and seamless transition to apply to supervision the same theoretical lens with which they view their counseling work comprised of views on interpersonal behavior, personality development, and abnormal psychology, whether in the counseling or supervisory domains (Topolinski & Hertel, 2007).

The cognitive behavioral therapy (CBT) supervision model is an example of a well-accepted theory-specific model of supervision (Aasheim, 2012). Through the CBT model, the supervisor will engage in a collaborative process that is educational, interpersonal, and skill based. CBT supervision offers a structured template for supervision sessions that details the arc of the session from check-in to conclusion, with specific touchpoints along the way. A CBT supervisor works with the supervisee to set an agenda, make a bridge between the last session and the current one, review homework, prioritize agenda items, assign new homework, summarize, and elicit feedback. While the process is systematic, session content is not prescribed and allows for discussion of affective aspects of clinical work.

The structured nature of CBT supervision would seem to lend itself to an easy transition online. Distance supervisors may wish to conduct some of the more logistical aspects of the sessions like setting the agenda, prioritizing discussion items, and completing homework via email so as to leave more time for substantive discussion. Intermingling modes of distance communication such as email or text with videoconferencing may work well with the CBT approach to online supervision.

Process

Process models approach supervision as an educational and relationship-driven encounter. Bernard's **discrimination model (DM)** is one of the most well-researched process models, known for its flexibility and eclecticism (Bernard & Goodyear, 2019). Within the DM, supervisors are encouraged to embrace three roles: **teacher, counselor,** and **consultant**. In navigating each of those roles, they may choose to focus on any or all of the following supervisee skills: intervention, conceptualization, and personalization. "As a consequence, the supervisor might be responding at any given moment in one of nine different ways (i.e., 3 roles x 3 foci)" (Bernard & Goodyear, 2019, p. 52). A distinguishing feature of the DM is that it is situation specific, which means that the supervisor's role and foci will change both within individual sessions and across sessions. Thus, the supervisor's conception of the supervisory process and relationship is ever changing. Process models do not typically differ significantly when implemented online versus in person. Distance supervisors who use the DM must be cognizant that it is a model predicated on relationship, so special attention should be paid to rapport building.

The Importance of a Supervision Plan

A supervision plan is a vital factor in effective and efficient counseling supervision (Bernard & Goodyear, 2019). A comprehensive overview of supervision explores ethical and multicultural considerations and outlines models, documentation, and methods that will be utilized throughout the supervisory relationship. The plan also serves as a roadmap outlining the scope of the relationship between supervisor and trainee and establishes the parameters of working together, including the duration of meetings, the modality, and the frequency. A thoughtful, thorough supervision plan lays a solid foundation for the supervision contract and minimizes the chance of misunderstandings that could mar this formative professional relationship.

Elements of a Solid Supervision Plan

A comprehensive supervision plan uses the supervisor's knowledge, expertise, and preplanning as a jumping-off point from which to provide information about the supervision process. This information typically takes shape as a contract between supervisor and supervisee and provides for the supervisee's informed consent. At minimum, the supervision documents should include information on the following topics:

- Modes of supervision
- When and how often will supervision be held and what is the duration of the contract
- Communication glitches and how to handle potential interruptions to sessions
- Financial information (if applicable)
- Cancellation policy
- Scope of competency
- Ethics
- Preparation for sessions
- Documentation requirements
- Emergency procedures
- Homework
- Termination
- Evaluation
- Appeal procedures (in the event a trainee disagrees with the supervisor's evaluation or feedback)

For an example of a supervision contract that touches on all of these subjects, please see the sample worksheet for this chapter.

Documentation

Supervision records should be maintained and kept in a secure location (ACES, 2011; Bernard & Goodyear, 2019), with online records being encrypted and password protected (Belsak & Simonič, 2018). Supervision records will contain the supervision agreement, supervision contract, statements of disclosure, proof of liability insurance, copy of performance evaluations, record of supervision sessions, notation of any missed sessions, supervision notes, and any other pertinent information (ACES, 2011; Bernard & Goodyear, 2019). Supervision notes should include the session date, time, modality of supervision, interventions utilized, and recommendations suggested during the session (Belsak & Simonič, 2018). Additionally, all communication, including emails, texts, instant messages, and phone conversation, should be documented in the supervision record.

Collaboration

Supervision does not occur in a vacuum; supervisors are responsible for providing endorsements for qualified supervisees and obtaining remedial assistance for supervisees with impairments (ACA, 2014). When supervising interns, supervisors will need to maintain communication with university faculty. Communication guidelines should be outlined in the supervision contract and performance evaluations should be provided in accordance with the program requirements or state regulations. Additionally, concerns related to ethical breaches should be reported to the appropriate party in a timely manner (ACES, 2011). Chapter 15 explores gatekeeping issues in detail.

Multicultural/Ethical/Social Justice Applications

Clinical supervision delivered online must adhere to the same ethical standards required in a face-to-face format with a few additional caveats. Consequently, multicultural and social justice concerns must be a part of supervision process regardless of the delivery modality.

Multicultural Considerations

ACES (2011) acknowledges that all supervision is multicultural. Therefore, supervisors must infuse multicultural considerations into their supervision approaches. Conversations regarding multicultural considerations should begin at the onset of the supervision process with cultural and advocacy competencies addressed in the supervision plan. Bernard and Goodyear (2019) assert that "multiculturalism responds to the diverse range of cultures and identities that people hold and the intersections between. These include but are not limited to gender, race, religion, ethnicity, sexual orientation and identity, ability status, age, and socioeconomic status" (p. 117). A multiculturally competent supervisor will attend to the interrelated dimensions of intrapersonal identity, interpersonal expectations, biases, and prejudice, interpersonal response to others' cultural identity and behaviors, and sociopolitical privilege, oppression and institutionalized "–isms" (Bernard & Goodyear, 2019). Adoption of a multicultural supervision model such as MECA can help ensure that supervisors are constantly viewing interactions from a cultural perspective, rather than simply checking off a competency. Viewing multiculturalism as a lens, not a skill, is an important distinction that supervisors can share with emerging counselors.

Ethical Considerations

Ethical responsibilities must be at the forefront of the supervisor's mind. Unethical behavior can have a detrimental impact in multiple ways, impacting "(a) the supervisory relationship, (b) the supervisees, (c) clients being served by the supervisees, and (d) even the general public" (Bernard & Goodyear, 2019, p. 252). Serving as both examples and gatekeepers of the professions, the supervisor bears the responsibility of modeling ethical behavior. To carry out this responsibility, the supervisor must maintain an intimate knowledge of the ACA (2014) Code of Ethics.

Section F of the Code of Ethics (ACA, 2014) outlines ethical guidelines in supervision, stating that supervisors are tasked with fostering "meaningful and respectful professional relationships" and maintaining "appropriate boundaries" (p. 12). Additionally, supervisors are to have a theoretical foundation and knowledge of supervision models (ACA, 2014). The following codes are especially pertinent to preparation of distance counseling: F.1.c., Informed Consent; F.2.c., Online Supervision; F.4.a., Informed Consent for Supervision; and F.4.b., Emergencies and Absences (ACA. 2014). Additional information on ethical codes related to online supervision is discussed in Chapters 14 and 15.

Informed Consent

Informed consent should not be a stagnant document, but an ongoing process beginning at the initiation of supervision and continuing to termination of the supervisory relationship (Belsak & Simonič, 2018). Within the supervision process, informed consent involves the supervisor, supervisee, and client. Code F.1.c. (Informed Consent for Client Rights) focuses on the clients right to be provided with the supervisee's professional disclosure and information regarding the supervision process, while code F.4.a. (Informed Consent for Supervision) focuses on the incorporation of the principles of informed consent into the supervision process (ACA, 2014). Informed consent for distance supervision is basically the same as face-to-face with one caveat.

Supervisees should be brought into the informed consent conversation as a partner and their emotional and learning needs assessed during informed consent discussions to determine the most efficacious supervision structure (Belsak & Simonič, 2018). Additionally, as part of the informed consent, supervisees must be made aware of the policies and procedures of supervision and mechanisms of due process (ACA, 2014, F.4.a.). Lastly, supervisors are instructed to include "issues unique to distance supervision" in the informed consent documentation (ACA, 2014, F.4.a.).

Online Supervision

There are additional risks to confidentiality inherent to distance supervision (Belsak & Simonič, 2018; Carlisle et al., 2016); consequently, ACA (2014) directly addresses the use of technology in supervision. In code F.2.c. (Online Supervision), distance supervisors are compelled to maintain competence in the use of any technologies they choice to utilize and "take the necessary precautions to protect" the electronic information of supervisees and clients (ACA, 2014, p. 13). To safeguard confidentiality, it is vital for supervisors to "regularly update their knowledge of technology" and awareness of how data breaches can occur (Belsak & Simonič, 2018, p. 242). Armed with this knowledge, supervisors should maintain up-to-date procedures for use of technology in supervision, outlining how data will be stored, transferred, and deleted, and how possible breaches of confidentiality will be addressed.

Emergencies and Absences

Regardless of the modality of supervision, supervisors are ethically obligated to provide supervisees with a protocol for contacting the supervisor and an alternative on-call supervisor for emergency situations (ACA, 2014, F.4.b.). According to ACES (2011), emergency protocols should include contact information, parameters for determining what merits an emergency, and emergency protocol instructions. Protocols specific to treatment issues such as violence, lethality, mandated reporting, and legal or ethical concerns must be clearly outlined. The emergency protocols should be determined at the onset of supervision and updated as needed throughout the supervision process (Belsak & Simonič, 2018; Vaccaro & Lambie, 2007). These protocols are especially important in distance counseling and supervision as the clients and supervisee may be in a different city or state than the supervisor. The distance requires counselors and supervisors to be extra cautious and ensure due diligence.

SUMMARY

Clinical supervision, which can be delivered in person or online, is a critical component of counselor development. While many of the elements of effective supervision remain the same across delivery methods, the distance format presents some unique challenges and opportunities that merit consideration. These considerations may include technological issues, making full use of opportunities for direct observation rather than relying on supervisee self-report, and tailoring activities and interventions to the online environment. Management of possible concerns regarding multicultural and ethical issues was outlined, and discussion of the importance of the informed consent and emergency management was explored. The online clinical supervisor is advised to begin with a carefully considered supervision model and a thorough supervision contract, which will facilitate good communication and a productive supervision experience.

CASE EXPLORATION

The case study involves Katrina, who is a provisionally licensed mental health counselor in her state, under the supervision of Eugene, a licensed professional counselor certified in telebehavioral health, who resides 2 hours away from Katrina in the same state. This chapter has the most applicability to Eugene, who in the development of his supervision plan needs to attend to several potential issues that may arise with Katrina in her work with the Levai family.

1. Katrina is provisionally licensed, which means that Eugene, as her fully licensed supervisor, assumes responsibility (liability) for her clinical work. It is important for Katrina to be aware of Eugene's assumption of risk and to keep Eugene well informed about the progression of therapy.

2. Eugene, as Katrina's supervisor for licensure, needs to assess Katrina's developmental needs as a trainee and her current level of competency, with an eye toward how best to address gaps in her proficiency.

3. It is important that both Eugene and Katrina continually reflect on scope-of-practice considerations and ensure that they have the requisite training and expertise (or can consult with other experts, as needed) to work effectively with the Levai family. When new issues arise that may be outside of their expertise, Eugene and Katrina must determine how best to handle client needs.

4. Given that Eugene, Katrina, and the Levai family are all geographically distant from one another, Eugene must work with Katrina on developing emergency protocols and a list of emergency resources local to the Levais.

Utilizing the MECA supervision model, Eugene takes time while reviewing the informed consent, to highlight the important role of multicultural factors.

Eugene: Each supervision and counseling relationship is multicultural, and multicultural competency is necessary for ethical work. As such, multiculturalism will be infused throughout the supervision process. In your multicultural counseling course, did you explore how you have multiple cultural identities?

Katrina: Do you mean, how I am female and from a middle-income socioeconomic status?

Eugene: Exactly. As part of supervision, we are going to explore how identities of power and oppression intersect to form our cultural identity and how that impacts our relationships. We will also explore both the similarities and differences in our cultures and the cultures of your clients. Now understand that this process may be difficult at times, especially as we address privilege, oppression, and social justice.

Katrina: I am excited to get started!

Eugene: That is great! I want you to feel comfortable discussing any concerns that may arise. Multicultural competency is not a goal that once achieved can be abandoned. It is something we must work to maintain and continuously grow. I am not all knowing and will make mistakes—and so will you.

Katrina: That is both a relief and scary at the same time. I worry that I will say the wrong thing.

Eugene: All counselors feel that way at some point. Providing online counseling can add to this fear due to the limited visual cues, but that is something we will explore later. Do you have any questions before we continue reviewing the supervision contract?

Worksheets

SUPERVISOR GOALS WORKSHEET

As the supervisor, there are specific deficits or areas of need that you see in your supervisees. Use this worksheet to identify areas of growth for the counselor in training and steps the supervisor can take to facilitate growth in the supervisee. This form is NOT intended for use with supervisee, but rather as a means for the supervisor to track progress during supervision toward specific goals that address deficits.

Goal (Identify specifically what the counselor in training needs to focus on during supervision)	Action steps toward completing goal (List specific steps you will take to support your supervisee)	Progress toward achieving goal (Use a scale or other means to determine progress)

* Please feel free to add additional goals and steps on the back of this worksheet or add additional sheets as you see necessary.

SUPERVISEE GOALS WORKSHEET

As a counselor in training, you are expected to reflect back on your work with clients to determine what areas you require additional support or training. Use this worksheet to identify areas of growth and steps to take to facilitate growth in the identified areas. Share this form with your supervisor during supervision to guide supervision sessions and ensure your professional needs are being met.

Goal (Identify specifically what areas you need to improve on)	Action steps toward completing goal (List specific steps you will take to strengthen each area)	Progress toward achieving goal (Use a scale or other means to determine progress and identify where additional support is needed)

* Please feel free to add additional goals and steps on the back of this worksheet or add additional sheets as you see necessary.

Basic Counseling Forms

SUPERVISION CONTRACT

Supervisor's name and credentials

Email address

Phone number

State license #: *******

Online Counselor Supervision Agreement

The purpose of this document is to establish the parameters of the supervisor–supervisee relationship, set clear expectations, outline supervisor and supervisee responsibilities, and serve as a guidepost for maintaining an ongoing collaborative and professional mentoring relationship.

Date: _____

This contract serves as verification and a description of the counseling supervision provided

by _____ to _____, enrolled in the Counselor Education program at

_____ _____ for the _____ semester. Supervision may extend beyond

the semester by the mutual agreement of supervisor and supervisees. Date of extension _____

Initials _____ and _____.

Supervisor Information and Background

Thank you so much for considering me to provide your clinical supervision. I am looking forward to sharing my passion for our chosen profession and to hearing about what brought you to the field, what energizes you about it, and what types of concerns you may have as you start your professional career in counseling. I am licensed in (state) as a (your credentials) and have a (type of degree) from (your graduate school). (*Feel free to share here more about your experience, the settings in which you have worked, and specialized trainings or certifications you have.*)

My approach to supervision is collaborative, with the goal of offering you professional support, guidance, and information as you join the profession of counseling, while also ensuring the welfare of the clients with whom you work during your training. By necessity and design, my role is also evaluative, meaning that I am required to make professional assessments regarding your competency and progress throughout the time we work together.

What You Can Expect From Online Supervision

Supervision will consist of 1 hour of individual supervision per week for a semester, with extension possible by mutual agreement.

Mode of supervision. Supervision will be conducted via electronic means of communication, including phone, videoconferencing, and email. Given that the delivery platform for this supervision is provided via distance communication methods, it is important to address specific issues that may arise due to the nature of technology and the limitations inherent in having the supervisor and supervisee in different physical locations.

Confidentiality, security, and privacy. Electronic communication is not 100% secure, unfortunately. It is possible for our communications to be intercepted or hacked, which can constitute a breach of confidentiality. Given the risks, it is important that we maintain best practices in the protection of client information. Please take care not to state the client's name or to reveal specific, identifying information that would increase the likelihood of a client's identity being revealed. It is also important to mutually remain cognizant of ways we can minimize the potential for being overheard or having our screens viewed by others. Please protect your devices with passwords, log off of relevant communication accounts when stepping away or when finished, and find a private location for online supervision.

Everything we discuss in supervision is confidential with a few notable exceptions. The exceptions are the same as yours in treatment of clients, adhering to legal and ethical standards set forth by government agencies and professional associations, and would include risk of self-harm, risk of harm to others, abuse of children, adults, elderly, or disabled persons, court orders, and instances in which you give written permission to disclose to others about the treatment that you provide. Additionally, please be mindful that—because this supervision is taking place under the auspices of my PhD studies—I may discuss supervision sessions and issues with my supervisor, who is also bound to keep client and supervisee information confidential. If you have any questions regarding confidentiality in general or the confidentiality of your sessions particularly, please ask. _____ Initials

Please also be advised that it is your obligation to inform your clients that you will be receiving supervision and that your supervisor will be privy to confidential information, bound by the same rules regarding their information as you. I maintain secure records of supervisees and their clients in the same way as I do with my therapy clients. The supervisee must inform the client they are in training, are being supervised and will be sharing clinical information with the supervisor, and receive written consent. Last, technology affords us enormous opportunities and greatly facilitates communication but can also present an area for concern with regard to confidentiality.

Finally, please be mindful about using HIPAA-compliant platforms for any confidential communications, safeguard client names and identifying information, and follow all protocols for the handling and storage of counseling records.

Communication glitches. While we can all appreciate the benefits of being able to conduct supervision via distance, we also need to acknowledge the real limitations of the online milieu. Unstable internet connections, frozen screens, phone crackling—combined with difficulty in reading body language over distance—can sometimes lead to miscommunications or clunky conversation. Maintaining a patient but proactive, problem-solving approach will help us to resolve even the most annoying technological challenges. Should we get disconnected during a supervision session, please phone me immediately at (phone number). If necessary, we will make every reasonable effort to reschedule any time we have missed. If you experience any issues with the mode of supervision we have mutually agreed on, please let me know. It is important that you get what you need out of your supervision experience.

Financial information. During the course of your practicum, supervision—which typically involves one hour per week of direct supervision—is included as part of your class. Once your practicum has ended, should we choose to extend supervision beyond the term and outside the bounds of your class, the hourly rate for supervision is _____, payable by check or Paypal. If any changes are made to the status of our supervisory relationship in terms of duration, we will mutually agree on an effective date for the financial obligation to change and note it (and fill in the hourly rate) here: Date: _____ Rate per hour: _____ Initials _____ and _____ Payment is due at the end of each session. Please discuss financial hardship with me as it arises so we can discuss how to proceed. Accrual of unpaid fees—other than by mutual agreement—can negatively impact the working relationship and therefore may be grounds for termination of the supervisory relationship with 2 weeks' notice.

Cancellation policy. In the event you need to cancel, please do so 24 hours in advance of our session as professional courtesy dictates; I will do the same. Should cancellations happen on a regular basis, our work may be impacted in that (a) you may not accrue the hours of supervision you need, (b) I will have less content to consider in offering feedback and completing evaluations, and (c) it will be noted in your feedback and evaluations.

Emergencies do happen; however, please discuss extenuating circumstances with me as they arise. It is the supervisee's responsibility to reschedule the session as needed to comply with their program requirements.

Preparation. During our supervision session, I will expect for you to come prepared with material to discuss; material may include case conceptualizations, sample treatment plans and psychotherapy notes, concerns, questions, examples to share of clinical situations you feel are going well, observations you are making about your work in counseling, observations about our shared collaboration, and more. Twice during our work together, please also bring a video or audiotape of a session you have conducted with a current client after obtaining the written consent of that client. In my experience, this is the part of supervision that can generate significant anxiety in the supervisee; however, it is typically of tremendous benefit because it gives us a shared experience to discuss and allows me the opportunity to see your clinical skills as they develop. I will be listening or watching to your recorded sessions with an ear to how I can most be of help to you, as well as evaluating your client engagement in terms of how you performed compared to what I would expect from a clinician at your level of preparation. Perfection is not a reasonable expectation. I do, however, expect that our supervisory relationship will include transparency and openness, as we work together in service of offering your clients quality care that is responsive, responsible, and ethical. Likewise, you can expect for me to come prepared to our sessions, which may mean having reviewed tapes you have given me in a timely fashion, formulated questions from the information you have shared, brought resources to share, completed forms required by your program, or otherwise demonstrated that I take my collaboration with you seriously.

Scope. Supervision will revolve around counseling conducted by supervisee on cases brought to supervision. Please note that if a case is not brought to supervision, the supervisor is not responsible for any of the supervisee's actions with that case.

Competency. Both supervisor and supervisee are bound to practice within the scope of their training and expertise. In practical terms, this means that we need to inform clients of our qualifications and represent our experience accurately, seek supervision in areas in which we are developing skills, and indicate when something is out of the scope of our practice. In supervision, for example, you may express interest in counseling modalities with which I have little to no experience; in that instance, I am obligated to share that I am not trained in that area but as your supervisor will work with you to find resources or contacts to pursue your interest further.

Documentation. In the field of counseling, documentation is extremely important; part of your training in counseling will be to learn to document early, often, and well. During your supervision experience, I will expect for you to complete notes regarding your work with clients in a timely manner (within the same week) and to share examples of your treatment notes for review, particularly in the beginning of our work together.

Ethics. The supervisor will ensure the supervisee understands the American Counseling Association (ACA) Code of Ethics and standards of practice and legal responsibilities. The supervisor and supervisee will discuss sections applicable to the beginning counselor. There is an absolute expectation that both supervisor and supervisee will uphold the Code of Ethics; failure to do so is grounds for malpractice, as well as termination of the supervisory relationship (see Termination).

Homework. From time to time, you may receive follow-up tasks, prompts for reflection, or other supervision-related assignments such as watching a video demonstrating a clinical skill, reviewing the Code of Ethics from the ACA, or completing the Emergency Preparedness Information form. The intent of any and all assignments is to further add to your competence and confidence. I do not believe in giving anyone "busy work."

Emergencies. Please notify me through a call or text (keeping in mind the need for confidentiality) as soon as possible. In the event that it is difficult to reach me, please follow the protocol of your work setting and crisis plans. An emergency may also warrant calling 9-1-1 as your professional judgment permits. We will discuss crisis plans for your clients in advance so that if a crisis should arise, you will feel more confident in knowing how to handle these situations. You may also contact the local mental health agency in your area to find the appropriate services to meet your client's needs.

Evaluation. Informal evaluation will be given in the form of feedback during each session. Formal evaluations will be given at midterm and at the end of the semester or may be offered additionally as determined by the supervisor. Self-reflection is also an important tool in our work as counselors; you can expect to have opportunities to self-assess throughout our work together. Evaluation is meant to further develop a counselor's professional competency by identifying those areas in which the counselor is proficient, where some development is needed, or where the counselor may not be meeting the expected level of skill. Maintenance of the strictest ethics, professional honesty, and compliance with all legal obligations of professional counselors are of the utmost importance and will be assessed throughout supervision. Evaluations are not meant to be a surprise but a reflection of the ongoing work you have completed, as well as the ongoing feedback you have received. I welcome your questions and concerns as we navigate this aspect of our work.

Appeal. As part of your formal evaluations, you have a right to respond to any critiques that you feel are inaccurate. I hope that we have a supervisory relationship that is comfortable enough for you to discuss your concerns with me. There is also a space for you to record a written response, to note any ratings with which you disagree, and to provide specific information to the contrary; that space is on the bottom of the rating form I will use midsemester and again at the end of the term to evaluate your clinical skills. If we have already spoken and you are not satisfied with the resolution to our conversation, the next step I would suggest is contacting your course professor. Once you have discussed the situation with them, it would be helpful for the three of us to have a discussion to clarify our viewpoints on the situation and to work toward resolution. While a mutually satisfactory resolution is the goal, in the end my primary responsibility is to uphold all professional, legal, and ethical standards for client care.

Termination of supervision. While I look forward to collaborating with you as you progress through your practicum experience, it is possible that something unexpected may arise within the context of the supervisory relationship that necessitates termination sooner than we anticipated, such as a relocation or change in circumstance. In this instance, the supervisor and supervisee each have the right to terminate supervision with 2 weeks' notice in writing. Maintaining sterling ethics is essential for counselors, including both supervisors and supervisees. Should the supervisor become aware of an ethics violation, failure to disclose information that pertains to the health and safety of clients, lying, misrepresenting one's work or hours, or any other issue that creates a relationship of mistrust between the supervisor and supervisee, the supervisor has a right to terminate the supervisory agreement effective immediately. The supervisor has an obligation to notify appropriate authorities and governing bodies should a situation like this arise.

Reporting complaints. I pride myself on maintaining a professional practice. However, if you should have complaints or concerns, please do not hesitate to let me know. I adhere to the ACA Code of Ethics. If you feel that I have violated those standards, you may contact the licensing boards for the state in which you are/were under supervision to report the breach of ethics.

Acknowledgement of Statement and Consent for Supervision

I, _____, understand the terms of this counseling supervision contract and have been provided with an opportunity to express questions or concerns.

_____

Supervisee   Date

_____

Supervisor   Date

Online Resources

- **American Counseling Association (ACA):** ACA membership information, Code of Ethics, and other resources for supervisors and counselors https://www.counseling.org

- **American Association of State Counseling Boards:** Membership information and resource. www.aascb.org/aws/AASCB/pt/sp/home_page

- **American Mental Health Counselors Association:** Membership information and resources for counselors. https://www.amhca.org/home

- **Association of Counselor Education and Supervision (ACES):** Membership information and resources for CES professionals. https://acesonline.net/

- **Chi Sigma Iota (CSI):** Counseling honor society membership information and resources. https://www.csi-net.org/group/wellness

- **Healthit.gov (HIPAA and Health IT):** Information on HIPPA, Title IX, and legislation regarding information technology as it applies to online health services. https://www.healthit.gov/policy-researchers-implementers/hipaa-and-health-it

- **Motivo:** Resources to assist in licensure for the counselor and supervisor. https://wearemotivo.com/

- **Zur Institute:** Resources for supervisors in both face-to-face and online platforms. https://www.zurinstitute.com/resources/supervision/

References

Aasheim, L. L. (2012). *Practical clinical supervision for counselors: An experiential guide.* Springer.

American Counseling Association. (2014). *2014 ACA Code of Ethics.* https://www.counseling.org/knowledge-center

Association for Counselor Education and Supervision. (2011). Best practices in clinical supervision. https://acesonline.net/wp-content/uploads/2018/11/ACES-Best-Practices-in-Clinical-Supervision-2011.pdf

Belsak, K., & Simonic, A. (2019). Ethical issues in the use of technology in clinical supervision. *Psihoterapija, 32*(2), 233–246. https://doi.org/10.24869/psihei.2018.233

Bernard, J. M., & Goodyear, R. K. (2014). *Fundamentals of clinical supervision* (5th ed.). Pearson.

Bernard, J. M., & Goodyear, R. K. (2019). *Fundamentals of clinical supervision* (6th ed.). Pearson.

Brandoff, R., & Lombardi, R. (2012) Miles apart: Two art therapists' experience of distance supervision. *Art Therapy, 29*(2), 93–96. https://doi.org/10.1080/07421656.2012.683729

Carlisle, R. M., Hays, D. G., Pribesh, S. L., & Wood, C. T. (2017). Educational technology and distance supervision in counselor education. *Counselor Education & Supervision, 56*(1), 33–49. http://dx.doi.org/10.1002/ceas.12058

Council for Accreditation of Counseling and Related Educational Programs. (2016). *2016 CACREP standards.* http://www.cacrep.org/wp-content/uploads/2018/05/2016-Standards-with-Glossary-5.3.2018.pdf

Falicov, C. J. (2014). Psychotherapy and supervision as cultural encounters: The multidimensional ecological comparative approach framework. In C. A. Falender, E. P. Shafranske, & C. J. Falicov (Eds.), *Multiculturalism and diversity in clinical supervision: A competency-based approach* (pp. 29–58). American Psychological Association. https://doi.org/10.1037/14370-002

Family Educational Rights and Privacy Act of 1974, 20 U.S.C. § 1232g (1974). https://www2.ed.gov/policy/gen/guid/fpco/ferpa/index.html#:~:text=The%20Family%20Educational%20Rights%20and,privacy%20of%20student%20education%20records.&text=Students%20to%20whom%20the%20rights%20have%20transferred%20are%20%22eligible%20students.%22

Health Insurance Portability and Accountability Act of 1996, Pub. L. No. 104-191, 110 Stat. 1936 (1996). https://www.govinfo.gov/content/pkg/PLAW-104publ191/pdf/PLAW-104publ191.pdf

Heron, J. (1989). *Six-category intervention analysis* (3rd ed.). Human Potential Resource Group, University of Surrey.

Jordan, S, & Shearer, E. (2019). An exploration of supervision delivered via clinical video telehealth (CVT). *Training and Education in Professional Psychology, 13*(4), 323–330. https://doi.org/10.1037/tep0000245

Mallen, M. J., Vogel, D. L., & Rochlen, A. B. (2005). The practical aspects of online counseling: Ethics, training, technology, and competency. *The Counseling Psychologist, 33*(6), 776–818. http://dx.doi.org/10.1177/0011000005278625

McAdams, C. R., & Wyatt, K. L. (2010). The regulation of technology-assisted distance counseling and supervision in the United States: An analysis of current extent, trends, and implications. *Counselor Education and Supervision, 49*, 179–192. https://psycnet.apa.org/doi/10.1002/j.1556-6978.2010.tb00097.x

Nelson, J. A., Nichter, M., & Henriksen, R. (2010). On-line supervision and face-to-face supervision in the counseling internship: An exploratory study of similarities and differences. https://www.counseling.org/docs/default-source/vistas/vistas_2010_article_46.pdf?sfvrsn=7

Topolinski, S., & Hertel, G. (2007). The role of personality in psychotherapists' careers: Relationships between personality traits, therapeutic schools, and job satisfaction. *Psychotherapy Research, 17*, 378–390. https://doi.org/10.1080/10503300600830736

Vaccaro, N., & Lambie, G.W. (2007). Computer-based counselor-in-training supervision: Ethical and practical implications for counselor educators and supervisors. *Counselor Education and Supervision, 47*(1), 46–57. https://doi.org/10.1002/j.1556-6978.2007.tb00037.x

14

Methods and Techniques of Effective Distance Supervision

Tina Pharr, Sabrina Wannamaker, and Elizabeth Brokamp

Distance supervision has been an option for several years, but the COVID-19 pandemic has made it a necessity, requiring both the supervisor and supervisee to transition from face-to-face meetings to the telebehavioral health format. Physical distance between a supervisee and a supervisor no longer presents an insurmountable barrier to clinical supervision. Distance communication mechanisms have created exciting opportunities, allowing trainees access to supervisors in clinical specialty areas and improving supervision's accessibility to counselors in underserved areas. Additional benefits include removing financial, practical, and geographical obstacles to securing supervision. At the same time, distance supervision involves a learning curve for both supervisor and supervisee. With careful planning and forethought, however, distance supervision can be a productive, meaningful experience.

Fundamentals of Distance Supervision

Distance supervision, which involves a supervisor and trainee engaging in a clinical mentorship from different physical locations, is in its relative infancy. Nevertheless, findings from numerous studies support the assertion that distance supervision is as effective as traditional in-person supervision (Belsak & Simonič, 2018; Coker & Schooley, 2012; Jordan & Shearer, 2019). Advances in technology have provided supervisors valuable options for providing distance supervision, giving supervisees greater access to supervisors regardless of their geographic location (Belsak & Simonič, 2018; Jordan & Shearer, 2019; McAdams & Wyatt, 2010; Vaccaro & Lambie, 2007).

Characteristics of effective distance supervision coincide with those of in-person supervision (Jordan & Shearer, 2019), and little to no difference in supervisory satisfaction between in-person and distance formats has been found (Coker &

Schooley, 2012). It is important that supervisors using the distant format consider factors impacting the mentoring alliance (Belsak & Simonič, 2018). Special attention needs to be placed on open communication, emotional processes of supervisees, and multicultural issues (Belsak & Simonič, 2018; Chamberlain & Smith, 2018; Falender et al., 2014; Kanz, 2001; Porter, 2014). Additionally, those professionals providing distance supervision need additional competencies related to the use of technology. Specifically, distance supervisors must be able to effectively use technology to enhance supervision while protecting confidentiality (American Counseling Association [ACA], 2014; Association for Counselor Education and Supervision [ACES], 2011).

Modalities for Technology-Assisted Supervision

Modalities for providing supervision from a distance have expanded beyond the phone to include videoconferencing, text messaging, instant messenger, and email. These methods of communication can be sorted into two major categories: synchronous (videoconferencing, live chatting, live streaming, and phone) and asynchronous (email, discussion board posts, social media communications, file sharing). Synchronous supervision may be required in some states.

With the proliferation of Health Insurance Portability and Accountability Act (HIPAA)-compliant tools and platforms for counseling and supervision, professionals have a choice among several methods of communication to use at a distance. Selection criteria may be based on three critical considerations: logistics, the supervisee's learning needs (Martin et al., 2017), and the supervisor's evaluative responsibilities. In order to make informed decisions, giving thought to *how* to discuss them is also important. This opening conversation helps to establish the foundation on which the supervisory relationship will develop.

Logistics

Discussing logistical considerations related to each modality can serve as an entry point for the supervisory relationship and sets the stage for collaboration. Logistical concerns related to technology may include the supervisee's access to the technology, the degree of tech-savviness required, the bandwidth, the reliability of the platform, and the cost. By utilizing modalities aligned with the supervisee's personal preference and level of comfort with technology, supervisors communicate an awareness of the supervisee's needs. The choice of a platform that is low in cost and easily accessible conveys consideration for the supervisee's personal and financial circumstances. The following questions can be used by supervisors to assess supervisee logistical needs:

- How comfortable are you with technology?
- Is this a platform that's readily available to you?
- What preferences, if any, do you have for the ways in which we keep in touch?

Supervisee Learning Needs

Supervisors should explain their style of supervision and the range of platforms and tools they use, then solicit information from supervisees about how they learn best. The supervisor can then use that information as a guide when selecting which modality may best showcase the supervisee's strengths and optimize their learning. For example, if a supervisee identifies as a visual learner, videoconferencing would be preferable to phone sessions for regular supervision meetings. For experiential learners, supervisors may want to use synchronous platforms that allow for role playing, role reversal, and case conceptualization activities. In selecting modalities compatible with the supervisee's learning style, what results is a collaborative exchange instead of a one-size-fits-all approach.

Evaluative Responsibilities

Evaluation is paramount to the supervisory relationship in the counseling profession, whether supervision takes place in person or online. While best practices in assessing the competence of supervisees remain the same regardless of modality (Belsak & Simonič, 2018), there are unique aspects of the virtual environment that merit careful consideration. For example, virtual environments do not always allow the same visibility and access to nonverbal behavior and cues. The supervisor's view is limited and can be distorted or delayed by technology glitches.

Limitations can be mitigated, however, by regular synchronous meetings and ongoing communication to check for understanding. The supervisor must remain aware of the potential for miscues and misinterpretations and continually ask questions such as, "What did you mean just then?" "It looked like your shoulders tensed up a bit when talking about that; did I read that right?" and "I'm having trouble picking up on how you felt about your session but would like to understand. Can you share that with me?" Using the basic skills of summarizing and paraphrasing will enhance the clarity. Matter-of-factly acknowledging the pitfalls of the virtual environment and soliciting more information can help build a relationship of trust.

The distance supervisor must be vigilant about maintaining the same high standards in an online environment as in real-world encounters. For the most accurate assessment of supervisee competence, supervisors should review a representative sample of the supervisee's work utilizing multiple counseling techniques and working with a range of clients (Belsak & Simonič, 2018). Supervisors can utilize various forms of technology to assist in direct observation of supervisee skills. Supervisees must have the client's permission to record or allow viewing or streaming of any sessions per the ACA (2014) Code of Ethics.

Live supervision is an experiential learning activity in which a clinical supervisor observes a counselor in training in session and provides guidance through direct intervention (Machuca et al., 2016). Live supervision was initially provided in person with supervisors observing counseling sessions via a one-way mirror, with the supervisor entering the counseling room to provide feedback (Machuca et al., 2016). As technology advanced, the methods of real-time intervention became less intrusive (Chamberlain & Smith, 2018) and expanded to include the telephone, the bug-in-the-ear apparatus, the bug in the eye, teleprompter, computer, and tablet.

Prerecorded counseling sessions that are streamed or shared via digital file provide an avenue for clinical collaboration. To stream a video, supervisee utilizes the share screen feature on the videoconferencing platform, enabling counseling recordings to be viewed during the supervision session. Watching video-recorded sessions together allows the supervisor and supervisee to identify therapeutic issues as they arise and isolate key moments for intervention. The supervisor can use actual data, rather than a case study or vignette, to help the emerging counselor with the development of clinical skills.

Supervisees may also review their own video-recorded sessions to gain a different perspective on their clinical work and learn to become self-supervisors (Abbass et al., 2011). Transcribing sections of a session, typically referred to as verbatims, is an excellent method of having the supervisee reflect on a counseling session, and it provides rich supervision material online or face-to-face. The process of reflecting is more likely to lead to transformative and more meaningful learning.

Synchronous Supervision Options

There are currently three primary synchronous mechanisms for distance supervision: video, telephone, and real-time chat (Carlisle et al., 2017), each of which has unique uses within the supervision context. Discussion of each is provided in the following sections, beginning with videoconferencing, which should be the primary mechanism for distance supervision. Special considerations for each are explored.

Videoconferencing

Unlike other synchronous or asynchronous communication methods, videoconferencing allows supervisors and supervisees to see each other in real time, allowing for the assessment of both verbal and nonverbal cues (Vaccaro & Lambie, 2007). Visual access gained through videoconferencing gives supervisors greater insight into their supervisees' skills and processes. The main disadvantage of videoconferencing is that it requires more bandwidth than voice or text-only communication, meaning reliable high-speed internet is needed. For individuals who cannot afford high-speed internet or live in rural areas where it is not available videoconferencing may not be a viable option.

Telephone

Telephones have been utilized for decades in distance supervision (Wetchler et al., 1993). While initially used in distance supervision as the primary means of communication, telephones are now predominately used between formal sessions to enhance supervision. Telephone communication can be helpful to facilitate supervision when there are scheduling limitations, such as either party needing to be at an alternate location, or when internet connectivity is compromised. The telephone can also be a preferred method for the supervisee to contact the supervisor in the event of an emergency, as most supervisors carry cell phones with them. However, telephone-based communication is limited to "verbal dialogue and exclude[s] the benefit of visual cues and subtleties" (Abbass et al., 2011, p. 109), and therefore should not be the primary mechanism for carrying out supervision.

Instant Messaging

Instant messaging (IM) allows the supervisor and supervisee to communicate instantly (Vaccaro & Lambie, 2007) and enables supervisees to obtain immediate feedback during a counseling session. To use IM during sessions, supervisees will need to have a tablet or computer in front of them, which could be distracting for them or clients. Additionally, as with email, there is considerable room for miscommunication. It is also important to note that with both IM and text messaging, communications may be synchronous or asynchronous, as there is no way to know if a person has received a message and will respond contemporaneously. Therefore, supervisors are advised to directly address IM shortcomings head-on and troubleshoot how to resolve potential disconnects, as well as establish rules for its use. Confidential information should never be sent via IM or text message as they are generally not secure and confidentiality cannot be guaranteed.

Asynchronous Supervision Options

Asynchronous communication is useful for augmenting synchronous supervision. For example, email can serve as a direct communication tool between the supervisor and supervisee, which, when used between sessions, can promote relational connections (Chamberlain & Smith, 2018). There are also asynchronous technologies such as streaming services that can assist the supervisor in performing training or evaluative functions. Apps can help track self-care and counselor wellness, as well as offer journal features that are beneficial to the supervisee's self-reflection. Supervisors are advised to consider incorporating asynchronous tools into the supervision plan as needed.

Email, while commonplace, merits special attention in the supervisory context due to security concerns. When utilizing email, care should be given to protecting confidentiality. Client consent should be obtained prior to sharing potentially identifying information via email or any other means (Vaccaro & Lambie, 2007). Best practices, however, supported by laws such as HIPAA and Family Educational Rights and Privacy Act (FERPA), mandates implementing additional measures for securing information, such as using HIPAA-compliant email providers that encrypt data, and scrubbing communications of names and instead using client numbers and other identifiers. It is important to note that utilizing secure servers with encrypted messages reduces threats; however, it is impossible to guarantee confidentiality against hackers (Vaccaro & Lambie, 2007).

File sharing, which enables the transfer of audio and video recordings, as well as documents, can be a useful tool in supervision. Access to the supervisee's recordings gives the supervisor data from which to offer feedback, determine what skills the supervisee needs to further develop, and to identify supervisee strengths. If viewed prior to meeting, the supervisor's feedback can shape the session's content.

Ethical and Multicultural Issues in Distance Supervision

The ACA (2014) explicitly addresses ethical issues related to the use of technology in supervision in code F.2.c. Supervisors are mandated to protect the confidential information of their supervisees and their supervisees' clients (ACA, 2014). To safeguard protected information, supervisors must only utilize HIPPA-compliant platforms. To decrease technical difficulties and data breaches, supervisors should maintain competence in the technologies they use (ACA, 2014; ACES, 2011; Belsak & Simonič, 2018). In addition to competently utilizing HIPPA-compliant platforms, it is essential that both supervisors and supervisees conduct supervision in appropriate locations. Supervisors and supervisees should avoid locations where information could be overheard or seen by others and avoid spaces with other people, including family rooms, shared office space, and restaurants. Public Wi-Fi that is not secure should not be used.

A second ethical concern related to distance supervision is the assurance of quality supervision (Belsak & Simonič, 2018). The ACES (2011) tasks distance supervisors with providing supervision that clearly approximates face-to-face synchronous contact and adheres to the same ethical standards as in-person supervision. No matter the platform used, supervisors are mandated to protect client welfare and assist supervisees in their professional development (ACA, 2014; Belsak & Simonič, 2018). For distance supervision, supervisors will engage in the same techniques utilized in person; however, additional technologies will need to be utilized to carry out the techniques (ACES, 2011). Supervisors are required to assess and provide feedback on the supervisee's performance (ACA, 2014). Supervisors engaging distance supervision, however, lack the ability to view the supervisee's work in person. Therefore, distance supervisors may use video streaming to review the supervisee's work with clients.

Multiculturalism

An exploration of the literature around multiculturalism and distance supervision reveals a noticeable gap. Consequently, it is important to look to professional best practices as reflected in standards and codes of conduct and apply them to the distance context. Given that social and cultural diversity is one of the eight core counseling competencies outlined in the Council for Accreditation of Counseling and Related Educational Programs (CACREP, 2016) standards and that "honoring diversity and embracing a multicultural approach in support of the worth, dignity, potential, and uniqueness of people within their social and cultural contexts" is a foundational counseling value (ACA, 2014, p. 3), distance counselors should give ample consideration to both their own multicultural competency, as well as how to effectively demonstrate it in an online environment.

In code F.2.b. of the ACA (2014) Code of Ethics, supervisors are called to not only be aware of the impact of multiculturalism, but to address its role in the supervisory relationship. While the ACA codes do not explicitly discuss multiculturalism in distance supervision, multicultural variables are present in every supervisory relationship and should be an in integral part of the distance supervision process (ACES, 2011; Belsak & Simonič, 2018). Power differentials, such as those based on role and authority, are endemic to supervisory relationships and intersect with multicultural factors (such as race, ethnicity, ability, sex, and gender) in the context of supervision. Supervisors must first recognize the professional power they hold in relation to supervisees, given that they provide assessments and evaluations that may determine a supervisee's ability to graduate or pursue licensure. Moreover, they need to develop a nuanced, research-informed perspective on how differing identities can combine with issues of power and authority to impact the supervisory relationship.

Unfortunately, these issues can be difficult to recognize and even more difficult to discuss. Supervisees may be wary of sharing their cultural biases and assumptions with supervisors, fearing that they could negatively impact the supervisor's evaluations or personally offend the supervisor. Ultimately, the supervisor bears primary responsibility for creating a supervisory context that feels safe and open, while modeling how and when and using what kind of language to address multicultural issues. In the first few supervision sessions with a new supervisee, the supervisor may want to address, for example (a) the importance of a multicultural lens, (b) power differentials, (c) the impact of the supervisor's evaluative role on the relationship, (d) cultural and societal biases, and (e) how personal differences could impact the supervisory dynamic. Monitoring the impact of role, culture, experiences, and personal perspectives throughout the supervision process is important as multicultural awareness requires constant cultivation and attention.

Supervisors may also want to weave assessments of multicultural competency—such as the multicultural counseling self-efficacy scale, racial diversity form (MCSE-RD; Sheu & Lent, 2007)—into the supervision process in order to identify areas of challenge versus areas of relative strength for the supervisee. Supervisors should assure supervisees that the assessment is meant to establish a baseline for showing supervisee growth over time. Identifying challenging areas through assessments can also help make supervision more efficient: Supervisees do not need to spend a lot of time on areas in which they are already proficient. In the online environment, the use of assessments is facilitated by easy and secure transmission of documents through HIPAA- and FERPA-compliant platforms.

Social Justice

In 2015, the ACA endorsed the "Multicultural and Social Justice Counseling Competencies," effectively linking advocacy work with multicultural competence (Field et al., 2019; Ratts et al., 2015). Furthermore, best practices in supervision call for supervisors to promote social justice through assisting supervisees in exploring diversity and engaging advocacy in their counseling practice (ACES, 2011). Advocacy is defined by the ACA (2014) as the "promotion of the well-being of individuals, groups, and the counseling profession within systems and organizations work" (p. 20). A key component of advocacy is the removal of "barriers and obstacles that inhibit access, growth, and development" (ACA, 2014, p. 20). COVID-19 has highlighted the numerous barriers to mental health care faced by many older individuals related to their age, ethnicity, race, economic status, and place of residency (Hames et al., 2020). Distance supervision provides supervisors with a unique opportunity to reach supervisees and clients in underserved areas. It is vital that supervisors assist supervisees in learning to consider and navigate client barriers to mental health care and advocate for greater access to care.

In addition to advocating for greater access of care, supervisors should engage in social justice through the promotion of equality to end oppression and injustice (ACA, 2014). Supervisees will be exposed to a plethora of social justice issues faced by their clients including barriers to education and social support housing insecurities, discrimination and oppression related to sexual orientation or identification, racism, incarceration, poverty, and difficulty finding work (Field et al., 2019). Supervisors should take an active role in assisting supervisees in recognizing the social injustices experienced by their clients and developing an advocacy plan. In distance supervision, both the supervisor and supervisee may be in different geographical locations than the client. This distance can mean less awareness and connection to agencies and resources close to the client. Supervisors can address geographical concerns by having the supervisee gather information on resources near the client and advocating for changes at the state and national levels. Additionally, active participation in state, regional, and national associations provides both supervisors and supervisees with opportunities to build connections and learn of social justice opportunities.

Skills Application

A key factor in counselor development is the supervisory relationship, this is true for face-to-face and distance supervision. Building this relationship should be intentional with clear goals and expectations. Supervisees will develop a stronger sense of counselor competence through measurable goal achievement.

Methods and Techniques Building the Supervisory Alliance

The importance of the **supervisory alliance** has been widely acknowledged in supervision literature (Belsak & Simonič, 2018; Bernard & Goodyear, 2014; Campbell, 2006; Chamberlain & Smith, 2018). "The supervisory working alliance is a collaborative relationship of change based on a mutual agreement on the goals and tasks of supervision along with a strong emotional bond of caring, trust, and respect" (Campbell, 2006, p. 162). Within the alliance, the primary responsibility of the supervisor is to facilitate supervisee growth and protect client welfare (Belsak & Simonič, 2018). The supervisory relationship has been shown to influence the quality of care provided to a client (Bernard & Goodyear, 2014). Strong supervisory alliances are linked with increased self-efficacy, self-disclosure, and supervision satisfaction by the supervisee (Chamberlain & Smith, 2018), as well as improved acquisition of counseling skills and development of professional identity (Coker & Schooley, 2012).

The supervisory relationship is both hierarchical and evaluative, evolving over time (Chamberlain & Smith, 2018). For effective distance supervision, supervisors must consider how the use of technology influences the supervision alliance (Belsak & Simonič, 2018). While deficiencies in communication related to visual constraints are the most frequently cited concerns related to distance supervision, the impact of these constraints are unclear (Rousmaniere et al., 2014). Since standard relational cues can be absent in some forms of distance communication, supervisors must be deliberate in establishing and maintaining the supervisory alliance (Kanz, 2001). Outlined next are seven steps to building a supervisory alliance in distance supervision.

Start With a Collaborative Supervision Plan

Utilizing a well–thought out collaborative supervision plan from the onset of the supervisory relationship is one of the best ways to establish a strong supervisory alliance and minimize supervisee anxiety (Campbell, 2006; Chamberlain & Smith, 2018; Falender et al., 2014; Luxton et al., 2016). Through collaborative planning, the supervisor and supervisee will create a shared vision of supervision with agreed-on goals and expectations, shared tasks facilitating goal attainment, and a strategy for resolving conflicts (Campbell, 2006; Chamberlain & Smith, 2018; Falender et al., 2014). "Such agreement will help create the supportive, trusting environment in which the trainee feels comfortable openly sharing thoughts, ideas, experiences, and feeling with the supervisor" (Luxton et al., 2016, p. 87). For additional information on the creation of supervision plans see Chapter 13.

Model Professional Growth

Supervisors sharing professional growth experiences with supervisees not only serves to reinforce the importance of professional growth, it also lays a foundation for bonding in the supervisory alliance. Supervisors serve as models for supervisees in relation to self-care, flexibility, openness, honesty, and vulnerability (Campbell, 2006; Chamberlain & Smith, 2018; Falender et al., 2014). Through appropriate self-disclosure, supervisors create an environment where it is safe for supervisees to self-monitor and discuss concerns. Appropriate use of disclosure is especially important in distance supervision where meetings tend to be more rigid and lack personalization (Chamberlain & Smith, 2018).

Attend to the Supervisee's Emotional Needs

According to Belsak and Simonič (2018), effective supervisory alliances are characterized by supervisees feeling safe enough to explore their emotional processes. However, emotional elements of supervision can get lost on the distance format, resulting in the need for intentional efforts to explore the supervisee's emotional and cognitive responses to their clinical work (Chamberlain & Smith, 2018). Supervisors should take a process-oriented approach that fosters openness and self-exploration while remaining noncoercive regarding disclosure by the supervisee (Chamberlain & Smith, 2018; Falender et al., 2014; Porter, 2014). A process-oriented approach can assist in the facilitation of dialogue about the interplay of supervisees' cultural background and experiences and work with their clients.

Approach Evaluation as a Collaborative Process

Supervisors have a dual responsibility to promote the growth of the supervisee and ensure the counseling client receives the best care possible (Porter, 2014). This responsibility is accomplished in part through ongoing assessments and feedback. While supervisees are encouraged to be open and honest regarding their mistakes, they often face anxiety related to the evaluation of their competence and suitability (Campbell, 2006). Supervisee anxiety can be minimized through the supervisor taking a collaborative approach to assessment and feedback. Collaborative evaluation allows the supervisee to participate in the process, for example, by conducting a self-assessment to share with the supervisor. The supervisee has an opportunity to compare their thoughts, feelings, and assessments with the supervisor's and to discuss where they overlap versus where they differ.

Adapt Communication for Online Platforms

A major concern related to distance supervision is the absence of relational cues and risk of miscommunication (Kanz, 2001). While "face-to-face contact, immediacy, unrestricted dialogue and flexibility" have been shown to promote to effective supervision, they may be impacted with distance supervision (Chamberlain & Smith, 2018, p. 9). During synchronous distance supervision, assessment of nonverbal language can be limited based on the positioning of the supervisee's webcam or size of the supervisor's monitor. Both tone of voice and nonverbal language are absent in asynchronous communication, which can lead to misinterpretation. Lastly, feedback may be delayed depending on the modality of distance supervision used (Chamberlain & Smith, 2018).

Despite these limitations both body language (facial expressions, posture, appearance, gestures, etc.) and paralanguage (vocal elements and changes) exist in the online environment and can still be observed and addressed by participants in real time (Al Tawil, 2019). Supervisors should pay attention to micro expressions, diverting of eyes, and changes in blinking patterns, posture, and breathing patterns to utilize as part of a comprehensive assessment the supervisee's engagement. Furthermore, supervisors can utilize various forms of synchronous and asynchronous communication between sessions to help facilitate and clarify topics covered in session. For example, it may be beneficial to send an email highlighting feedback given following a videoconference session. Additionally, check-in emails sent between sessions can increase communication and strengthen the supervisory alliance (Chamberlain & Smith, 2018).

Provide Multiculturally Competent Supervision

Cultural influences may impact the way supervisors and supervisees perceive the supervisory alliance (Chamberlain & Smith, 2018) and can contribute to misunderstandings in supervision and counseling (Belsak & Simonič, 2018). As such, supervisors should make evident the importance of multiculturalism within supervisory and counseling relationships, from the onset of the supervision process (ACES, 2011). Supervisors should attend to the full range of cultural factors, use culturally sensitive interventions, be aware of issues of privilege and oppression, assist supervisee in broaching difficult topics, and engage in ongoing self-monitoring (ACES, 2011).

Address Strains in the Alliance

Numerous issues can lead to friction in the supervisory alliance, including distrust, role confusion, dual relationships, conflicts in clinical judgment, and misunderstandings in communication (Campbell, 2006). These issues can be exacerbated by the communication limitations inherent in distance supervision and, if left unaddressed, can undermine the supervisory alliance. The supervisor is responsible for identifying and resolving the source of alliance strains (Falender et al., 2014). For example, it is the supervisor's responsibility to be aware of how the supervisee perceives and responds to feedback sent through email, and to ensure that any miscommunication of tone or meaning is resolved. Supervisors can best mitigate alliance strains through being invested in the supervision process, modeling warmth and flexibility, grounding feedback in clinical data, and providing ample opportunity for clarification during and between sessions (Abbass et al., 2011). Supervisors can utilize asynchronous communication to send a review of the supervision session and should use the first part of each session to address any concerns regarding between session communication. When issues that can lead to strains are identified early, an appropriate response by the supervisor can provide an opportunity for growth and the development of problem solving and social development skills.

Supervisee Competency Development

Working from an egalitarian perspective, the supervisor–supervisee relationship is collaborative, built on mutual respect and trust, and includes goals for helping supervisees become effective clinicians (Bornsheuer-Boswell et al., 2013). In the initial phase of the supervision process, the supervisor should inquire of the supervisee if they have identified any strengths, deficits, and areas of interest for additional clinical and professional development. These identified factors form a foundation for setting the supervisee's goals in clinical supervision. Collaborative goal setting is highly correlated with a positive supervisory alliance (Borders & Ledick, 1987) and with supervisee satisfaction (Lehrman-Waterman & Ladany, 2001).

Effective goal setting requires developing goals that are specific, measurable, and ambitious but realistic. The goal "I would like to become a better clinician" might therefore be re-stated as "Demonstrate three new counseling techniques within 3 months, as evidenced by videotaped sessions." Many of the components of good supervision, including goal setting, have a meta quality to them, in that the supervisor models approaches, skills, and techniques that the supervisee may later apply in session with their clients.

Once the goals for supervision have been articulated, the supervisor must consider how best to structure the supervision process in ways that facilitate goal realization leading to competency development. At this point, it is vital for the supervisor to have a model of supervision guiding their plan. For example, a supervisor ascribing to the discrimination model (DM) may use Bernard's three foci of interventions, conceptualization, and personalization as guideposts in determining supervision activities (Bernard & Goodyear, 2019). Other supervisors may choose a more reactive stance, focusing on topics as they arise during weekly sessions. Whether their approach is planned or spontaneous, it is important for supervisors to check in with supervisees to ensure they are getting their personal and professional needs met. Professional needs are initially addressed in the development of supervision goals, which are explored in detail in Chapter 13.

Supervision Interventions

Supervisors have a wide range of activities and interventions at their disposal, which can be adapted as necessary for the online environment. Many of these activities need no special adaptation, but do require advance preparation and comfort with technology. Popular supervision interventions include the following:

- Case conceptualization
- Narrative activities
- Modeling/demonstration
- Experiential methods (role play, role reversal, family sculpting, genograms)
- Audio/videotaping review
- Live supervision opportunities

For case conceptualization, narrative activities, and recording review, supervisors and supervisees will need to be familiar with videoconference screen-sharing functions. Technologies such as **bug in the ear**, **bug in the eye**, and virtual one-way mirrors provide minimally obtrusive avenues for live supervision. Supervisors use bug-in-the-ear technology to speak to the supervisee during the session through an earbud, while instant messaging is used for bug in the eye (Jencius & Baltrinic, 2016). Both "bugs" can be utilized with the supervisor viewing the session through three-way videoconferencing or through a virtual one-way mirror. Each option provides live video and audio feed directly to the supervisor via HIPAA-compliant platforms that are used for telehealth service.

The kind of information gathered from live supervision mechanisms can be useful for supervisors in fulfilling their evaluative responsibilities.

In evaluating a supervision activity's utility in the online environment, supervisors should consider the following questions:

- Will the online environment in any way lessen the impact of this supervision activity? If so, is there a way to mitigate limitations of the online environment?
- Are there ways to communicate this lesson that are easier, more accessible, or more effective?
- Is the technology needed to implement this activity readily available and free?
- Are there any security or confidentiality risks associated with this supervision activity?
- Will this activity assist the supervisor in evaluating the supervisee on a key counseling competency?
- Is this activity likely to assist the supervisee in reaching their supervision goals?
- Is the timing of this activity appropriate and helpful given the supervisee's stage of development and the current level of trust in the supervisory relationship?

Thoughtful consideration of these and other issues will help create a context for supervision that maximizes supervisee comfort, learning, and growth.

SUMMARY

Supervision delivered by distance has experienced a surge, with advances in technology paving the way for varied and ever-expanding forms of communication. While online supervision shares many of its fundamental principles and methods with face-to-face supervision, the technology required to access distance supervision presents its own challenges and opportunities. Supervisors and supervisees engaged in distance supervision should discuss the impact of distance and reliance on technology on the supervision dynamic. The logistics and supervisee learning needs must be considered, as well as the process for evaluating the supervisee's fitness for duty and gatekeeping issues. Synchronous supervision may include the use of videoconferencing, phone calls, or instant messages, while asynchronous supervision may use emails or file sharing. Supervisors need to be familiar with and assist supervisees in developing competency in considering and managing multicultural, ethical and social justice issues. Increasing familiarity and comfort with online platforms, as well as taking advantage of varied methods for delivering supervision information, will enhance their working relationship.

CASE EXPLORATION

Supervisors oversee the clinical work of their supervisees in order to ensure that the care clients receive from trainees meets minimum standards. In this case, in which Eugene (the supervisor), Katrina (the counselor trainee), and the Levai family (the clients) are all in different physical locations, Eugene must take special care to ensure that Katrina has the support, skills, and knowledge she needs in order to work effectively with her clients' issues. Eugene must also work with Katrina on emergency protocols in the event that one of her clients experiences a mental health emergency, something arises in the counseling context that Katrina feels ill-equipped to handle, or Katrina perceives a risk of which Eugene should be made aware. Eugene should help Katrina establish a clear plan for when and how to access his help and how to access community resources within the clients' home community.

Two additional areas of focus within supervision between Eugene and Katrina should include multicultural competency and development of clinical skills. The assessment of Katrina's competency development will begin at the initial supervision session and will be addressed through supervision goals. To assess and build competency skills, during their videoconferencing supervision session, Eugene and Katrina can collaboratively watch a recording of Katrina working with the Levai family. While watching the session, the recording can be paused to allow for discussion regarding Katrina's internal process related to working with the Levai family, as well as the interventions and techniques she chooses to employ.

The Levai family includes members with a diversity of social identities who are navigating issues within individuals, dyads, and the larger family system. Katrina will need to learn about issues related to divorce, changing family dynamics, transgender issues, and more. Utilizing the multidimensional, ecological, and comparative approach (MECA) to supervision, discussed in Chapter 13, Eugene can effectively assist Katrina in gaining a greater understanding of Levai's cultural norms without assuming cultural generalizations hold true for the family.

Eugene: Welcome back Katrina. During our last session you mentioned starting sessions with the family who were all located in different physical locations; how did that session go?

Katrina: Well it was initially a challenge trying to coordinate schedules due to different time zones, but the session actually turned out really well. I was surprised that all of the family members actually attended and that there were no major issues with even coordinating the second session. So, it seems like all of the family members are at least interested and ready to engage in services.

Eugene: That is always great to hear. If you had to highlight two takeaways from that session where you would need the greatest support from me, what would that be?

Katrina: Honestly, the father kept mentioning that his biggest issue is surrounding the breakdown of cultural values in the family, but he would never really go into details. And I truly don't want to inadvertently offend my clients in any way. And I don't know how to approach the situation. I don't want to come off like I don't know what I'm doing.

Eugene: Do you think that your clients would see you as incompetent if you were to ask them more about their cultural values?

Katrina: I just don't want to offend them.

Eugene: So how do you think you could approach that conversation?

Katrina: I mean, maybe I could just ask the father in the moment if he could explain exactly what he means. I really don't want to assume that certain things apply simply because that they are a particular heritage or practice a particular religion. Because that's not always the case. And I also don't want it to all be about dad.

Eugene: I can understand that. Keeping all family members engaged in the process is extremely important. So how do you think you can do that moving forward? Can you give me an example of how you could phrase a question to the family about their cultural values?

Katrina: Could I do a round where each family member names at least one value that they practice within their family? Sort of like what we learned about in our group therapy class.

Eugene: That is actually a great idea. What do you think would be the benefits of utilizing this method?

Katrina: I think it would give everyone an opportunity to speak and the kids and adults would get to share a value from their perspective or at least what they viewed as a family value. So, I think it would give everyone a chance to be heard and feel included in the session.

Eugene: What would your plan of action be if there was a disagreement on what one member said before another one was able to speak?

Katrina: Could I establish the expectation at the beginning that each family member would speak first before anyone could verbalize agreement or disagreement with what they said?

Eugene: I think that would be a great idea. What other benefits do you think posing the question to the family could have?

Katrina: I think it would also help me to build rapport with the family.

Eugene: Really? How?

Katrina: I think that by asking them about their family values it shows a genuine interest in learning more about them and not drawing my own assumptions and conclusions. And isn't that what counseling is all about?

Eugene: You are absolutely right.

Worksheets

SUPERVISION TECHNOLOGY TIP SHEET

Technology can be a wild card in conducting professional, well-organized online supervision sessions. In order to maximize the distance supervision experience and minimize the chance of technological impediments, follow these tips for best practice in online environments.

Choose a professional setting for distance supervision. Distance supervision allows for the supervisor or supervisee to conduct sessions from anywhere where there is connectivity, however, pay attention to the adage "Just because you can does not mean you should."

Make your background appealing and professional by either choosing a neutral option from your platform's background features or by carefully selecting where you are physically situated. This means

- not videoconferencing from bed or lying on the couch,
- checking the view of what is behind you to ensure it is free from visual distraction,
- ensuring privacy, and
- appearing alert and ready for work.

Minimize Distractions

Cell phones – Place your phone face-down, set on vibrate and silent. (Do ensure your phone is charged in the event you need it as a backup.)

Preparation – Set expectations of privacy with household members and consider using a sign or signal that indicates you are engaged in a professional meeting. If applicable, take care of kids' snacks and entertainment as much as possible prior to the session.

Computer applications – Consider closing all other applications not being used or needed for session.

Mute yourself when unexpected noise, such as doorbells ringing or dogs barking, interrupts the session.

Troubleshoot

When possible, test equipment, connections, and audio prior to the start of session in order to minimize delays and disruption. Do not use an application for the first time during session; always take time to develop a working familiarity with the platforms you are using in advance of your work together to minimize frustration and maximize professionalism.

Develop a Backup Plan

Technology, while useful, can also be unreliable and frustrating. Work together to develop a protocol in the case of the loss of connectivity or dropped calls, identifying who will reach out to whom, by what methods, and when.

Attend to Camera Placement

Roy Huggins (2016), of Person-Centered Tech, shares geometric calculations for the proper "gaze angle" to maximize simulation of eye contact online. But if the mention of geometry makes you want to run, heed this advice:

- Sit a little further back from the screen because distance gives more latitude in perception of eye contact.
- Stay engaged.

People tend to associate engagement with eye contact and may accommodate more variations in gaze onscreen if the other signals of presence are there.

Basic Counseling Forms

SUPERVISION FORMS

Supervisee name:

Date:

EE- Exceeds expectations ME – Meets expectations NI – Needs improvement NR – Needs remediation (areas rated as NI & NR must be detailed in the comments)

Area	EE	ME	NI	NR	Comments
Professional development					
Collaborative approach to supervision					
Motivated to learn					

Appropriately challenges colleagues and supervisors					
Exhibits growing autonomy					
Exercises good judgment with seeking help					
Exercises good judgment when acting independently					

Clinical presentation

Performs thorough case presentations					
Understands cultural background of client's presentation					
Recognizes nonverbal and metaphorical communication					
Addresses client's need through prescriptive versus generic interventions					

Interventions reflect knowledge of cognitive behavioral, time-limited, crisis intervention and systemic intervention					
Accurate diagnosis formulated based on client presentation					

Documentation

Notes are comprehensive and thorough					
Treatment plans are detailed, identifying problems, goals, and interventions					

Summation:

Online Resources

- **American Counseling Association (ACA)**

  The American Counseling Association website includes information about governmental initiatives salient to counselors, professional research articles, continuing education opportunities, career information, and more. https://www.counseling.org

- **American Association of State Counseling Boards**

  This site offers information about counseling board policies across the states, information about licensure and portability, ethics resources, and membership information. www.aascb.org/aws/AASCB/pt/sp/home_page

- **American Mental Health Counselors Association**

  AMHCA's site offers listings of news and events, advocacy and professional development opportunities, and online interest groups related to counseling topics. https://www.amhca.org/home

- **Association of Counselor Education and Supervision (ACES)**

  The ACES site includes information about regional groups, webinars, conference information, and information about the *Counselor Education and Supervision Journal*. https://acesonline.net/

- **Chi Sigma Iota (CSI)**

  CSI is the national honor society for academic and professional counselors. Its site offers information about its chapters across the United States, awards and grants available to members, links to professional publications, and professional development opportunities. https://www.csi-net.org/group/wellness

- **Healthit.gov (HIPAA and Health IT)**

  This government site offers detailed information about HIPAA policies and requirements. https://www.healthit.gov/policy-researchers-implementers/hipaa-and-health-it

- **Motivo**

  Motivo is a site where supervisees seeking an independently hired supervisor are able to find a licensed clinical supervisor in their state for hire. https://wearemotivo.com/

- **The National Center for Cultural Competence**

  This site, sponsored by Georgetown University, offers resources to help counselors to develop and deliver programs and initiatives that are multiculturally competent. Includes self-assessments, reading, and resources. http://nccc.georgetown.edu

References

Abbass, A., Arthey, S. M., Elliott, J., Fedak, T., Nowoweiski, D., Markovski, J., & Nowoweiski, S. (2011). Web-conference supervision for advanced psychotherapy training: A practical guide. *Psychotherapy, 48*(2), 109–118. https://doi.org/10.1037/a0022427

Al Tawil, R. (2019). Nonverbal communication in text-based, asynchronous online education. *International Review of Research in Open and Distance Learning, 20*(1), 145–164. https://doi.org/10.19173/irrodl.v20i1.3705

American Counseling Association. (2014) *2014 ACA code of ethics.* https://www.counseling.org/knowledge-center

Association for Counselor Education and Supervision. (2011). *Best practices in clinical supervision.* Author. https://acesonline.net/wp-content/uploads/2018/11/ACES-Best-Practices-in-Clinical-Supervision-2011.pdf

Belsak, K., & Simonič, A. (2019). Ethical issues in the use of technology in clinical supervision. *Psihoterapija, 32*(2), 233–246. https://www.researchgate.net/deref/http%3A%2F%2Fdx.doi.org%2F10.24869%2Fpsihei.2018.233

Bernard, J. M., & Goodyear, R. K. (2014). *Fundamentals of clinical supervision* (5th ed.). Pearson.

Bernard, J. M., & Goodyear, R. K. (2019). *Fundamentals of clinical supervision* (6th ed.). Pearson.

Borders, L. D., & Leddick, G. R. (1987). *Handbook of counseling supervision.* Association for Counselor Education and Supervision.

Bornsheuer-Boswell, J., Polonyi, M., & Watts, R. (2013). Integrating Adlerian and integrated developmental model approaches to supervision of counseling trainees. *Journal of Individual Psychology, 69*(4), 328–343. https://www.researchgate.net/publication/265161349_Integrating_Adlerian_and_IDM_approaches_to_supervision

Campbell, J. (2006). *Essentials of Clinical Supervision.* John Wiley and Sons, Inc.

Carlisle, R. M., Hays, D. G., Pribesh, S. L., & Wood, C. T. (2017, March). Educational technology and distance supervision in counselor education. *Counselor Education & Supervision, 56*(1), 33–49. http://dx.doi.org/10.1002/ceas.12058

Chamberlain, T., & Smith, C. (2018). Shaping supervisory working alliance from a distance. *Journal of Counselor Preparation & Supervision, 11*(2), 1–28. https://repository.wcsu.edu/jcps/vol11/iss2/2

Coker, K., & Schooley, A. (2012). *Investigating the effectiveness of clinical supervision in a CACREP-accredited online counseling program.* https://www.counseling.org/docs/default-source/vistas/vistas_2012_article_42.pdf?sfvrsn=dbff9031_11

Council for Accreditation of Counseling and Related Educational Programs. (2016). *2016 CACREP standards.* http://www.cacrep.org/wp-content/uploads/2018/05/2016-Standards-with-Glossary-5.3.2018.pdf

Falender, C. A., Shafranske, E. P., & Falicov, C. J. (Eds.). (2014). Diversity and multiculturalism in supervision. In C. A. Falender, E. P. Shafranske, & C. J. Falicov (Eds.), *Multiculturalism and diversity in clinical supervision: A competency-based approach* (pp. 3–28). American Psychological Association. https://doi.org/10.1037/14370-001

Field, T. A., Ghoston, M. R., Grimes, T. O., Sturm, D. C., Kaur, M., Aninditya, A., & Toomey, M. (2019). Trainee counselor development of social justice counseling competencies. *Journal for Social Action in Counseling & Psychology, 11*(1), 33–50. https://doi.org/10.33043/jsacp.11.1.33-50

Hames, J. L., Bell, D. J., Perez-Lima, L. M., Holm-Denoma, J. M., Rooney, T., Charles, N. E., Thompson, S. E., Mehlenbeck, R. S., Tawfik, S. H., Fondacaro, K. M., Simmons, K. T., & Hoersting, R. C. (2020). Navigating uncharted waters: Considerations for training clinics in the rapid transition to telepsychology and telesupervision during COVID-19. *Journal of Psychotherapy Integration, 30*(2), 348–365. http://dx.doi.org/10.1037/int0000224

Huggins, R. (2016, November 2). *Making eye contact over video in telemental health services.* Person Centered Tech. https://personcenteredtech.com/2016/11/02/making-eye-contact-over-video-in-telemental-health-services/

Jencius, M., & Baltrinic, E. R. (2016). Training counselors to provide online supervision. In T. Rousmaniere & E. Renfro-Michel (Eds.), *Using technology to enhance clinical supervision* (pp. 251–268). American Counseling Association.

Jordan, S. E., & Shearer, E. M. (2019). An exploration of supervision delivered via clinical video telehealth (CVT). *Training and Education in Professional Psychology, 13*(4), 323–330. https://doi.org/10.1037/tep0000245

Kanz, J. E. (2001). Clinical-supervision.com: Issues in the provision of online supervision. *Professional Psychology: Research and Practice, 32,* 415–420. https://www.researchgate.net/deref/http%3A%2F%2Fdx.doi.org%2F10.1037%2F%2F0735-7028.32.4.415

Lehrman-Waterman, D., & Ladany, N. (2001). Development and validation of the evaluation process within supervision inventory. *Journal of Counseling Psychology, 48*(2), 168–177. https://psycnet.apa.org/doi/10.1037/0022-0167.48.2.168

Luxton, D. D., Nelson, E. L., & Maheu, M. M. (2016). Telesupervision and training in telepractice. In D. D. Luxton, E. L. Nelson, & M. M. Maheu (Eds.), *The practitioner's guide to telemental health: How to conduct legal, ethical, and evidence-based practice* (pp. 97–107). American Psychological Association. https://doi.org/10.1037/14938-009

Machuca, R., Johnson, T., & Moro, R. R. (2016). Tablet-assisted live supervision: Eye-bug supervision. https://www.counseling.org/knowledge-center/vistas/by-subject2/vistas-education-and-supervision/docs/default-source/vistas/article_5547f227f16116603abcacff0000bee5e7

Martin, P., Kumar, S., & Lizarondo, L. (2017). Effective use of technology in clinical supervision. *Internet Interventions, 8*(C), 35–39. http://dx.doi.org/10.1016/j.invent.2017.03.001

McAdams, C. R., & Wyatt, K. L. (2010). The regulation of technology-assisted distance counseling and supervision in the United States: An analysis of current extent, trends, and implications. *Counselor Education and Supervision, 49*, 179–192. https://doi.org/10.1002/j.1556-6978.2010.tb00097.x

Porter, N. (2014). *Women, culture, and social justice: Supervision across the intersections.* In C. A. Falender, E. P. Shafranske, & C. J. Falicov (Eds.), *Multiculturalism and diversity in clinical supervision: A competency-based approach* (p. 59–82). American Psychological Association. https://doi.org/10.1037/14370-003

Ratts, M. J., Singh, A. A., Nassar-McMillan, S., Butler, S. K., McCullough, J. R. (2015). *Multicultural and social justice counseling competencies.* https://www.counseling.org/docs/default-source/competencies/multicultural-and-social-justice-counseling-competencies.pdf?sfvrsn=8573422c_20

Rousmaniere, T., Abbass, A., & Frederickson, J. (2014). New developments in technology-assisted supervision and training: A practical overview. *Journal of Clinical Psychology: In Session, 70*(11), 1082–1093. doi: 10.1002/jclp.22129.

Sheu, H.-B., & Lent, R. W. (2007). Development and initial validation of the multicultural counseling self-efficacy scale–racial diversity form. *Psychotherapy: Theory, Research, Practice, Training, 44*(1), 30–45. doi: 10.1037/0033-3204.44.1.30.

Stoltenberg, C. D., Bailey, K. C., Cruzan, C. B., Hart, J. T., & Ukuku, U. (2014). The Integrative Developmental Model of Supervision. In C. E. Watkins, Jr. & D. Milne (Eds.), *The Wiley International Handbook of Clinical Supervision* (1st ed., pp. 567–597). Wiley Blackwell.

Vaccaro, N., & Lambie, G. W. (2007), Computer-based counselor-in-training supervision: Ethical and practical implications for counselor educators and supervisors. *Counselor Education and Supervision, 47*(1), 46–57. https://doi.org/10.1002/j.1556-6978.2007.tb00037.x

Wetchler, J. L., Trepper, T. S., McCullum, E. E, & Nelson, T. S. (1993). Videotape supervision via-long-distance telephone. *American Journal of Family Therapy. 20*(3), 242–247. https://psycnet.apa.org/doi/10.1080/01926189308250922

Gatekeeping

Elizabeth Brokamp

The coronavirus pandemic of 2020 intensified reliance on technology for delivery of counseling and supervision, making it more critical than ever to explore opportunities presented by conducting supervision online. However, clinical supervision conducted via distance, through videoconferencing, or through other electronic means, can create unique challenges for supervisors in their gatekeeping role. Since ensuring the competency of counseling students and **pre-licensed** counselors remains a fundamental responsibility of the profession, any issues in distance supervision should be proactively addressed for the protection of both supervisor and supervisee.

Gatekeeping as Foundational to the Profession

Council for Accreditation of Counseling and Related Educational Programs (CACREP, 2015) defines **gatekeeping** as "the ethical responsibility of counselor educators and supervisors to monitor and evaluate an individual's knowledge, skills, and professional dispositions required by competent professional counselors and to remediate or prevent those that are lacking in professional competence from becoming counselors." (p. 45). Three major counseling organizations, CACREP (2016), the American Counseling Association (2014) and the American Mental Health Counselors Association (2015) mandate gatekeeping responsibilities in their Codes of Ethics, emphasizing the importance of gatekeeping to preserving the integrity of the counseling profession. As such, gatekeeping is an ethical imperative for counselor educators when they feel that a student or supervisee presents a threat to the public through the substandard practice of counseling. The supervisor's gatekeeping responsibilities exist therefore, regardless of whether the supervision is delivered in person or online.

The Implications of Growth in Online Supervision for Gatekeeping

Clinical supervision via online platforms has undergone explosive growth in the past decade. Increased access to technology, enhanced means of digitally sharing information, and technological advancements that allow synchronous communication have spurred the use of electronic communication systems in counselor education, including in the provision of supervision. In a signal that distance supervision is poised for growth in years ahead, in 2019 the American Counseling Association (ACA) endorsed Motivo, a company that touts itself as the first "HIPAA (Health Insurance Portability and Accountability Act)-compliant network for connecting therapists to clinical supervisors for live video supervision" (Motivo, 2019, para. 1). As counselor educators and clinical supervisors increasingly rely on virtual modalities such as Motivo for supervision, they must also grapple with how to address counselor competency issues that arise in the online setting.

Two Primary Contexts for Gatekeeping

There are two main stages in an emerging counselor's professional development in which gatekeeping is a primary consideration. The first occurs when a student-counselor receives university-based supervision under the auspices of a counselor preparation program (Cook et al., 2020) as mandated by CACREP (2016). **Counselors in training** at this stage must participate in clinical experiences, participate in clinical experiences, practicum and internship, and demonstrate competency in order to satisfy requirements for their graduate degree. The second stage at which emerging counselors receive clinical supervision is when they have attained pre-licensure status. Pre-licensed counselors have already earned their counseling degree but must complete postgraduate supervised experience in order to obtain a state license to practice independently. These pre-licensed clinicians may work with clients in an agency, school, organization, or private practice under the supervision of a licensed counselor who may or may not work for the same organization.

While there is much overlap in supervisory and gatekeeping responsibilities in each of these stages, there are also differences that merit consideration. Supervisors who are overseeing the work of counselors in training through an academic program have an organizational structure underpinning their work. For example, the counseling program and the larger university may have both formal and informal institutional supports such as gatekeeping policies and procedures, legal counsel, and colleagues and administrators with whom to consult to aid counselor-educators in fulfilling their gatekeeping responsibilities. Similarly, supervisors working for agencies, schools, hospitals, and other organizations are likely to have existing workplace supports, including policies and procedures, to guide their supervisory role.

In contrast, supervisors who provide clinical supervision independently perform these functions outside of an organizational structure and as a result may experience unique challenges with gatekeeping, whether face-to-face or online.

Challenges to Supervising and Gatekeeping Online

Clinical supervision is critical to ensuring that student-counselors and pre-licensed counselors meet a minimum standard in the provision of counseling to members of the public. The provision of clinical supervision online presents some unique challenges to the supervisory context and relationship that should be acknowledged. Addressing differences between face-to-face and **online supervision** may help mitigate potential pitfalls in the online environment.

The Distance in Distance Supervision

Off-site supervision is not a new concept; counselor educators who oversee practicum and internship experiences have traditionally provided supervision to students, regardless of where the student's placement is located. However, online supervision introduces a new layer of distance. It is possible that the supervisee and supervisor are in different geographical locations while discussing a work setting that the supervisor may never physically visit and with which the supervisor may have no other professional ties. These additional dimensions of distance in which the supervisor and supervisee may live cities or states apart and lack any shared community reference points may present a subtle challenge to developing a working alliance. Supervisors, in recognizing the barrier of geographical distance, should consider talking with the supervisee about their community and learning more about the context in which they live and work. These types of overtures can personalize virtual interactions and may assist in developing rapport.

Relational Impact

Gatekeeping, because it involves injecting an evaluative and potentially critical dimension into a mentoring relationship, can be challenging. The supervisor, while working closely with the supervisee to help prepare them for entry into the profession, must simultaneously retain an objective view of the supervisee's performance, skills, and disposition. Managing the tension between these roles and responsibilities can take a toll on supervisors. Potential fallout can include personal stress (Russell & Peterson, 2003), fear of litigation (Gaubatz & Vera, 2002; Jacobs et al., 2011; McAdams et al., 2007), and significant expenditures of time and energy above and beyond typical job responsibilities (Russell & Peterson, 2003).

Unfortunately, distance supervisors who provide university-based supervision may also be physically distant from their colleagues and fellow faculty, making it difficult to get peer support, consultation, and commiseration. This collegial support and validation is important for mitigating stress due to gatekeeping, however (Wissel, 2011). The distance supervisor must, therefore, make extra effort to reach out to peers who can offer guidance and support. This guidance can take many forms, from informal consultation to regular peer supervision to formal discussion within an academic department. Weekly meetings with fellow supervisors are perceived as offering greater support than ad hoc consultation (Gizara & Forrest, 2004), so supervisors are encouraged to engage regularly with professional peers.

Qualitative Differences

Research comparing supervisee perceptions of effectiveness of online supervision with face-to-face supervision have largely shown no significant difference between the two formats (Coker et al., 2002; Nelson et al., 2010; Reese et al., 2009). While this finding is reassuring, some researchers have speculated that supervisees' favorable impressions of online supervision are influenced by factors of convenience (Coker et al., 2002) and flexibility (Nelson et al., 2010). Furthermore, online counselors and supervisors are often cautioned about limitations in reading nonverbal cues in online environments. Given these mixed messages, it is important for the online supervisor to remain vigilant to ways in which distance could impact the supervisory dynamic and attempt to mitigate negative differences (Chamberlain & Smith, 2018).

Independent Clinical Supervisors: Pitfalls and Challenges

It is clear that counselor educators play a critical role in ensuring that counseling students possess the necessary qualities, temperament, training, and experience to counsel clients before they are permitted graduation (Bryant et al., 2013). However, once a student has graduated, these gatekeeping responsibilities become the purview of clinical supervisors, who may have been assigned by the supervisee's workplace or whom the supervisee may have hired. No longer under the auspices of a degree-granting institution, clinical supervision for pre-licensed counselors has been described as a "business relationship" (Magnuson et al., 2000, p. 177). This description is apt and differentiates postgraduate supervision from university-based supervision in two primary ways: Postgraduate supervisors are often selected by the supervisee, rather than assigned, and the pre-licensed supervisee may be directly paying their postgraduate supervisor for supervision services. The monetary tie between supervisor and supervisee, in this instance, can present either the appearance of or an actual conflict of interest with regard to gatekeeping.

Workplace-assigned supervisors, while they may not have a direct financial relationship with the supervisee, may have a different kind of conflict of interest regarding potentially overlapping and conflicting roles. Having the same person serve as both clinical supervisor and administrative supervisor, for example, may impact the supervisee's comfort with disclosure in supervision since it could have potentially negative repercussions for employment (Cook et al., 2020). Maintaining multiple roles could also be problematic for the supervisor, who may face challenges when navigating between their role as clinical supervisor and their role as workplace administrator. The clinical supervisor's primary allegiances are to the counseling profession, ethics and laws that govern professional conduct, and their duty to protect the public from harm may conflict. Workplace supervisors may have additional interests that are driven by employment-related motives, however, such as wanting to protect the organization from reputational harm. It is not difficult to imagine situations in which the two roles are in conflict and the supervisor is faced with a hard choice.

The differences between university-based supervision and postgraduate supervision extend to the supervisory dynamic. For example, pre-licensed counselors tend to self-direct the supervision experience far more than counselors in training (Cook & Sackett, 2018). This means that rather than relying on the supervisor to take the lead, self-directed supervisees drive the content of supervision sessions with their own clinical concerns and their proactive requests for guidance (Cook & Sackett, 2018).

Unfortunately, self-direction may also take a contrary turn; an estimated 60 to 97.2% of counselors in training (Cook et al., 2018; Ladany et al., 1996; Mehr et al., 2010) and 95.3% of pre-licensed counselors (Cook et al., 2020) engage in supervisee nondisclosure in clinical supervision. Whether it is intentional or not, withholding concerns about clients and the supervision experience can pose a risk for supervisors (Cook et al., 2020). Supervisors are advised, therefore, to take proactive steps to educate supervisees about the pitfalls of withholding information, explain the risk to their license, and detail expectations for what information should be shared. Establishing a supervisory alliance that is predicated on safety and trust may also go a long way in encouraging disclosure.

Solo Oversight and Liability

Supervision requires that the supervisor assume responsibility for a supervisee's professional conduct, a responsibility that rests on the supervisor's license and professional reputation. Prior to commencing a supervisory relationship, therefore, distance supervisors would be advised to do due diligence in assessing the emerging counselor and getting to know them. Prospective supervisors may seek additional background information by interviewing the supervisee, requesting transcripts and a curriculum vitae (CV), and contacting personal and professional references. For distance supervisors outside of an employment or academic setting, gathering this kind of background information may provide a measure of reassurance regarding the supervisee's disposition and basic competency.

Lack of an Umbrella Organization

Unlike counselor-educators who provide student-counselors with supervision in an academic context, many distance supervisors may lack the support and shared liability of a larger organization. This lack of institutional backing may increase the sense of vulnerability experienced by both supervisors and supervisees, particularly in the event of challenges in the supervisory relationship. At an extreme, independent supervisors may fear litigation if supervisees perceive them as inappropriately impeding their progress in the field. Independent distance supervisors may also lack collegial support for fulfilling their gatekeeping responsibilities, depending on their practice circumstances. Solo private practitioners, who do not have peers on premises, may be particularly isolated should problems arise in supervision.

Lack of Partnership With the Workplace

The supervisee's workplace, unlike the student's former academic institution, may not see itself as the distance supervisor's partner in gatekeeping. This lack of coordination may be due to a lack of appreciation for gatekeeping responsibilities, a lack of perceived benefit of licensure, or ignorance that an outside supervisor exists. Pre-licensed clinicians, who have hired independent supervision and are paying for it themselves also may not voluntarily facilitate communication between their workplace and their independent supervisor.

Unfortunately, lack of coordination and cooperation can substantively affect the quality of supervision. One of the chief drawbacks may be difficulty the supervisor faces in accessing videotaped sessions, session notes, and other samples of the supervisee's work. For example, some counseling centers utilize electronic health record (EHR) systems that can only be accessed on site via a password-protected account. Other workplaces have policies prohibiting sending videotape files outside of their secure system for fear of violating laws regarding security and confidentiality. These kinds of policies, while understandable, mean that the distance supervisor is often left relying on the supervisee's self-report. While it has a positive role to play in supervision (Noelle, 2002), self-report offers an incomplete picture of the supervisee's functioning (Cook et al., 2020; Ladany et al., 1996) and should be paired with direct observation (Borders, 2014).

Another drawback of lack of coordination is that the distance supervisor may have limited options in terms of remedies and consequences should the supervisee fail to meet expected practice standards. In the event of concern, the distance supervisor may talk to the supervisee, note the issues on any licensure paperwork, or discontinue the supervision relationship. However, if a cooperative relationship existed with the site, the distance supervisor and site supervisor could work together to devise a **remediation** plan, offer a united front in terms of expectations, and presumably better address the supervisee's professional challenges.

The boundaries around these differing relationships and contexts may present an issue, however. For example, what would happen if the distance supervisor's feedback to the site supervisor resulted in the supervisee being terminated? What if the workplace supervisor shares personal information about the supervisee with the distance supervisor and it complicates the relationship? There is a risk of triangulation within this dynamic; coordinated work efforts should be well thought out and have clearly defined boundaries at the outset.

Prior to agreeing to a distance supervision relationship, supervisors should gather information about workplace limitations concerning the sharing of materials related to the supervisee's performance. Possible questions that may be helpful to ask a prospective supervisee include the following:

- What is the record-keeping system your site uses?
- What are your site's policies for allowing your outside supervisor to see videotaped sessions or read over progress notes?
- Is your **on-site supervisor** willing to consult with your outside supervisor as needed?
- Are you willing to sign a release of information to allow your supervisors to speak with one another regarding your progress?
- Are you and your site supervisor willing to meet with me together?

Supervisors can address these potential drawbacks in the supervision agreement signed with the supervisee prior to initiating supervision. Additionally, distance supervisors should consult with their attorneys and malpractice insurance to determine best practices.

Online Rating Sites

Online rating sites, which allow supervisees a means to publicly comment on their supervisor-clinicians, may pose a unique challenge to the independent supervisory relationship. While ratings may encourage supervisors to maintain high professional standards and offer potentially valuable information to other consumers, they could also impede the gatekeeping role. Poor online ratings from a disgruntled supervisee could negatively impact the livelihoods of online supervisors and, as such, present a conflict of interest. Online supervisors may also be reluctant to confront questionable behavior or to share concerns with the state's licensing board if the supervisee can retaliate on platforms such as Yelp or Healthgrades.

It is advised that the supervisor and supervisee review the ACA (2014) Code of Ethics Standard H.6.a. This standard discusses the use of responsible social media for counselors. An understanding of this standard may assist supervisee's in the appropriate professional use of social media and related internet platforms. Supervisors may also wish to include a media policy in their supervision contract, incompliance with expectations from the ACA Code of Ethics.

Gatekeeping and the Supervision Contract

Enormous variability is evident in the content of supervision contracts, depending on the setting and the personality, preferences, theoretical orientation, role, and sensibilities of the clinical supervisor. Some contracts are simple single-page agreements, while others spell out the process in far greater detail. Samples may be obtained in the Online Resources section (please see Dr. Carole Fallender's website). Supervisors who work in academic settings, community agencies, and institutions such as hospitals and schools may be provided with a supervision contract that has been vetted by the employer. Independent clinical supervisors, however, may have to supply their own. Chapter 13 provides an example of a supervisory contract.

For the purposes of gatekeeping, supervisors may wish to give specific attention to the following parts of the supervision contract:

- The roles and responsibilities of the supervisor
- The roles and responsibilities of the supervisee
- Logistics (when, how often, and for how long meetings will take place, as well as the format and location for meetings)
- Expectations for attendance
- Expectations regarding demonstration of skills, knowledge, and ethics
- Assessment and **evaluation** in supervision, including how often it will be delivered formally and informally, how feedback will be given, what measures or standards will be applied, what constitutes successful completion of supervision, what will happen in the event of a supervisor concern, and what entities may be contacted or involved in the event of a competency concern
- Due process considerations including what process is in place in the event the supervisee disagrees with the supervisor assessment, to whom the supervisee can report concerns, and what recourse is available for resolution
- The supervisor's scope of practice

It is critical to remember that, above all, any contract has legal ramifications that may become particularly relevant if conflict arises in the supervisory relationship. Regardless of setting, supervisors should familiarize themselves with the contract terms and thoroughly review them with supervisees. Independent supervisors are also advised to have their supervision contract reviewed by legal counsel.

Discussing the Online Context to Gatekeeping

As supervisors are reviewing the supervision contract with their supervisees, they would be advised to discuss the virtual environment and how it may impact the supervision process, including the therapeutic alliance, the structure of supervision sessions, assessment, and evaluation. While most supervision activities, interventions, and strategies can be easily translated online without significant fallout, perception of the effectiveness of online supervision, as well as comfort with technology, are likely to play an important role in supervisee satisfaction. Gauging how the supervisee feels with regard to these issues may dictate how much time and effort the supervisor expends to address the online supervision context. For the purposes of assessment and evaluation, this conversation is also important because it minimizes the chance that the supervisor will mistake challenges the supervisee has with technology for competency issues. Topics that may be particularly helpful to address include best practices for simulating eye contact virtually, eliminating environmental distractions, and troubleshooting internet connections and sound prior to sessions.

An Important Consideration

When talking about how technological quirks or glitches may impact perception, it is even more important to discuss how the supervisor will acknowledge and grapple with individual and identity differences in the online environment. Supervisors must cultivate a habit of using a variety of assessment mechanisms in order to adequately determine if an issue related to competency, and being curious, rather than judgmental, when they make observations. An example may be, "I notice that I don't perceive you online as having eye contact with me. That could be for lots of reasons: the angle of my screen, the angle of yours, a personal reaction, a different cultural standard, or something else entirely. But it's something I observed that I wanted to bring up and see what your thoughts are." Engaging with gentle observations and questions is preferable to making snap judgments about what is informing the supervisees' behavior.

The Role of Assessment and Evaluation in Online Clinical Supervision

Gatekeeping has been recognized as a critical responsibility of counselor educators and supervisors. Out of this recognition, numerous researchers have advocated best practices in order to support, structure, and systematize the gatekeeping process (Forrest et al., 1999; Gaubatz & Vera, 2002; Homrich, 2009; Wilkerson, 2006). Homrich, for example, asserted that the three best practices in gatekeeping are establishing expectations, communicating them clearly, and consistently enforcing them. These practices can easily be applied in both face-to-face and virtual supervision.

Competency

At its most basic level, competency refers to a minimum standard of professional conduct. However, competency in counselor education and supervision is a much more complex concept than is implied by meeting a minimum standard.

> Competencies involve the whole person; are teachable, observable, measurable, containable, practical, derived by experts, flexible, and transferable; are required for effective performance; correlate with performance; can be evaluated against standards; can be enhanced through training; and should be continually reevaluated and redefined. (Kaslow et al., 2007, p. 480)

Counselors, including students and supervisors, are also ethically bound to operate within their scope of practice, which is another way of describing their zone of competence. Typically, counselors' scope of practice includes counseling issues, modalities, and populations with which the counselor has had special training and experience. Supervisors work with counselors in training to determine with what populations and issues they are suited to work, and to expand their scope of practice through continuing education and on-the-job experience. Because counselors will undoubtedly have clients on their caseloads who differ with regard to aspects of identity, such as gender, sexual orientation, religion, ethnicity, race, socioeconomic status, and ability, competency with multicultural counseling is essential. Supervisors should prepare supervisees for assessment and evaluation in the area of multicultural competence.

Increasing efforts have been made to develop research-supported assessments of competency, such as the Counselors' Competency Scale (Lambie et al., 2018), which measures counseling student's skills and development using the main domains of counseling skills and therapeutic conditions, including nonverbal skills, encouragers, questions, and counseling dispositions and behaviors, such as ethics, multicultural competencies, and openness to feedback. Supervisors should consider using such established measures with their supervisees in order to get a more nuanced picture of their skills, to identify areas of strength versus areas of weakness, to assist in the development of clinical supervision goals, and to establish a baseline at the beginning of supervision that can be revisited at later stages in order to measure progress. Using this kind of structured feedback instrument can ensure that online supervision stays focused and on track.

Assessment in Online Supervision

Effective gatekeeping requires that a supervisor develop a proactive plan for supervisee assessment. In the online environment, as well as in the face-to-face sessions, this means determining the ways in which the supervisor will gather data about the supervisee's skills, knowledge, and disposition. Sources of data about the supervisee include the following:

- Self-report
- Observation
- Discussion
- Inventories and assessments, such as the Counselors' Competency Scale

- Audio and video-recorded sessions
- Experiential exercises like role plays and case studies
- Written reports including progress notes and diagnostic evaluations
- Presentations such as case study or general topic
- Advocacy initiatives including letters and emails
- Self-assessments

Supervisors and their supervisees may wish to discuss the blend of assessments they would like to use in their work together, with the supervisor retaining the right to additional forms of assessment as the need arises. Gathering a rich array of assessment data over time sets the stage for effective evaluation.

Evaluation

Evaluation flows from assessment, meaning that if ample data that is of sufficient variety has been gathered, the evaluation process is likely to proceed with relative ease. Typically, clinical supervisors are provided with standard evaluations that are generated by the academic program, the workplace, or the state through its licensure process. At the start of supervision, supervisors should familiarize themselves with these forms, if possible, as the evaluation criteria they contain could inform supervision content, as well as help with the development of goals.

While the fundamentals of evaluation are the same online as in person, the online supervisor is cautioned to engage in best practices with regard to organized and timely communication and HIPAA- and FERPA-compliant protection of the supervisee's personal data. Organized and timely communication is important because it conveys respect to the supervisee as they anticipate evaluation results, and because often evaluation paperwork is time sensitive, and depending on its contents can have a significant impact on the supervisee's next steps. Typically, a **counselor in training**, also known as a student-counselor, who is providing counseling services in practicum and/or internship under the supervision of faculty members and site supervisors as part of their academic degree program, must receive a satisfactory final evaluation at their practicum site in order to pass the course. Similarly, a pre-licensed counselor must meet minimum evaluation standards in order to progress in their licensure process. Secure handling of the supervisee's evaluation data is important for compliance with regulations regarding privacy and confidentiality.

Remediation

Mandated by both the CACREP (2016) standards and the ACA (2014) Code of Ethics (Standard F.6.b.), counselor educators and supervisors are tasked with addressing problems of professional competency in emerging counselors. This responsibility requires clinical supervisors to first identify supervisees' problematic behaviors, beliefs, and dispositions that could threaten the welfare of clients such as monitoring and evaluation, and second, to determine appropriate remedies or interventions of remediation.

Academic settings, in accordance with CACREP (2016) standards, typically have policies and procedures that can offer guidance to clinical supervisors in gatekeeping with students. The university setting also has a wide range of interventions at its disposal, since they can include academic tasks such as writing a paper, receiving tutoring, increasing academic supervision, or repeating a course (Forrest et al., 1999). Universities also have significant leverage in terms of compliance with remediation plans, since withholding graduation, albeit an extreme measure, is a potential consequence for the most egregious competency issues. Likewise, work-affiliated clinical supervisors have effective leverage in remediation given that successfully addressing competency problems is likely to be a condition of continued employment.

In contrast, independent supervisors may have a more challenging context in which to require remediation. Supervisees who have hired their own supervisors can also fire them rather than completing a remediation plan. Supervisors do have an ultimate remedy that they may employ in extreme circumstances, which is notifying the state licensure board of their concerns. Short of contacting the appropriate licensing body, remediation options for independent supervisors may involve a range of interventions, including recommending increased supervision (Forrest et al., 1999), suggesting workshops or additional trainings, requiring increased audio or videotaping for review in session, suggesting temporary leave from practicing counseling (Campbell, 2006), and requiring the supervisee to seek individual counseling (Elman & Forrest, 2004). When using personal counseling as an intervention within a remediation plan, supervisors must be mindful of protecting the rights of the supervisees and maintaining appropriate boundaries. In this way, they balance supervisees' rights to privacy with the potential risk of harm to clients (Henderson & Dufrene, 2018).

All of the remediation options listed are compatible with online supervision. Online clinical supervisors need to consider their supervision context and their relationship with the supervisee to determine which remediation options are both viable as well as appropriate to address the student's issue. Consistent monitoring of the supervisee and the supervisory relationship is highly recommended.

Best Practices to Support the Distance Gatekeeping Role

Independent online clinical supervisors should consider the adoption of the following best practices, in order to uphold their professional gatekeeping responsibilities. Careful attention should be paid to the supervision contract, which provides foundational understanding between online supervisor and supervisee.

- **Require proof of identity.** The supervisor must do due diligence in ensuring that the person whom they are supervising is who they purport to be.
- **Hold synchronous sessions.** Synchronous sessions allow the supervisor to get a sense of the supervisee's presence and to observe body language, tone, pacing, and other communication skills in real time albeit with limitations. The supervisor can use their powers of clinical observation more readily in service of the gatekeeping role if they have synchronous interactions.

- **Explain the gatekeeping role in the supervision contract.** The supervisor should be explicit in sharing their obligation to the profession of counseling, not just to the supervisee's training and development. It is important to articulate what process would be followed in the event the supervisor and supervisee have a significant disagreement or should the supervisor have significant concerns about the supervisee's professionalism (Dugger & Francis, 2014). Details may include examples of issues that could prompt gatekeeping concerns, who may be called in to help mediate, what due process would look like, and what entities the supervisor would notify. See Chapter 13 for supervision contract information.

- **Require periodic communication with the supervisee's workplace supervisor.** Establishing contact with the supervisee's place of employment may help improve communication about the supervisee and their professional conduct, ensure that gatekeeping responsibilities are shared between both supervising entities, and may provide some continuity in expectations.

- **Ensure opportunities for direct observation of the supervisee's clinical skills.** Supervisees should be required to videotape counseling sessions for periodic supervisor review (Gray & Erickson, 2013). Viewing videotape of the counselor's session in its entirety rather than having the supervisee select excerpts may offer the supervisor a more accurate overall picture of the supervisee's skills. Additionally, the supervisor should have access to samples of the supervisee's progress notes and reports. If access to workplace material is not possible, the supervisor should require that the supervisee furnish videotape of a mock session and a copy of mock progress notes.

- **Use established assessments at regular intervals.** In fulfillment of the gatekeeping role, supervisors should take care to accumulate as much objective information as possible regarding the supervisee's clinical skill using measures such as the Counseling Competencies Scale, which was designed as a comprehensive measure of counseling trainees' competencies (Lambie et al., 2018). Information from assessments may be used to help the supervisor to develop a plan of remediation by targeting specific problem areas and growth opportunities. In addition, should the supervisor feel uncertain about their concerns related to the supervisee's professionalism, data may help support the supervisor's position.

- **Keep thorough documentation.** Documentation offers an important protection for both parties and should be kept regularly, particularly throughout remediation (Henderson & Dufresne, 2018). In a distance relationship in which clarity of communication is particularly important, having a written record of events is good precedent. Documentation may consist of supervision agendas, supervisory session notes, chat transcripts, and dictation summaries, and in the event of a remediation plan should include descriptions of any behaviors associated with impairment, rationale for plan requirements, use of consultation, communication with the student, evaluation methods used, and student progress.

- **Address the issue of supervision session recordings.** Some supervisors and supervisees may wish to record sessions for the purpose of future review. However, in a contentious situation, session recordings and their acceptable use may become an issue between supervisor and supervisee. Session recordings could be taken out of context and posted by the supervisee as a retaliatory measure against the supervisor, for example, in the event of a disagreement. Supervision contracts should therefore explicitly address the need for mutual agreement for recording; the supervisor may also wish to make it clear that the recordings should not be released, posted, or otherwise made public.

- **Seek peer supervision and consultation.** In the end, gatekeeping relies on the supervisor's professional opinion; it is helpful for the supervisor to seek the counsel of other colleagues in the field in the event of a gatekeeping crisis.
- **Attend to process.** This should be done in the supervision of the supervisee's clinical work, as well as in the supervisory relationship (Reese et al., 2009). While it is relatively easy to misrepresent when reporting factual information from a distance, such as how many sessions a supervisee held during the week, it is more difficult for the supervisee to hide weak or inadequate skills in processing, particularly if the supervisor is engaging in discussion, analysis, and experiential exercises with the supervisee.

SUMMARY

Gatekeeping is a challenging but essential supervisory function that merits careful consideration and planning, particularly in the online environment. The supervisee's stage of professional development either pre- or postgraduate and the nature of the supervisory relationship, be it university based, work based, or independent, can impact the supervisory dynamic and have implications for assessment, evaluation, and remediation. Effective clinical supervisors will consider these factors, as well as the opportunities and challenges afforded by the online environment, in laying the groundwork for a productive, rewarding supervisory relationship.

CASE EXPLORATION

In addition to having a base-level competency with a myriad of counseling issues, Katrina must also have intrapersonal awareness that allows her to reflect on her thoughts, feelings, reactions, and potential biases related to the Levai family. She will need to explore questions such as, "What frames my understanding of the family dynamic and relationships? Do I feel tugged toward certain family members and away from others? Why might that be happening?" Quality supervision between Eugene (LPC) and Katrina (provisionally licensed counselor) will involve time, space, and a safe context in which to explore these issues and how they may impact the therapeutic relationship.

It is important that as Katrina's licensure supervisor Eugene gives time and attention to how he will effectively evaluate Katrina's disposition, knowledge, and skills. The distance considerations, as well as the complexity of this family system, make it critical for Eugene to require recordings of Katrina's sessions with the family. Recordings will allow Eugene to evaluate nonverbal behaviors, pick up on dynamics that Katrina may have overlooked, identify areas in which she could grow in insight and skill, challenge blind spots, and offer suggestions for future interventions as well as for the evaluation of any personal or professional gatekeeping issues, which may be evident for Katrina. Eugene should also consider how he will help remediate areas in which Katrina has opportunities for growth, including recommending training, reading, and discussion in supervision.

Should Eugene have serious gatekeeping concerns about Katrina's competence in dealing with the Levai family's issues that remain unresolved after remediation attempts or that are so egregious that they merit immediate intervention, he may need to consult with colleagues, representatives from professional counseling organizations, his malpractice insurance, an attorney, and/or the state licensing board. The most important consideration in this counseling context is protection of the Levai family, particularly the minor children, and both Eugene and Katrina are ethically and legally bound to "do no harm."

Eugene: Thank you for meeting with me today, Katrina, and for sharing your self-assessment. I wanted to share my evaluation with you, too, so we can take a look at the areas in which are in alignment and where we may differ.

Katrina: Okay. Did I do something wrong? Because the Levai family is really challenging to work with. They have so many issues!

Eugene: I'm interested to hear about your experiences with them, but first, I want to assure you that I don't see feedback as a gotcha moment, when I look for what's wrong. No matter the experience level of the counselor, seasoned or new, it's important to be open to different ways of seeing things. We all have blind spots sometimes and could use someone else's perspective.

Katrina: That makes sense, but first can you tell me what it was that I did wrong?

Eugene: Before I go over my notes with you about your session recording, I would love to hear more about the challenges you've experienced with the Levai family because that's also an important piece for me to know as I offer you support and guidance. It might be helpful for you to leave this session with some ideas for how you might approach those challenges as you continue to meet with them.

Katrina: Well, I don't know if it's okay to say this, but for one thing, I don't think the Levai parents should be dating other people so soon. It isn't fair to their kids, so when they talk about their new relationships, it makes me really uncomfortable. I've tried to just push those feelings aside but it's not really working.

Eugene: I hear you saying that their family's choices make you personally uncomfortable. Let me ask you this: How helpful do you think you can be to them when you are focusing in session on your own reactions and judgments? Can you see how that might impact your ability to help them?

Katrina: That's what I am supposed to do, right? Pay attention to my own reactions?

Eugene: You most definitely want to pay attention to your own feelings, but at the same time you don't want to impose those on other people, whose pasts and experiences and worldviews and beliefs may be very different from your own. I would love to see you replace judgment with curiosity. What makes the members of the Levai family tick? What roles do you see people play in the family? What led up to the divorce and how has it impacted each person in the family? Answers to those kinds of questions will give you more insight into how they function and will enable you to be a better helper to them.

Katrina: I get what you are saying, but I don't know if I'll be able to do that. There's just something about them that bugs me.

Eugene: I'm hearing how much this bothers you and wondering if it's possible that there might be some countertransference going on here. Sometimes if we've experienced similar issues in our personal lives, we can have a hard time separating those experiences from what our clients are experiencing. You don't have to share anything personal with me if you don't feel comfortable, but I'd like to invite you to give that some thought and be prepared to talk about it in general in our next session. Does that work for you?

Katrina: Without going too much into it, yeah; my parents got divorced when I was a kid and both of them remarried really fast. I didn't get along with my stepmom at all.

Eugene: I'm really sorry to hear that, Katrina. That can have a big impact on a child.

Katrina: Yep.

Eugene: You've shared something important and personal and I really appreciate that. I know that can be hard to do. I want to invite you again to think about it this week and give some thought to what might help you in those situations and relationship discussions to re-focus on the Levais, rather than feeling triggered into thinking about your own past. Some counselors decide that doing their own counseling can really help, for example.

Katrina: Oh, boy. Is it that bad?

Eugene: I am not thinking about it as bad or good at this point but as something that may get in the way of you both being there for your clients and feeling better yourself.

Katrina: Wow, I hadn't really thought about it like that.

Eugene: Let's keep our eyes out and see how much this is impacting your work; then we can decide what is the best way to deal with it. I would like to put our heads together about this issue so we can both make sure that the Levais get their needs met, but also so you have more tools to handle uncomfortable situations with clients. Let's add this as a competency goal to our supervision agreement; how about "As evidenced by self-report and supervisor observation, the supervisee will demonstrate the ability to bracket her own experience and approach clients with openness and curiosity.

Katrina: Okay, but I'm not really sure how to do that.

Eugene: I know you don't know yet, but I assure you, I will work with you on it and make suggestions as we go along. I'd like for you to bring another recording to our next session so we can watch together with an eye toward these issues. Sound okay?

Katrina: Okay. Thank you.

Worksheets

SUPERVISOR RESOURCE: ENTITIES GOVERNING ETHICAL, LEGAL, AND PROFESSIONAL PRACTICE

Each supervisor must take into account five critical entities when providing distance supervision that is ethical, lawful, and professional. These entities include the Council for Accreditation of Counseling and Related Education Programs (CACREP), the American Counseling Association (ACA), the law, the state licensing board, and the supervisor's professional liability insurance agency.

The Council for Accreditation of Counseling and Related Education Programs (CACREP)

www.cacrep.org

CACREP establishes foundational expectations for clinical supervision that may be applied to both in-person and online settings. In its 2016 standards, CACREP requires that counseling students receive supervision (Section 3, Standard N), but does not specify the modality: in person or online. In declining to explicitly address virtual supervision and how distance may impact these supervision requirements, CACREP places the responsibility on participants in distance supervision to determine how to maintain the same standards as their face-to-face counterparts. Distance supervisors, therefore, must carefully and thoughtfully select digital means with which they may accomplish the same ends.

American Counseling Association (ACA)

www.counseling.org

The ACA (2014) Code of Ethics differs from the CACREP 2016 standards in its specificity regarding online supervision, stating in Standard F.2.c, "When using technology in supervision, counselor supervisors are competent in the use of those technologies. Supervisors take the necessary precautions to protect the confidentiality of all information transmitted through any electronic means" (p. 13). Additionally, Section H of the ACA (2014) code is dedicated to "Distance Counseling, Technology, and Social Media" and outlines best practices regarding the integration of technology into counseling interactions. While Section H does not specifically reference distance supervision, the guidelines it contains are highly relevant to the supervisory context. For example, topics such as the limits of confidentiality when using technology (Standard H.2.c), the security measures such as encryption that will be used to protect information (Standard H.2.d), and the benefits and limitations of using a technology application (Standard H.4.a) are also important for supervisors to discuss with the counselors they supervise. Chapter 4 explores this in detail for counselors.

The Law

Familiarity with the law as it pertains to telebehavioral health is essential for clinical supervisors. Two significant federal laws that govern counseling practice around privacy and confidentiality are the Family Educational Rights and Privacy Act (FERPA) and the Health Insurance Portability and Accountability Act (HIPAA). Supervisors must also pay careful attention to state laws, which have jurisdiction over the practices of counseling and supervision.

FERPA

Family Educational Rights and Privacy Act of 1974

FERPA (1974) is a set of statutes that requires educational institutions to safeguard the confidentiality of student information, including student educational records and personally identifiable information.

FERPA would therefore be applicable to in-person or distance supervision that occurs between faculty and students, such as is required for clinical coursework in CACREP-approved programs. While FERPA does not specifically address the protection of digital information, supervisors should assume that "student information" includes both digital and hard-copy files. Appropriate measures must be taken to protect documents such as formative and summative evaluations and supervision contracts, which may be digitally exchanged during distance supervision.

HIPAA

Health Insurance Portability and Accountability Act

https://www.hhs.gov/hipaa/index.html

HIPAA (1996) mandates the protection of clients' personal health information and is applicable to anyone who is practicing in a health-related capacity with clients, including supervisors and supervisees. Several subsequent additions and refinements to HIPAA address the increasing use of technology in health care, including

- client confidentiality is safeguarded;
- the privacy and security of electronic personal health information is addressed;
- appropriate security standards and encryption when exchanging information digitally are mandated; and
- business associate's agreement (BAA) with purveyors of third-party software is required.

BAAs must ensure HIPAA compliance and must include information about how information will be maintained, explain how potential data breaches will be handled, and offer technical support to users.

In academic settings, the university should provide access to a learning management system (like Canvas or Blackboard) and an email system that are compliant with FERPA and HIPAA. Likewise, if a supervisor is providing the supervision as a condition of employment for a mental health organization, the employer must provide protocols and programs that adhere to the law. However, supervisors operating independently of an umbrella agency or institution will need to personally ensure HIPAA compliance and should choose the platforms and messaging systems they use accordingly. Gatekeeping HIPPA compliance needs to focus on consistent application of the privacy rule, the transactions and code sets rule, the security rule, the unique identifiers rule, and the enforcement rule. Each of these is discussed in detail in Chapter 3.

State Law

In addition to federal law, clinical supervisors should be familiar with the laws in all potentially pertinent localities, which may include the laws of the state in which they are licensed, where they are physically located when the supervision is provided, and the jurisdiction in which the student-counselor or resident in counseling is located. Unfortunately, in the absence of national telebehavioral health laws and standards, online counseling and supervision has largely been regulated on a state-by-state basis, resulting in significant variability in state laws around online counseling and its corollaries. Additionally, not all states currently count distance supervision toward licensure requirements, so it is important for supervisors to check their state laws to determine what modes of supervision are permissible for licensure. Prompted by the COVID-19 pandemic in 2020, Congress has begun to consider national initiatives to regulate telebehavioral health, a change that would impact Medicare providers and recipients, as well as the larger behavioral health community.

Counselor educators, professionals, students, and supervisors would be advised to seek legal counsel to fully understand the responsibilities pertaining to their respective roles and the provision of ethical client care. Being knowledgeable about the laws in all practice-related municipalities can help supervisors to stay within the scope of legal practice, as well as be able to competently advise and support supervisees.

The State Licensure Board

https://www.counseling.org/knowledge-center/licensure-requirements/state-professional-counselor-licensure-boards

Counselor licensing is regulated by the states under the purview of a licensing entity (for example, in the state of Virginia, this entity is the Board of Health Professions). Each state, therefore, has its own policies and procedures that regulate the provision of telebehavioral health, including the criteria for acceptable licensure supervision that occurs by clinicians operating within state borders. State requirements may include requiring supervisors to register, mandating formal training in supervision, and requiring regular documentation of the supervisee's progress.

Supervisors need to assess their supervisee's counseling competencies in accordance with these policies and procedures, providing remediation should gatekeeping issues arise. Such issues may arise around problematic behaviors, ethical violations, or lack of proper training or education (Homrich & Henderson, 2018. Appropriate interventions to assist the supervisee may range from educational interventions for minimal concerns to formal remediation. These are explored in detail in Chapter 3.

Liability Insurance

Supervisors who are employed by an agency or university likely have malpractice coverage under their employer, but it is recommended that they also seek individual liability protection. Employer-provided liability insurance exists first and foremost to protect the interests of the organization, and those interests may not align with what would be best for an individual provider. Independent supervisors will need to secure coverage themselves at the outset. All providers, whether employed or self-employed, should confirm that the coverage they have includes telebehavioral health. Confirmation in this instance means getting a copy of the coverage in writing and making sure that it spells out the conditions under which distance services (including supervision) will be covered. Distance supervisors are also advised to consult state licensing boards and the other entities (federal law, codes of ethics, and CACREP) with a stake in guiding or regulating behavioral health practice. Gatekeeping issues on this topic may include the lack of appropriate liability insurance on behalf of the supervisee. Appropriate interventions or formal remediation may be necessary depending on the issues that arise regarding liability insurance.

GATEKEEPING SELF-ASSESSMENT

As a professional counselor in supervision, it is important to understand gatekeeping and our areas of need that require strengthening. Please complete the worksheet and bring it to your next supervision session to provide an outline for your discussion on gatekeeping and goals with your supervisor.

Please rate yourself on each of the elements on the following scale:

1. Had not considered it, not a problem

2. Addressing it actively

3. Considering it but have not addressed it

4. Achieved and continue to monitor own management

5. Actively addressing it but need assistance

Professional behaviors	Self-rating	Steps you are taking to manage this	Questions/concerns for your supervisor regarding this item	Supervisor feedback (complete with supervisor)
Openness to feedback				
Application of feedback				
Ability to manage conflict				
Ability to manage confrontation				
Application of ethics to work				
Professional boundaries with clients				
Appropriate boundaries with supervisor				
Appropriate boundaries with coworkers				
Professional presentation of self as a counselor				
Appropriate use of supervision				
Appropriate use of consultation				
Compliance with agency policies/procedures				

Professional behaviors	Self-rating	Steps you are taking to manage this	Questions/concerns for your supervisor regarding this item	Supervisor feedback (complete with supervisor)
Completion of documentation timely and professional				
Completion of document thorough and complete				
Additional item #1:				
Additional item #2:				

Personal aspects	Self-rating	Steps you are taking to manage this	Questions/concerns for your supervisor regarding this item	Supervisor feedback (complete with supervisor)
Maturity				
Flexibility				
Cooperation				
Interpersonal communication skills				
Ability to express self effectively				

Personal aspects	Self-rating	Steps you are taking to manage this	Questions/concerns for your supervisor regarding this item	Supervisor feedback (complete with supervisor)
Appropriate personal boundaries				
Appropriate stress management				
Awareness of impact of own behaviors on others				
Awareness of impact of own emotions/expression on others				
Willingness to self-examine own behaviors, thoughts, choices				
Impact of substance use on self				
Impact or presence of mental health concerns on self				
Impact or presence of emotional concerns on self				
Relationship issues or concerns				
Family issues or concerns				
Financial stressors or concerns				
Physical stressors or concerns				
Impact/presence of stressor on self				

* Please feel free to add additional goals and steps on the back of this worksheet or add additional sheets as you see necessary.

Basic Counseling Forms

SUPERVISOR EVALUATION OF SUPERVISEE

Feedback to supervisees is an important part of the supervision process. Use the scale to evaluate your supervisee and provide support for areas of need and encouragement for areas of strength. This is not a complete list. Feel free to add or delete to meet your needs.

1: Poor/never, **2**: Below Average/occasionally, **3**: Average/regularly, **4**: Above average/almost always, **5**: Excellent/always

Competency	1	2	3	4	5
Knowledge					
Supervisee has chosen a theory and clearly operates from that theory during work with clients					
Supervisee understands how to complete online paperwork and completes all paperwork on time					
Supervisee understands how to diagnose online and is accurate in diagnoses					
Supervisee understands Code of Ethics and provides online services in an ethical manner					
Supervisee understands multicultural considerations and is respectful of differences in their clients					
Supervisee is competent in utilizing technology and understands and complies with standards surrounding online services					
Supervisee demonstrates appropriate understanding of the environment and necessary technical requirements for online work					
Intervention					
Supervisee develops rapport online and builds the relationship with clients					
Supervisee uses appropriate nonverbal skills during online sessions and understands the limitations of these skills					
Supervisee uses appropriate verbal skills during online sessions and understands the limitations of these skills					
Supervisee accurately chooses and applies appropriate online intervention strategies					
Supervisee accurately navigates stages of treatment					
Supervisee successfully collaborates with clients to create appropriate treatment goals and uses them to guide therapy					
Supervisee can provide interventions synchronously and asynchronously					
Client Conceptualization					
Supervisee accurately conceptualizes client online understanding the impact of the online platform					
Supervisee accurately recognizes multicultural considerations and responds appropriately					

Competency	1	2	3	4	5
Supervisee recognizes subtle patterns and themes presented by the client and responds appropriately					
Supervisee can discriminate important information and respond accurately					
Personal Awareness					
Supervisee is aware of their own biases, the impact each has on the client, and the differences in the online setting					
Supervisee understands their own place of power and privilege and appropriately addresses each within the therapeutic relationship					
Supervisee is aware of any areas that could impair ability to provide ethical treatment online					
Supervisee can accurately identify areas of strength and limitations					
Supervisee is open to feedback and regularly applies feedback as a means of growth					
Supervisee seeks supervision when confronted with an uncomfortable or unclear situation					
Supervisee understands the manner in which the client views them through the online platform					

Online Resources

- **Dr. Carole Falender's website** includes a comprehensive list of resources for clinical supervision, including sample contracts, assessments, and evaluations of both supervisor and supervisee. http://www.cfalender.com/clinical-supervision-resources.html

- **Substance Abuse and Mental Health Services Administration (SAMHSA)**: Clinical Supervision and Professional Development of the Substance Abuse Counselor. This handbook is a "treatment improvement protocol" produced to help clinical supervisors who work in substance abuse treatment to improve the quality of the clinical supervision they provide to substance abuse counselors. https://store.samhsa.gov/sites/default/files/d7/priv/sma14-4435.pdf

- **County of Santa Clara Behavioral Health Services: Toolkit for Clinical Supervision**. This resource site includes tips for effective supervision, suggested documentation, sample contracts, and more. https://www.sccgov.org/sites/bhd-p/QI/PQIC/Pages/TOOLKIT-For-Clinical-Supervision.aspx

References

American Counseling Association. (2014). *2014 ACA code of ethics*. https://www.counseling.org/resources/aca-code-of-ethics.pdf

Borders, L. (2014). Best practices in clinical supervision: Another step in delineating effective supervision practice. *American Journal of Psychotherapy, 68*(2), 151–162. https://doi.org/10.1176/appi.psychotherapy.2014.68.2.151

Bryant, J. K., Druyos, M., & Strabavy, D. (2013). Gatekeeping in counselor education programs: An examination of current trends. *Vistas Online*, 1–12. https://www.counseling.org/docs/default-source/vistas/gatekeeping-in-counselor-education-programs.pdf?sfvrsn=7f6e77b5_13

Campbell, J. (2006). *Essentials of clinical supervision*. Wiley.

Chamberlain, T., & Smith, C. (2018). Shaping supervisory working alliance from a distance. *Journal of Counselor Preparation & Supervision, 11*(2), 1–28. https://repository.wcsu.edu/jcps/vol11/iss2/2/

Coker, J. K., Jones, W. P., Staples, P. A., & Harbach, R. L. (2002). Cyber-supervision in the first practicum: Implications for research and practice. *Guidance & Counseling, 18*, 33–39.

Cook, R. M., & Sackett, C. R. (2018). Exploration of prelicensed counselors' experiences prioritizing information for clinical supervision. *Journal of Counseling & Development, 96*, 449–460. https://doi.org/10.1002/jcad.12226

Cook, R. M., Welfare, L. E., & Jones, C. T. (2020). Incidence of intentional nondisclosure in clinical supervision by prelicensed counselors. *Professional Counselor, 10*(1), 25–38. https://doi.org/10.15241/rmc.10.1.25

Cook, R. M., Welfare, L. E., & Romero, D. E. (2018). Counselor-in-training intentional nondisclosure in onsite supervision: A content analysis. *The Professional Counselor, 8*(2), 115–130. https://doi.org/10.15241/rmc.8.2.115

Council for Accreditation of Counseling and Related Educational Programs. (2015). In *Council for Accreditation of Counseling and Related Educational Programs (CACREP) online glossary*. Retrieved from https://www.cacrep.org/glossary/

Council for Accreditation of Counseling and Related Educational Programs. (2016). *2016 CACREP standards*. http://www.cacrep.org/wp-content/uploads/2018/05/2016-Standards-with-Glossary-5.3.2018.pdf

Dugger, S. M., & Francis, P. C. (2014, April 1). Surviving a lawsuit against a counseling program: Lessons learned from *Ward v. Wilbanks*. *Journal of Counseling & Development, 92*(2), 135–141. http://dx.doi.org/10.1002/j.1556-6676.2014.00139.x

Elman, N. S., & Forrest, L. (2004). Psychotherapy in the remediation of psychology trainees: Exploratory interviews with training directors. *Professional Psychology: Research and Practice, 35*(2), 123–130. https://doi.org/10.1037/0735-7028.35.2.123

Forrest, L., Elman, N., Gizara, S., & Vacha-Haase. (1999). Trainee impairment: A review of identification, remediation, dismissal, and legal issues. *The Counseling Psychologist, 27*, 627–686. https://doi.org/10.1177%2F0011000099275001

Gaubatz, M. D., & Vera, E. M. (2002, June). Do formalized gatekeeping procedures increase programs' follow-up with deficient trainees? *Counselor Education and Supervision, 40*(4), 294–305. http://dx.doi.org/10.1002/j.1556-6978.2002.tb01292.x

Gizara, S., & Forrest, L. (2004). Supervisors' experiences of training and incompetence at APA-accredited internship sites. *Professional Psychology: Research & Practice, 35*(2), 131–140. https://psycnet.apa.org/doi/10.1037/0735-7028.35.2.131

Gray, N. D., & Erickson, P. (2013, January 1). Standardizing the pre-licensure supervision process: A commentary on advocating for direct observation of skills. *The Professional Counselor, 13*(1), 34–39. http://dx.doi.org/10.15241/ndg.3.1.34

Health Insurance Portability and Accountability Act of 1996 (HIPAA), Public Law 104-191, (1996). https://aspe.hhs.gov/report/health-insurance-portability-and-accountability-act-1996

Healthgrades. (n.d.). *Home page.* www.healthgrades.com

Henderson, K. L., & Dufrene, R. L. (2018). Remedial interventions used with students enrolled in counseling graduate programs. *The Journal of Counselor Preparation and Supervision, 10*(1). https://repository.wcsu.edu/jcps/vol10/iss1/7

Homrich, A. M. (2009). Gatekeeping for personal and professional competence in graduate counseling programs. *Counseling & Human Development, 41*(7), 1–23.

Homrich, A.M. & Henderson, K.L. (Eds.) (2018). Gatekeeping in the mental health professions: American Counseling Association.

Jacobs, S. C., Huprich, S. K., Grus, C. L., Cage, E. A., Elman, N. S., Forrest, L., & Kaslow, N. J. (2011). Trainees with professional competency problems: Preparing trainers for difficult but necessary conversations. *Training and Education in Professional Psychology, 5(3),* 175–184. http://dx.doi.org/10.1037/a0024656

Kaslow, N. J., Rubin, N. J., Forrest, L., Elman, N. S., Van Horne, B. A., Jacobs, S. C., Huprich, S. K., Benton, S. A., Pantesco, V. F., Dollinger, S. J., Grus, C. L., Behnke, S. H., Miller, D. S. S., Shealy, C. N., Mintz, L. B., Schwartz-Mette, R., Van Sickle, K., & Thorn, B. E. (2007). *Recognizing, assessing, and intervening with problems of professional competence. Professional Psychology: Research and Practice, 38*(5), 479–492. https://doi.org/10.1037/0735-7028.38.5.479

Ladany, N., Hill, C. E., Corbett, M. M., & Nutt, E. A. (1996). Nature, extent, and importance of what psychotherapy trainees do not disclose to their supervisors. *Journal of Counseling Psychology, 43,* 10–24. https://doi.org/10.1037/0022-0167.43.1.10

Lambie, G. W., Mullen, P. R., Swank, J. M., & Blount, A. (2018, January 1). The counseling competencies scale: Validation and refinement. *Measurement & Evaluation in Counseling & Development, 51*(1), 1–15. https://doi.org/10.1080/07481756.2017.1358964

Magnuson, S., Norem, K., & Wilcoxon, S. A. (2000). Clinical supervision of prelicensed counselors: Recommendations for consideration and practice. *Journal of Mental Health Counseling, 22,* 176–188.

McAdams, C. R., III, Foster, V. A., & Ward, T. J. (2007). Remediation and dismissal policies in Counselor education: Lessons learned from a challenge in federal court. *Counselor Education and Supervision, 46,* 212–229. https://doi.org/10.1002/j.1556-6978.2007.tb00026.x

Mehr, K. E., Ladany, N., & Caskie, G. I. L. (2010). Trainee nondisclosure in supervision: What are they not telling you? *Counselling and Psychotherapy Research, 10,* 103–113. https://doi.org/10.1080/14733141003712301

Motivo. (2019). *Motivo and the American Counseling Association partner for online clinical supervision* [Press release]. https://www.counseling.org/docs/default-source/default-document-library/final---aca-motivo-press-release.pdf?sfvrsn=bed3562c_2

Nelson, J. A., Nichter, M., & Henriksen, R. (2010). *On-line supervision and face-to-face supervision in the counseling internship: An exploratory study of similarities and differences.* https://www.counseling.org/docs/default-source/vistas/vistas_2010_article_46.pdf?sfvrsn=7

Noelle, M. (2002). Self-report in supervision: Positive and negative slants. *The Clinical Supervisor, 21,* 125–134. https://doi.org/10.1300/J001v21n01_10

Reese, J. R., Aldarondo, F., Anderson, R. C., Lee, S., Miller, W. T., & Burton, D. (2009). Telehealth in clinical supervision: A comparison of supervision formats. *Journal of Telemedicine and Telecare, 15*(7), 356–361. http://dx.doi.org/10.1258/jtt.2009.090401

Russell, C. S., & Peterson, C. M. (2003). Student impairment and remediation in accredited marriage and family therapy programs. *Journal of Marital & Family Therapy, 29*(3), 329–337. https://doi.org/10.1111/j.1752-0606.2003.tb01210.x

Wilkerson, K. (2006). Impaired students: Applying the therapeutic process model to graduate training programs. *Counselor Education & Supervision, 45*(3), 207–217. https://doi.org/10.1002/j.1556-6978.2006.tb00143.x

Wissel, A. M. (2011). *Gatekeeping in counselor education: Experiences of terminating students for nonacademic concerns* [Doctoral dissertation]. ProQuest Dissertations and Theses Global.

GLOSSARY

Accurate empathetic understanding Humanistic ability to understand the subjective world of another on behalf of the counselor but also a skill to develop in the client, thereby creating an appreciation and understanding of other's thoughts, feelings, and values, resulting in the client becoming more able to accurately assess their interpretation of the behaviors of others

Adding The therapist will incorporate other interventions into the current theoretic approach to enhance its effectiveness with the individual client

Additive approach Modifying their theoretic approach to enhance its effectiveness; also called an integrative approach

Adjunct online interventions Educational material accessed over the internet that can be used as ancillary to in-person or online counseling

Affirmative counseling Intentionally validating, affirming, and supporting the client; often used with the LBGTQ+ population

Alliance Shared goals, completed tasks and a strong therapeutic attachment between client and counselor

Ambivalence The central barrier to change that is explored with the client

Asexual Little or no sexual attraction to other people. Asexual individuals may still be romantically attracted to other people

Assessment The evaluation of someone or someone

Asynchronous Communication and interactions not happening instantaneously or at the same time

Attending Fully and actively listening to the client, which allows the client to feel understood and accepted; this requires the counselor to orient their body toward the client and be free of distractions, focusing only on the client and encompasses eye contact, head nods, mirroring body positioning, leaning forward, and facial expressions.

Barriers Factors that limit or otherwise restrict access to counseling services

Bibliotherapy The use of books or other print media materials in a therapeutic manner

Bisexual Attraction to people of the same gender as well as members of another gender. May also be defined as attraction to both feminine and masculine individuals

Boundaries Professional limitations to the nature, purpose, and occurrence of the clinical relationship between the client(s) and counselor

Brainstorming With clients is asking them to "picture in their mind" what something else could look like, or consider all the possibilities that exist

Bug in the ear A method of facilitating supervision through earbuds worn by counselors while conducting sessions

Bug in the eye A method of facilitating supervision through typing prompts on a screen (computer, tablet, or phone)

Cancellation/no-show policy A policy for client cancellations that describes what will happen if the client does not cancel in a timely manner, include the no-show fee, and the appropriate timeframe for canceling an appointment to avoid a fee

Cisgender Gender identity matches the sex assigned at birth

Cissexism Prioritizing the experiences and perspectives of cisgender people while ignoring or devaluing those of transgender people

Client contact statement Provides clients the counselor's contact information, times available, and acceptable means of communication and helps to establish boundaries around the client-counselor relationship

Client verification In telebehavioral health it is important that the client's identity is verified prior to the beginning of treatment, especially if insurance is being utilized, to ensure privacy and confidentiality; may be accomplished by comparing a photo ID picture to the client on the screen and making sure the identification matches the name on the insurance card

Closed group Group members must be screened and invited to participate

Cognitive behavioral therapy (CBT) supervision model An orientation-specific supervision model based on Aaron Beck's theory of cognitive behavioral therapy, which uses the structure and lens of CBT to guide the supervisor's work with the supervisee

Comfortability The degree to which someone is comfortable

Conceptualization The building of a mental picture, working idea, or theory; often informed by a theoretical orientation that can help guide a counselor's understanding of a client and the client's feelings, thoughts, behaviors, and motivations

Confidentiality Refers to the clinician's requirement to protect the privacy of clients by only disclosing information shared within the therapeutic relationship with the client's permission

Confrontation The challenging of the client's thoughts, perceptions, or choices by means of highlighting incongruencies; allows the client to consider underlying emotions and conflicts they may have otherwise been overlooked. Confrontation is an advanced skill and requires a good rapport with the client

Congruency A key concept of the humanistic approach; the genuineness or realness of the therapist, or the ability of the therapist to be professional yet real with their client in their thoughts and reactions

Consciousness The sum of physical sensations, memories and dreams, and emotions

Consultant Used in the discrimination model of supervision as one of three roles that may be adopted by the supervisor. In this role, the supervisor serves as a supporting expert for the supervisee

Contact information Information including phone number, address, and emergency contact; provided to local emergency services during instances of medical and mental health emergencies

Conversational map A tool of narrative therapy that helps the client give voice to and make sense of their story and trauma

Counselor A person trained to give guidance on personal, social, or psychological problems. Used in the discrimination model of supervision as one of three roles that may be adopted by the supervisor

Counselor availability statement Explains when the counselor is available and where to call during that time, establishing business hours so to speak; defines who to call and what to do if the counselor is unavailable; client expectations of response time need to be clearly delineated and procedures in place

Counselor in training A counselor-in-training is a student-counselor who is providing counseling services in practicum and/or internship under the supervision of faculty members and site supervisors as part of their academic degree program

Countertransference The counselor's emotional reaction and projection of expectations based on the client's behavior or experiences presented in session

Crisis A response to an event perceived as critical or traumatic, resulting in distress, followed by the ineffectiveness of previously used coping mechanisms

Crisis intervention The counseling service provided to reduce a crisis reaction or response, with the goal of stabilization

Crisis reaction Synonymous with crisis response, the experience of the individual after a traumatic event or critical incident

Critical incident An event with the potential to illicit distress, leading to a crisis response

De-escalation Therapeutic techniques and interventions intended to diminish the intensity of the experience of adverse emotions or distresses.

Discrimination model (DM) Originally developed by Janine Bernard who later collaborated with Rodney Goodyear, the discrimination model is a process-oriented model of supervision that divides supervisory functions into three roles: teacher, counselor, or consultant. Within these roles, supervisors may choose to focus on the clinical skills of intervention, conceptualization, and personalization

Domestic violence Emotional, psychological, sexual, and/or physical violence occurring between romantic partners, family members, or others residing in a home together

Duty to warn Counselors requirement to use reasonable care to protect an identifiable or foreseeable victim when a patient is deemed to be a danger to others

Empathy The counselor's ability to understand the client's lived experiences and reflect them back in a manner that conveys understanding, which enhances the therapeutic relationship

End-to-end encryption A method of secure telecommunication that encrypts and decrypts communication between parties and prevents unauthorized third parties from accessing the communication

Evaluation In counselor education involves professional counselor educators making judgments about the suitability of students for the counseling profession by assessing their knowledge, skills, dispositions, and ethics

Evidence-based practices Therapeutic practices that are well-researched and based on scientific evidence

Exaggeration exercises Gestalt technique that requires the client to focus by repeating and exaggerating a behavior or expression, such as a leg bounce or an eye roll, to gain insight into the emotions related to the action, thus allowing a client to focus on the root emotion of the behavior, gaining clarity at the origins of the behavior, and addressing the underlying emotion in a direct manner

Existentialism is a philosophical approach to counseling for those considering the nature of humans and the experiences of anxiety, grief, isolation, and death that we all share

Experiment The Gestalt technique in which an individual tries on a new behavior prior to accepting it into their daily life

Eye movement desensitization reprocessing A therapy pioneered by Francine Shapiro involving bilateral stimulation (involving both sides of the brain)

Family system A theoretical approach to conceptualizing and understanding each individual within the family as having a unique role and function, which operates within and constitutes the collaborative system

Flipped classroom A learning model where the students are presented with material, traditionally given in lecture format (recorded presentations, etc.) to explore on their own, encouraging processing and assimilation through dynamic classroom interaction

Floatback technique Used in EMDR, a technique that helps the client to identify and associate earlier events with a current disturbing event

Flooded The overwhelming experience of intense emotions where an individual becomes unable to process further without first de-escalating

Free will The concept that individuals are free to make decisions for themselves, based on their experiences, thoughts, perceptions and emotions. Subsequently, the individual needs to accept responsibility for the resulting consequences, both positive and negative

Functionalism Theoretic approach that explores the purpose of behaviors and their benefits to the client with an emphasis on freewill and voluntary behaviors

Gatekeeping Refers to the ethical responsibility that counselors and counselor educators to intervene with counselors with competency issues and thereby protect the public from potential harm

Genuineness The counselor's ability to congruently be themselves. The way someone feels about a topic or situation remains consistent regardless of the setting

Gestalt theory The theoretic approach built on the belief that individuals become more whole by integrating all aspects of themselves, including those previously denied or dismissed

HIPAA The acronym for the Health Insurance Portability and Accountability Act of 1996. The act covers four main areas, which include portability of health coverage, reduction in health care fraud and abuse, standards for health care information and electronic processes, and protection and confidential handling of protected health information

Hitech An acronym for the Health Information Technology for Economic and Clinical Health Act. This act address privacy and security as it relates to electronic transmission of health information. It also dictates what practitioners must do if disclosure of PHI occurs, including informing patients of the disclosure of PHI. The act extended HIPAA compliance to business associates of health care organizations

Holism In Gestalt theory, viewing the value of experiences as a whole without denying any aspect of it

Human trafficking The intentional and illegal transporting of a person from one country or one area to another for the purpose of forced labor or sexual exploitation

Humanism The theoretic approach that holds to the fundamental belief that humans are inherently good and will make healthy choices as they move to more self-actualized versions of themselves

Hybrid Methods that use a blend of synchronous and asynchronous client contact

Individualized education plan (IEP) A legally binding written statement of the goals and supports a team of educators, caregivers, and administrators will provide a student with special needs

Integrated developmental model of supervision (IDM) A model in which the supervisor promotes the supervisee's growth by paying attention to three areas of supervisee functioning—self and other awareness, motivation, and autonomy—across eight areas of clinical practice, including intervention skills competence, assessment techniques, interpersonal assessment, client conceptualization/diagnosis, attention to individual differences in client work, theoretical orientation, treatment plans and goals, and professional ethics

Integrating Utilizing one or more theoretic approaches throughout counseling

Integrative approach Another term for additive approach; combining of theoretic approaches to be able to provide the best treatment to an array of clients and problems effectively. This approach draws from the strengths of individual theories and combines them in an additive manner to provide the counselor with a variety of skills and techniques to personalize to the client at hand

Internal dialogue exercises The Gestalt technique that allows the client to externally process an internal conflict though processing them through writing (**phantom letter**, a letter written but never sent to the recipient) or verbal (**empty chair**, verbally expressing emotions to another who is represented by the empty chair) expression

Internet-delivered parent-child interaction therapy A family intervention where the therapist can observe in-home parent-child interactions via videoconferencing and provide live feedback

Intervention The method or tool the supervisor uses in order to facilitate the supervisee's growth, development, change, or insight

Intimate partner violence Emotional, psychological, sexual, and/or physical violence occurring between dating or married partners

Introspection The process of looking inward at one's self, exploring one's own values and perceptions and how they shape and influence their choice of behaviors

Lengthening the protocol The protocol increases the number of sessions while maintaining the evidenced-based protocol

Lengthening the session The session maintains the protocol while extending the number of sessions with the clients

LGBTQIA+ Acronym for lesbian, gay, bisexual, transgender, queer or question, intersex, and asexual or ally. Sometimes also written as LGBTQIA+ to encompass additional identities

Live supervision A synchronous approach to supervision that allows the supervisor to observe the supervisee's work with a client in real time and to unobtrusively share feedback with the supervisee

Long-distance relationship A romantic relationship where involved parties live at a geographical distance, which limits the frequency of their physical contact and interactions

Loosening The structure of the protocol for the approach is made less restrictive by the therapist to modify the treatment approach to the client and their individual needs

Mandatory reporter A professional (e.g., doctor, teacher, counselor, daycare provider) who is required by law to report suspected or known abuse or neglect of a minor

Marriage, couple, and family counseling (MCFC) The application of counseling services to a marriage, couple, or family system

Microcosm A community or group that is a parallel representation of a larger group

Multicultural competency The counselor's awareness of and ability to navigate the unique cultural and ethnic considerations that impact the process and delivery of therapy

Multidimensional ecological comparative approach (MECA) A multicultural model of supervision in which the supervisor and supervisor are encouraged to examine their own and one another's cultural maps and to continually explore within supervision and clinical work how power, authority, difference, oppression, and discrimination are contributing to a context or situation

Multi-stressed families Family units that face a variety of obstacles and barriers, which prevent or otherwise limit access to counseling services such as childcare, finances, schedules, etc.

Needs assessment Include data from a variety of stakeholders to answer questions that will ultimately inform the business plan regarding the practice process and procedures

Normed A test or assessment that has been proven to show validity and reliability for a specific population when administered in a specific way which will be clearly identified on each assessment

Online supervision Online supervision refers to distance clinical supervision that is provided via video conferencing platform

On-site supervisor An on-site supervisor provides clinical supervision to a counselor in training or pre-licensed counselor at the practice site, whether a fieldwork placement or place of employment

Open group A group open to newly joining participants at any time

Pansexual Attraction to individuals based on personality characteristics rather than gender or sex. Sometimes used interchangeably with bisexual

Parallel form reliability Two tests administered to measure the same thing and/or achieve the same result

Paraphrasing Repeating back to the client portions of what they have shared with the counselor for clarification and to show understanding

Personalization Based on the work of Aaron Beck and David Burns, personalization is a kind of distorted thinking that involves a person believing, despite reasonable evidence to the contrary, that the words and actions of others are relevant and personal

Play therapy The facilitation of the client's exploration of thoughts, feelings, and interaction with the environment through the use of imagination, creativity, and selected objects. Includes a variety of theoretical orientations

Positive asset search Where upon the counselor and client explore the client's strengths, support system, and available resources, which allows the exploration of possible avenues for change

Postvention Counseling services provided after crisis intervention and/or hospitalization, aimed at addressing the causal diagnosis and unresolved trauma

Pre-licensed Counselors who have earned their counseling degree but have not yet attained professional licensure

Prevention Counseling services designed to build coping skills and supports prior to the occurrence of ineffective or harmful coping strategies

Privacy Refers to the clients right to determine what information is shared or withheld from others.

Privacy rule Set of national standards for the protection of individually identifiable health information by three types of covered entities: health plans, health care clearinghouses, and health care providers who conduct the standard health care transactions electronically.

Privileged communication A legal concept that protects clients from having confidential communications with their counselors disclosed in a court of law without their permission.

Protected Health Information Commonly referred to as PHI, represents any individually identifiable information relating to the past, present, or future health status of an individual that is created, collected, transmitted, or maintained by a HIPAA-covered entity in relation to the provision of healthcare, payment for health care services, or use in health care operations. Health information such as diagnoses, treatment information, medical test results, and prescription information are considered protected health information under HIPAA. Additionally, national identification numbers, demographic information such as birth dates, gender, ethnicity, and contact and emergency contact information are also protected. PHI relates to physical records, while ePHI is any PHI that is created, stored, transmitted, or received electronically

Psychoanalysis The counselor facilitates bringing the unconscious drives into consciousness

(often through dreams), identifying defense mechanisms and paying attention to transference and countertransference

Psychoeducational groups Groups that are informative in nature where the group leader takes on a teacher role; participants are generally less participative and may parallel a traditional classroom

Reflecting back to the client An additional skill that fosters the therapeutic alliance by conveying active listening and understanding

Reflection The ability to say back to the client what the counselor heard the client say, as well as summarize their emotions

Rehearsal exercises Gestalt technique practiced within a support group or supported environment in which a client may attempt to use a new behavior without the fear of failure, for example a role play of how to handle a difficult situation

Reliability A test consistently measures the same thing or achieve the same result even after multiple administration points

Remediation Remediation is the process of attempting to rectify deficits in a counselor or counselor in training's skill set, knowledge, disposition, ethics, or behavior, which may otherwise undermine their ability to ethically and effectively practice

Removing Removing one or more elements of a theoretic orientation to adjust to the client while maintaining the core aspects of the approach

Reordering Allows the counselor to modify and rearrange the order in which interventions are provided

Repeating The counselor uses the interventions prescribed by a protocol once numerous times during the duration of treatment

Reversal techniques Gestalt technique that allows a client to explore repressed aspects of their personality by acting in the opposite manner they may be used to

Rural populations Individuals and families who live in geographical areas that are not urbanized, usually with a low population density

Sandplay A nondirective form of play therapy developed by Dora Kalff, utilizing sand, water, miniatures, mindfulness practices, and a Jungian theoretical orientation

Schema Core beliefs, or a cognitive framework, that help to organize knowledge into categories and interpret new information

Scope of practice Refers to the services that a counseling professional is competent to provide based on training, knowledge, experience, and disposition and in accordance with their professional license

Security rule Set of national standards for protecting the confidentiality, integrity, and availability of electronic protected health information

Self-actualization The last stage of Maslow's hierarchy in which an individual is capable of using their talents to their fullest while finding a realistic balance of their limitations

Self-regulation Allows each individual to interpret the impact of changing experiences on their definition of themselves and the choices they perceive to have for their actions

Sex trafficking The practice of forcing or coercing another person into sexual acts for one's own monetary gain

Shortening the protocol is reducing the number of sessions with the client while maintaining the evidence base

Shortening the session is accomplished by Reducing the time spent with the patient in each session

Silence The stillness, or lack of movement in the room, can benefit the counselor willing to listen, which enhances the counselor and client connection. Providing silence ensures the counselor is not talking over the client and that the message is being processed to its fullest extent

Social justice The advocacy and efforts to provide equitable access to counseling services for underserved populations

Socratic questioning is a cognitive technique which facilitates guided discovery and can be used to help clients identify core beliefs and maladaptive behaviors while provideing a safe space for clients to explore what they are thinking and feeling and how it connects to their behavior

Staying with the feeling Gestalt technique that encourages a client to go deeper into uncomfortable emotions rather than avoid them, allowing a client to gain insight into their range of emotions and realize that regardless of their initial emotional reaction intensity, they ultimately have control over how they choose to express their emotions, and allowing the client to increase their sense of personal responsibility and accountability for their actions while simultaneously increasing their honesty with themselves and others

Stigma The experience of prejudice, discrimination, or social shame associated with having a negatively perceived identity, status, or attribute

Stigmatizing To become disgraced or invite blame

Structuralism Theoretic approach that values the subjective introspection of the client to assist in understanding their own emotions, perceptions, and behaviors

Summarizing Using a brief statement of the main points shared by the client to bring the key points into focus and provide clarification and understanding

Supervisory alliance The collaborative relationship with mutually agreed-on goals and tasks shared by the supervisor and supervisee characterized by care, trust, and respect

Support groups Gathering of people to offer support to each other through a shared challenge, sometimes lead by a professional counselor, at other times peer led

Synchronous Communications and interactions that occur over a telecommunication platform, which enables instantaneous live communication between parties

Tailoring The therapist will modify the treatment protocol to meet the client's need but maintain the core focus and values of the therapeutic approach

Task/work groups Groups with focused attention to an outcome, usually in the form of an assignment

Teacher A person who instructs. Used in the discrimination model of supervision as one of three roles that may be adopted by the supervisor

Telebehavioral health The provision of mental health counseling and support over the internet, through email, video conferencing, online chat, or telephone. Also called online counseling, distance counseling, telehealth, and telecounseling

Telehealth The provision of clinical care over telecommunications technology or a distance platform

Telepresent/telepresence The developmental skill of being emotionally engaged and well-regulated online, such as in the therapeutic alliance in an online counseling session

Termination of counseling Begins in the first session and is incorporated as a goal from the start, with evaluation of the process throughout the counseling process regardless of setting and includes incorporation of ongoing support and additional services that will be incorporated as they fit the client and regardless of treatment length, thus requiring the counselor to be aware of available services in the client's area

Therapeutic alliance The therapeutic relationship between client and counselor in which the two connect and behave with one another

Therapeutic groups Groups in which participants are encouraged to collaboratively explore the root causes and/or current impacts of problems

Therapeutic relationship The professional relationship between counselor and client, guided by ethics and professional boundaries, which assist the client in sharing personal information and increasing introspection and change

Time-off statement Defines steps to take if counselor has taken time off, such as who the client is to contact in the counselor's absence; it is a good practice to have a covering clinician able to respond to client crises providing clear parameters of the time off with expected return date for availability

Transference The client's emotional reaction to someone else is redirected to the counselor

Transgender Gender identity does not match the sex assigned at birth

Trauma-informed care Recognizing the prevalence and role trauma plays in a person's life and promoting a culture of safety, healing, and recovery

Unconditional positive regard The humanistic concept of accepting the client for who they are and where they are in their development combined with care about the person and their well-being without juedgementwhile challenging the client to become a healthier version of themselves, which furthers the theraputic relationship and increases the client's comfort with disclosure

Underserved youth Those who do not have equitable services or access to care (e.g., healthcare, education). Underserved youth may include those from low-income homes and racial/ethnic minorities

Validity Factual and correct. A test or measurement tool is considered valid if it measures what it intends to measure

Verbal tracking skills Includes paraphrasing and summarizing; the main difference in the online environment is that these skills are used with greater care and more intentionality due to the potential delay in audio or video technology

Videoconferencing A synchronous internet or mobile-based distance platform in which participants can both see and hear one another by use of a webcam, microphone, or other video- and audio-enabled device

Vocal quality Includes the volume, speed, and tone of voice and is different in the online format, as some of what is heard is controlled by the speakers on the computer

Voluntary behaviors Those behaviors of an individual that are not automatic, those that are decision of the individual based in thought, perception and emotion

Working alliance The therapeutic relationship that forms between counselor and supervisor rooted in shared goals and completed tasks, which guides the counselor in working with the client

INDEX

ABOUT THE EDITORS

Sherry M. Todd, Ph.D., LPC, ATR-BC, CTTS, TFTdx earned a Ph.D. from Old Dominion University and a M.S. from Eastern Virginia Medical School in graduate art therapy. Currently, she is a core faculty member in the Counselor Education and Supervision Ph.D. Program at the University of the Cumberlands and was formerly tenured faculty at Regent University where she co-directed the Center for Trauma Studies. She is the clinical director of New Vita Neurotherapy and the Tidewater Emergency Medical Services Critical Incident Stress Management Team. She has over two decades of crisis intervention, trauma evaluation/treatment, and risk of lethality assessment experience. Dr. Todd is a diplomate in the American Academy of Experts in Traumatic Stress, a premier speaker with the National Center for Crisis Management, an approved instructor with the International Critical Incident Stress Foundation and serves on the Green Cross Board of Directors. Her recognitions and awards include the Founder's Award from Green Cross Academy of Traumatology for lifelong service dedicated to healing those suffering from severe trauma and leadership in deployment in difficult situations; the 2014 William Hathaway Outstanding Faculty Award, School of Psychology and Counseling, Regent University; the 2010 Golden Starfish Award and the 2009 Making a Difference Award, Tidewater Emergency Medical Services CISM Team; the 2008 Chi Sigma Iota National Outstanding Practitioner/Supervisor Award; the Outstanding Practitioner/Supervisor Award, 2008 Omega Delta, Chi Sigma Iota; and the Paul Fink, M.D. Outstanding Art Therapist Award, 1994 Eastern Virginia Medical School. Dr. Todd has taught in an online platform for over a decade and has provided supervision for counselors for more than twenty years and at a distance for a decade.

Tricia M. Mikolon, Ph.D., CRC, LPC, BC-TMH earned her Ph.D. in counselor education and supervision from Regent University. Her master's degree is in rehabilitation counseling from the University of Scranton and her bachelor's degree is in psychology from Elizabethtown College. She is a Certified Rehabilitation Counselor and holds an LPC in Pennsylvania and is a Board Certified Telebehavioral Health Provider. Dr. Mikolon's interests include correctional fatigue, the impact of self-definition and coping skills on holistic recovery, and the use of art therapy techniques in counseling. She is employed in the Counseling Department at the University of the Cumberlands as an assistant professor and has been on numerous dissertation committees. Additionally, she retired from the Pennsylvania Department of Corrections as a psychological services specialist after 20 years. While there she served on the Critical Incident Stress Management Team (CISM) and provided instruction to staff on various training topics including mental health issues, suicide prevention, reinforcing positive behaviors, and cognitive behavioral interventions on both the student and instructor training levels. She has authored works on rehabilitation counseling and corrections fatigue and has presented on the topics of corrections fatigue, motivational interviewing, and co-occurring disorders. She is an active member of Chi Sigma Iota, the American Counseling Association, the Fraternal Order of Police (Pennsylvania), and Psi Chi.

Debra M. Perez, M.A., LPCC, BCTP-II, SCPG earned her masters of arts degree with honors from New Mexico Highlands University over 16 years ago. She worked at a community mental health agency with children through adults, utilizing community supports to assist clients on their path to wellness, self-acceptance, and healing. She then worked in a day treatment program with adolescents transitioning out of treatment, foster care, or residential treatment, reintegrating back into their families, and navigating probation and the juvenile judicial system. She then opened her own private practice, serving children, teens, adults, and seniors, providing individual, family, and couples therapy. She now provides telebehavioral health services online in a private practice serving rural New Mexico. She is a Board Certified Telebehavioral Health Provider and holds a special credential in problem gambling treatment and a certification in aromatherapy. She is currently a doctoral candidate in counselor education and supervision at the University of the Cumberlands and is a member of Chi Sigma Iota.

ABOUT THE CONTRIBUTORS

Elizabeth Brokamp (Chapters 13, 14, and 15)

Elizabeth Brokamp, LPC, MA, EDM, is a licensed professional counselor in Virginia with over 20 years of experience. Currently a PhD candidate in Counselor Education and Supervision at the University of the Cumberlands (CACREP), Elizabeth is board certified in telemental health and has practiced online for several years.

Collette Brooks-Salaam (Chapter 3)

Colette Brooks-Salaam is a licensed professional counselor in the state of Virginia. She holds certifications as a national certified counselor, certified clinical trauma professional, thought field therapy practitioner, and EMDR therapist. Colette graduated from George Washington University with a master's in education and human development and a master's in clinical mental health from the University of the Cumberlands CACREP-accredited program. She has provided telehealth services for 5 years.

Marcus Folkes (Chapter 3)

Marcus Folkes is a licensed mental health counselor in the state of Florida. He currently holds certification as a national certified counselor. He is also a 2020 NBCC Doctoral Minority fellow. Marcus graduated for the great Bethune Cookman University in 2015, where his passion drove him to work with foster care adolescent youth in a residential group home setting.

Shara B. Goudreau (Chapter 9)

Dr. Shara B. Goudreau is a licensed mental health counselor (LMHC) and qualified supervisor (QS) in the state of Florida, as well as a national certified counselor (NCC) and certified clinical mental health counselor (CCMHC). While she has treated various populations in private practice, community mental health, middle school, and college, her work has focused on teens and young adults with attention deficit hyperactivity disorder (ADHD) transitioning to higher education. She authored a multitouch electronic workbook, *Transitioning From High School to College: An Interactive Workbook to Enhance Students' Executive Function Skills*, and coauthored peer-reviewed journal articles *"Executive Function Coaching: Assisting With Transitioning From Secondary to Postsecondary Education"* and *"Executive Function Coaching as a Tool for Transition to College for Students with ADHD."* Dr. Goudreau earned her

PhD in counselor education and supervision with the University of the Cumberlands in 2019. She currently provides counseling services via telehealth and teaches various graduate courses in the Clinical Mental Health Counseling programs with Lynn University and the University of the Cumberlands.

Colleen Grunhaus (Chapter 10)

Dr. Colleen Grunhaus is an assistant professor at University of the Cumberlands and the CEO of Second Order Consulting and Supervision. She is a licensed professional counselor in Virginia and a licensed clinical mental health counselor in North Carolina. Dr. Grunhaus earned a PhD in counselor education from William & Mary and is a board-certified counselor and approved clinical supervisor. Her research and teaching passions include organizational wellness, general systems theory, suicide prevention, leadership, and marriage, couples, and family counseling.

Michelle Harrision (Chapters 5 and 9)

Michelle Harrison earned her PhD in counseling education and supervision, with a specialization in leadership at the University of the Cumberlands.

She is licensed as a professional clinical counselor and supervisor and a national certified counselor. Michelle speaks at a variety of national, state, and local conferences and events educating people how to recognize and respond to human trafficking. She addresses the importance of trauma-informed care and shares about her experience working in a residential and private practice setting with women who have been sexually exploited and trafficked.

Kristal James (Chapters 6 and 12)

Kristal James is a licensed clinical mental health counselor in the state of Utah. She holds certifications as a national certified counselor, approved clinical supervisor, and board-certified telemental health provider through the National Board for Certified Counselors. Kristal graduated from the University of Phoenix CACREP-accredited ground campus in 2005 and has been teaching students seeking a master's degree in counseling since 2009. Kristal is enrolled in a CACREP-accredited doctoral program through the University of the Cumberlands with an anticipated graduation date of 2021. Her area of research interest includes supervision and mentorship relationships.

Andrea Josephs (Chapter 8)

Andrea Josephs holds a master's degree in higher education teaching and learning from Walden University, a master's degree in clinical mental health counseling from Regent University and is currently a counselor education and supervision doctoral candidate at the University of the Cumberlands. She is passionate about innovation in online delivery in the field of counseling. She is currently developing CES identity and publication prowess under the CES mentorship of Dr. Sherry Todd.

Sarah Littlebear (Chapter 7)

Dr. Sarah Littlebear is core counseling faculty at the University of the Cumberlands and is a licensed professional counselor in the state of Georgia. She graduated with her PhD in counselor education from Auburn University in 2014 and has worked in the counseling field since 2008. Dr. Littlebear continues to grow in clinical work with a small practice alongside her passion for teaching.

Erin Lofties (Chapter 9)

Erin Lofties, MEd, LPC, lives and works in the state of Oklahoma. She works primarily with members of the LGBTQ community and survivors of IPV, DV, and sexual assault. She is currently pursuing a PhD in counselor education and supervision.

Rachel McRoberts (Chapter 11)

Rachel McRoberts is a doctoral candidate at the University of the Cumberlands with research interests in creativity, expressive therapies, heutagogy, and professional development. She is a licensed professional counselor, mental health service provider (TN), approved clinical supervisor, and registered play therapist-supervisor with nearly 20 years in the field.

Jerimiah Peck (Chapter 10)

Jeremiah Peck, MA is a licensed mental health counselor and clinical director of a group counseling practice in Vancouver, Washington, where he works with couples and families and supervises and trains developing clinicians. In addition to his clinical work, Jeremiah is also faculty in the Master of Arts in Counseling program at Multnomah University in Portland, Oregon, instructing and supervising student counselors.

Tina Pharr (Chapters 8, 13, and 14)

Tina Pharr is a licensed clinical mental health counselor in North Carolina, with 5 years' experience as an adjunct professor and 15 years of clinical experience. Her counseling experience includes intensive in-home counseling with families impacted by trauma, individual community-based counseling, telemental health services, and college counseling. As a doctoral candidate at the University of the Cumberlands, she is completing her dissertation, *A Phenomenological Exploration of Counselor Educators Initiating Remediation*.

Anita M. Pool (Chapter 11)

Dr. Anita M. Pool is an assistant professor of counseling and is the subject matter expert on child and adolescent counseling in her department. As a national certified counselor and national certified school counselor, she has worked with young children for over 16 years. She currently teaches child and adolescent counseling to students earning their master's degree in counseling at the University of the Cumberlands.

Tera Rumbaugh Crawford (Chapter 2)

Tera Rumbaugh Crawford is a licensed professional counselor associate in the state of Kentucky. She holds a certification as a national certified counselor. Tera graduated from the University of Louisville's education bachelor's program and CACREP-accredited counseling master's program. She is currently continuing her education in the counselor education and supervision PhD program at the University of the Cumberlands.

Diedre Wade (Chapter 2)

Diedre Wade is a licensed professional clinical counselor supervisor in Kentucky and a licensed mental health counselor in Florida. She graduated from Liberty University with a master's in professional counseling in 2012. Diedre has experience working in drug court, in-patient behavioral health, and residential treatment, all while working in her private practice. She is a Counselor Education and Supervision PhD student at the University of the Cumberlands.

David C. Walther (Chapter 3)

David C. Walther, PhD, University of the Cumberlands, MDiv, Phoenix Seminary, is a licensed professional counselor (LPC) in Arizona. He is a national certified counselor (NCC), approved clinical supervisor (ACS), and board-certified telemental health provider (BC-TMH). Dr. Walther oversees a large church-based counseling ministry in Scottsdale, Arizona, and has been providing clinical supervision to interns since 2004.

Sabrina Wannamaker (Chapter 14)

Sabrina Wannamaker is a licensed professional counselor and supervisor in South Carolina. She holds certifications as a national certified counselor and employee assistance specialist–clinical, and is a board-certified case manager. She is a graduate of Webster University and is a current doctoral student at University of the Cumberlands in the Counselor Education and Supervision program. She is the proud owner and chief clinician with Just-Us Counseling & Consulting, LLC.

CPSIA information can be obtained
at www.ICGtesting.com
Printed in the USA
LVHW011743200422
716609LV00007B/459